BETWEEN
JEWISH TRADITION
AND MODERNITY

David Ellenson. Photograph by Richard Lobell.

BETWEEN JEWISH TRADITION and MODERNITY

rethinking an old opposition

Edited by Michael A. Meyer and David N. Myers

• • • • • •

Essays in Honor of David Ellenson

Wayne State University Press
Detroit

18 17 16 15 14   5 4 3 2 1

Library of Congress Control Number: 2014936565

ISBN 978-0-8143-3859-9 (cloth)
ISBN 978-0-8143-3860-5 (e-book)

Designed and Typeset by Bryce Schimanski
Composed in Gentium and Trade Gothic

CONTENTS

PART 4: CULTURE

PREFACE
AND ACKNOWLEDGMENTS

In popular consciousness, the poles of "tradition" and "modernity" have often been understood to be opposed, with the latter assumed to have displaced the former. This assumption belies the way in which tradition itself was understood by religious adherents in premodern times. Gershom Scholem, the great scholar of Jewish mysticism, made this point amply clear in his powerfully succinct article from 1966, "Revelation and Tradition as Religious Categories in Judaism." Scholem asserted there, on the basis of his review of rabbinic and kabbalistic literature, that "every religious experience after revelation is a mediated one"—mediated, that is, by decidedly human interpreters seeking to grasp the word of God. Their constant efforts to arrive at new and deeper meanings of Scripture assure ceaseless interpretive dynamism. In this way, "tradition," Scholem proposes, "undergoes change with the times, new facets of its meaning shining forth and lighting its way."[1]

But the perception persists that tradition is immutable and immune to the passage of time, often promoted by "traditionalists" who regard themselves as links in an unbroken chain of transmission. They cast their foes as mindless avatars of modernity, unmoored from their roots. But the chasm between traditionalists and moderns is not nearly so wide. The former engage in the creative "invention of tradition," as Eric Hobsbawm and Terrence Ranger described the phenomenon in 1983. Invariably, they borrow insights, methods, and communication strategies from the very modern world they criticize. Meanwhile, the proudly modern, for all of their claims of innovation, inevitably draw from the rich repository of the past, reshaping the contours of tradition in the process. And thus, tradition and modernity rest on a continuum whose extremes are more imagined than real.

Few have grasped this proposition as deeply as David Ellenson, one of the leading contemporary scholars of modern Jewish thought. In a series of books and a long stream of articles, Ellenson has skillfully demonstrated the complex and dialectical interplay of tradition and modernity, showing how tradition is renewed and reimagined in response to modernizing currents, as well as how avowedly modern currents bear traces of traditional impulses. Ellenson's work has been especially influential in his study of two forms of traditional Jewish expression, rabbinic responsa and liturgy, both of which figure prominently in this volume. Like Ellenson, the contributors examine the permutations and adaptations of these intertwined forms of Jewish expression and assess their ongoing relevance for contemporary Jewish culture and religion. Drawing from a diverse range of disciplines and scholarly interests, they present essays that range in subject from the theological to the liturgical, the sociological to the literary. The geographic and historical focus of these essays is on the United States and the State of Israel, both of which have been major sites of inquiry in Ellenson's work.

The volume opens with David Myers's examination of the place of tradition and modernity in David Ellenson's scholarly oeuvre. Myers explores the development of Ellenson's writing, focusing on his analysis of halakhic and liturgical changes in Germany, America, and Israel. The twenty essays that follow, which we have placed under the headings of Law, Ritual, Thought and Culture, represent key sites of contestation and negotiation between tradition and modernity in modern Judaism.

The first group of essays explores the way in which Jewish law (halakhah) has been rethought, reformulated, and reinforced in responding to the challenges of modernity. Zvi Zohar shows how a traditional Sephardic rabbi, Rabbi Ben-Zion Meir Hai Uzziel, and some of his colleagues were able to interpret Jewish law in such a manner as to facilitate the entry of prospective converts into the Jewish community. That Jewish law, leniently construed, remains an important source of moral guidance that Jewish ethicists should not abandon is the argument of Elliott N. Dorff. In an essay that juxtaposes an ethic that draws on a "legal approach" with the "covenantal ethics" David Ellenson has advocated, Dorff illustrates the differences between them by applying the two approaches to a number of moral issues.

For Orthodox Jews tradition sets boundaries that affect their relationships with their non-Orthodox counterparts. Yet the conditions of modern Jewish life require coming to grips with those who have "deviated" from the traditional faith. Adam Ferziger examines how Zionist Orthodox rabbis in Israel have stigmatized the Reform movement, thereby moving closer to the stance of their non-Zionist ultra-Orthodox colleagues. But he also notes that there is a small movement in the other direction, whose adherents suggest that in public policy, though not in halakhah, less traditional religious Jews should be granted recognition. Orthodox awareness of the non-Orthodox Jewish world is likewise a theme of Jack Wertheimer's essay on Jewish outreach workers. Focusing on the United States, he analyzes how, in a reversal of earlier separatism, thousands of Orthodox missionaries, especially from Chabad Hasidism, have overcome long-standing inhibitions to engage fellow Jews who do not adhere to Jewish law in the manner they do—indeed, who may flout it (e.g., the prohibition on driving on the Sabbath) quite demonstrably. The final essay in this section shifts the temporal focus to the nineteenth century. Utilizing hitherto unused sources, Jonathan Sarna explores how the issue of constructing a fitting monument to the Jewish philanthropist Judah Touro resulted in conflicting points of view regarding the permissibility of sculpture in Jewish law and commemoration, each anchored within the spirits of both tradition and modernity.

The second section of the volume engages a related bellwether of change in Judaism to which David Ellenson has devoted much attention: ritual. The essays in this section reveal the way in which ritual, deemed an essential element of Jewish tradition, has in fact undergone revision in response to new life circumstances. The first two articles deal with ritual changes in the American synagogue in the late twentieth and early twenty-first centuries. Isa Aron examines the current practice and problems attending the Bar/Bat Mitzvah ceremony. The Bar Mitzvah ceremony, which in Reform Judaism had been displaced by Confirmation and to which the Bat Mitzvah was added, provided the movement with a degree of personalization it had previously lacked. However, as Aron argues, it has become a graduation ceremony increasingly followed by the child's dropout from further Jewish education. Her essay suggests ways in which the B'nai Mitzvah experience can be "reverse engineered" so as to assume its proper role within Jewish education. An important site of ritual change is synagogue music. Deborah Lipstadt analyzes the controversy that surrounded the popular Jewish singer and composer Debbie Friedman, which pitted traditionalist cantors against musical innovators within the Reform and Conservative movements—culminating in the decision by the Reform movement to rename its School of Sacred Music after Friedman. Shifting away from the United States, Dalia Marx's essay demonstrates how within the context of secular Israeli kibbutzim, the traditional Kaddish prayer has undergone verbal transformations that connect it more closely to its nontraditional context. Whereas the Kaddish has retained its place within modern Judaism, the mikveh (the ritual bath), after its abandonment as irreconcilable with modernity, has made a recent comeback among non-Orthodox Jews who have imbued it with old and new meanings. Michael A. Meyer traces the history of this development across the spectrum of modern Jewish religious movements, while focusing on its recovery within the Reform movement. The section concludes with Steven M. Lowenstein's comparison of the paths to modernization of the Jewish communities in Germany and the Netherlands. Lowenstein explores ritual differences between the two communities in the early nineteenth century, as well as differing markers of economic growth and social integration to argue that Dutch Jewry followed a different and more traditional path than German Jewry into the twentieth century.

The third section of the volume follows varied byways in Jewish thought. David Ellenson's colleague as the head of a Jewish seminary, Arnold Eisen, explores the transformation of the traditional doctrine of the centrality of Zion into the Zionist ideology of negation of the diaspora, thereby creating deeply problematic relationships. As against the doctrine of negation, Eisen observes that the two main bodies of world Jewry, in Israel and the United States, represent equally unprecedented forms of modern Jewish reality, each drawing selectively on Jewish tradition. In the next essay, Michael Marmur unearths eight early articles by Abraham Joshua Heschel dealing with Tannaitic sages. Marmur examines how this modern Jewish thinker appropriated the spirit of the rabbis as sources for enriching Judaism in a secular world. He then supplements his analysis of Heschel's treatment of these pillars of Jewish tradition with a comparison with their treatment by other writers of recent times. Among modern Orthodox Jewish thinkers, one of the most prominent is certainly Joseph Baer Soloveitchik. Deftly utilizing Soloveitchik's writings, Rachel Adler in her essay discusses his attitude toward gender equality, focusing specifically on the apparent contradiction between his willingness to provide equivalent Jewish education for girls and women and his unvarying support for masculine privilege in other areas. The final two essays in this section deal with the encounter of traditional Jewish sources and sensibilities with prominent strains of modern intellectual culture. Thus, William Cutter shows how "narrative thinking" can prompt new understandings of traditional genres and thereby shed important light on ethical dilemmas relating to end-of-life situations. Similarly, Lewis M. Barth, in contrasting midrash with secular psychoanalysis, finds that they complement one another when their respective perspectives on forgiveness are juxtaposed. Following an examination of texts in both areas, Barth concludes that these two traditions, one ancient and one modern, converge in significant and helpful respects.

The fourth section deals with the diverse realms of modern Jewish culture. It opens with Lawrence A. Hoffman's discussion of the profound impact of secularism on New York Jewish intellectuals. For them, universalism replaced religion, though the Conservative movement sought, and for a time succeeded, in integrating ethnic with religious identity. The next two essays probe two significant episodes in late twentieth-century Jewish cultural history in America. Riv-Ellen Prell analyzes the tension in the Conservative movement in 1968 when students at the Jewish Theological Seminary challenged its chancellor, Louis Finkelstein, on issues of social justice. For the students, the struggle for social justice demanded a response by and from within the Jewish tradition. No less bitter was the controversy that arose in the inherently modern Reform movement over how to respond to the failed passage of the Equal Rights Amendment. In her essay Carole Balin examines the deep division that arose within Reform when its union of congregations was scheduled to hold a biennial convention at a hotel located in the state of Arizona, which had failed to ratify the amendment. As she notes, the decision revolved around whether the union would uphold gender equality, which by then had become a "tradition" of Reform Judaism.

The last two essays of this section shift attention to literary and visual culture. Wendy Zierler's essay places ideas drawn from the German Jewish philosopher Franz Rosenzweig and other representatives of ancient and modern Judaism into dialogue with Christopher Nolan's film *Memento*, on the subject of the construction of memory. In making this comparison, she observes that an embrace of "inner remembering" may result in a creative reenvisioning of tradition. Arnold Band examines the balance of tradition and modernity in his essay devoted to the great Hebrew writer Shmuel Yosef Agnon. Band shows how Agnon made ample use of motifs from a Hasidic tale, while at the same time writing very much in the mainstream of modern prose fiction. Indeed, Agnon masterfully fused traditional elements within Judaism with the stylistic idioms and sensibilities of a cosmopolitan secular culture.

Finally, we close on a poignant note. When we began this project, Paula E. Hyman was our third editor. She played a large role in formulating the conception of the volume and in advancing its progress. We deeply mourn the premature death of this outstanding scholar of modern Jewry, who contributed immensely to the field. And we profoundly regret that she did not live to present this volume to her dear friend David Ellenson. From her daughter, Dr. Judith Rosenbaum, we received an unpublished lecture on the transformation of Jewish women in post-Holocaust Poland from tradition to radicalism. We include this essay in tribute to the memory of Paula Hyman and as a coda to this volume on tradition and modernity, inspired by the work of David Ellenson.

We wish to thank especially Lindsay King, who undertook the rather complicated task of coordinating the mechanics of this volume, and did so with great skill and devotion. Without her efficient assistance our task would have been far more arduous. Working with Wayne State University Press has been a genuine pleasure. We are grateful to editors Kathryn Wildfong and Kristin Harpster, to our copyeditor Sue Breckenridge, and to our designer Bryce Schimanski. We also owe a considerable debt of gratitude to a group of devoted admirers of David Ellenson's, Rob Bildner and Elisa Spungen Bildner, Marvin Israelow and Dorian Goldman, Peter Joseph and Elizabeth Scheuer, and Ilana and Skip Vichness, who have expressed appreciation for their friend and teacher by providing a generous subvention for this volume. Finally, Rabbi Jacqueline Koch Ellenson has been a source of encouragement, sound advice, and support throughout the process of producing the book.

Michael A. Meyer and David N. Myers

---

1. Scholem's essay, "Revelation and Tradition as Religious Categories in Judaism," was republished in Gershom Scholem, *The Messianic Idea in Judaism* (New York: Schocken, 1971), 292–96.

BETWEEN
JEWISH TRADITION
AND MODERNITY

INTRODUCTION

At the Border

David Ellenson and the Study of Modern Judaism

DAVID N. MYERS

In the thirty-five years during which he has been studying the changing face of modern Judaism, David Ellenson has been drawn over and again to the permeable boundary between the forces of tradition and modernity. Given his keen analytical sophistication, worn lightly beneath his legendary affability, Ellenson knows well that tradition and modernity are less precise historical markers than ideal constructs. And yet, like Max Weber, one of Ellenson's most important guides in the sociology of religion, who advocated the use of such constructs, Ellenson has made frequent use of these poles, between which he probes the malleability of forms of Jewish religious expression and behavior from the nineteenth century to the present. Through a large body of work that impressively expanded during his tenure as president of Hebrew Union College—Jewish Institute of Religion, David Ellenson has emerged as one of the most insightful observers of this complex relationship in Judaism in our generation.

That the tension-filled relationship between tradition and modernity preoccupied him from an early stage is evident in the titles and major themes of his first books. In his 1989 collection of essays, *Tradition in Transition: Orthodoxy, Halakhah, and the Boundaries of Modern Jewish Identity*, he set out to unpack "the central problem of modern Judaism"—namely, the challenge of remaining "'authentically' Jewish while simultaneously affirming the worth of western culture."[1] Shortly thereafter, Ellenson published his first monograph, *Rabbi Esriel Hildesheimer and the Creation of a Modern Jewish Orthodoxy* (1990), based on his 1981 Columbia University dissertation. As he noted in the book's introduction, one of the major goals of that book was "to highlight the blend of and dissonance between tradition and modernity" that the German Orthodox rabbi Esriel Hildesheimer represented.[2] Four year later, Ellenson put out another collection of papers, entitled *Between Tradition and Culture: The Dialectics of*

Jewish Religion and Identity. He introduced that volume by arguing that "[o]ne can only comprehend the nature of Judaism . . . by appreciating the dialectical interplay between Jewish tradition on the one hand and the social and cultural world in which it finds itself on the other."[3]

Ellenson understood well that the shifting of the sands of "tradition," whose adepts constantly had to adapt to the new conditions of modernity, was not unique to the Jews. His interest in the phenomenon was rooted in a broader sociological perspective that he associated with Max Weber. This perspective rested on the premise that "[c]ontemporary religious phenomena are . . . the result of a dialectical interplay between past tradition and present-day cultural settings and needs."[4] Even more than Weber, who spoke famously of the *Entzauberung* ("disenchantment") of the modern age, Ellenson has been alive to the resilience and regenerative capacity of religion in the modern age. In this regard, he makes his own contribution to the ongoing debates over the utility of the secularization thesis originally attributed to Weber and those sociological theorists who followed in his wake (e.g., Thomas Luckmann, Peter Berger, and José Casanova). In public speeches, Ellenson often quotes Berger's well-known claim from *The Sacred Canopy* that the modern age spelled the dismantling of the "plausibility structure" of traditional religion.[5] It is important to note that, over the years, Berger, like Luckmann and Casanova, came to realize that a simple, unidirectional view of religion's decline under the weight of modernity missed a great deal of its resurgent force. To wit, Berger edited in 1999 a collection that captured his new approach, entitled *The Desecularization of the World: Resurgent Religion and World Politics.*

Ellenson's work resonated with this new approach, as he made clear in his 2001 essay "Judaism Resurgent? American Jews and the Evolving Expression of Jewish Values and Jewish Identity." That is not to say that he offered the opposite of a declensionist view of religion in the form of a linear triumphalism that heralded the victory of religion over secularization. With characteristic nuance, honed by his reading of Berger and Casanova, Ellenson observed instances of a newly emboldened and deprivatized Judaism alongside unmistakable signs of the attenuation of faith, ritual, and identity.[6]

Although he has not promoted himself (or even been acknowledged) as such, Ellenson is one of the most important sociological theorists of Judaism today. He is known for his close studies of modern responsa and liturgy, sources that he approaches and analyzes with an impressive degree of theoretical range and precision. In an important biographical sense, this should not surprise us. He was not only trained as a rabbi at Hebrew Union College, where he gained a lifelong interest in German Jewry through his relationship with Professor Fritz Bamberger, but he also was a student of the sociology of religion, initially as a master's student at the University of Virginia, where he was introduced to the field by David Little. It was in the seminar with Little that Ellenson was exposed to the grand figures of modern social theory: Marx, Durkheim, Freud, and Weber. This encounter, Ellenson averred, "changed my life" by providing the requisite "tools to understand my own existence and the existence of my people."[7] Indeed, he found in the seminar with Little a vocabulary with which to understand religion as the product of specific and evolving contexts.

To be sure, Ellenson's formative upbringing in Newport News, Virginia, did not afford the kind of critical scrutiny that he would later develop. In Newport News, he lived within the confines of a close-knit Jewish community; his family belonged to the main Orthodox synagogue in town, and he was trained in the ritual and liturgical practices of Orthodox Judaism. The Jewish observance of the Ellensons—their adherence to the laws of kashrut and Sabbath observance—clearly distinguished them from most others in the city. At the same time, it did not prevent their successful integration into the fabric of Newport News—or at least, of white Newport News—in professional, civic, and educational terms.[8]

It was exactly this kind of juxtaposition—between preservation of tradition and acculturation—that would exercise David Ellenson's scholarly imagination, beginning with his early formative studies of Orthodoxy. But even before undertaking those close examinations, he continued to lay a firm theoretical foundation for his emerging scholarly approach. After his master's work at Virginia, he continued on to Columbia University, where he pursued a PhD. There he worked under the supervision of Gillian Lindt, the scholar of American religion who advised Ellenson's dissertation on Esriel Hildesheimer. He also took courses with the sociologist Robert Nisbet, as well as with several leading scholars in Jewish studies, in particular Arthur Hertzberg and Joseph Blau.[9] During his time at Columbia, Ellenson deepened his reading of Weber. He came to adopt a critical view of Weber's theories about Judaism and the persistent particularism of the Jewish people. But he nonetheless recognized Weber as "one of the truly seminal thinkers in the history of western intellectual thought."[10]

If Weber served as the theoretical foil to Ellenson's developing sense of method, it was Jacob Katz who demonstrated to him how to apply a sociological approach to history. Ellenson met the eminent Israeli historian at Columbia, where he had come from Jerusalem as a visiting professor. Trained as a sociologist under Karl Mannheim in Frankfurt, Katz pioneered the study of rabbinic responsa as vital and to revealing historical sources in a long series of studies, none better known than *Tradition and Crisis*. He also devoted much of his long and fertile career to examining the way in which Jewish religious tradition was altered and challenged but not vanquished by forces of modernity. Katz's impact on Ellenson was vast. Not only did Katz guide him to the study of modern responsa, whose authors were constantly engaged in the act of balancing tradition and modernity, but he taught Ellenson, fresh from his studies of sociological theory, "to write Jewish history from the inside, relying on its own sources and articulations."[11] From his early meetings with Katz to his last, Ellenson was deeply affected by Katz's thematic interests, methodological approach, and personal attention. He concluded in an appreciation to Katz after his death: "No one more brilliantly analyzed the course and complexity of modern European Jewish history than he did."[12]

In fact, what Ellenson meant was that no scholar of Jewish history offered—in both empirical and theoretical terms—as textured a sense of the balance of tradition and modernity as did Katz. Although himself a lifelong Orthodox Jew, Katz too did not treat Orthodoxy as an unchanging religious form. On the contrary, he noted that traditionalists in the modern age wrapped themselves in the cloak of antiquity, claiming unbroken continuity with the distant past while staking out new positions and adopting new modes of communication and organizational strategy.[13] Ellenson followed in Katz's path, devoting a good portion of his career to exploring two traditional forms of religious expression, responsa and liturgy, that were in fact bellwethers—and agents—of change. Grasping their surprising elasticity was more than an academic pursuit for Ellenson, more than an illuminating insight into the dynamism of religion. It was a profoundly personal lesson. For after encountering Katz and his unique arsenal of methods and sources, Ellenson averred that "the study of Judaism had become, and remains, a religious quest, an attempt at self-knowledge and discovery."[14]

Curiously, Katz, who remained true to his Orthodox roots throughout his life, was more circumspect about the link between his scholarship and his spiritual or existential impulses than Ellenson, who left Orthodoxy as a young man. Katz bore the reserve and *wissenschaftliche* commitments of his native Europe, whereas Ellenson, the ebullient American, was far more open in acknowledging the inseparable bond between the scholarly and spiritual planes in his life.

In the remainder of this essay, I would like to focus on two key sites of significance to David Ellenson's scholarly work: Germany and Israel. These are hardly the only areas of scholarly interest to him; he also has written a great deal on American Judaism and Jewish life. The focus on Germany and Israel owes to the fact that, for Ellenson, the two serve as key testing grounds on which Judaism was constantly being recalibrated between the poles of tradition and modernity. In both settings, Ellenson has used similar prisms to gauge this ongoing work of recalibration: rabbinic opinions and prayer books. These media provided him with an opportunity not only to investigate the process of historical change in religion; they also have afforded him an opportunity to understand better—and, to a degree, work through—his own religious transformation.

Notwithstanding the similarities between them, the two settings possess different valences for Ellenson and his sense of personal engagement. Whereas the earlier German scene evokes a distinctive Orthodox world that once existed, the contemporary Israeli setting reflects an ongoing and vibrant reality with which Ellenson feels a profound and ongoing identification. Moreover, the abstractions of halakhic discourse in nineteenth- and early twentieth-century Germany, when most Jews had left behind stringent observance, are quite different from the real-life implications of halakhic discourse in a polity in which Jewish law is taken seriously by a substantial portion of the population. Accordingly, there is a greater sense of immediacy in the Israel-based studies than in the work on Germany, though in both Ellenson attends to the ever-shifting pendulum between tradition and modernity with finely grained detail.

Halakhah under Duress: The German Case

David Ellenson opened his first collection of essays with an unmistakable methodological challenge: "Students of modern Judaism (Jacob Katz is a notable exception) have largely ignored the responsa literature as a source for comprehending the nature and development of Jewish history and thought during the last two hundred years."[15] From an early point in his career, even before he received his doctorate from Columbia in 1981, he set out to correct the neglect of previous generations of scholars. In one of his first major articles, Ellenson focused on a usual figure in an unusual setting to address what would become a regular concern. The figure was one of the leading—and few—Orthodox rabbis in the United States in the mid-nineteenth century, Bernard Illowy, who emigrated from Europe in 1853. The setting was New Orleans, Louisiana, which neither was then nor is now a major center of Orthodox activity. The issue that Illowy took up—and Ellenson in his wake—was the question of whether local mohalim could perform ritual circumcisions on sons born of a Jewish father and Christian mother, who were thus not deemed Jewish according to the traditional halakhic criterion. Although mohalim in New Orleans had previously circumcised such children, Illowy ruled that henceforth they should desist. In situating Illowy's ruling in context, Ellenson's article offered a helpful historical sociological profile of the state of Jewish ritual observance in the United States—and more specifically, New Orleans—in the mid-nineteenth century. It also unearthed an interesting transnational rabbinical discourse insofar as Illowy sent his legal opinion on to Germany for affirmation. The German rabbis with whom Illowy consulted, including Esriel Hildesheimer, concurred with his decision. One European rabbi, however, dissented, the proto-Zionist Zvi Hirsch Kalischer, who chose to describe the baby boys with Jewish fathers as *zera' kodesh* (holy offspring) for whom ritual circumcision was, in fact, an obligation.

Already in this early essay, we can identify a recurrent concern in David Ellenson's work: his attention to the process by which various groups of Jews sought to define boundaries of communal membership at a time of great social and religious change. Whether to err on the side of leniency in order to allow for a larger and more inclusive Jewish community or to hold fast to established, exclusionary norms was and remains one of the most enduring questions that Ellenson's scholarship has posed. Circumcision was one site of contestation over boundary maintenance. Indeed, he followed up on his discussion of Rabbi Illowy in New Orleans with a paper in 1981 devoted to a similar case in Frankfurt, Germany. In that instance, Rabbi Markus Horovitz, a former student of Esriel Hildesheimer at his Hungarian yeshivah, issued rulings on a number of occasions in the late nineteenth century regarding the circumcision of a son born to a Gentile mother. Unlike Illowy, Horovitz adopted the position of Zvi Hirsch Kalischer and permitted the circumcision. Like Kalischer, he favored laxity as a way of encouraging Jews on the margins to remain within the fold.

From this pair of case studies on circumcision, Ellenson concluded that the halakhic system in its modern guise was neither "monolithic" nor did it yield "a single response" from its decisors. Multiple variables came into play in the formulation of a legal decision, including the personal proclivities of the jurist, the interpretive strategy employed, the particular social conditions of the day, and, of course, fealty to the halakhic system. In assessing this admixture, Ellenson thought it advisable to resist the dichotomy between "accommodation" and "resistance"—the two poles identified by Peter Berger in *The Sacred Canopy* to understand the confrontation of religious institutions with forces of secularization.[16] In fact, his study of the circumcision cases suggests that modern halakhic decisors often operate in the gray area between accommodation and resistance, as they seek to balance the competing impulses of boundary maintenance and responsiveness to rapidly changing circumstances.

In Ellenson's early studies Germany was the preferred historical venue in which to examine this balancing act. Germany had been, after all, the site of extensive Jewish acculturation since the late eighteenth century, as manifested in a wide variety of sociological and intellectual factors: university attendance, denominational reform, intermarriage, and conversion. Concomitantly, it was a milieu in which halakhic observance among Jews declined precipitously, undergoing a rapid transformation in the course of a generation—from the time of Moses Mendelssohn (1729–86) to that of his children.

And yet, Germany was also the site of a resurgent Orthodoxy that sought to reconcile "Torah 'im derekh erets," in the famous phrase of the mid-nineteenth-century rabbi Samson Raphael Hirsch. That is, Hirsch and others who marched under the banner of "Neo-Orthodoxy" sought to balance the centrality of Torah (and accompanying adherence to Jewish law) with appreciation for contemporary German cultural norms and attitudes. This negotiation deeply interested David Ellenson. The particular lens through which he most often chose to explore it was law. As one who recalls that he entered college "resigned to become an attorney" (like his father and brother), Ellenson was something of a lawyer manqué.[17] His interest in studying Jewish law may well have issued from this source, as well as from his own personal journey down a path away from Orthodoxy. What we can say with greater certainty is that the notion of law to which he was drawn was not a static or brittle conception, but rather a fluid and ever-shifting one. "Jewish law," he declared at the end of his article on Markus Horovitz, "even when interpreted by Orthodox authorities, displays the same dynamism of pluralism and variability that characterizes all living legal systems."[18]

Just as circumcision was an important marker of the boundaries of halakhic permissibility in Germany, so too were a number of related issues, including conversion, intermarriage, and the degree of tolerance accorded Reform Judaism. In dozens of essays and a number of books devoted to these issues, Ellenson repeatedly dispensed with the assumption of a univocal and predictable halakhic system.[19] His body of work revealed a much more textured view of the relationship between tradition and modernity than the received image of diametric opposition suggests.

Indeed, from his perch as a scholar trained and employed at a Reform institution, he recognized, with a fair measure of denominational magnanimity, the extent to which the halakhic system could be open ended. His heroes, if we may call them that, were precisely those German Orthodox figures who defied the stereotype of rigid and unvarying legalists—rabbis such as Markus Horovitz, David Zvi Hoffmann, and Esriel Hildesheimer. It was the last of these figures who anchored Ellenson's Columbia dissertation and later his first book, *Rabbi Esriel Hildesheimer and the Creation of a Modern Jewish Orthodoxy*. Hildesheimer (1820–99) was the son of a well-known rabbi and raised in a traditional home. From an early age, he was exposed to modern educational standards, culminating in his doctoral studies in Berlin and in Halle, from which he received his PhD in 1846. Five years later, Hildesheimer assumed the position of rabbi of the Jewish community of Eisenstadt, Hungary, where he established what Ellenson described as "the first yeshiva in the modern world to have a secular component in its regular course of study."[20]

As in his other studies of German Orthodox rabbis, Ellenson was fascinated by Hildesheimer's ability to navigate between his deep commitments to halakhic observance, on the one hand, and to educational and cultural openness, on the other. Indeed, Hildesheimer appears in the book as the embodiment of *Bildung*, the vaunted German ideal of self-cultivation and self-formation through education that found large numbers of Jewish adepts throughout the nineteenth century. Hildesheimer hardly saw his Orthodoxy as an obstacle to the realization of *Bildung*. It was Ellenson's task to explain the worldview of an Orthodox rabbi for whom university study and general cultural literacy were not merely tolerable, but essential to the mission of social, moral, and spiritual edification. In this regard, the epitome of Hildesheimer's career was his involvement in the creation of a modern rabbinical seminary in Berlin in 1873. As the first director of the seminary, he was instrumental in shaping the philosophical and curricular contours of the institution. Thus, in addition to Bible, Talmud, and rabbinic codes, students studied Hebrew language, Jewish philosophy, ethics, and history, as well as homiletics. Moreover, Hildesheimer quite consciously—and controversially, among his fellow Orthodox Jews—encouraged a limited degree of openness to the approach and standards of *Wissenschaft des Judentums*, critical modern Jewish studies, in classes (though with limits, such as in discussions of the Hebrew Bible). In similar fashion, he insisted that students for the rabbinate at the seminary simultaneously enroll for PhD studies at the university. The result of such training would be a well-rounded rabbi able to serve the Jewish community with an impressive degree of intellectual and cultural authority.

The Hildesheimer seminary was the last of three new-style rabbinical seminaries that arose in Germany in the latter half of the nineteenth century. Each of the seminaries represented a distinct denominational strand within German Judaism: the Breslau Jüdisch-Theologisches Seminar (Positive-Historical or Conservative), the Berlin Hochschule für die Wissenschaft des Judentums (Liberal or Reform), and the Hildesheimer Seminary (Orthodox). In studying the three, Ellenson noticed a curious phenomenon. Notwithstanding their differences in religious ideology, "[t]he commonalities between the courses of instruction at all three seminaries is apparent." All three required students to study the same subjects and, more or less, in the same proportions. All three required students to work toward a PhD at a university. And all three, he added, shared a commitment to *Wissenschaft des Judentums*. In fact, the seminaries were among the few places where trained scholars in Jewish studies could gain employment in Germany.[21]

These commonalities in curriculum and scholarly standards did not, however, spell harmony and collaboration among the three. One of the reasons Esriel Hildesheimer felt an urgent need to create an Orthodox seminary was to combat the Liberal Hochschule in Berlin, which he regarded with great suspicion and concern. Under the veil of *Wissenschaft*, faculty members such as Abraham Geiger and Heymann Steinthal promoted what he regarded as heretical ideas.[22] Hildesheimer's mission therefore was to provide a safe alternative for Jewish students without surrendering the commitment to modern scholarly methods.

In analyzing Hildesheimer's efforts, Ellenson was intent on demonstrating that his subject had deeply and irreversibly embraced a modern worldview, but that the result was not a boundless religious ecumenism. On the contrary, Hildesheimer felt a constant need to draw a border between himself and those to the left of him religiously (just as he faced a steady stream of criticism from those to his right). In this sense, he embodied the space between the poles of outright accommodation and resistance that so persistently intrigued David Ellenson.

Ellenson devoted a large portion of his early research to studying the evolution of German Orthodoxy in that space. At the same time, he recognized that Orthodoxy's denominational opponents also dwelt in that middle ground, striking a somewhat different balance between accommodation and resistance. One especially illuminating source in gauging that balance was liturgy. Along with his interest in rabbinic responsa, Ellenson followed in the path of his HUC teachers Jakob Petuchowski and Lawrence Hoffmann in examining prayer books as a key measure of historical change. In one of his first published essays on liturgy in 1991, Ellenson studied the new prayer books produced by three non-Orthodox rabbis in mid-nineteenth-century central Europe: Isak Noa Mannheimer in Vienna, Abraham Geiger in Breslau, and Leopold Stein in Frankfurt-am-Main. On the one hand, all three strained to preserve the structure and formulations of earlier prayer books, at times against their own judgment and theological instincts. On the other hand, the "ubiquitous and relentless pressure of a larger central European cultural world" impelled modifications and alterations (for example, regarding the aspirations of Jews to return to Zion or reference to the ancient sacrificial cult).[23]

In a later essay devoted to a comparison of prayer books produced by Geiger and his successor as rabbi in Breslau, Manuel Joël, Ellenson was able to take stock of the similarities—and also differences—between Reform and Positive-Historical positions on the non-Orthodox side of the German Jewish spectrum. This textured analysis of two proximate and yet distinct positions on that spectrum affirmed a pair of principles that guided David Ellenson in his work on German Judaism: first, the nineteenth century, to which he devoted a great deal of attention, was "a time of great liturgical ferment in the life of the German-Jewish community," for indeed, change was everywhere about; and second, prayer books are "ideal barometers for measuring the moods and attitudes of the variegated religious streams of Judaism in Germany in modern times."[24] To study them closely required the kind of intimate familiarity with the siddur that Ellenson's background afforded him. At the same time, to read them as texts that reveal not stasis, but the dynamic and evolving character of religion required the kind of nuanced sociological approach that he acquired at Columbia. In this regard, he was animated by the words of his Columbia teacher Joseph Blau, who once wrote: "Not the least of the elements of the paradox that enter into the very nature of religion is the necessity that lies upon it, in its organized and institutionalized forms, to change while both seeming changeless and protesting its changelessness."[25] Indeed, the quality of appearing changeless while undergoing constant, if incremental, change was what attracted David Ellenson to the study of German Judaism, a task to which he brought a rare mix of textual erudition and theoretical sophistication.

Halakhah in Practice: The Israeli Case

Ellenson's scholarship has not been restricted, to be sure, to an examination of German Judaism. It has ranged widely, touching on many aspects of modern Jewish theology and philosophy, American Jewish life, and Jewish feminism and gender studies, among other topics. One of his most frequent sites of investigation has been Israel (or the pre-State Yishuv) where his favored genres of inquiry, responsa and prayer books, have operated in a very different context than in Germany.[26] That is, they have functioned in a Jewish majoritarian society whose leaders have tended to be secular in orientation and practice, who have harbored concerns over the specter of a Jewish theocracy, and who yet have maintained a respectful attitude to rabbinical figures (if only, at times, to advance the interests of their respective political coalitions).

In writing about the Israeli setting, David Ellenson has brought his own particular outlook and sense of commitment. If, as we noted earlier, he approached the study of halakhic responsa as a lawyer manqué, then we must also note that he approaches Israel as a sort of Israeli manqué. Indeed, his connection to Israel may well be the foundation of his entire Jewish sense of self. He relates in his autobiographical reflections that after spending eight months in Israel in 1972–73, he felt "a wholeness and completion I had never felt before or since"—to the point that he considers himself a "failed Zionist" for not having made aliyah.[27] Ellenson returned to Israel in 1997–98 and renewed his deep connection to the country, to his erstwhile professor, Jacob Katz, and to colleagues at Israeli universities as well as at the Shalom Hartman Institute, with which he has been affiliated ever since. As a general matter, his passionate Zionism adds a layer of personal significance and engagement to his study of responsa and liturgy in Israel, which possess a degree of authority and relevance to public life that they lack elsewhere.

In one of his earliest papers on an Israel-related subject, Ellenson presented a detailed review of a three-volume collection of responsa produced by Israeli Masorti rabbis (affiliated with the Conservative movement). He understood well that Masorti rabbis were and still are accorded little authority by the state, which recognizes only Orthodoxy as the official form of Judaism. Moreover, he opened the article by repeating the question posed by rabbi and scholar David Novak in 1974: is halakhah a meaningful or relevant category for Conservative Jews?[28] Nevertheless, he proceeded to offer a careful reading of the theoretical and practical conclusions of Masorti rabbis. In doing so, he eschewed a narrow, formalist understanding of legal decision-making as operating only according to its own internal rules. Instead, he drew on two leading legal theorists, Robert Cover and Ronald Dworkin, to understand the formation of law in a broader context. From Cover's famous article "Nomos and Narrative," he adopted the principle that law is "not merely a system of rules, but a world in which we live."[29] And from Dworkin, he came to the realization that law functions not only as legal prescription, but as "policy" that seeks to fulfill "the community's highest principles and ideals in the light of limitations imposed by a contemporary situation."[30] This very role of law as policy—and for that matter, as a scale of justice that must balance between allegiance to the past and responsiveness to an ever-changing present—is not unique to Masorti/Conservative Halakhah, but is shared by Orthodox Jews as well. In the particular case at hand, Ellenson noted how the Masorti responsa dealt with issues of a ritual nature (e.g., the use of a *mehitsah*, the barrier separating men and women in synagogue), as well as with issues of broader civic/national significance (for example, the question of whether women must serve in the Israeli Defense Forces).

The point in his paying attention to this compendium of responsa was, first, to make clear that there is a Masorti constituency for whom halakhah is relevant, if not determinative, in their lives. But second, it provided a lens through which Ellenson could trace the permeable boundary between religious and national considerations within the Jewish majority in Israel. This latter point comes into clearer view in a series of essays devoted to Orthodox halakhic decision-making in the Yishuv or Israel published in 2000–2001 and reprinted in *After Emancipation*. Of particular importance is the paper devoted to the attitude of three chief rabbis of Palestine and later Israel—Rabbis Kook, Ouziel, and Herzog—to the question of women's suffrage. Here, as in Ellenson's earlier studies of German Orthodox responsa, a key concern was the matter of membership. Who belongs to the Jewish polity? Who qualifies to participate in its governance? These questions reflect yet another version of the negotiation between tradition and modernity that has long fascinated Ellenson. But in this case, the stakes were somewhat higher, for they involved "the challenge of adapting Halakhah to the demands of a modern nation."[31] The first of the decisors to be studied, Rabbi Abraham Isaac Ha-Kohen Kook, was the chief rabbi of Palestine when the question arose whether women should be allowed to vote for the *Asefat Nivharim* (Elected Assembly) of the Jewish community. The issue prompted an intense debate in the Yishuv, with a particularly vocal role played by various non-Zionist haredi (ultra-Orthodox) groups. As Ellenson notes, Rabbi Kook was widely expected to endorse the right of women to vote in line with the desires of the broader Zionist movement. As it turns out, he unequivocally rejected the proposition as a violation of Jewish law and national spirit, though notably without relying on "a single halakhic precedent."[32] By contrast, the first Sephardi chief rabbi of the State of Israel, Rabbi Ben-Zion Meir Hai Ouziel, published a responsum in 1948, apparently written decades earlier when the Yishuv was in the throes of impassioned debate over the question, in which he unequivocally supported the right of women to vote. He took a further step and affirmed the right of women to serve in public office. Meanwhile, his Ashkenazic counterpart, Chief Rabbi Isaac Herzog, offered a somewhat less robust affirmation of the right of women to vote (and to serve in public office). Ellenson took note of the way in which Ouziel and Herzog confronted and then dispensed with the classical halakhic category of kingship as the relevant model in their deliberations.[33]

In so doing, each was expanding, according to his own style and degree of enthusiasm, the bounds of halakhic—and more broadly, national—inclusion in response to shifting gender demands.

Like his colleague and friend Zvi Zohar (see chapter 1), Ellenson has been especially interested in the distinctive path of Sephardic decisors in balancing tradition and modernity in Israel. In figures such as Rabbi Ouziel and his outstanding student Rabbi Hayim David Halevi, Ellenson found an open-minded, tolerant, and searching approach to halakhah that stood in contrast to that of many Ashkenazic decisors. Ellenson analyzed, and admired, this approach in an article on Rabbi Halevi's responsa on the obligations of the State of Israel toward its Arab minority. He argued that Halevi skillfully "mined" biblical and rabbinic sources in order to present "a moral vision" of humane treatment by the Israeli government toward its minority citizens. Halevi, who served as chief rabbi of Tel Aviv–Jaffa, was well aware that his responsa "did not have the force of law," but he did at the same time appreciate the extent of his moral and spiritual authority over "vast sectors of the Israeli public."[34] He used the form of the halakhic responsum to offer novel readings of biblical texts—not the normal source material of the decisor—in order to formulate clear moral directives for a broad public. Thus, he condemned King Saul for his role in the death of the foreign Gibeonites (II Samuel 21:1), insisting that it is "the obligation of every government to be concerned for the subsistence of its citizens, whether they are permanent residents or strangers." This obligation was the "great moral" to be learned and internalized by governments in their regular interaction with minority residents in their midst. Failure to discharge that obligation, Ellenson added, would bring "shame upon the Jewish people" and the God of Israel.[35]

As he had in countless other instances, David Ellenson aimed to demonstrate here through his study of Rabbi Hayim David Halevi both the elasticity and relevance of the halakhic system. His larger message was directed at multiple audiences. On one hand, he wanted to reveal to halakhically observant Jews that the boundaries of halakhah were constantly shifting—indeed, that jurists continually recalibrated the tradition to meet the exigencies of the day, particularly in the modern age. On the other, he concluded his Halevi article by acknowledging the decline of the plausibility structure of rabbinical authority in recent centuries, but still insisting—no doubt with his fellow non-Orthodox Jews in mind—that halakhah is "a crucial resource for the expression of Jewish teachings and a fundamental part of our patrimony as Jews."[36] In this sentiment is contained David Ellenson's own rich and complex connection to a traditional system to whose tenets he no longer adheres. That said, he studies it with as much acuity and empathy as any living scholar. His way is not dispassionate and disengaged study. It is study that can serve, he avers, as "the conduit to my soul."[37]

All who have encountered David Ellenson know of his passion, his engagement, his love for study as a way of understanding himself and his people. He studies law not only because of the intellectual pleasure in deciphering the tortuous turns of thought of halakhic decisors. Like Hayim David Halevi, he studies law in order to mine the tradition for moral principles to guide his community in the present. While not yielding a single Kantian "categorical imperative," these principles nourish David Ellenson's undiluted goodness and generosity of spirit, which, in turn, radiate out to the broader Jewish world. Rare is the person who combines such virtues with keen intelligence, clarity of mind, and moving eloquence. These are the qualities not only of a gifted scholar, but of an uncommon leader.

It is the great good fortune of the Jewish community to have David Ellenson—*talmid hakham* (scholar), *moreh derekh* (guide), *tsadik* (righteous one)—as one of its most important and beloved servants. His ability to balance the forces of tradition and modernity has served as an example worthy of emulation for thousands of students whom he has taught and inspired. May he continue to be, as the Psalms remind us with liturgical frequency, a *tsadik ke-tamar* (Ps. 92), a righteous one like a palm tree who brings forth fruit for many years to come.

Notes

1. David Ellenson, *Tradition in Transition: Orthodoxy, Halakhah, and the Boundaries of Modern Jewish Identity* (Lanham, Md., 1989), 2.
2. David Ellenson, *Rabbi Esriel Hildesheimer and the Creation of a Modern Jewish Orthodoxy* (Tuscaloosa, Ala., 1990), xi.
3. David Ellenson, *Between Tradition and Culture: The Dialectics of Modern Jewish Religion and Identity* (Atlanta, 1994), xi.
4. Ibid., xii.
5. Peter Berger, *The Sacred Canopy: Elements of a Sociological Theory of Religion* (Garden City, N.Y., 1967), passim. See also José Casanova, *Public Religions in the Modern World* (Chicago, 2004), 17–18.
6. See David Ellenson, "Judaism Resurgent? American Jews and the Evolving Expression of Jewish Values and Jewish Identity," *Studies in Contemporary Jewry* 17 (2001), 156–71, reprinted in the collection of Ellenson's essays that was awarded the National Jewish Book Award for 2004, *After Emancipation: Jewish Religious Responses to Modernity* (Cincinnati, 2004), 27–50.
7. Ellenson, *After Emancipation*, 16.

8. See Ellenson's autobiographical reflections in "A Separate Life," in *Jewish Spiritual Journeys: 20 Essays Written to Honor the Occasion of the 70th Birthday of Eugene B. Borowitz*, ed. Lawrence A. Hoffman and Arnold Jacob Wolf, 93–101 (West Orange, N.J., 1997).
9. See the autobiographical review in Ellenson, *After Emancipation*, 16–18.
10. See "Max Weber on Judaism and the Jews: A Reflection on the Position of Jews in the Modern World," originally in *What Is Modern about the Modern Jewish Experience?*, ed. Marc Lee Raphael, 78–88 (Williamsburg, Va., 1997), and reprinted in Ellenson, *After Emancipation*, 80–95.
11. Ellenson, *After Emancipation*, 18.
12. See "Jacob Katz on the Origins and Dimensions of Jewish Modernity: The Centrality of the German Experience," originally published in *The Pride of Jacob: Essays on Jacob Katz and His Work*, ed. Jay M. Harris, 97–123 (Cambridge, Mass., 2002), and reprinted in Ellenson, *After Emancipation*, 51.
13. See Jacob Katz, "Orthodoxy in Historical Perspective," *Studies in Contemporary Jewry* 2 (1986): 3–17. See also the important essay by Katz's student Michael Silber, "The Emergence of Ultra-Orthodoxy: The Invention of Tradition," in *The Uses of Tradition: Jewish Continuity in the Modern Era*, ed. Jack Wertheimer, 23–84 (New York: Jewish Theological Seminary, 1999).
14. Ellenson, "A Separate Life," 99.
15. Ellenson, introduction to *Tradition in Transition*, 1.
16. See Berger, *The Sacred Canopy*, 156, quoted in Ellenson, "Accommodation, Resistance, and the Halakhic Process: A Case Study of Two Responsa by Rabbi Marcus Horovitz," originally published in *Jewish Civilization: Essays and Studies Honoring the One Hundredth Birthday of Mordecai Kaplan*, vol. 2, *Jewish Law*, ed. Ronald Brauner, 83–100 (Philadelphia, 1981), and reprinted in Ellenson, *Tradition in Transition*, 123.
17. Ellenson, "A Separate Life," 96.
18. Ellenson, "Accommodation, Resistance, and the Halakhic Process," 139.
19. Of particular note is Ellenson's most recent book, co-authored with Daniel Gordis, *Pledges of Jewish Allegiance: Conversion, Law, and Policymaking in Nineteenth- and Twentieth-Century Orthodox Responsa* (Stanford: Stanford University Press, 2012).
20. *Rabbi Esriel Hildesheimer*, 2.
21. Ibid., 159–61 (quote at 161).
22. Ibid., 139.
23. See "The Mannheimer Prayerbook and Central European Communal Liturgies," in *Between Tradition and Culture*, 78.
24. See "The *Israelitische Gebetbücher* of Abraham Geiger and Manuel Joël," *Leo Baeck Institute Year Book* 44 (1999), 143–64, reprinted in Ellenson, *After Emancipation*, 193–222 (quotes at 193).
25. Joseph L. Blau, "Tradition and Innovation," in the volume that he co-edited, *Essays on Jewish Life and Thought Presented in Honor of Salo W. Baron* (New York, 1959), 95, quoted in Ellenson, *Rabbi Esriel Hildesheimer*, 21.
26. As Ellenson and co-author Daniel Gordis observe in *Pledges of Jewish Allegiance*, "[i]t seems almost inevitable that defining Jewishness in a Jewish state would be a different enterprise from doing so in a context in which Jews were a minority, often a powerless one" (121).

27. Ellenson, "A Separate Life," 97–98.
28. See David Novak, "Is Conservative Halakhah Possible?" *Judaism* (1976): 494, quoted in Ellenson, "Conservative Halakhah in Israel: A Consideration of the Rabbinical Assembly of Israel Law Committee Responsa, Volumes 1–3," in *Between Tradition and Culture*, 101.
29. Robert Cover, "Nomos and Narrative," *Harvard Law Review* 97, no. 1 (1983): 5, quoted in "Conservative Halakhah in Israel: Consideration," 104.
30. Ellenson, "Conservative Halakhah in Israel: Consideration," 105.
31. See David Ellenson and Michael Rosen, "Gender, Halakhah, and Women's Suffrage: Responsa of the First Three Chief Rabbis on the Public Role of Women in the Jewish State," in *Gender Issues in Jewish Law*, ed. W. Jacob and M. Zemer (New York, 2001), reprinted in Ellenson, *After Emancipation*, 347.
32. Ibid., 351.
33. Ibid., 364.
34. David Ellenson, "Jewish Legal Interpretation and Moral Values: Two Responsa by Rabbi Hayim David Halevi on the Obligations of the Israeli Government toward Its Minority Population," *CCAR Journal* 48, no. 3 (2001): 5–20, reprinted in *After Emancipation*, 412.
35. Ibid., 416.
36. Ibid., 421.
37. Ellenson, "A Separate Life," 97.

1

CARING FOR AN INTERMARRIED JEW BY CONVERTING HIS PARTNER

Rabbi Uzziel's Earliest Responsum on *Giyur* (Salonica, c. 1922)

ZVI ZOHAR

Preliminary Remarks

If one imagines tradition and modernity as two poles of a continuum, Reform Judaism would be regarded by many as modern rather than as traditional. However, Reform's position on this continuum has not been static over the movement's history. Thus, three of David Ellenson's manifold research interests are halakhah, conversion to Judaism, and Sephardic rabbinical creativity in modern times. Such a characterization of a person's interests, had it been made fifty or even thirty years ago, would have been enough to indicate that the person being referred to was *not* the president of the Hebrew Union College–Jewish Institute of Religion or a leader of the Reform movement in the United States and Israel. It is hard to imagine Nelson Glueck (HUC president 1947–71) or his successor Alfred Gottschalk poring over responsa by Esriel Hildesheimer, Moshe Feinstein, or Hayim David HaLevy—let alone regarding conversation with these sources as significant for contemporary Reform Judaism. David Ellenson's ability to engage such texts meaningfully, without in any way relinquishing the forward-looking intellectual and spiritual autonomy that is the hallmark of Reform Judaism at its best, is but one indication of his inspiring ability to span broad realms of Jewish creativity and life—as well as a signifier of dynamism within the Reform movement itself. His intellectual capabilities, together with his warm and friendly personality, reflect well upon the wisdom of those who saw fit to choose him as the intellectual and religious leader of Reform Jewry at the outset of the twenty-first century. That choice itself reflects in a most positive way the evolving nature of Reform Judaism, now able to interact in a more relaxed and balanced way with aspects of traditional Judaism against which it earlier vigorously contested.

The intersection of halakhah, conversion to Judaism, and Sephardic rabbinical creativity in modern times is itself an expression of interaction between tradition and modernity. Before modernity, intermarriage was very limited, and conversion to Judaism entailed great risks. The option of healing the social and religious anomaly created by intermarriage through inclusion of the non-Jewish partner into the community via conversion became a topos of halakhic thought primarily in the context of modernity. A leading halakhic author who devoted some twenty responsa to this issue was Rabbi Ben-Zion Meir Hai Uzziel (1880–1953), chief rabbi of Jaffa–Tel Aviv from 1912 until 1939 and subsequently chief Sephardic rabbi of Mandatory Palestine and of the State of Israel.[1]

In the following pages, I conduct a close reading of Uzziel's first responsum on *giyur* (conversion to Judaism), composed during his two-year stay in Salonica in the early 1920s.[2]

Salonica: Halakhic Questions Regarding Intermarriage and Giyur

In 1921 Rabbi Jacob Meir (Jerusalem, 1856–1939), who had been serving as chief rabbi of Salonica for more than a decade, was elected chief Sephardi rabbi of Mandatory Palestine.[3] Salonica had a large Jewish population, and under Ottoman rule had been a great center of rabbinical scholarship and creativity; Rabbi Meir was concerned for the community's future and asked Rabbi Uzziel to fill that post temporarily.[4] Rabbi Uzziel agreed and received a two-year leave of absence from his position in Tel Aviv–Jaffa.[5] It was in Salonica that he authored his first two responsa relating to giyur.[6]

As related in the she'elah (halakhic query) posed to Rabbi Uzziel, a Jewish man had married a non-Jewish woman in a civil ceremony, whereupon they approached the rabbinical authorities in Salonica seeking for her to become a Jew and to subsequently contract a Jewish marriage. Before 1982 civil marriage was neither possible nor recognized in Greece.[7] It is thus apparent that the man had spent time abroad, where he met and married his spouse. They returned to his native town and sought her giyur there so that their union would be recognized under Greek law and so that she could become part of his family and of the Salonican Jewish community at large. As Rabbi Uzziel explained: "When she enters the covenant of Judaism, she will be drawn nearer and nearer to her husband's family." Rabbi Uzziel presents the case as follows: "When I was serving as rabbi of the Salonican community, I was asked with regard to a [Jewish] man who had married a non-Jewish woman. They had lived together for several years and she bore him several sons. Now she requested to undergo giyur and to marry him in a Jewish ceremony." Rabbi Uzziel asked several questions:

1. May the [rabbinical] court agree to convert her, given that it stands to reason that her motivation is not for conversion per se but in order to marry him according to Jewish tradition?
2. May her husband marry her in a Jewish ceremony after her conversion, or is she forbidden to him because of the law concerning a person who was suspected with regard to a bondswoman or a gentile, who a priori may not marry her?
3. If he may marry her, is she required to separate from him for three "months of separation" before the marriage?[8]

Clearly, each subsequent question is contingent on a positive answer to the previous one. Rabbi Uzziel deals with each question separately and in detail. I shall now focus on a discussion and analysis of the content and method of his response.

May a Rabbinical Court Convert a Woman Linked to a Jewish Man?

The phenomenon of a non-Jew seeking to become Jewish for the sake of marriage is age-old.[9] Rabbi Uzziel begins his halakhic discussion with the *Shulhan ʻarukh*, cites additional material from Maimonides's *Mishneh Torah*, and notes the *Mordekhai*'s view,[10] as presented in Joseph Caro's *Beit Yosef*. All three sources instruct the court to reject a candidate for giyur whose motivation is utilitarian. If so, the correct response to the first question should be negative: a rabbinical court may *not* convert a woman seeking giyur for the sake of a Jewish man. But Rabbi Uzziel now introduces a different view, advanced by the Tosafot.[11]

The Tosafot sought to reconcile the implications of several Talmudic sources. *BYevamot* 24b indicates that rabbis should refrain from accepting candidates whose motivations are utilitarian. However, great scholars acted otherwise: Hillel converted a man who chose Jewishness for the sole declared purpose of wearing the ornate robes of the High Priest, and Rabbi Hiyya converted a woman who declared that she wanted to become a Jew in order to marry one of Hiyya's students.[12] The Tosafot resolved this matter by positing that it is permissible to convert a person who openly declares utilitarian motivation if the court is convinced that the convert will subsequently identify with his Jewishness "for the sake of Heaven." Citing this resolution in his magnum opus *Beit Yosef*, Rabbi Caro added: "From here we learn that all is contingent upon how it is viewed by the court." Rabbi Uzziel applies this principle to the couple in Salonica and concludes that the court may convert the woman based on their assessment of the consequences:

> The conclusion with regard to our case is that this gentile woman is already married to this Jew, and by now entering into the covenant of Judaism she will be drawn nearer and nearer to the family and the Torah of her husband; and furthermore, the children already born to her and those still to be born will be fully Jewish. Thus, this resembles the cases of Hillel and of Rabbi Hiyya, as it is certain that eventually they will be fully Jewish. Or, more correctly: it is a *mitsvah* for the court to draw them near, to bring them into the covenant of Israel's Torah, and to be rid of the affliction of intermarriage that is a cancerous affliction in the vineyard of Israel.[13]

Rabbi Uzziel's conclusion is far from self-evident. In the *Beit Yosef*, Rabbi Caro accorded the court discretion; however, he did not include this rule in his *Shulhan 'arukh*. Perhaps he had retracted his earlier view on the matter. Even if he hadn't, the meaning of the clause "eventually he would be [Jewish] for the sake of Heaven [*sofo le-shem shamayim*]" was moot; some rabbis explained it to mean that the convert would become a devout Jew.[14] Rabbi Uzziel, in contrast, interprets it as meaning that ultimately the convert's identification as a Jew will not be contingent on the fulfillment of his original utilitarian reason for giyur. In the case at hand, he judges that after conversion the woman will experience a gradual change of attitude due to several factors: increased closeness to her husband's family, greater closeness to Torah,[15] and self-identification as the mother of Jewish children. All these will synergistically transform her identity—and, knowing this, the court not only *may* accept her for giyur but is *commanded* to do so.

This imperative derives from a general teleological consideration: Religious leaders bear responsibility for furthering the progress of the entire Jewish people, *including the sinners*, toward a more positive condition in which estranged and liminal Jews become integrated within the community. In situations of intermarriage, this can be done by transforming the non-Jewish spouses—and the couple's children—into Jews. Therefore, if the rabbis judge that the non-Jewish spouse will ultimately internalize a noncontingent identification as a Jew, they are commanded by Torah to accept her or him for giyur.

May Her Jewish Spouse Marry Her after Her Giyur?

After determining that the non-Jewish wife should be accepted for giyur, Rabbi Uzziel moved on to the second question: Could she now marry the Jew with whom she had lived while still a gentile? Prima facie, this question seems strange: If we were to rule that they would not be allowed to marry each other, would she decide to convert nevertheless? Obviously not! Furthermore, Rabbi Uzziel above justified the assessment that she would ultimately remain Jewish "for the sake of Heaven" by explaining that "she will be drawn ever nearer to the family and the Torah of her husband." Thus, her acceptance for giyur was predicated upon her remaining together with her Jewish spouse. In addition, Uzziel thinks a general policy should guide rabbis: "To get rid of the affliction of intermarriage, which is a cancerous affliction in the vineyard of Israel," requires transforming a mixed union into a marriage between two Jews.

Clearly, the woman's conversion and her subsequent marriage to her Jewish spouse must function as an indivisible "package deal." What, then, led Rabbi Uzziel to suggest the possibility that their marriage after the giyur was not self-evident?

MYevamot 2:8 states that if a Jewish man is suspected of conducting an illicit relationship with a non-Jewish woman and she subsequently converts, she may marry any Jewish man—except one who had been suspected of sleeping with her, for such a union would set tongues wagging.[16] It might seem to follow that if their earlier liaison was not merely "rumored" but a public fact, there would be no reason to bar their marriage.[17] However, the Tosefta forbids their marriage after giyur when illicit relations were not rumor but certain.[18] Rabbi Uzziel therefore posits the following:

> We must understand the Mishnah to be taking a more radical position [than the Tosefta]: According to the Mishnah, even when there had been merely a rumor and the only concern is to prevent strengthening that rumor, he may not marry her [after she converted]. It thus goes without saying that if he had openly been in a relationship with her, their subsequent marriage would lead all the more to "dissembling mouths and perverse lips" with regard to his sin [and is

therefore also forbidden].[19] This understanding is supported also by the words of *Nimukei Yosef*,[20] [which holds] that the Mishnah's term "suspected" should not be specifically construed, rather, even if he *definitely* had sex with her the law is that a priori he may not marry her. But if he [nevertheless] did so, he should not divorce her. And so too wrote Rabbi Hayyim Shabbetai—see *Yad Aharon*, first edition, comments on *Beit Yosef*, §41.[21]

After analyzing another interpretation, that of Ramban in his novellae on *bYevamot*,[22] Rabbi Uzziel concludes: "It follows from the above that in the case under consideration [in Salonica], although it is known with certainty that he had intimate relations with her when she was not Jewish, and although he intends to remain married to her by renewing the marriage with *hupah* and *kidushin* [bridal canopy and marriage contract], he is a priori not permitted to do so because of [the consideration] 'Put away from thee a dissembling mouth.'"

Rabbi Uzziel's analysis thus leads to the clear conclusion that whereas it was a mitzvah to convert the non-Jewish spouse, the couple could not subsequently be permitted to marry each other.

In the next section of his responsum, Rabbi Uzziel critiques the positions of two recent rabbis—Rabbi Ya'akov Elyashar and Rabbi Shmuel Matalon—each of whom had permitted a Jew to marry his non-Jewish spouse after she had converted. We shall now present and consider his discussion of each.

> I saw that our pride, the Rishon le-Tsiyon Yisa Berakhah (in his book *Yisa Ish, even ha-'ezer* #7)[23] was asked about such a situation and permitted her marriage to her Jewish husband after her conversion, for since she had been married to him under their [i.e. civil] law, there was no cause to require them to separate as this is a[n a posteriori] situation of "if he married her he is not required to divorce her." And he relied upon what was written by our master the HIDA in *Hayim Sha'al* part 1 #49.[24] But in my opinion this is unreasonable; for their civil marriage is [halakhically] void and his sexual activity with her was illicit, and when we are asked to conduct a [Jewish] marriage ceremony for them, it is as if he is marrying her ab initio.

Rabbi Ya'akov Shaul Elyashar (1817–1906), known as Yisa Berakhah,[25] was Jerusalem's greatest rabbinical scholar during the latter decades of the nineteenth century and served as Rishon le-Tsiyon (Chief Rabbi of Jerusalem) from

1893 until his death. In 1894 he received a halakhic question from Melbourne: a Jewish man had lived in civil marriage with a non-Jewish woman, and then she underwent giyur. Could they now marry? In his responsum, Elyashar cited a ruling by Rabbenu Tam,[26] concerning a case in which a Jewish woman had converted to Christianity, married a non-Jew, and returned to Judaism, and her Christian spouse had then undergone giyur. Rabbenu Tam had allowed them to marry as Jews.[27] Elyashar wrote that HIDA had proposed the following resolution of the apparent conflict between this ruling and the Tosefta: when living as a Christian the woman had married her spouse in an official ceremony, and thus they had been living in a recognized legal union even before he became Jewish. Rabbenu Tam considered this an ex post facto situation governed by the rule "if he married her he is not required to divorce her." Rabbi Elyashar's conclusion with regard to the couple in Australia was that "Rabbenu Tam's ruling should be applied to our case as they have already married each other according to their [civil] laws, and the applicable norm is that of a situation where he disregarded [the a priori prohibition] and married her, and thus the court need not try to separate them and he may now cohabit with her licitly [in a Jewish marriage]." Australian civil marriage was halakhically equivalent to a situation of "he [already had] married her"; ergo "he is not required to divorce her." The rabbis in Australia should therefore conduct a Jewish marriage ceremony for the husband and his newly Jewish spouse.

Rabbi Uzziel rejects Elyashar's conclusion and writes: "This is unreasonable; for their civil marriage is [halakhically] void." The fact that their union was recognized by the non-Jewish legal system is of no halakhic consequence.[28] When such a couple applies for a Jewish marriage, they are like any other unmarried couple applying for marriage—and ab initio "he may not marry her." It is worthy of note that Uzziel does not feel called upon to suggest an alternative explanation for Rabbenu Tam's ruling and feels secure in his outright critique of Rabbis Azulai and Elyashar—each a halakhic authority of the first rank. His ground for negating their position is reason per se: "This is unreasonable."

Rabbi Uzziel next relates to the position of Rabbi Shmuel Matalon.[29] In the late 1860s Rabbi Matalon was asked about a Jewish man who had left his Jewish wife and moved to a different city, where he lived with a non-Jewish woman.[30] After some time, he divorced his Jewish wife. His non-Jewish partner sought "to convert and to live with that man according to the law of our holy Torah, to marry him with hupah and kidushin and seven benedictions according to the religion of Moses and Israel. Thus he will not eat the [nonkosher] meat of animals that died of natural causes."[31] In a long responsum, covering sixteen dense columns on folio-sized pages, Rabbi Matalon discussed two main halakhic issues. The first: Was it permissible to accept for conversion a woman whose choice of giyur was clearly affected by her living together with a Jewish man? The second: If she were to become Jewish, would it be permissible for her to marry the Jewish man with whom she had previously cohabited illicitly?

Rabbi Matalon's detailed analysis of these two issues was based on citations from a wide range of sources that situate him as part and parcel of the cultural-religious rabbinic tradition of the Jewish communities in the heartlands of the Ottoman Empire.[32] His response to the first question was that the prohibition against giyur for the sake of a Jewish man applies only when the woman could not become that man's spouse unless she converted. However, in the case at hand, they were already living together openly. Her current application for giyur was thus not "to obtain" a Jewish man, and she could therefore be accepted.

His response to the second question was reached after an extremely detailed analysis of the variety of ways in which halakhists had interpreted the Mishnah and the Tosefta constraining the marriage of converts who before their giyur had engaged in liaisons with Jewish partners. He devoted special attention to the position of Rabbenu Tam and the ways in which it had been understood by halakhic scholars. He noted that those who (unlike Tam) refused to permit the marriage of that Jewish woman to her (formerly Christian) partner did so because she had been married before her apostasy. Although her Jewish husband later divorced her, she could not marry the specific man with whom she had betrayed her husband. This consideration was not relevant to the case facing Matalon.[33] Therefore, those same rabbis would agree here with the conclusion to be drawn from Rabbenu Tam's position as construed by HIDA: since the couple had already married before her conversion, this should be seen as an ex post facto situation in which the relevant maxim was: "He is not required to divorce her."

Rabbi Matalon added that Rabbi Solomon ben Adret (Rashba) had forbidden a Jewish man who had cohabited with his female slave to marry her after she became a Jew, thus disagreeing with Rabbenu Tam.[34] Yet Matalon argued that this was irrelevant to the case at hand. First, Rabbi Caro in the *Shulhan 'arukh*—and other eminent authorities—had ruled according to Rabbenu Tam. Second, Tam's position was more lenient than that of Rashba, and "since the matter under deliberation is one of rabbinic law (*de-rabanan*), the general procedural rule for resolving which opinion to prefer is: "In matters of rabbinic law, follow the more lenient opinion."[35] Earlier, we noted that Rabbi Uzziel had rejected as "unreasonable" the attribution of any halakhic significance to civil marriage. He therefore disregarded Rabbi Matalon's conclusion and attributed validity only to Rashba's view forbidding a mixed couple to marry after the wife's conversion. It thus emerges that according to Rashba, the Jewish husband of this convert may not marry her after her giyur. The upshot of Rabbi Uzziel's analysis was, therefore, that after the non-Jewish wife of the Salonican Jew undergoes giyur, she may not marry her erstwhile partner.

Overriding Standard Halakhah

At this point, however, Uzziel introduces a surprising twist: Whereas standard halakhah indeed forbids their marriage, other considerations—specified by Maimonides—override that prohibition. Maimonides was asked about a young Jewish man who had acquired a bondwoman and was suspected of cohabiting with her. He noted that according to the Mishnah even were she to become a Jew, her erstwhile master could not marry her. However, Maimonides gave three justifications for overriding the Mishnaic rule. Uzziel writes:

> Maimonides of blessed memory wrote (in *Pe'er ha-dor* #132)[36]: Despite the [Mishnaic] rule that if a man was suspected [of intercourse] with a bondwoman and she was released and [thus] became a Jewess, *ab initio* he may not marry her. We have already ruled several times that, in such cases, he should release her and marry her. And the reason we did this is because of the enactment for the encouragement of penitents;[37] and we said: "He should rather eat gravy than the meat itself."[38] And we relied on the words of the rabbis, may their memory be blessed: "It is time to act for the Lord: they have made void thy Torah." (Ps. 119:126)[39]

Thus, it is preferable in the eyes of God that the young man and his bondwoman continue their relationship in the framework of Jewish marriage—and Maimonides concludes his responsum with a directive to the local court that the young man "is to be helped to marry her, kindly and gently."[40]

Rabbi Uzziel states that the considerations that guided Maimonides also apply to such cases as the one before him in Salonica: "These precious words of his are our guide in all matters that do not involve an absolute prohibition, and such is the case with regard to him who is suspected of cohabiting with a non-Jewish woman or to he who has actually done so. For if we will not permit her to marry him after her giyur, they will remain together forever without her converting, and their children will be mixed offspring, uprooted from Israel's soil." That is to say, if rabbis would apply the law as it stood and forbid them to marry after her conversion, she will not convert. Her Jewish partner would not abandon her, and thus they would live in a state of permanent sin. In order to encourage him to become a penitent with respect to this sin, it is right to suspend application of the original Mishnaic law in the spirit of an "enactment for the encouragement of penitents." But passive restraint is not enough: positive action is required of the rabbis, namely to conduct a Jewish wedding for the couple. Such positive action contrary to the Mishnah ("if she converted he may not marry her") is analogous to what is done when a pregnant woman is seized by a craving for nonkosher food. It does not say there that "she *may* eat the gravy" but rather "they *should feed her* the gravy." Saving the husband from the negative consequences of remaining with a non-Jewish wife merits active rabbinical participation in conducting the couple's marriage although it is forbidden by the Mishnah.

Other negative consequences to be overcome pertain to the fate of the couple's children: "Their children will be mixed offspring, uprooted from Israel's soil." Rabbi Uzziel's concern for these children is worthy of note. The Salonican couple's children were halakhically non-Jewish. How then could they be "uprooted" from an identity they never had? Even the term "*their* children" is not self-evident. According to halakhah, in any mixed marriage there is no genealogical connection between the male progenitor and the children—in other words, they are not "his," but considered the descendants of the mother alone.

In the responsum we are analyzing Rabbi Uzziel gives no explanation for his concern for ensuring the Jewishness of these children. However, in a responsum written in 1936 to Rabbi Benzion Lichtman of Beirut,[41] Rabbi Uzziel explains the rationale that guided his decision in Salonica in order "to rescue the children from their gentilehood," saying, "For as long as the mother is a non-Jew, they are as she is. But now, when she will convert, her children—who are seed of Israel [zera' yisrael]—will be converted with her. And it is certainly a benefit for these innocent souls to be rescued from assimilation, and it is a mitzvah for us to draw them near, so that those who are distant shall not be severed from us [she-lo yidah mimenu nidah]." Rabbi Uzziel's very first responsum on giyur thus reveals key elements of his religious worldview, elements that were to become explicit in his later writings. Rabbis bear responsibility for ensuring that the offspring of a Jewish parent will be Jews. This responsibility applies also to offspring who are not halakhically Jewish. It entails that rabbis do all they can to bestow upon these children—and their non-Jewish parent—the halakhic status of Jewishness. In order to do so, the rabbis must utilize the powerful halakhic tools set forth in Maimonides's responsum. By converting the non-Jewish spouse of the Jewish man in Salonica, together with her (and his) offspring and enabling the couple to join together in a Jewish marriage after her giyur, Rabbi Uzziel acted to fulfill his rabbinical responsibility with regard to prevention of their assimilation and toward the inclusion of the "seed of Israel" under the wings of the Shekhinah.

Postscript: Ellenson and Uzziel

As David Ellenson has cogently argued, even were rabbis willing to convert all the non-Jewish spouses of Jewish men or women, this would not suffice per se as a response to intermarriage and its consequences. Many intermarried Jews, and their spouses and children, are currently uninterested in conversion and have at best an ambivalent attitude toward the Jewish aspect of their identity. Rather, Ellenson (and Kerry Olitzky) go on to say:

> Outreach, not conversion, is the best strategy to draw people, born Jewish or not, from the periphery into a revitalized Jewish community. If we can create an open Jewish community through effective outreach—a community that is welcoming, embracing and meaningful—then people will want to join our ranks. . . . Our community has to demonstrate—through experience—why living a Jewish life will add meaning to their lives and the lives of their children. We must be prepared to do this, and we must do so in a spirit that Rabbi Zvi Hirsch Kalischer articulated in the 19th century when he labeled children born of gentile mothers and Jewish fathers as holy offspring. He argued that the community should do everything in its power to facilitate the entry of such children into the Jewish community.[42]

Rabbi Uzziel's characterization of such children as "seed of Israel" resonates closely with Rabbi Kalischer's view. Both set forth the concept of a particular human collective characterized by a core that consists of persons who are halakhically Jews (*Yisrael*) and a penumbra consisting of persons of Jewish origin (*zera' Yisrael / zera' kodesh*). Those in the penumbra are "estranged" (or "far off")—*nidahim*. It is the responsibility of the Jewish leadership—specifically, of rabbis—to prevent the total severance of these persons from the Jewish people "so that those who are distant shall not be severed from us [*she-lo yidaḥ mimenu nidaḥ*]."[43] Rabbis are bound to extend themselves to the utmost so as to (re)include these persons within the core community of *Yisrael*. Since the core community comprises all persons who are halakhically Jews, a sine qua non for (re)inclusion within that community is giyur.

At this point, I believe, a difference in nuance between two viewpoints may be perceived. Rabbis Ellenson and Olitzky hold that membership in the Jewish community is significant because it adds vital meaning to a person's life. Individuals will be motivated to join that community if they have come to appreciate and acknowledge that meaning. To arrive at such appreciation and acknowledgment, one must experience it directly. Personal participation in the life of a vibrant Jewish community is therefore the path of entry into Jewishness. That is, de facto membership in the community, by active involvement in religious activities such as synagogue and home rituals as well as Jewish education and learning, should precede de jure inclusion via conversion.

If one were to apply here a historical-cultural methodology as favored by David Ellenson in many of his works,[44] one might read this position as situated within contemporary American religious reality. A major 2007 survey of religion in America described the United States as "a very competitive religious marketplace. . . . Constant movement characterizes the American religious marketplace, as every major religious group is simultaneously gaining and losing adherents."[45] The extent of such movement is great: "More than one-quarter of American adults (28 percent) have left the faith in which they were raised in favor of another religion—or no religion at all." A Jewish think-tank declared that this was a positive phenomenon: "Church-switching reflects the vigorous good health of American religion."[46] In this reality, religious affiliation is increasingly based not on birth and ethnic origin, but is rather a personal choice founded on individual conviction and existential preference—that is, on the perceived merits of the various religions. Under such circumstances, conversion to Judaism will be the outcome of individuals' positive regard for the Jewish religion and of their positive experiences of participation in religious activities within the Jewish community. This is precisely what Ellenson and Olitzky posit: "If we can create an open Jewish community through effective outreach—a community that is welcoming, embracing and meaningful—then people will want to join our ranks."

Uzziel and Kalischer, however, were not situated within a society embracing the "Marketplace of Religions" cultural model. Rather, they were working under another paradigm, according to which Jews are first and foremost not a religion, but an extended kinship group. The primary mode of affiliation with this group is thus, naturally, by birth. Membership in this group entails rights and duties. The rights include, among others, the right to benefit from the support and goodwill of other members, to marry a member of the group, and to enjoy a special covenantal relationship with God. The duties mirror the rights: extending support and goodwill to other Jews, marrying within the group, and following the way of life outlined in the covenant, that is, Judaism. However, while membership entails duties, it is not contingent on their fulfillment: as in other families, a person born into the family remains kin, however inappropriately they conduct themselves. Given the kinship paradigm of membership, giyur is best understood as a rite through which a person originally born as a non-Jew becomes kin. Having done so, their Jewishness is as irrevocable as that of any other member.[47]

While Uzziel and Kalischer would certainly prefer that a person's decision in favor of giyur be based on, and motivated by, deep appreciation of Torah and of Jewish life, such subjective identification does not seem to them a *necessary* precondition for accepting a person into the group. Especially in situations of boundary ambiguity (such as couples or families in which only one partner or parent is currently Jewish), the prime consideration should be to extend support and goodwill to the Jewish partner and to resolve the ambiguity by including the non-Jewish partner (and the couple's children) within the kinship group. In other words, Uzziel and Kalischer attach significance to membership in the core community of Yisrael even if this is not subjectively experienced as adding vital meaning to a person's life, and even if the choice to become a Jew was motivated by seemingly mundane considerations. Once a person is within the core community, she or he is in the company of all other Jews, many of whom are themselves far from perfect in their awareness of the vitality and meaningfulness of Jewish life. Now unequivocally part of Yisrael, the convert can—together with his or her sisters and brothers in the kinship group—progress toward ever-increasing comprehension of what being Jewish means and entails. And even if the convert does not progress at all, she or he has undergone the crucial transformation from "outsider" to "insider" that creates the foundation for his or her children or grandchildren to achieve great things. As Kalischer wrote, there is a real "possibility that great leaders of Israel will spring from among them."

Returning now to David Ellenson, if the only justification for Jewish affiliation is because it adds vital meaning to an individual's life, why should he (or any Jew) advocate outreach? Why should the Jewish community per se try to influence the individual choices of non-Jews by making Jewishness meaningful and attractive? As I understand it, David Ellenson here—as in many other realms—is personally and existentially at the convergence of the two viewpoints outlined above. Resonating deeply with the kinship paradigm of Jewishness, as reflected in his admiration for Kalischer, it is precisely out of concern for the future of that group that he advocates outreach. Given a culture in which there is a "marketplace of religions," he realizes that the kinship group may not remain viable if it does not adapt to the fluid reality of American religious life by openly manifesting its most attractive and meaningful aspects both to Jews by birth and to others. And given Ellenson's deep and serious acquaintance with the treasures of Jewish creativity throughout the ages, as well as his own lifelong experience, there is no doubt in his mind that Judaism is indeed replete with attraction and meaning. As a leader of Reform Judaism in these complex times, Ellenson is doing his utmost to enable the group's members (and their families) to live in the light of those treasures—and thus to enjoy the fullest blessings of membership in the ancient but constantly renewing covenantal kinship community of Yisrael.

Notes

1. I analyze and discuss these responsa in my recent book *Ve-lo yidah mimenu nidah* (Jerusalem, 5773/2012).
2. *Mishpetei 'Uzziel*, vol. 1, Yoreh de'ah, responsum 14; also included in *Piskei 'Uzziel* (1977). As such, it is briefly referred to in David Ellenson and Daniel Gordis, *Pledges of Jewish Allegiance: Conversion, Law, and Policymaking in Nineteenth- and Twentieth-Century Orthodox Responsa* (Stanford, Calif., 2012), 130. The first part of this article presents main points of the very detailed analysis of this responsum in chapter 1 of my book cited above; the second part of this article, comparing the strategy of Uzziel (and Kalischer) to that of Ellenson (and Olitzky), is completely new.
3. On Rabbi Meir's career up to this point see David Ashkenazi, "From Jerusalem to Saloniki: Rabbi Jacob Meir's Leadership as 'Haham Bashi' in Jerusalem and Grand Rabbi in Saloniki" [in Hebrew] (PhD diss., Bar Ilan, 2008).
4. An excellent work on Salonica under Ottoman and then Greek rule is Mark Mazower, *Salonica, City of Ghosts* (London, 2004). Salonica had been conquered by Greece in 1912. The transfer to Greek Christian rule after more than four centuries in a Muslim milieu was not easy for the city's Jews, and the difficulties of the war years, compounded by a great fire in 1917 that devastated the Jewish neighborhood, had a powerfully negative effect upon the community. Rabbi Meir's sense of concern was therefore well grounded.
5. On his activities in Salonica and his continued relationship with that community after his return to Israel, see Yitzchak Kerem, "Rabbi Uzziel as Chief Rabbi of

Salonica and His Subsequent Links with the Community," in *Rabbi Uzziel and His Contemporaries*, ed. Z. Zohar, 166–89 [in Hebrew] (Jerusalem, 2009).

6. *Mishpetei 'Uzziel*, vol. 1, Yoreh de'ah, responsa 13 and 14; these deal with different aspects of the same case. In number 14 the question is raised whether a Jewish man's non-Jewish wife may be converted to Judaism and then celebrate a Jewish marriage with him. In responsum number 13 the question is: Given that she may be accepted for conversion, how should her immersion for giyur be accomplished, seeing that there was no possibility for men (i.e. the conversion "court") to accompany her to the mikveh? *Mishpetei 'Uzziel* was arranged in accordance with the order of topics in the *Shulhan 'Arukh*, and thus responsum 14 was placed after responsum 13.

7. See Charalambos K. Papastathis, "Greece: A Faithful Orthodox Christian State," *Religion and the Secular State*, ed. J. Martinez-Torrón and W. C. Durham Jr., 339–75 (Provo, Utah, 2010) (online at www.iclrs.org/content/blurb/files/Greece.2.pdf [accessed December 30, 2013]). The relevant legal acts that enabled civil marriage were: Law 1250/1982 on Civil Marriage; Presidential Decree 391/1982 regulating civil marriage issues; and Act 1329/1983 on the modernization of family law.

8. *Mishpetei 'Uzziel*, vol. 1, Yoreh de'ah, responsum 14. All further quotations are from this source, unless otherwise indicated. All translations are mine.

9. For a survey and analysis of halakhic positions from antiquity to the present regarding conversion for nonreligious reasons, see: Avi Sagi and Zvi Zohar, *Transforming Identity* (London, 2007), 9–103.

10. Mordekhai ben Hillel Hacohen (c. 1250–98) was a leading Ashkenazic halakhic scholar. His position is discussed in Sagi and Zohar, *Transforming Identity*, 19–21.

11. Tosafot on *bYevamot* 24 s.v. *lo bi'mei David*.

12. *bShabbat* 31a; *bMenahot* 44a.

13. This paragraph is quoted in Ellenson and Gordis, *Pledges of Jewish Allegiance*, 130–31.

14. Thus, Rabbi Yitzchak Schmelkes (1828–1905) allowed a court to convert a person whose current motivation was utilitarian only if the court is convinced that "subsequently he will be God-fearing" (Responsa *Beit Yitshak*, 2, Yore de'ah, responsum 100, §4).

15. It should be noted that he does not speak of her becoming God-fearing or observant of specific commandments.

16. In *bYevamot* 24b Rabbi Assi cites Prov. 4:24: "'Put away from thee a dissembling mouth, and perverse lips put far from thee.'" He derives from these verses a guideline for Jewish communal authorities: they should prevent community members from acting in a way that will raise gossip. Specifically, if we were to allow this man to marry the convert with whom he had been suspected of having had an illicit relationship, this would lead to gossip. Therefore, the marriage should be prevented."

17. That is, their subsequent marriage would not strengthen any rumor, as their earlier relationship had been public knowledge. If so, the Mishnah's restriction would not apply and the couple in Salonica, whose relationship had been overt, could marry after her conversion.

18. *tYevamot* 4.6: "If a non-Jew . . . cohabited with a Jewish woman, then, even if the non-Jew underwent giyur . . . he may not marry her."

19. According to this interpretation, the Mishnah accepts the Tosefta's position and extends it to include cases in which the liaison had merely been *suspected*. Logically, another possibility exists: that the two sources disagree, with the Tosefta

forbidding the subsequent marriage only if the earlier relationship had been *explicit* and the Mishnah forbidding such marriage only if the relationship had been merely *suspected*. If so, we would rule according to the Mishnah (whose authority outranks that of the Tosefta) and there would be no bar to the marriage of the couple in Salonica.

20. *Nimukei Yosef* is a commentary on the Talmud and on the rulings of Rabbi Yitshak Alfasi (1013–1103) authored by Rabbi Yosef Haviva of fifteenth-century Spain.

21. *Yad Aharon*, vol. 1 (Istanbul, 1756), by Rabbi Aaron Alfandari (Izmir c. 1700–Hebron 1774) is a compendium of comments and glosses on the major fourteenth-century code *Arba'ah Turim* and on Rabbi Joseph Caro's composition *Beit Yosef*. In the section cited by Uzziel, Alfandari focuses among other things on the compatibility (or lack thereof) between the Mishnah and the Tosefta. He quotes Rabbi Hayyim Shabbetai (1551–1647) as determining that the Mishnah accepts the Tosefta's position and expands on it.

22. Ramban is the acronym of Moses Nahmanides (Spain 1194–Jerusalem 1270).

23. Rabbi Ya'akov Shaul Elyashar (see below).

24. HIDA—Hayim Yosef David Azulai (1724–1806)—was one of the greatest Jewish scholars of the eighteenth century. In *Hayim Sha'al* (vol. 1, responsum 49) he discusses the case of a non-Jewish man who had engaged in a relationship with a married Jewish woman. Then two developments occurred: Her (Jewish) husband divorced her and her non-Jewish paramour underwent giyur. Rabbi Azulai was asked if she could now marry him.

25. In Psalm 24:5 the words *yisa berakhah* relate to the Heavenly blessing conferred upon the righteous person who is worthy to ascend God's mountain. This was applied to Rabbi Elyashar as a righteous and worthy rabbinical leader of Jerusalem's Jewish community.

26. The great twelfth-century Ashkenazi scholar Ya'akov ben Meir.

27. HIDA notes that this ruling is cited in *Terumat ha-Deshen* no. 219 and by the Tosafot (*Yoma* 82b, *Sanhedrin* 74b, and *Ketubot* 3b).

28. In a later responsum, dated 1947, Rabbi Uzziel expresses a different, positive view of Rabbi Elyashar's position. See *Mishpetei 'Uzziel,* mahadurah tinyana, vol. 2, *Yore de'ah,* #58.

29. One of Salonica's leading rabbis in the latter part of the nineteenth century, Rabbi Matalon passed away in 1891. See Yitzhak Emmanuel, *Matsevot Saloniki* (Jerusalem, 1968), 2:852–53.

30. The time framework of this responsum may be deduced from the fact that he quotes "the recently published" *Nediv Lev*, vol. 2, referencing the author as alive. The second volume of *Nediv Lev* was published in 1866 and its author, Rabbi Hayyim David Hazan, died in 1869. Thus, Matalon's responsum was written between those two dates.

31. *'Avodat ha-Shem*, fol. 47b. The words "Thus he will not eat the [nonkosher] flesh of animals who died of natural causes" allude to the Talmudic explanation for the Torah's permitting an Israelite warrior to marry a non-Israelite captive of war: "The Torah took the evil inclination into account—better that Israel should eat the flesh of animals who had been on the verge of death when [properly] slaughtered rather than eat the flesh of animals who died of natural causes" (*bKiddushin* 21b). This is an allegorical formulation of the principle of preferring the lesser evil.

32. He cites, among others, the following works: *Kise Rahamim* (authored by HIDA); Responsa *Maharhash* (Hayyim Shabbetai, Salonica, 1557–1647); *Mishneh la-Melekh* (Yehuda Rosanes, Istanbul, 1657–1727); *Zer'a Emet* (Ishm'ael ben Avraham haCohen, Modena, 1723–1811); *'Erekh he-Shulhan* (Yitshak Tayeb, Tunis, 1786–1828), *Sha'ar ha-Melekh* (Yitzchak Nunez Belmonte, Izmir, eighteenth–nineteenth centuries); *Hiqre lev* (Rafael Yosef Hazan, Izmir 1741–Jerusalem 1822); *Tosefet Yom ha-Kipurim* (Moshe ben Haviv, Salonica 1654–Jerusalem 1696); *Shoreshe ha-Yam* (Rafael Yitshak Mayo, Izmir, d. 1810); *Admat kodesh* (Nissim Mizrahi, Jerusalem, d. 1749); *Hayim ve-shalom* (Hayyim Palache, Izmir, 1788–1868); *'Erekh Lehem* (Ya'akov Castro, Cairo, 1525–1610).

33. In the case discussed by Matalon, the betrayer was not the wife but the husband. According to classic halakhah, polygamy is a lesser sin than polyandry. Thus, a married woman who has sex with another man faces much greater sanctions than does a married man who has sex with an unmarried woman.

34. Rashba, Spain, 1235–1310.

35. *'Avodat ha-Shem*, fol. 50a. Rabbi Matalon added to this a general policy consideration: "Due to our many sins, the current generation is lesser than previous ones, and there are many individuals who refuse to follow the instructions of rabbis. There is thus reason for concern that if we do not permit him to marry her after her giyur, he will distance himself even more from Judaism [and continue to cohabit with her outside of wedlock]. Therefore, we should be lenient even though doing so requires us to act in a slightly prohibited way. For it is best that he should eat the flesh of animals who had been on the verge of death when [properly] slaughtered, rather than eat the flesh of animals who died of natural causes" (ibid., 50d). These words resonate with the problem as presented to Matalon (above). A similar consideration had been applied by Maimonides—and was adopted by Uzziel (see below).

36. A collection of responsa by Maimonides printed in Amsterdam, 1765. Our translation here follows the superior text of this responsum, published in vol. 2 of the scientific edition of Maimonides' responsa, ed. Joseph Blau (Jerusalem, 1960), 374–75. The differences between the two editions do not affect the content of the points noted by Uzziel.

37. The rabbis struck a balance between a thief's desire to repent and his psychological inability to return the stolen article itself, as required by Torah. Their enactment allowed him to retain possession of the article itself, returning only its *value* (cf. *mGittin* 5.5; *bGittin* 55a). Similarly, Maimonides rules that the Jew living with the bondwoman should be allowed to mend his ways without breaking up the relationship (as required by the Mishnah) by marrying her after she becomes a Jew.

38. A *beraita* in *bYoma* 82a discusses the case of a pregnant woman suddenly overwhelmed by a craving for nonkosher meat. Since eating nonkosher gravy is a less severe transgression than eating forbidden meat, "'they should feed her the gravy.'" Similarly, given the worse option (that the young man would continue the relationship "as is"), the less negative option should be chosen: having him free her and then marry her, *pace* the Mishnah.

39. The plain meaning of that verse is: For God's sake, strong action must be taken against those who void the Torah. However, the rabbinic-midrashic reading—powerfully stated in *mBerakhot* 9.5—is: In order to act for the Lord, it is sometimes proper to void the Torah, i.e., in certain situations the religiously correct path of

action is to directly transgress an injunction of Torah so as to attain a result that God would consider preferable.

40. Blau edition, 375.

41. Born in the Ukraine (1892), Rabbi Lichtman studied in Lithuanian yeshivot and was ordained by Rabbi Isser Zalman Meltzer. In the 1920s he made aliyah to mandatory Palestine, then moved to Beirut (1932). In 1936 he was serving there as a *dayan* (rabbinical judge). Rabbi Uzziel's responsum to Rabbi Lichtman, dated 29 Tevet 5696 [= January 24, 1936], was discovered in the Tel Aviv Municipal archives by Dr. Naama Sat and included in her PhD dissertation: "Rabbi Uzziel's Halakhic Rulings on Matters of Family Law" [in Hebrew] (Bar Ilan University, 2008), appended after 307. I discuss the correspondence between Lichtman and Uzziel in *Ve-lo yidah mimenu nidah*, chap. 3.

42. David Ellenson and Kerry Olitzky, "Conversion Is Not an Outreach Strategy," *Forward Newspaper Online: Forward Forum*, May 12, 2006, http://forward.com/articles/1396/conversion-is-not-an-outreach-strategy/ (accessed January 23, 2014).

43. Uzziel, responsum to Lichtman.

44. Including major parts of his outstanding recent book on giyur, co-authored with Daniel Gordis, *Pledges of Jewish Allegiance*.

45. *U.S. Religious Landscape Survey*, conducted by the Pew Forum on Religion and Public Life, http://religions.pewforum.org/reports (accessed January 2, 2014). The survey is based on interviews with more than 35,000 residents of the United States age eighteen and over, conducted in 2007.

46. Rodney Stark and Gary Tobin, "Competition and the American Religious Marketplace," *Institute for Jewish and Community Research*, March 2008, www.jewishresearch.org/v2/2008/articles/demography/03_08.htm (accessed January 2, 2014).

47. On this and other aspects of giyur/conversion, see Sagi and Zohar, *Transforming Identity*.

2

GAINING MORAL GUIDANCE FROM THE JEWISH TRADITION

Four Examples to Test David Ellenson's Approach and Mine

ELLIOT N. DORFF

Tradition and Modernity

As this volume illustrates in multiple ways, the interaction between tradition and modernity is not a new phenomenon. In fact, the Jewish tradition responded to cultures surrounding it from its earliest sources in the Bible and Rabbinic literature. Sometimes it completely borrowed outside ideas or practices (e.g., commercial law); sometimes it completely rejected the foreign idea or practice (e.g., the idolatry demanded by the Seleucid Greeks in the Hanukkah story as told in the Books of Maccabees); and most often it assimilated some parts but not all of the input from other cultures, generally giving even these influences a distinctively Jewish rationale and form.[1]

One also must distinguish what the religious elite were doing in any age from what the masses of Jews were doing. So, for example, even though the Bible rails against idolatry in laws and in the hortatory speeches of Moses and many of the Prophets, we see repeated Israelite engagement with idolatry from the Golden Calf incident through the stories of Former Prophets and in archaeological evidence.[2] Thus, on the very first day of a course that I took with Professor Moshe Greenberg, he distinguished between biblical religion and Israelite religion, the former being what the leaders of the people, the ones who wrote the books of the Bible, were thinking and doing, with the latter being what the members of the Israelite community were thinking and doing. That distinction continues to our own day.

It is important to recognize, however, that the leaders and the people they lead are ultimately part of the same community, and so it should not be surprising that the leaders' thought and practices influence the people, and, conversely, the people's thought and practices influence the leaders. Jewish religion, law, and culture, then, are always the product of the *interaction* between the leaders and the people they lead.[3]

Furthermore, the interaction between tradition and modernity affects every aspect of the Jewish tradition—its thought, culture (dress patterns, foods, music, art, dance, literature, etc.), its interactions with non-Jews and their cultures, and its hopes for the future. It also affects its law and ethics. As I discuss in detail in my book *Love Your Neighbor and Yourself: A Jewish Approach to Modern Personal Ethics*,[4] Classical Judaism from antiquity to early modernity derives ethics from a whole series of sources, including stories, proverbs, history, theology, prayer, and study, but it especially uses law as its vehicle to guide Jews' behavior, to decide hard moral questions, and to motivate Jews to be moral. In gaining moral guidance from the Jewish tradition, then, it is critical to determine whether Jewish law is still to be used at all as a resource for morality, and, if so, how.

Nonlegal vs. Legal Methods of Gaining Moral Guidance from the Jewish Tradition

To honor David Ellenson in this volume, then, I have chosen to continue a conversation that he and I have had in both oral and written form for decades about this very issue of whether and how to use Jewish law in determining and motivating Jewish morals. The written form of our discussion began with Ellenson's essay "How to Draw Guidance from a Heritage: Jewish Approaches to Moral Choices."[5] Based on the medical decisions he had to make when his mother was dying, Ellenson describes first what he calls the position of "halakhic formalism." In that approach the Jew with a question goes to his or her rabbi, who learns the facts of the case and then applies Jewish law to it, and then the questioner is supposed to follow the ruling of the rabbi. As he says, "This approach to medical ethics, while text-centered, is hardly univocal. Different authorities read the same texts in diverse ways. They offer different opinions as to which texts provide appropriate analogues for understanding a contemporary situation."[6] Moreover, advocates of this approach can take modern science into account because of the principle embedded in Jewish law of *shinui ha-itim*, a changed reality. Furthermore, "the methodological direction provided by 'halakhic formalism' does not preclude lenient or demand stringent positions. Tremendous discretion in how the sources are read remains with the rabbi who is issuing the decision. Rather, the methodology simply demands that the decision be warranted by a text taken from the tradition."[7]

Ellenson, however, finds this approach wanting in several ways. First, "individual autonomy is not prized as an independent variable in this approach to Jewish medical ethics."[8] Rabbis can have great compassion for the people involved, but ultimately it is rabbis who make the decisions, not patients, let alone their families or physicians. This undermines the authority of individuals to determine what will happen to them in their medical treatment, which, minimally, undermines the strong sense of individual autonomy that Western liberalism has taught Jews in Western countries to value highly.

Worse, this method takes away a sense of responsibility for whatever decision is made, for now the patient or surrogate can say that it was the rabbi's decision, not his/her own. In the wake of claims of Nazi subordinates that they were just following orders, Jews in particular need to be wary of removing responsibility from the person who rightfully has it—in our case, the patient or surrogate. Indeed, Ellenson cites Rabbi Irving Greenberg, who says, "The proper lesson to be derived from this horrific event [the Holocaust] is that bureaucracy, when left unchecked, can totally deprive people of power and lead to excesses of evil behavior."[9] Ellenson, like Greenberg, seeks instead "to assert an ethic of power, an ethic of human beings charged with responsibility and control for their own decisions."[10]

Moreover, the technology of modern medicine is so vastly different from that of even the recent past that none of the texts of our tradition until very recent times even contemplated modern medical realities, let alone dealt with them. This means that any rabbi trying to use classical Jewish texts to determine whether or not, for example, to remove a heart-lung machine is reading whatever he or she wants into the text, not honestly basing the decision on the text. This is eisegesis, not exegesis—that is, this is reading into the text (the etymological meaning of "eisegesis") whatever one wants to read into the text, often pretending that it is the actual meaning of the text, in contrast to exegesis (literally, reading out of the text), which is either an honest attempt to determine the original meaning of the text (*peshat*) or to provide a reasonable derivation or application of the text (*midrash*).

In light of these issues, Ellenson proposes instead what he calls "covenantal ethics," which differs from "halakhic formalism" in two primary respects. First, the person facing the decision makes it, not a rabbi. The person involved may consult with a rabbi—and, for that matter, with family members and people with other forms of expertise relevant to the issue at hand—but ultimately it is the person involved who makes, and has responsibility for, the decision.

Second, the Jewish materials that the person (and his or her rabbi) should use include not only whatever legal precedents might be relevant, but also any other Jewish materials that might guide one's decision. This includes the theology and anthropology of the tradition—that is, how it perceives God, humans, and the relationships between them. It is important to note that Ellenson demands that Jews consult these materials, including the legal ones: "This means that one must search out the tradition for those precedents relevant to the making of an ethical decision. Not to do so would provide an unwarranted break with a huge dimension of the tradition and would deny Jews the continuity and wisdom such precedents have to offer."[11] Still, in the end, it is the individual who should make the decision, and thus the Covenant to which Ellenson refers in his methodology of "covenantal ethics" is ultimately one between the individual Jew and God in the context of the Jewish people, *not*, as traditionally conceived and as I would maintain, a Covenant between God and the Jewish people as a whole.

I felt a need to respond to Ellenson because, in my view, there is much in his proposal that is right but also much with which I disagree. To take the latter first, I am one of the people he identifies as an exemplar of "halakhic formalism." This is very ironic, because my own approach to halakhah is anything but formalistic. Legal formalism is a school in legal thought that identifies the law only with authoritative legal texts; any other considerations—moral, economic, social, pragmatic, and so forth—are, in the words of a genuine proponent of legal formalism in Jewish law, Joel Roth, "extra-halakhic," that is, outside the law.[12]

There are, however, other schools of legal thought about how law does and should operate, which Ellenson fails to take into account. My own approach is contextual, and in my later articles and in my book on Jewish law, *For the Love of God and People*,[13] I argue *against* legal formalism as applied to Jewish law. Instead, I advocate seeing Jewish law as an organism, much like a human being.

Human beings are body and soul, and the two constantly interact and affect each other. What we think, feel, and desire and our relationships with other people—what I call collectively our "soul"—have major effects on our bodies, and the reverse is true as well. Jewish law has a number of properties that are common to the body of every legal system. Just as people's bodies differ, however, the body of each legal system has distinctive features, including its particular way of addressing the issues common to all human beings (its substance) and its particular mode of operation (its methods).

The most significant differences among people, however, are functions of their personalities—their thoughts, emotions, aspirations, and associations. The same is true for communities and their legal systems: Law has not only organic, physical features (which I describe in chapter 2 of *For the Love of God and People*—the *corpus juris*, literally, the body of the law), but also properties rooted in its community's philosophical vision and its emotions—that is, the particular way the members of a society understand and feel about themselves, others, and the world in which they live. These internal qualities determine the role of law in their lives.

So, for example, in contrast to the Enlightenment's view of human beings as individuals with rights, which leads people in Western countries to think that the purpose of law is to preserve rights, with major implications for law's limits and methods, the Jewish tradition understands Jews as members of a thick, organic community that has chosen to respond to God's commandments and fulfill its mission of fixing the world. The aim of law, then, is to help the Jewish community accomplish that goal. Such underlying perceptions of the source and purposes of the law directly affect its scope, content, procedures, and tone, making, in our example, Jewish law significantly different from Western legal systems like that of the United States. American Jews, of course, inherit both the Western liberal and Jewish traditions, and many of the extra-halakhic considerations that affect Jewish law in our time arise in the attempt to reconcile the two. Other extra-halakhic factors, however, come from within the Jewish tradition itself.

David Ellenson, of course, could not have known what I was later going to write, but by bundling all approaches to Jewish law into the sweeping category of "halakhic formalism," he abandons Jewish law as a method to gain moral guidance much too quickly. Thus in 1991, the year after his article appeared in print, I wrote an article in response to his that makes the following points: "My view ultimately rests upon three factors: (a) my appreciation of the *strengths* of a legal approach to the moral issues in life, and the corresponding weaknesses of the suggested alternative; (b) my conviction that personal responsibility *can* be retained in a properly understood halakhic system; and (c) my confidence that, *when properly understood and applied*, legal methods can enable Jewish law to treat realities as new as contemporary medical phenomena."[14]

As I explain these points in the article, the strengths of a legal approach to moral issues include "the continuity, authority, and coherence that this method produces, together with its ability to balance the past with the needs of the present. . . . In contrast, a method that seeks to determine morality on the basis of each individual's interaction with God poses a severe danger of anarchy, for each person will be on his or her own in determining what is right and good. One wonders how community is supposed to be maintained under such a system. . . . Moreover, this 'covenantal' method ironically robs individuals of precisely what they seek when they turn to religion for guidance in these matters, for it tells them to seek God and decide for themselves!"[15] My appreciation of the weight of these factors has led me to affiliate with the Conservative movement, which takes Jewish law to be authoritative; conversely, the emphasis on individual autonomy embedded in Ellenson's approach has led him to identify as a Reform Jew.

At the same time, a legal way of gaining guidance from the tradition does not necessarily remove personal responsibility for one's decisions because even in a legal system, "individuals retain the obligation to examine any law or ruling for its morality and to disobey all laws and rulings that are immoral on their face."[16] This is not a new phenomenon in Jewish law; the Torah already warns us not to follow leaders who would lead us astray theologically or morally,[17] and the Mishnah and Talmud include an entire tractate, *Horayot*, which provides guidelines about when one should follow a court's instructions and when not.

Finally, Jewish law can, in my view, be used effectively and wisely only if it is applied in an intelligent way. We clearly cannot simply look up chapter and verse, as we would if we wanted, say, to build a sukkah, for building a sukkah has not changed much in two thousand years, while many of the moral questions we are now asking arise in contemporary contexts that our ancestors never even contemplated, let alone rendered authoritative answers. We need to develop a keen sense of *judgment* so that we can, among other things, weigh the applicability of precedents; distinguish among rules, principles, and policies; balance general rules and individual cases; and recognize the impact of the individual reader and the community of readers on the classical materials we are now interpreting and applying. In addition, we need to bring into our legal discussions moral, theological, economic, social, and practical concerns—not as extralegal considerations, but as part and parcel of how an organic system of law operates. Furthermore, we need to recognize when Jewish narratives, proverbs, history, liturgy, and philosophy can help us decide hard moral issues—again, as an integral part of the process of determining law, with no embarrassment or apologies for calling on sources beyond legal texts.

As readers should recognize, I come close here to what Ellenson advocates in asking us to do what I call "depth theology," that is, bring to bear our deepest concepts and convictions about God, humans, and the interactions between them in making concrete decisions of practice. The difference between us is that Ellenson wants us to go directly to such sources and to ask each individual Jew to know and apply them to the decision at hand. In contrast, I want rabbis who really know such sources to apply them to their legal analysis of what Jews should do in such circumstances, and then that decision can guide a Jewish community. Different Jewish communities may interpret and apply the law differently, varying by movement and even within each movement, and one must remember the interaction that I described earlier between leaders and the people they lead; but ultimately the law as articulated by rabbis is, for me, a critical guide in determining what is moral and in making that decision identifiably Jewish.

End-of-Life Decisions

Subsequent to that interchange, in two articles I have illustrated how my method would work in two areas where contemporary realities are radically different from those of the past. In one I addressed medical decisions at the end of life, which is exactly the example Ellenson uses in his article.[18]

There are exactly four sources in classical and medieval Jewish literature that even contemplate that human beings might have the power sustain life medically or to choose to remove all interventions to allow nature to take its course. None of these sources assumes modern medicine, though, and so none is directly on point.

Thus, we have three choices: at one end of the spectrum, we can decide that because no source directly deals with the current question, Judaism has nothing to say about it. This approach has the advantages of honesty—for it is indeed true that the tradition has nothing directly to say about the issue at hand—and of freedom, for if the tradition says nothing, one may choose to do whatever one wants. The disadvantages of this approach, however, are serious. After all, there are many areas of life where modern technology, science, political and economic circumstances, and moral views are different from those of the past, and so if one follows this approach one will effectively make the Jewish tradition irrelevant to many areas of life. We Jews, though, value our tradition in part because it gives us moral guidance, and this approach would deprive the tradition of that role, making our tie to the Jewish tradition weaker. Furthermore, if we cannot turn to the Jewish tradition for moral guidance, where should we turn? The same factors that, according to this approach, make the Jewish tradition irrelevant to end-of-life decisions make all other traditions irrelevant as well, for no ancient or modern tradition has dealt with contemporary medical decisions until and unless they have been stretched to do so in recent times. This response to the Jewish tradition, then, leaves us bereft of any source of moral guidance.

At the other end of the spectrum, there are those who, quoting the Mishnah, say, "Turn it over, and turn it over again, for everything is in it."[19] They search the tradition for any source that, by hook or by crook, can be used as a source of authority for a particular decision, even if the source does not really speak to the question. The advantage of this approach is that it reaffirms the continuity of the tradition and confers the authority of the tradition upon the particular decision. It also makes the tradition relevant to every question. The disadvantages of this approach, though, are very serious, for it is disingenuous. It is making texts mean things they never contemplated, let alone dealt with directly. It is eisegesis, not exegesis. Thus this approach is inherently dishonest, for it pretends to announce what the tradition would have us do, but the interpreter is actually inserting whatever decision he or she wants into the text rather than gaining moral guidance from it. Finally, if Jews want to call on the Jewish tradition for its wisdom or even for what God wants of us, this approach will not afford us either of those things, for it is the individual interpreter that is responding to the tradition, not the texts of the tradition or God's will as derived from those texts.

What I proposed in the article, then, is the use of the approach I am advocating now. Specifically, where there are indeed texts on point, we should definitely use them. Thus at the other end of life, the Torah and later the Mishnah and Talmud announce the very specific view that the fetus is not a person and therefore does not have the protections that full-fledged people do—that, in fact, if the mother's life or health is threatened, the fetus must be aborted to save the mother's life.[20] That line of precedents can and should guide us not only on the issue of abortion, but also on embryonic stem cell research.[21]

When texts of our tradition are not on point, however, as is the case with end-of-life decisions, then we should use "depth theology," identifying and applying the fundamental Jewish perspectives and values to the issue at hand. In the case of end-of-life decisions, this will involve, for example, the legal

principle based on the four sources that do exist—namely, that we may neither hasten nor delay the dying process. It will also involve the Jewish theological assertion that we are mortal, that "there is a time to be born and a
time to die,"[22] and the moral demand that we do what is in the best interests
of the patient. Other factors will also play a role, as, for example, the need of
the community to spend its resources wisely. In my book on Jewish medical
ethics, *Matters of Life and Death,* I spell out what applying these precedents and
principles means for specific medical decisions.[23]

War

The same question about how to derive moral guidance from the Jewish tradition when contemporary circumstances are vastly different from those of
the past arises in many areas outside medical ethics. In this and the following
two sections of this essay, I will illustrate how my method of deriving such
guidance applies to very different categories of questions in terms of their
complexity and scale of magnitude, and how David Ellenson's approach would
differ from mine.

One such topic in which there seems to be a lack of relevant sources is that
of war. Jews as a nation decided whether to go to war only in three periods of
history: from Moses to the end of the First Temple period; during the century of
Hasmonean rule; and since 1948 in the modern State of Israel. Jews have been
drafted into other people's armies, but only in those three periods did Jews as
Jews have both the power and the responsibility to decide whether to go to war
and how to wage it. As a result, Jewish sources about the motivations and procedures to decide to go to war and the proper conduct within war and thereafter
are either very ancient or very modern. Rabbinic, medieval, and early modern
treatments of war were all formulated in a vacuum of actual military experience. How, then, should we articulate a contemporary Jewish ethic of war?

In responding to the same facts, Professor Michael Walzer suggested at a
conference to which he and I both contributed papers that we should import
secular and Catholic just war theory. There is much precedent for Jews using
the legal institutions and thought of other peoples in defining their own law
and philosophy. As a result, Walzer's proposal is not outlandish or somehow
traitorous to the Jewish tradition. I argued, however, that we should instead
identify the Jewish concepts of God, human beings, society, and international
relations as well as what we know about modern warfare and politics to articulate a modern Jewish ethic of war. Both papers have since been published

in *Philosophia*.[24] Note, though, that neither of us suggested what Ellenson proposes, in part because his methodology applies at most to individual decisions and not to national ones, a major problem for his theory.

Providing References for Schools or Jobs

In the previous cases of end-of-life decisions and war, Jewish sources were written in contexts that were so dissimilar to our own that few, if any, of the sources were helpful in gaining moral guidance for our time, and depth theology had to be used to its fullest. In what follows, I will consider two rabbinic rulings that I have written on moral issues for the Conservative Movement's Committee on Jewish Law and Standards, in which some of Jewish law applies quite clearly to the case at hand, but factors about the American environment require that a contemporary rabbi use judgment about when and how to apply it. Furthermore, in each of these cases there is a communal dimension that a legal approach like the one I am advocating is able to address in a way that Ellenson's method does not do nearly as well.

Judgment, of course, has always been required of judges and rabbis in applying the law to a specific circumstance. Even when the issue before the decision-maker was not new at all, his (and now her) good judgment marked the character of a good ruling rather than just a mechanical application of the law, sometimes with very harmful consequences. The first story I heard about Jewish law, in fact, was the one my father told me. My grandparents lived in Milwaukee, across the street from a large Orthodox synagogue, of which they were members. Because of the proximity, they often hosted guests of the congregation for the Sabbath. One Friday afternoon my grandmother sent my father, then a lad of fifteen, to ask Rabbi Solomon Scheinfeld whether guests were expected that week. Rabbi Scheinfeld served that congregation from 1902 to 1943, and, according to the *Encyclopedia Judaica*, "was the recognized head of the city's Orthodox congregations during his tenure." When my father entered the rabbi's office, Rabbi Scheinfeld was in the process of deciding whether a chicken was kosher. As he turned the slaughtered chicken over in his hands, he asked the woman who had brought it many questions about the physical and economic health of her husband and family. After he pronounced the chicken kosher and the woman left the room, my father asked him why he had asked so many questions about her family. The rabbi turned to my father and said, "If you think that the kosher status of chickens depends only on their physical state, you understand nothing about Jewish law!" What the rabbi had determined through his questions was that if he pronounced the chicken unkosher, the family would have nothing to eat that night, and that affected how stringently he would apply the relevant criteria. Thus judgment is required even if the question is the very old and narrow one of the kosher status of a chicken.

Modernity, however, makes this quality all the more critical, for now rabbis must deal with some very new questions. They then must learn about the new circumstances or technologies; probe the tradition for anything relevant to their decision about how to act in the face of these new conditions (and determining what is or may be relevant is itself often a hard task); and then sensitively apply such precedents, concepts, and values to the issue at hand.

One such case is the question of what one should say when asked to give a reference for an applicant for a school or job. The Jewish tradition provides a very sophisticated and nuanced ethics of speech, much more so than American law. Jewish law forbids not only slander and libel, but lies, gossip, and even true but defamatory information about someone unless the hearer has a practical need to know it. In the case of potential schools and employers, that practical need exists, and so the strong commitment of the Jewish tradition to truth would instruct Jews asked for a reference to tell the truth as they see it, including the negative as well as the positive factors that should affect the school's or employer's decision.

American law, though, allows people to sue for virtually anything. So do Jews following Jewish law on this matter open themselves up to at minimum a court case, and possibly serious monetary damages for conveying negative information about someone? My wife served as personnel director for the Bureau of Jewish Education of Los Angeles for a time, and she was told that when asked for a reference, she may only affirm that a teacher was employed by a particular school from date x to date y. She was not allowed to convey even positive comments about the teacher, let alone negative ones.

As part of the work of the Conservative Movement's Committee on Jewish Law and Standards, I asked a lawyer who is a lay member of the committee to write a section on how American law affects Jews asked for such references. He pointed out that there are some protections built into American law to shield those providing references from liability, and that therefore Jews should follow the directions of Jewish law when asked for references. Still, one still might find oneself in court defending against a lawsuit if one provides negative information about someone, and even if one prevails, who wants to risk the time and expense of being involved in a court case?

This, then, is a case in which Jewish law gives clear instruction on a moral matter, but the American legal environment makes following Jewish law risky.

A legal analysis of the case, though, provides contemporary Jews with all the factors involved, including the Jewish values at stake as well as the relevant information about American law.

How would David Ellenson's approach deal with this case? The individual can—and probably should—consult both a rabbi and lawyer as part of his or her process of making a decision, but the decision is a matter of individual choice. In the end, of course, individuals must decide what to do on either theory, but in mine they get the benefit of a careful legal and moral analysis of the tradition and a communal norm to guide them, while in Ellenson's, each individual must determine how to balance the competing factors involved in the larger context of their individual Covenant with God.

Furthermore, if the person consults his or her rabbi, that person may do a thorough job of probing the tradition on this issue, but the chances are that the rabbi will have neither the time nor the expertise to do that on every issue. That is the reason that the Central Conference of American [Reform] Rabbis has a Responsa Committee to guide its members on a variety of issues. There is no clear role for the work of that committee in Ellenson's model except indirectly—specifically, if the rabbi consulted by an individual chooses to check for a responsum on the issue. In contrast, the commitment to Jewish law embedded in my approach means that both rabbis and individual Jews confronted with this issue would be more likely to examine what Jewish law says about it. Thus, the Jewish character of the individual's ultimate decision is likely to be much deeper in my approach than in Ellenson's.

Violent and Defamatory Video Games

Well over 90 percent of boys and men—and high percentages of girls and women as well—play video games. Although the amount of time they spend on these games is often excessive, the content of the vast majority of the games raises no moral problems. Some are even educational. A small percentage of them, however, are violent and/or defamatory, in which the player scores points for killing human-like figures, raping them, or maiming them, and often the targets are women, minorities, or police officers. These games are unfortunately among the most popular.

Although the video game industry rates the games in a manner parallel to the movie industry to indicate which games should be reserved for adults, the courts have held that the Constitutional right of free speech protects these games from censure. Therefore, to justify a ban of such games would require proof that such games lead to violent behavior in real life. The professional organizations in the field of psychology have warned that these games have this dangerous potential (though recent discussion suggests no link between them and gun violence), but the fact of the matter is that very few of those who play these games perpetrate the portrayed actions in real life. Thus, it is hard to argue for a ban of such games based on their alleged consequences.

Some have sought to ban these games on the basis of moral principles, such as Kant's categorical imperative that people should do only that which they would want permitted to all others. Kant's imperative applies, though, only to real life, not to the world of fantasy.

So how shall we characterize and deal with the moral problems that these games raise? In a rabbinic ruling I wrote for the Conservative Movement's Committee on Jewish Law and Standards along with a former student of mine, Rabbi Joshua Hearshen,[25] I traced how Jewish law would respond to the argument based on the potential consequences of playing such games and the moral principles involved, with an extensive treatment of how Judaism understands the relationship between one's mental states and one's physical actions. In the end, though, it was a third approach that was the most instructive—namely, Judaism's concern for creating good moral character. The ultimate rulings, then, were as follows:

1. "To do the right and the good in God's eyes" (Deut. 6:18) and to help us make progress toward fulfilling our aspiration to be "a kingdom of priests and a holy people" (Exod. 19:6), Jews of all ages ought not to play violent or defamatory video games. The games that are inappropriate are any that have the following in them: coercive sex, violence and encouragement to kill in settings where those are not required for self-defense, or negative portrayals of women, police officers, or minority groups, whether of religion, ethnicity, race, or sexual orientation. In addition, children and teenagers ought not to play sex or war games that are rated "M" for mature. Video games with other themes may be played but, like all games, should not occupy so much time that the player ceases to engage in the other worthwhile activities of life. As a matter of aspiring to be a holy people and in recognition that we are all created in the image of God, we must examine the games that we and our children play to determine what they say about us as individual Jews and as a people, and we must then select only those games that are not violent or

defamatory. Parents are asked to reinforce these goals by modeling the same standards in their homes and in their own lives.

2. On an institutional level, Jewish goals of character development require that violent or defamatory video games, as defined in (1) above, not be allowed at any program of any Conservative/Masorti movement–affiliated institution. This includes, but is not limited to: Camp Ramah, United Synagogue Youth, day schools, supplementary schools, and any social events or parties held at a synagogue or under synagogue auspices, whether for children, teenagers, or adults.

Although the conclusion just cited invokes the Torah's verses that ground the later Rabbinic legal discussion and ultimately the ruling, the responsum draws heavily on Jewish legal precedents to indicate how these biblical principles are to be applied. It then expands on those earlier interpretations and applications of these biblical principles to apply them to the case at hand—namely, violent or defamatory video games. The responsum thus illustrates that using Jewish law in the expansive way that I advocate enables it not only to treat moral choices faced by individuals, but also to set communal norms, including those intended to produce the kinds of people that Judaism aspires to help us be.

How would David Ellenson's method approach this question? Even if questioners take seriously their individual Covenant with God, and even if they consult with many people, they would be deprived of the richness of this kind of legal treatment of the issue. Moreover, individuals could decide only for themselves; communal norms could emerge only if everyone agreed—and even then, individuals might change their minds and opt out of the communal consensus. Here again, Ellenson's method needs at least to be supplemented to accomplish these character-building and communal functions of Jewish law.

Conclusion

In exploring David Ellenson's example of end-of-life decisions and also the example of war, I have illustrated how his approach and mine would respond to issues where classical sources address a radically different reality from our own. In probing the examples of providing references and playing violent and/ or defamatory video games, I have suggested how his approach and mine would respond to issues where a communal norm is needed. In both sorts of cases, I think that my legal approach provides a clearer and more Jewishly rooted guide for both individual Jews and Jewish communities than his does. This means that in this ongoing conversation of ours, the ball is now in David's court!

Notes

1. Shaye J. D. Cohen has illustrated these varying processes of assimilation in the last two centuries BCE and the first two centuries CE in his book *From the Maccabees to the Mishnah* (Philadelphia, 1987).
2. See Ziony Zevit's documentation of this based on the archaeological evidence: Ziony Zevit, *The Religions of Ancient Israel* (London, 2001).
3. For an exposition of this theme with regard to Jewish law, see Elliot N. Dorff, *For the Love of God and People: A Philosophy of Jewish Law* (Philadelphia, 2007), chap. 7.
4. Elliot N. Dorff, *Love Your Neighbor and Yourself: A Jewish Approach to Modern Personal Ethics* (Philadelphia, 2003), 311–44.
5. In *A Time to Be Born and a Time to Die: The Ethics of Choice,* ed. Barry Kogan, 219–32 (Hawthorne, N.Y., 1990); reprinted in *Contemporary Jewish Ethics and Morality: A Reader,* ed. Elliot N. Dorff and Louis E. Newman, 129–39 (New York, 1995).
6. Ibid., in Dorff and Newman, *Contemporary Jewish Ethics and Morality,* 133.
7. Ibid., 135.
8. Ibid.
9. Ibid., 137.
10. Ibid.
11. Ibid.
12. Joel Roth, *The Halakhic Process: A Systemic Analysis* (New York, 1986), 1–12, 231–34, 302–4; I have reprinted these sections and analyzed his theory in Elliot N. Dorff, *The Unfolding Tradition: Philosophies of Jewish Law,* 2nd ed. (New York, 2011), 208–32.
13. Elliot N. Dorff, *For the Love of God and People: A Philosophy of Jewish Law* (Philadelphia, 2007). For my own critique of my own theory, see Dorff, *The Unfolding Tradition,* 311–52.
14. Elliot N. Dorff, "A Methodology for Jewish Medical Ethics," *Jewish Law Association Studies* 7 (1991): 35–57; reprinted in Dorff and Newman, *Contemporary Jewish Ethics and Morality,* 161–76 (quotation on 163).
15. Ibid., in Dorff and Newman, *Contemporary Jewish Ethics and Morality,* 164.
16. Ibid., 165.
17. Deut. 13:2–19, 17:2–7, 18:9–22.
18. Elliot N. Dorff, "Applying Jewish Law to New Circumstances," in *Teferet Leyisrael: Jubilee Volume in Honor of Israel Francus,* ed. J. Roth, M. Schmelzer, and Y. Francus, 189–99 (New York, 2010).
19. *mAvot* (*Ethics of the Fathers*), 5:22.
20. Exod. 21:22–25; *mOhalot* 7:6; *bYevamot* 69b (during the first forty days of gestation, the fetus is "simply water"); *bHullin* 58a and elsewhere (after the first forty days, the fetus has the status of the thigh of its mother).
21. Elliot N. Dorff, "Stem Cell Research," *Conservative Judaism* 55, no. 3 (2003): 3–29.
22. Eccl. 3:2.
23. Elliot N. Dorff, *Matters of Life and Death: A Jewish Approach to Modern Medical Ethics* (Philadelphia, 1998), chaps. 8 and 9.
24. Michael Walzer, "The Ethics of Warfare in the Jewish Tradition," *Philosophia* 40 (2012): 633–41, http://link.springer.com/content/pdf/10.1007%2Fs11406-012-9390-5 (accessed January 5, 2014); Elliot N. Dorff, "War and Peace: A Methodology to Formulate a Contemporary Jewish Approach," *Philosophia* 40 (2012): 643–61, http://link.

springer.com/article/10.1007%2Fs11406-012-9391-4/fulltext.html (accessed January 5, 2014).

25. Elliot Dorff and Joshua Hearshen, "Violent and Defamatory Video Games," February 4, 2010, available on the Rabbinical Assembly's website at www.rabbinicalassembly.org/sites/default/files/public/halakhah/teshuvot/20052010/videogames%20 Dorff%20Hearshen%20Final.pdf (accessed January 6, 2014).

3

THE ROLE OF REFORM
IN ISRAELI ORTHODOXY

ADAM S. FERZIGER

I first came across an article by David Ellenson, titled "The Role of Reform in Selected German-Jewish Orthodox Responsa: A Sociological Analysis," during my graduate studies at Bar-Ilan University in the early 1990s.[1] The author employed the functional approach to the sociology of deviance to examine how responses of prominent nineteenth-century German rabbis to Reform facilitated their efforts to cultivate internal Orthodox group identity. This was my first exposure to the application of such an apparatus. It inspired me both to explore additional ways in which this perspective could offer insight into modern Jewish religious life and more broadly to seek out further writings from the author of this enlightening study. The following discussion is dedicated to David—long since a dear friend and academic mentor—and introduces a similar methodological perspective to consider developments within contemporary Israeli Orthodoxy.

One of the key perceptions emphasized by Emile Durkheim is that deviance plays a central role in coalescing mainstream society. The appearance of deviant behavior, he argued, causes those who reject it to solidify their connections with one another by emphasizing what they share in common.[2] Expanding on this theory, Kai Erikson wrote, "The deviant is a person whose activities have moved outside the margins of the group, and when the community calls him to account for that vagrancy it is making a statement about the nature and placement of its boundaries. It is declaring how much variability and diversity can be tolerated within the group before it begins to lose its distinctive shape, its unique identity."[3] If Durkheim called attention to the usefulness of deviance in group building and the need for it to make regular appearances, Erikson came closer to saying that societies often actually look for opportunities to utilize deviance in this manner.[4] Both their works suggest that it is simply easier to define what one is not than it is to articulate an identity in clear, positive terms. By labeling certain people as "outsiders," the rest understand who belongs to the group.

Building on this approach, Ellenson's article focuses on a selection of German Orthodox rabbis who themselves were secularly educated and had adopted a positive attitude toward many aspects of modern culture. Nonetheless, they were adamant in defining certain theological doctrines as well as aesthetic and ritual changes that were adopted by German Reform as beyond the boundary of authentic Judaism. This they did despite the availability of lenient precedents that permitted such adjustments. Indeed, it was only once these behaviors or attitudes were associated with Reform that they took on symbolic meaning as declarations of departure from accepted religious tenets. Thus, for example, numerous individual premodern synagogues had organs, but after this innovation was adopted universally by Reform it became emblematic of a more fundamental ideological digression from accepted tradition. By highlighting the responses of moderate figures who were open to other aspects of contemporary culture, Ellenson demonstrated that the issues they chose to forbid in their boundary-defining rulings solidified their own association with the broader Orthodox camp, including those who rejected all aspects of modernity.[5]

In the following discussion I focus on contemporary Israel, an environment in which the Reform movement has made limited inroads and where few people are familiar with the details of its worldview. All the same, the label "Reform" is drafted consistently within Orthodox discourse as a tool for demonizing ideological opponents and rendering them outside the margin of normative religious life. In this context, I examine cases in which Israeli religious Zionist rabbis and organizations utilize attacks against Reform representatives to solidify their own place within the Orthodox spectrum. Moreover, I will consider episodes of internal debate within the Orthodox camp in which conservative ranks attack their liberal Orthodox compatriots. The main claim of the more traditionalist critics is that the religious legal policies and educational approaches of the moderates share much in common with the nineteenth-century Reformers demonized already in the literature that David Ellenson has analyzed with great acumen and erudition. By raising this analogy, the contemporary polemicists distinguish themselves from their colleagues and diminish the differences between the conservative religious Zionist rabbinate and the non-Zionist haredi rabbinate.

Rabbi Moses Sofer (1762–1839), the Hatam Sofer, was one of the most vociferous opponents of the Reform movement during its initial rise in early nineteenth-century central Europe.[6] In an 1819 letter, which upon its posthumous publication achieved almost canonic status among Sofer's students and followers,[7] he articulated a sharply adversarial approach to Reform that resonated in much of the subsequent Orthodox discourse on the topic: "If we had the power over them, my opinion would be to separate them from us, we should not give our daughters to their sons and their sons should not be accepted for our daughters so as not to be drawn after them. Their sect should be considered like those of Zadok and Boethus, Anan and Saul, they among themselves and we among ourselves."[8] From Sofer's perspective, Reform was the archenemy of "authentic Judaism." It was a direct threat to the majority of Jews in his day who were still allegiant to observance of the halakhah and traditional customs. Therefore, he sought to delegitimize his contemporary foes by equating them with well-known examples of heretical groups. This, in turn, he hoped would dissuade the majority of Jews from associating with the Reformers and adopting their ideology and religious behavior. Such attempts to vilify Reform, as Jacob Katz emphasized, served to transform those who remained loyal to tradition into a modern movement that became known as Orthodoxy.[9]

Whereas the neo-Orthodox Rabbi Samson Raphael Hirsch articulated a decidedly more positive attitude toward modern culture than did Sofer, so far as Reform was concerned, his opposition was equally strident. Hirsch never actually proposed prohibiting marriage with Reform Jews, but according to a follower, when the rabbi's strongest financial supporter requested that he perform such a ceremony for his daughter, Hirsch refused.[10] David Ellenson and Michael Silber have each demonstrated that in subsequent generations, especially in Hungary, the terms "Reform" or "Reformer" took on an additional role within Orthodoxy. These terms became the designated accusations rendered by zealous voices within internal Orthodox polemics against more moderate forces.[11]

Moving to the Western Hemisphere, by the turn of the twentieth century Reform Judaism had succeeded in establishing itself as the religion of America's Jewish elite, most of them of central European origin. While some cooperation existed between Reform and the predominantly eastern European Orthodox leaders regarding social welfare and personal freedom issues, in so far as religious affairs and theology were concerned, the gulf between the streams had only widened.[12] Indeed, as late as 1993 even a liberal-thinking Orthodox leader like Rabbi Jonathan Sacks, the British United Synagogue chief rabbi, could remark that Reform decisions such as recognition of patrilineal descent "increase the likelihood that at some time Orthodoxy will see Reform as it saw Christianity: as a separate religion."[13]

Although the idea of an official split has found some outspoken Orthodox proponents, predictions that such a policy would become the majority opinion within American Orthodoxy have not come to fruition during the first decade of the twenty-first century. It would appear that the differences between the two denominations have become so clear that the Orthodox have been relieved of the need to aggressively assert distinctions.[14] In parallel, efforts within Reform to reengage aspects of tradition, combined with American Orthodoxy's increased self-assurance, have actually engendered less confrontational environments for certain types of Orthodox–Reform interactions.[15]

No doubt, instances of direct debates between American Orthodoxy and Reform still persist. Yet the more likely contemporary scenario is the application of the "Reform" appellation by Orthodox traditionalists to those within their own camp who promote more liberal ideas and interpretations. Thus, in 2003 a prominent Yeshiva University Talmudic authority described supporters of Orthodox feminism as following in the path of a series of historical heresies, including the Sadducees, early Christianity, and Reform Judaism.[16]

Unlike in the United States, Jewish religious life in Israel has been dominated by Orthodoxy since the founding of the state in 1948.[17] Consistent with its distinctive religious ambiance, the new spirit of nonconfrontation of American Jewish denominational relations has not arrived in Israel. Rather, open animus has actually grown since the 1990s in parallel to the expansion of the Israeli Conservative and Reform movements. Even among the nonobservant majority, the popular saying has long been that "the synagogue that I do not attend is the Orthodox one." In fact, the Israeli environment accounts in part for remaining tensions among the American movements.

With the exception of mostly ephemeral efforts by German Jews during the 1930s, the first Israeli Reform and Conservative congregations can date their founding back to the 1950s and 1960s, and both groups began to sprout branches in larger numbers after 1967.[18] But these were almost exclusively to be found among English-speaking immigrants who sought to transfer their familiar religious lifestyles to Israeli soil and generally maintained their distance from mainstream Israeli religious politics.[19] From the late 1980s the

Israeli Conservative (*Masorti*) and Reform (*Yahadut Mitkademet*) movements experienced considerable expansion. In addition to growth in congregational branches with sizeable Israeli-born contingents, their Jerusalem-based institutions of higher learning drew locals to their various study programs, including their rabbinical training seminaries. By the twenty-first century these movements were increasingly led by native Israelis or figures who had spent their formative years in Israel.[20]

For the foreseeable future, Orthodoxy will remain the exclusive option for most Israeli Jews. Nevertheless, liberal Jewish denominations have gained a greater foothold within Israeli society. By no means are their rabbis and institutions recognized by the state rabbinical bureaucracy, but a rising number of Israelis have chosen to forego official sanction in order celebrate their religious life-cycle events in liberal synagogues and invite Reform and Conservative rabbis to perform their weddings. As to the particular role of Reform, rarely do any Israeli Orthodox figures demonstrate awareness of distinctions between them and the Conservatives.[21]

From the perspective of the state Orthodox rabbinate, this increased prominence of the Reform and Conservative movements has raised deep concerns. These have arisen both on account of Orthodox ideological animosity and because the new options are among the factors that have led to an overall decline in the numbers of people who make use of state-sponsored religious services. Expressions of anxiety on the part of the state rabbinate can be identified from time to time in vituperative public statements and in ongoing efforts to prevent non-Orthodox denominations from receiving state funding or from having their representatives sit on local religious councils.[22] Even if the liberal groups cannot undermine the Orthodox foundation, they challenge its absolute hegemony and can compete for a piece of the funds on which the various Orthodox organizations depend.[23]

Efforts to malign the Israeli non-Orthodox movements in order to prevent them from gaining recognition and funding certainly lead to interdenominational conflicts. The most explosive source of friction between Orthodoxy and liberal streams, however, relates to issues of Jewish identity and the status of non-Orthodox conversions. Regarding these topics, the Israeli and American branches of the various denominations join hands in battle, and little of the nonconfrontational spirit is evident in either Jewish stronghold.[24] Questions of "who is a Jew" have a history of contentiousness within Israel, and the mass influx of Russian speaking immigrants—many of whom were not Jewish according the halakhah—only intensified the struggle. In the hope of attracting new members and with the claim that their brands of Judaism were more suited to the totally secular former Soviet Jews, liberal denominations campaigned to have their conversions recognized. Eventually the government-appointed Neeman Commission achieved a compromise by which Reform and Conservative representatives would participate in teaching the candidates, but the actual conversion would be under the auspices of Orthodox halakhic authorities. This agreement was accepted by prominent leaders within the religious Zionist camp, and an umbrella institute to orchestrate implementation of the guidelines has been functioning since 2000.[25] Yet even if the candidates do eventually succeed in passing through the arduous process and attaining official certification of their conversions, the Haredim (non-Zionist fervently Orthodox) do not necessarily view them as valid. Although this is partially related to struggles between the haredi and religious Zionist camps, it is expressive of the underlying tensions with the non-Orthodox as well. As Rabbi Gedalyahu Axelrod, a religious court judge from Haifa known for his strict approach to conversion, said in reference to the religious Zionist approved conversions: "If you want to perform conversions, then do so, but at least admit that they are Reform conversions."[26] Thus, Orthodox versus non-Orthodox tension in Israel has actually engendered the emergence of a hybrid class of citizens who are considered Jewish by some Orthodox authorities but not by others.[27]

Regarding fully Reform or Conservative conversions performed in Israel or abroad, there is no Orthodox debate. All contemporary Orthodox authorities in Israel and in the Diaspora reject them. To be sure, non-Orthodox conversions performed in the Diaspora cause an intensification of existing local tensions as well, but they are no longer a major casus belli there. The child of an American Reform convert who was brought up Jewish from birth can appreciate to a certain degree that each local stream has its own standards, and those who choose to associate with a given group must meet its particular criteria. When it comes to Israel, Orthodoxy's role as the sole arbiter of "who is a Jew" creates deep resentment among liberal Jews worldwide. Even if particular Orthodox standards can be countenanced on a local level, when the only sovereign Jewish state renders one's Jewish identity invalid, it is seen as highly offensive and even belligerent. This in turn reinvigorates interdenominational confrontations in the Diaspora as well.[28] From the American Orthodox perspective, meanwhile, even if some can appreciate aspects of the Jewish identity of Reform Jews in the context of contemporary assimilatory trends, when it comes to Israel they adopt a far more exclusivist approach. For just the same reasons that the Reform Jew is troubled by Israeli rejection, the Orthodox Jew feels that compromises that can be tolerated in the Diaspora are totally unacceptable in the "authentic Jewish homeland."[29]

To a far greater extent than vis-à-vis Reform, the major battle of the state rabbinate is actually with the non-state-employed Orthodox religious Zionist rabbinate. In this conflict, however, the existence of liberal denominations plays a useful role for both parties. The non-state Orthodox rabbinate has been represented most prominently since the mid-1990s by the Tzohar organization, which has succeeded in drafting a relatively wide coalition of hundreds of religious Zionist rabbis. Its main goal is to provide free rabbinical services to the broader Israeli population in a more sensitive and attractive way than the official rabbinate.[30] Unlike the liberal denominations, Tzohar's representatives are Orthodox and do not perform weddings without the official license of the state rabbinate. As Rabbi Yuval Cherlow, an outspoken figure in the more progressive Israeli Orthodox rabbinate and one of the founders of Tzohar, opined in 2005, "As far as I am concerned . . . we are trying to change the rabbinate from within."[31] Indeed, this view received its most concrete expression in the fall of 2012 when Tzohar began a full-fledged campaign for the election of Rabbi David Stav, another one of its founders and leaders, as the new Ashkenazic chief rabbi.[32]

Not surprisingly, then, the state rabbinate has long viewed this "upstart" organization as a serious challenge to its hegemony and has used its leverage as the arbiter of who is sanctioned to perform weddings as a tool for neutralizing the Tzohar rabbis. Yet the rabbinate is reluctant to acknowledge that these stricter policies are aimed at Tzohar. Rather, the claim is that these measures were enacted to prevent non-Orthodox rabbis from slipping through the cracks and succeeding in gaining halakhic recognition.[33] This may partially be the case. However, the rabbinate's guidelines primarily affect the Tzohar rabbis, and the unspoken implication is that all liberal rabbis who challenge the state rabbinate's hegemony—be they Reform and Conservative or Orthodox ones—should be subject to intense skepticism. Thus the existence of non-Orthodox denominations is once again useful to the state rabbinate, this time in its struggle with its Orthodox competitors.

The Tzohar rabbis have acknowledged the potential minefield resulting from their association with liberal non-Orthodox groups and have made a point of taking sharp stands against liberal denominations as a way to clarify the great degree to which Tzohar differs from them. Thus Cherlow argued in 2006: "The claims against the Reform are stronger than those against

Christianity and Islam. Despite the fact that the believers [in the non-Jewish faiths] are enemies and idolaters . . . the Reform Jews are impostors."[34] Indeed, already in 1999, Cherlow took pains to distinguish between Reform and fresh efforts to introduce greater spirituality and creativity into what appeared to religious Zionist youth as dry and moribund synagogue life. In an article that appeared in 2000 in the journal *Akdamot*, published by the moderate Beit Morasha Institute, Cherlow implored: "How is it feasible to distinguish between holy and profane, between the Reform movement that led to the collapse of the connection between Israel and its Father in Heaven and a call for spiritual renaissance[?] . . . If the faith renewal will be accompanied by efforts to find favor with the multitudes and to translate the Torah of Israel into the colloquial language of contemporary Israeli culture, it will turn into the Reform movement."[35]

In the spirit of conflict that continues to define the Israeli environment, Rabbi Gilad Kariv, currently the director of the Israeli Reform movement and formerly head of its Israel Religious Action Center, shot back at Cherlow's invectives: "Tzohar believes if they attack us they will increase their status in extreme national-religious groups. They are mistaken. With all due respect for the good intentions of its leadership, and some of the important things it did, Tzohar is nothing more than packaging for the rabbinic establishment and all of its defects and flaws."[36] In demonizing Reform, Cherlow was being consistent with time-honored Orthodox approaches. As Ellenson emphasized in his article on German Orthodox rabbinical responses to Reform, by highlighting the distinctions between themselves and the Reform movement, the moderate Orthodox figures shored up their own Orthodox credentials and deepened their connections to their traditionalist colleagues. In a response to Cherlow's *Akdamot* piece that appeared in the following volume, Jewish law and theology scholar Meir Roth noted the connection between the author and historical Orthodox polemics: "Cherlow's article does not truly attempt to answer the question of what religious renewal is desirable. . . . Rather it tries to tag all who desire change as Reformers, Heaven forbid. . . . The effort to combat religious renewal by labeling it as Reform will not deter anyone. If anything, it will just revive a sprouting of the type of religious zealotry regarding which we religious Zionists thought naively ourselves to be immune."[37]

Cherlow's initial efforts to highlight Reform's deviant status in order to shore up the bonds of the various strands of Israeli Orthodoxy notwithstanding, more recently the "Reform" heading has even been drafted by forces within religious Zionism to combat internal liberal initiatives. Cherlow himself has been a principal target of these invectives. Indeed, a deepening ideological rift has arisen within the religious Zionist rabbinate itself. One camp known as the "Hardalim" (the Hebrew word *hardal* literally means mustard, but it is used here as an acronym for *haredi-leumi*—nationalist and fervently Orthodox) supports the state but resonates toward the narrow interpretations and strictness that characterize non-Zionist Haredim in most areas of Jewish law. Many of its proponents studied in the Merkaz Harav yeshivah in Jerusalem or in offshoots or splinter institutions. The opposing liberal segment, for which Cherlow is one of the best-known figures, believes that the social and political realities of the State of Israel, and for that matter modern society in general, demand broader reassessments of religious policies and even certain areas of Jewish law.[38] This is by no means a neat divide, and many individuals sympathize with aspects of each Orthodox stream. All the same, in the winter of 2012 a group of rabbis—many of them Tzohar members—and female religious leaders reached the collective conclusion that Tzohar's efforts to maintain a big tent of religious Zionist rabbis were stifling their abilities to present a more flexible and tolerant rabbinical voice to the Israeli public. Without necessarily resigning from Tzohar, they founded an independent organization, Beit Hillel, whose mission statement declares, "Recent events have presented our Holy Torah to the Israeli public in an inappropriately narrow-minded, exclusionary light. We, who are engaged daily in teaching and studying the Torah, believe that this has misrepresented Judaism, and that only the authentic, enlightened, inclusive Judaism—whose ways are pleasant and peaceful—has a true message for Israel today."[39]

The establishment of Beit Hillel reflects the frustration of a growing number of congregational rabbis and educators who feel that much of the religious Zionist rabbinical leadership is out of touch with the realities of their constituencies and has abandoned the ideal of synthesizing tradition and modernity that once characterized this group. Moreover, it is a reaction to vociferous attacks rendered by some mainstream figures against Cherlow and others for putting forward lenient positions on such issues as the role of women in religious life, single motherhood, the status of religious homosexuals, and even for examining human imperfections when teaching about hallowed biblical figures.

One of the most celebrated of such public polemics took place in the spring of 2009. Rabbi Yehoshua Shapira of the Yeshivat Ramat Gan announced before a convention of counselors from the Ezra youth movement that a breach had developed within religious Zionism that demands rending one's garment in mourning. Despite numerous troubles, "the most difficult problem in my eyes is the Neo-Reform movement . . . [which] challenges the Godly nature of the Torah and its continuation in the Oral Law of our day. . . . There is growing within us a new Reform movement—this is my opinion—and it has many of the characteristics of the first Reform. . . . The Neo-Reform movement . . . destabilizes the sanctity of the Jewish home and the sanctity of modesty and purity in the nation of Israel."[40]

Shapira is one of the most charismatic and popular leaders of the hardal stream. In 1994 he established a new yeshivah and nurtured a dynamic urban religious community around it by promoting a brand of Orthodoxy that combines meticulous observance, loyalty to the state due to its position as the "beginning of the redemption," and Hasidic spirituality. His accusations of "neo-reformism" against the liberal ranks reflect his ongoing project of asserting the "normative" character of his more zealous brand of religious Zionism. In doing so he also minimizes the differences between his religious approach and that of non-Zionist haredi society.

Another prominent figure who advances a hardal outlook is the ubiquitous Rabbi Shlomo Aviner. Along with leading the Yeshivat Ateret Kohanim in Jerusalem's Muslim Quarter and serving as rabbi in the Beit El settlement, he has recorded all of his many lectures, had them transcribed by an industrious staff, and then uploaded to his yeshivah's website. These form the basis for a series of paperbacks that are distributed throughout bookstores as well as by representatives in various Zionist yeshivahs. He also provides a text message service that enables people to send him queries from their cell phones and receive almost immediate responses on any matter of halakhah or general conduct for which they desire guidance. The highlights of these "tweet"-like responsa are published in a bulletin that is distributed each Sabbath in hundreds of religious Zionist–oriented synagogues throughout Israel. Like Shapira, Aviner too sees merit in assailing the approach of his ideological adversaries within religious Zionism by describing them as "Reform."

The impetus for Aviner's criticism was the summer Bible study seminars sponsored by the Yeshivat Har-Etzion's Herzog College, which attract thousands of attendees annually. This institution—known colloquially as "Gush" ("bloc") due to its location in Gush Etzion ("Etzion bloc") south of Jerusalem—counts Cherlow among its prominent graduates. It has been at the forefront of disseminating an alternative religious Zionist ideology to that set out in the Merkaz Harav circles: less deterministic regarding the redemptive character of the state and more open to the positive aspects of secular learning and culture.[41] Indeed, a good percentage of the founders of Beit Hillel are Gush alumni, including a few of its leading faculty members. Among Yeshivat Har-Etzion's distinctions is that through its teachers' college it has developed and spread an analytical approach to Bible study that utilizes mainly literary but also archeological and historical tools without compromising on commitment to the Divine authorship of the text. This has become known as the "*Tanakh be-govah ha-enayim*" ("the Bible at eye level") school. As part of this development, and despite a certain ambivalence on the part of one its founding leaders, the yeshivah has created a vehicle for discourse and interaction with academic biblical studies. In fact, some of its products are themselves distinguished Bible scholars who occupy academic positions in Israeli and American universities. Others have gained responsibility for designing the Bible study curriculum for the state religious school system and have labored to integrate their technique into primary and secondary school pedagogy.

The Gush method, argue the hardal leaders, undermines the divine holiness of the *Tanakh*. Furthermore, by exploring the flaws of the biblical forefathers and foremothers, it minimizes their greatness and, as such, the power and truth that emerge from their lives. In line with this position, a more doctrinally conservative Bible study seminar was initiated by the hardal rabbinate in the summer of 2012—with Aviner as one of its central advocates—as an alternative to the veteran Gush event. In explaining the need for this program, Aviner emphasized that the problem with the existing highly successful framework was that it was essentially aimed at inculcating in its students "humanistic moral values and fitting conduct." As such, it is simply "an old adversary of which we have been eating its rotten fruit for a few hundred years. For is this not the utterance of the Reform movement, which inscribed upon its banner that the essence of Judaism is universal religious principles and that the rest of the commandments and laws are not appropriate for modern society?"[42]

Aviner highlights the intellectual and spiritual degeneracy that results from the liberal Orthodox Israeli camp,[43] while Shapira underscores the sexual decadence condoned by its leniencies. Interestingly, both these critical dissections are empowered by adopting the strategy identified by John Henderson as common to heresiologists in numerous religions, namely associating the new target with an "already defeated heresy."[44] This is not to say that Reform has disappeared, and as discussed above, the inroads it has made in Israeli society have engendered an aggressive atmosphere, just as animus has dissipated in the United States in recent years. All the same, it is not the contemporary Reform movement that chiefly concerns the hardal rabbis. It is, rather, its nineteenth-century forerunners who pioneered a new worldview that wrested the reins from traditionalist authorities and changed the face of Jewish religious life forever—those the Hatam Sofer compared for posterity to Sadducees, Karaites, and Christians.

In the United States, Reform Judaism is one among numerous possibilities that are available to the twenty-first-century Jew. Indeed, the interdenominational battles of the past have dissipated. Nevertheless, the "Reform" epithet continues to be employed, as noted above, by Orthodox polemicists in internal struggles such as that over Orthodox feminism. In Israel, Reform is not even a viable option for most citizens. Nonetheless, it has retained its status as the symbol of modern deviation. The more actual and visceral religious battles in Israel are between the Haredim and the religious Zionists, and increasingly between the Hardalim and the moderate religious Zionist camp. Any indication that the opinions and policies of the latter bear resemblance to the revolutionary approaches introduced by early Reform invites the opponents of the liberal wing of religious Zionism to raise this accusation as a black flag that delegitimizes the entire religious ideology of their internal disputants.

In the course of this discussion I have emphasized that the decline in direct Orthodox animus toward Reform that has recently characterized contemporary American Judaism has not been felt in the Israeli environment. Most Israelis are ignorant about Reform and rarely distinguish it from other liberal branches. Whenever attempts to gain state recognition for Reform do arise, the Orthodox are vigilant in their efforts to protect their nearly exclusive position as the arbiters of Israeli Jewish religious life. In parallel, Reform's historic role in Orthodox eyes as the principal symbol of deviation from Jewish tradition in modern times remains viable. It has been employed by liberal figures like Yuval Cherlow as a foil through which comparison lends credence to their own worldviews within Orthodoxy. In direct contrast, the haredi and more conservative hardal rabbis such as Yehoshua Shapira and Shlomo Aviner have raised the specter of Reform as justification for vilifying those exact innovations for which Cherlow and his cohorts seek legitimacy.

In December 2012, however, the distinctive Israeli and American Orthodox–Reform dynamics gravitated toward greater confluence. Reacting to a trip to the United States during which he met with Jews from across the religious spectrum, Yuval Cherlow penned a letter to his yeshivah students that articulated a transformation in his thinking. In light of the alarming rates of intermarriage and detachment of American Jews from active Jewish participation, he now feels that the State of Israel must take dramatic steps that will neutralize those aspects of Israeli life that alienate American Jews and undermine the state's role as an inspiration for strengthening Jewish connection. He acknowledges the "distancing" of American Jews from Israel's political positions, especially regarding the Palestinian conflict, but does not offer a specific remedy. The issue about which he delineates a concrete reevaluation is the Orthodox establishment's attitudes and policies toward non-Orthodox movements, including Reform and its followers. In so far as technical halakhah is concerned, he encourages suspension of rules that prohibit cooperation with non-Orthodox movements and leniency regarding inclusion of Reform Jews in prayer quorums. As to the State of Israel, Cherlow recommends differentiating between codified religious legal standards that are unchallengeable and public policy regarding who is welcomed into Israeli society. Thus the government should recognize non-Orthodox movements, accept their conversions for citizenship purposes, and provide them funds that will facilitate a more "free market" approach to religious involvement.[45] These shifts, he proposes, will neutralize the growing estrangement of many American Jews from Israel.

Are Cherlow's pronouncements indicative of a more fundamental change in the role of Reform in Israeli Orthodoxy? It is premature to draw any expansive conclusions beyond acknowledging the fact that a leading figure in the moderate wing of religious Zionism has moved toward a model of reconciliation that is closer to the postdenominational dynamic prevalent in the United States. This is especially significant since, as emphasized, in the past the same personality did not hesitate to denounce Reform. For the time being, the official position of all Israeli Orthodox sectors remains somewhere between deep hostility and unyielding conflict. To the non-Zionist Orthodox, Cherlow's comments simply gave ammunition for condemning him and his Tzohar partners in typical fashion. In the words of Haredi spokesman Dov Halbertal, "Cherlow and his gang, and the Tzohar rabbis organization, are themselves Reform. They are a greater danger to the Jewish people than the Reform [movement]."[46] More noteworthy, the Tzohar presidium itself rushed to differentiate Cherlow's views from the association's accepted positions, announcing that it "opposes any official recognition of Reform Judaism by the State of Israel, in terms of conversions or its general way."[47] Such efforts, however, did not appear to placate the hardal camp who subsequently refused to support the candidacy of Tzohar chairman, David Stav, for Ashkenazi chief rabbi. This ultimately paved the way for the 2013 election of Haredi oriented Rabbi David Lau to the post.[48]

Notes

1. David H. Ellenson, "The Role of Reform in Selected German-Jewish Orthodox Responsa: A Sociological Analysis," *Hebrew Union College Annual* 53 (1982): 357–80 (republished in his *Tradition in Transition: Orthodoxy, Halakhah, and the Boundaries of Modern Jewish Identity* [Lanham, Md.: University Press of America, 1989], 33–60).
2. Emile Durkheim, *The Division of Labor in Society*, trans. George Simpson (Glencoe, Ill., 1960), 70–110.
3. Kai T. Erikson, *Wayward Puritans: A Study in the Sociology of Deviance* (New York, 1966), 10.
4. For a discussion of how Erikson expanded on Durkheim, see David Downes and Paul Rock, *Understanding Deviance* (Oxford, 1982), 86–89.
5. Ellenson, "The Role of Reform."
6. On Sofer's approach to Reform, see, for example: David Ellenson, "Traditional Reactions to Modern Jewish Reform: The Paradigm of German Orthodoxy," *History of Jewish Philosophy*, ed. D. Frank and O. Leaman (London, 1997), 735 (republished in his *After Emancipation* [Cincinnati: Hebrew Union College Press, 2004], 154–83); Jacob Katz, "Towards a Biography of the Hatam Sofer," in *Divine Law in Human Hands*, trans. David Ellenson (Jerusalem, 1998), 403–5.
7. See Michael K. Silber, "The Emergence of Ultra-Orthodoxy: The Invention of a Tradition," in *The Uses of Tradition: Jewish Continuity in the Modern Era*, ed. J. Wertheimer (New York, 1992), 30n.11.
8. Moses Sofer, *Shu"t Hatam Sofer* 6 [Likutim], #89.
9. Jacob Katz, "Orthodoxy in Historical Perspective," *Studies in Contemporary Jewry* 2 (1982): 3–17.
10. Adam S. Ferziger, *Exclusion and Hierarchy: Orthodoxy, Nonobservance, and the Emergence of Modern Jewish Identity* (Philadelphia, 2005), 122–25.
11. David Ellenson, *Rabbi Esriel Hildesheimer and the Creation of a Modern Jewish Orthodoxy* (Tuscaloosa, Ala., 1990), 43–44; Silber, "The Emergence of Ultra-Orthodoxy," 30n.11.
12. Jonathan Sarna, *American Judaism* (New Haven, Conn., 2004), 193–201.
13. Jonathan Sacks, *One People? Tradition, Modernity and Jewish Unity* (London, 1993), 224.
14. Jack Wertheimer, *All Quiet on the Religious Front: Jewish Unity, Denominationalism, and Postdenominationalism in the United States* (New York, 2005), 17.
15. Adam S. Ferziger, "From Demonic Deviant to Drowning Brother: Reform Judaism in the Eyes of American Orthodoxy," *Jewish Social Studies* 15, no. 3 (2009): 56–88.
16. Herschel (Zvi) Schachter, "On the Matter of Masorah," www.torahweb.org/torah/special/2003/rsch_masorah.html (accessed December 30, 2012).
17. Eliezer Don-Yehiya, "Orthodox Jewry in Israel and in North America," *Israel Studies* 10, no. 1 (2005): 159–61.
18. On early attempts at establishing Reform in 1930s Palestine, see Michael A. Meyer, *Response to Modernity: A History of the Reform Movement in Judaism* (New York, 1988), 344–45.
19. See Ephraim Tabory and Bernard Lazerwitz, "Americans in the Israeli Reform and Conservative Denominations: Religiosity under an Ethnic Shield?" *Review of Religious Research* 24, no. 3 (1983): 177–87; Meyer, *Response to Modernity*, 348–52.
20. See Harvey Meirovitch, "The Shaping of Masorti Judaism in Israel,"*Contemporary Jewish Life*, January 10, 1999, www.ajc.org/atf/cf/%7B42d75369-d582-4380-8395-d25925b85eaf%7D/SHAPINGMASORTIJUDAISMISRAEL.PDF (accessed January 6,

2014); Ephraim Tabory, "The Influence of Liberal Judaism on Israeli Religious Life," *Israel Studies* 5.1 (2000): 183–203.

21. Yael Israel-Shamsian, "The Israeli Religious Market and Penetration of the Conservative and Reform Movements" (MA thesis, Tel Aviv University, 2004), 56–57.

22. Samuel G. Freedman, *Jew vs. Jew: The Struggle for the Soul of American Jewry* (New York, 2000), 17–23.

23. See, for example, Martin Edelman, "A Portion of Animosity: The Politics of Disenfranchisement of Religion in Israel," *Israel Studies* 5, no. 1 (2000): 219.

24. See, for example, Chaim Eisen, "Rx for Orthodox Intolerance," *Jewish Action* 58, no. 1 (1997): 92–93; Sarna, *American Judaism*, 367.

25. Asher Cohen, *Yehudim lo-Yehudim: Zehut Yehudit Yisraelit ve-etgar harhavat ha-le'om ha-Yehudi* (Jerusalem, 2005), 144.

26. The statement was made at the First Annual Conference of the Rappaport Center for Assimilation Research, Bar-Ilan University, Ramat-Gan, Summer 2002. In my capacity as chair of this session, I heard Axelrod's presentation. The citation appears in Cohen, *Yehudim lo-Yehudim*, 138.

27. The 2013 Israeli election campaign offered evidence that apprehension regarding the Jewish identity of new immigrants and "wholesale" conversions remain explosive issues that the Haredi political parties draft to stir up xenophobic tendencies that will translate into electoral votes. See the commercial produced by the Shas party that was eventually banned, www.youtube.com/watch?v=Y5wCALTOhCU (accessed January 13, 2013).

28. Ephraim Tabory, "The Legitimacy of Reform Judaism: The Impact of Israel on the United States," in *Contemporary Debates in American Reform Judaism*, ed. Dana Evan Kaplan (New York, 2001), 221–34; Jack Wertheimer, *A People Divided: Judaism in Contemporary America* (New York, 1993), 175–77.

29. See, for example, J. David Bleich, "Another Look at the Pluralism Debate: Synagogue and State in Israel," *Jewish Action* 58, no. 1 (1997): 94–95. For the roots of such a position, see Ehud Luz, *Parallels Meet* (Philadelphia, 1988), 58–59.

30. On Tzohar, see Adam S. Ferziger, "Religion for the Secular: The New Israeli Rabbinate," *Journal of Modern Jewish Studies* 7, no. 1 (2008): 67–90.

31. Cited in Amiram Barkat, "The Reform Movement as a 'Caricature,'" *Haaretz*, December 11, 2005, www.haaretz.com/hasen/pages/ShArt.jhtml?itemNo=583429&contra ssID=19 (accessed December 30, 2012).

32. Matti Friedman, "A Battle for the Rabbinate, and for Israel's Soul," *Times of Israel*, September 11, 2012, www.timesofisrael.com/a-battle-for-the-rabbinate-and-for-israels-soul (accessed January 1, 2013).

33. Kobi Nahshoni, "Ha-ma'avak mithamem: Ha-im rabbanei Tzohar lo yukhlu lehaten," *Yediot aharonot*, July 7, 2007, www.ynet.co.il/articles/0,7340,L-3426359,00.html (accessed January 22, 2014).

34. Neta Sela, "Ha-Rav Lior: kol maga im ha-Reformim asur hilkhatit," *Yediot aharonot*, October 24, 2006, www.ynet.co.il/articles/0,7340,L-3319195,00.html (accessed January 14, 2013).

35. Yuval Cherlow, "Al ha-havhanah ben Reformah le-hithadshut," *Akdamot* 7 (2000), www.bmj.org.il/akdama/35/t (accessed January 13, 2013).

36. Barkat, "The Reform Movement as a 'Caricature.'"

37. Meir Roth, "Ben hashdanut le-hadshanut," *Akdamot* 8 (2000), www.bmj.org.il/akdama/35/t (accessed January 1, 2013).

38. Yoel Finkelman, "On the Irrelevance of Religious-Zionism: Jewish National Culture from A Religious-Zionist Perspective," *Tradition* 35, no. 1 (2005): 21–39.

39. Beit Hillel website, www.beithillel.org.il/english.asp (accessed January 7, 2014).

40. Gil Ronen, "Rabbi Shapira: Time to Fight Neo-Reformists in Our Midst," *Arutz sheva*, May 7, 2009, www.israelnationalnews.com/News/News.aspx/132217#.UNxojeSTy0g (accessed December 27, 2012). Shapira expanded on his approach in a lecture to his students, which was transcribed and made available on the yeshivah's website: Yehoshua Shapira, "Me-Hashem yatsah ha-davar, al ha-neoreformah," www.yrg.org.il/show.asp?id=33537 (accessed December 27, 2012).

41. See Adam S. Ferziger, "Religious Zionism, Galut, and Globalization: Exploring 'Gush' Exceptionalism," *That Godly Mountain*, ed. Reuven Ziegler (Alon Shevut, 2012), 109–21. Full disclosure, I studied at Yeshivat Har-Etzion in 1983–84, as did one of my sons from 2006 to 2011.

42. Cited in Uri Falk, "Midrashot 'ha-kav' yozmot yame iyun be-Tanakh, ke-kontrah li-me ha-iyun shel 'ha-gush,'" *Kipah*, June 6, 2012, www.kipa.co.il/now/48769.html (accessed December 28, 2012).

43. Aviner, of course, is no less determined to rein in diversity regarding issues of modesty and sexuality. See, for example, this report on his directives regarding proper dress for prepubescent girls: Kobi Nahshoni, "Kelale tseniyut shel ha-Rav Aviner: Kakh tilbeshi mi-gil shalosh," *YNET*, December 30, 2012, www.ynet.co.il/articles/0,7340,L-4326091,00.html (accessed December 30, 2012).

44. John B. Henderson, *The Construction of Orthodoxy and Heresy* (Albany, N.Y., 1998), 157–60.

45. Yuval Cherlow, "Reshamim ve-lebatim mi-shelihut be-Arzot ha-Berit," *Yeshivat ha-Hesder Orot Shaul be-Petah Tikva*, December 6, 2012, www.ypt.co.il/show.asp?id=56143 (accessed December 8, 2012).

46. Yair Ettinger, "Tzohar Rabbis Oppose Recognition of non-Orthodox Jewish Movements," *Haaretz*, December 13, 2012, www.haaretz.com/jewish-world/jewish-world-news/tzohar-rabbis-oppose-recognition-of-non-orthodox-jewish-movements.premium-1.484456 (accessed December 30, 2012).

47. Ibid.

48. David M. Weinberg, "The Rabbinic Race Wreckage," *Jerusalem Post*, April 25, 2013, www.jpost.com/Opinion/Op-Ed-Contributors/The-Rabbinate-race-wreckage-311139 (accessed January 22, 2014).

4

BETWEEN "WEST POINT STANDARDS" AND LIFE IN THE TRENCHES

The Halakhic Dilemmas of Orthodox Outreach Workers

JACK WERTHEIMER

For much of the modern era, traditional Jews have been on the defensive, watching with a mixture of horror and defiance as ever-growing populations of their coreligionists defected to non-Orthodox religious movements or became completely indifferent to the demands of Jewish religious observance. Among our most important historians of how traditionalist rabbis responded to the abandonment of their religious way of life has been David Ellenson, who in numerous articles and books has analyzed the policies and rationales offered by Orthodox communal leaders and *poskim*, decisors of Jewish law, as they established clear lines in the sand to set their followers apart from the nonobservant. Writing about developments of the nineteenth century and the early part of the twentieth century, he has focused on issues of boundary maintenance, the stigmatizing of behaviors and ideas as "deviant," and "attacks on what were seen as unwarranted departures from traditional Jewish customs and practices."[1] Ever sensitive to nuance, he has delineated splits within the ranks of the Orthodox rabbinate concerning the desirability of making common cause with non-Orthodox groups under any circumstances, with some favoring cooperation on matters of communal and philanthropic, as opposed to religious, concern, and others intent on enforcing a policy of strict separatism in all dealings with non-Orthodox groups.[2]

In appreciation of our many years of friendship, dating back to our days as graduate students at Columbia University, I propose in this essay to offer an exploratory discussion linked to an area of David Ellenson's expertise: the responses of Orthodox rabbis to Jews who do not observe halakhah (Jewish law) *according to their traditionalist standards*. Rather than look to the distant past, though, my focus here is on a contemporary revolution sweeping some quarters of the Orthodox world that is bringing an army of outreach workers into contact with vast numbers of non-Orthodox Jews annually. Reversing 150 years of Orthodox separatism, *kiruv* workers (a term denoting those who seek to draw other Jews near to God and the commandments)[3] are finding their way to every nook and cranny of the globe to serve, teach, and inspire their non-Orthodox fellow Jews. These new forms of engagement are bound to raise a host of questions about how Orthodox Jews should comport themselves in the cause of kiruv. What makes the current situation novel, however, is that the large majority of kiruv workers are drawn from populations that in the past had deliberately pursued a policy of separating themselves from their nonobservant coreligionists. Moreover, rather than confine their activities to more benign communal cooperation, activities sanctioned by some Orthodox leaders in the past, today's kiruv workers are dealing frontally with religious issues, a kind of engagement even the most moderate Orthodox rabbis of the past had shunned. This present-day encounter adds new layers of complexity to the fraught relationship between tradition and modernity in the different sectors of the Jewish world, the central theme of this volume.

Organized Orthodox outreach activities in the United States have a history dating back to the decade immediately after World War II, when the Torah Umesorah movement was energetically planting Orthodox day schools in communities around the country for a student body that did not come from fully observant homes. Several additional educational programs were launched in the 1950s by the Modern Orthodox world under the banner of the National Council of Synagogue Youth and the Young Israel movement.[4] And, of greatest import in the long term, some time around 1958 Rabbi Menahem Mendel Schneerson recruited the first small cadre of emissaries (*sheluchim* and *sheluchos*) to fan out to areas across the United States and abroad with the mission of remaking those communities.[5] These efforts picked up momentum in the 1960s with the launching of yeshivahs in Israel aimed at potential *ba'ale teshuvah* ("returnees" to Jewish practice), most notably by Rabbi Noach Weinberg, who would eventually go on to create a vast kiruv enterprise known as Aish HaTorah, with outposts across the globe.

Without gainsaying the importance of these initial forays in setting a foundation for Orthodox outreach, the greatest growth has occurred in the past quarter century. The number of Chabad emissary families jumped in the United States from 400 in the mid-1990s to 1,600 by 2012, a growth all the more remarkable because it occurred after the death of the last Lubavitcher Rebbe.[6] In addition to Chabad, the yeshivah world has been sending ever-larger numbers of *mekarvim* (outreach workers) into the American Jewish community. Symptomatically, by the late 1980s enough non-Chabad kiruv workers were functioning to warrant the establishment of AJOP, the Association of Jewish Outreach Programs.

How many kiruv workers are there? One estimate from the former head of AJOP puts the number of current full-time outreach workers in 2012 at 3,500.[7] This figure seems far too modest when we consider Chabad's contribution alone: if there are 1,600 Chabad families that means 3,200 *sheluchim* and *sheluchos* are engaged in kiruv because virtually all wives of *sheluchim* are active partners in the work of outreach. Moreover, many Chabad schools, centers and programs are staffed by younger people who are training to become *sheluchim* or *sheluchos*, and they, in turn, are augmented by a back-office staff, which produces publications and educational materials and also maintains Chabad. org (probably the most frequently visited Jewish website in the world). The Chabad enterprise alone may consist of more than 5,000 people engaged full-time in kiruv. And then there are the non-Chabad outreach centers sponsored by Aish HaTorah, Partners in Torah, Ner LeElef (a kiruv training program claiming 1,200 graduates), various Modern Orthodox organizations such as the Manhattan Jewish Experience, community *kollelim* (advanced study programs), and a not insignificant number of independent operators.[8] Currently, more than 2,000 members belong to the AJOP—none of whom are associated with Chabad.[9] To make plain what all this means: the estimated 5,000–7,000 men and women working full-time across the country in kiruv represent more than double the number of active Conservative, Reform, and Reconstructionist rabbis combined.

This is not the place to document the dense network of institutions created by Orthodox outreach workers, which in the case of Chabad alone offers a cradle-to-grave panoply of support services. Nor is it the place to assess the impact of these efforts, whether from a numerical perspective—the numbers of nonobservant Jews brought to Orthodoxy or the numbers who have not bought the entire package but nonetheless have become more engaged with Jewish life—or from a fiscal perspective, that is, whether the investment yielded sufficient dividends.[10] Suffice it to say that at present, kiruv is no longer monopolized by Chabad, but now is also staffed by thousands of men and women educated in the so-called yeshivah world, in such places as Ner Israel of Baltimore and the Lakewood Yeshiva in New Jersey.[11]

Though no one has definitive figures documenting how many non-Orthodox Jews are touched annually by the growing kiruv movement, a quick back-of-the-envelope estimate yields eye-opening results: assuming that there are between five and seven thousand kiruv workers today and each one interacts annually with an average of no more than one hundred non-Orthodox Jews (a conservative figure given the size of many Chabad centers and the sizeable attendance at kiruv events), the collective effort of Orthodox outreach may touch between a half million and seven hundred thousand Jews each year.

These contacts are fraught with complications for the *mekarvim*, the outreach workers, often placing them in quandaries where they must choose between the dictates of halakhah as they learned it and the opportunity to work with nonobservant Jews to bring them closer to God and the commandments. Here is a partial list of the kinds of predicaments in which they often find themselves:[12]

1. Activities such as traveling in a car or smoking or going to work or using electrical devices are all considered to be desecrations of the Sabbath if performed on that day of the week. A Jew who desecrates the Sabbath is classified by halakhah as being an *'akum*, literally a worshiper of stars and astrology, or an idolater. Those classified as 'akum may not be granted synagogue honors, such as being called to the Torah for an aliyah or leading services or being counted as part of the minyan (the prayer quorum). The predicament is that by definition, virtually all who attend services in kiruv synagogues desecrate the Sabbath according to Orthodox lights. How are they to be treated? If they are barred from full participation, they may never return—and then they certainly would not have the chance to learn about the error of their ways. If they are included as full participants, the prayer service will not have proceeded properly and that means the kiruv worker will not have fulfilled his religious obligations by praying in such a setting.[13]

2. May an outreach worker invite someone to attend Sabbath services or a Sabbath meal knowing that the invitee will desecrate the

Sabbath by driving in a car when returning home? The kiruv worker is torn between providing opportunities for the nonobservant to experience Jewish life guided by Orthodox standards or avoiding a situation that will result in Sabbath desecration, but thereby foreclosing the opportunity for the nonobservant Jew to participate.

3. One of the features of outreach centers is a lavish food spread typically prepared for attendees. But the question arises: may one offer a nonobservant Jew a meal if that Jew in all likelihood will not say grace after meals? By actively feeding a fellow Jew, the kiruv worker is creating a situation whereby Jewish law will be desecrated.[14] The alternative is to inform the nonobservant Jew of the requirement to say grace after meals, but if the individual declines to do so, the kiruv worker will have made matters far worse from the perspective of Jewish law, because the failure to utter the correct blessings will result from an intentional decision, rather than inadvertence— that is, ignorance.[15]

4. May a male kiruv worker teach women who are not dressed properly according to standards of modesty assumed by Jewish law—for example, their clothing is too revealing, their hair is not covered, or they are wearing pants? The outreach worker is caught between the goal of teaching Torah to the nonobservant and his understanding of the proper standards of modest dress.

5. The pervasiveness of intermarriage creates a host of dilemmas: May a child born of a non-Jewish mother be enrolled in a kiruv school or summer camp? At what point should a kiruv worker make clear that he or she does not consider such a child to be Jewish according to halakhah and therefore would not allow such a child to celebrate a bar or bat mitzvah? If the kiruv worker speaks openly about the standards of halakhah, families may be driven away before there is even a chance to draw them into Jewish life; on the other hand, if this information is withheld, families may consider it cruel when told that despite their child's years of studying Judaism, the kiruv worker does not accept the Jewishness of that child.

6. On a related matter, how should a kiruv worker who believes that it is forbidden to teach Torah to non-Jews respond when a gentile accompanies a Jewish spouse to a class on Torah?

7. And what is an outreach worker to do when interacting with an intermarried Jew: encourage the Jew to get divorced, try to encourage the

non-Jew to convert, or simply say nothing? None of these options is palatable.

8. Since an intermarried couple by definition is not married according to Jewish law, what is a kiruv worker to do when such a couple stays for the Sabbath—offer the partners a room together, or insist they sleep in separate quarters? One need not elaborate on how off-putting it would be to the couple if the question is even raised, but wouldn't the kiruv worker feel compromised in avoiding the subject?

9. With so many non-halakhic Jews attending functions in kiruv settings, how are outreach workers to manage Jewish laws forbidding the drinking of wine touched by individuals not deemed Jewish according to halakhah?

10. And then there are questions about what kinds of interactions with Conservative and Reform rabbis are permissible. Many responsa written over the past 150 years have categorized such rabbis as nonbelievers. Is it permissible to offer such rabbis synagogue honors? And even in nonreligious settings, may a kiruv worker participate with Conservative or Reform rabbis in a panel discussion, a communitywide event, or a study session when all public activities are bound to be interpreted as acts of legitimation?[16]

This brief listing barely scrapes the surface of issues confronting the modern-day kiruv worker almost on a daily basis. Fortunately, guidance is available in two recently published volumes, both offering compendia of responsa on "matters that arise among those who engage in *kiruv rehokim*" (bringing those who are distant back to Judaism), as the sub-titles of both books put it. And indeed, virtually all the questions itemized above are treated in these compendia.[17] The limitation of any such collection, though, is that the application of a responsum to specific situations is not easily determined.

To illustrate the point, we will focus on two very different kinds of opinions offered by Orthodox *poskim* (legal decisors) since the rise of the contemporary kiruv movement. The first is a letter written specifically in response to an inquiry by a large yeshivah training kiruv workers—Ohr Somayach, the primary academy of the Aish HaTorah movement. The *posek* was the late Rabbi Shlomo Zalman Auerbach (1910–95), a prolific author of halakhic decisions who lived in Jerusalem. The letter is dated the fourth of Nissan 5748 (March 22, 1988).

To my honored friend, Rabbi Mikhoel Schon, Shelita, a member of the administration of the Yeshiva Ohr Somayach in the holy city of Jerusalem . . .

I hereby respond briefly to questions he [meaning the questioner] posed to me in connection to the conduct of a minyan for those who are distant from Judaism [rehokim] that we wish to bring nearer to the Torah and commandments through their participation in worship, and as we rely upon the important book Melamed le-ho'il [by Rabbi David Zvi Hoffmann], number 29, that is cited by many great rabbinic authorities to find leniencies for those who desecrate the Sabbath in our time because [these desecrators] are like captured children [who have lived only among Gentiles], and as this is done specifically for the holy purposes of bringing Jews who are distant to the Torah and fear of God, therefore in my humble opinion the simple answer is as follows: A) It is permissible to invite even someone who lives at a distance from the place of worship and to offer him a place to sleep nearby in order to obviate the need for him to desecrate the Sabbath [by traveling]. And even if the invitee will not accept this offer, we are not obligated to tell the invitee to forego attendance at the worship service [because he resides at some distance from the place of prayer], and it is unnecessary to warn him that it is forbidden to arrive in an automobile. B) The parking lot of a synagogue where such services are held must be closed at all times on the Sabbath and holidays. C) It is desirable not to count someone who continues to desecrate the Sabbath publicly in the prayer quorum for every davar she-bi-kedushah [a technical terms denoting parts of the prayer deemed especially sacred, such as Kaddish and Barkhu] that requires a quorum of ten. D) If there are ten who observe the laws apart from them [those who desecrate the Sabbath publicly], it is permissible both to call them [the Sabbath desecrators] to the Torah [for an aliyah] and to permit them to participate in the priestly blessings.

And I hereby conclude with my blessings that the Giver of the Torah will help you to bring the hearts of Jews to our Father in Heaven and may He hasten the eternal salvation.[18]

His respectful friend

Shlomo Zalman Auerbach[19]

This letter seeks to balance two halakhic imperatives: one is to condemn the public desecration of the Sabbath and the second is to open the door to contact with those who through no fault of their own are far removed from religious observance. Hence it displays a willingness to classify them as akin to a *tinok she-nishbah*, a kidnapped baby who had been raised by gentiles and therefore does not know better. Rabbi Auerbach resolved the dilemma by holding a firm line when it came to maintaining Orthodox standards in public ways—for example, parking lots may not operate on the Sabbath and holidays, even though many who come to kiruv centers drive; and according to him, a proper minyan still requires ten Jewish males who observe the laws. On the other hand, he offers leniencies by permitting kiruv workers to invite people to join them for the Sabbath even though they know that their guests in all likelihood will drive. And once a kosher minyan exists, he permits the granting of Torah honors and the opportunity to participate in the priestly blessings to nonobservant Jews.

The warrant cited in support of the leniencies is the opinion of Rabbi David Zvi Hoffmann, an early twentieth-century rabbinical authority who lived in Germany and who classified most nonobservant Jews of his time as falling into the category of *tinok she-nishbah*. It is a judgment about modern Jews who are not observant with a pedigree dating back to the writings of Rabbi Jacob Ettlinger in a publication that appeared in 1868.[20] This position has been upheld by quite a few late twentieth-century rabbinical authorities, most notably the last Lubavitcher Rebbe, and before him Rabbi Moshe Feinstein, the preeminent American posek of the postwar era. Though nonobservant Jews might take umbrage at this classification, it is designed to absolve them from responsibility for their own actions.

Much is left unstated in this letter: it does not, for example, directly address the question of whether a nonobservant Jew may be counted in a minyan or lead the services *if there is no other option*, and it does not explain whether the intention is to prohibit counting a Sabbath desecrator in a minyan, for if it is, why not forbid counting them in a minyan explicitly rather than state it is "desirable" not to do so? The letter also does not explain why only two *devarim she-bi-kedushah* may be performed by nonobservant men, and not many others. Even more important, it does not place limits on the elasticity of *tinok she-nishbah* as a category. After all, in theory virtually any kind of non-observance might be excused by invoking this category. Kiruv workers must determine when and under which circumstance it applies.

Moreover, the category of *mehalel shabat be-farhesyah*, the public desecrator of the Sabbath, invoked by this letter, is equally unclear: ever since modern poskim determined that it was not to be understood literally, but only described someone who did not shy away from desecrating the Sabbath with impunity *in the presence of an important Jew, such as a rabbi*,[21] all kinds of leniencies could become options, including some prohibited by Rabbi Auerbach—for example, counting some desecrators in a minyan. In short, even leniencies supported by a major decisor such as Rabbi Auerbach do not offer clear-cut solutions to many of the predicaments faced by kiruv workers.

We now turn to a second halakhic opinion about kiruv work, in this case an unpublished letter. The co-authors of the letter summarize their understanding of a ruling issued orally by a "distinguished rosh yeshivah"[22] concerning a program sponsored by the National Jewish Outreach Program (NJOP).[23] Before the ruling, NJOP had sponsored Hebrew language and basic Judaism classes in "hundreds of Conservative synagogues and Reform temples." Now the group sought approval to organize "Turn Friday Night into Shabbos" at those non-Orthodox synagogues, but was concerned about the ramifications if the laws of the Sabbath and kashrut (Jewish dietary restrictions) would not be observed during those programs. The letter does not make clear why this would be problematic, but presumably by cooperating with these synagogues NJOP might be complicit in the desecration of basic Jewish laws. Still, the yeshivah head consulted was prepared to sanction the program, provided certain conditions were met:

> Based on the advice offered by the *Rosh Yeshiva*, we will insist that there be a commitment by all locations to observe the *Shabbos* and *Kashrus*. Those locations which cannot, or will not, make a commitment will not be allowed to participate. However, those that do make such a commitment will be allowed to join our campaign, regardless of their affiliation, and despite the fact that no one from our staff will be there to confirm their adherence.

Like the letter of Rabbi Auerbach, this missive approves of a significant leniency: it allows the program to be run in Conservative and Reform congregations if they pledge to observe the Sabbath and dietary laws. Given the long

and bitter history of Orthodox scorn directed at the "deviant" religious practices of other movements, it is stunning that under this ruling the commitment of a Conservative or Reform congregation should be taken at face value.
Moreover, what does it mean that the Sabbath will be observed when in all
those congregations a microphone is employed, a very public desecration of
the Sabbath according to Orthodox standards? And to add to the mystery, how
is it that Orthodox rabbis running this program won approval to work with
Conservative and Reform temples and their rabbis when the governing policy
put forth by heads of major yeshivahs unequivocally forbids such interaction?
("We have ruled that it is forbidden by the law of our sacred Torah to participate with them [Conservative and Reform organizations] either as an individual or as an organized communal body?")[24]

Our point here is not to judge the policies and politics of this letter but to
note that there are all kinds of gray areas in kiruv work. Even the ban on cooperating with organizations and officials of other Jewish religious movements
apparently is subject to leeway for the sake of kiruv. This hardly means that
anything goes, but Orthodox outreach workers now routinely teach classes in
Conservative and Reform synagogues (provided they are not censored); they
appear on platforms at communal events along with non-Orthodox rabbis;
they teach in Solomon Schechter day schools; and they study together with
and befriend non-Orthodox rabbis, even as they negotiate the fine line of not
offering public legitimacy to people they do not recognize as rabbis and institutions they believe are leading the Jewish people astray.

How then is an Orthodox outreach worker to walk that tightrope? The
answer given by the authoritative heads of Orthodox outreach programs is
to urge kiruv workers to consult on a regular basis with a rabbi who has no
personal or financial stake in the resolution of an issue. Only by speaking regularly with a rosh yeshivah will they avoid compromising halakhah.

Here is how one prominent yeshivah head describes the trade-off inherent in arriving at a proper decision and still remaining on the proper halakhic
path. In an interview, Rabbi Sholom Kamenetsky, head of the Talmudical
Yeshiva of Philadelphia, quoted his own father, a leading light of Agudas
Israel: "'Always remember that you are not *HaKadosh Baruch Hu's apotropis*
[God's guardian].' He is responsible for the results, not you, and you have no
right to bend *Shulchan Aruch* in the pursuit of 'better results.'" In other words,
he warned of the seductions of kiruv work and of heedlessly pursuing as many
kiruv targets as possible in order to justify philanthropic support. But then the
younger rabbi Kamenetsky went on to say the following: "No one should go

into kiruv imagining that he will always be able to preserve 'West Point standards' in the field. We are not talking about doing anything in contravention of *Shulchan Aruch*. . . . [But] just the fact that any kiruv professional in the field will find himself engaged in many types of activities that he never imagined himself doing in the yeshiva or kollel" should alert us to the challenges. He therefore urged all kiruv workers to consult weekly with a *rav* (a rabbinic mentor) to "navigate their program."[25] Similarly, the Lubavitcher Rebbe exhorted his sheluchim to consult regularly with a rosh yeshivah about halakhic challenges they face.[26]

But as one Chabad rabbi candidly admitted to me off the record, the men in the field are not fully convinced *rashe yeshivah* understand the pressures of working in a community far removed from the rarified atmosphere of the Jewish academy, and where they must confront issues that are unimaginable to one living in the insular world of the yeshivah. Interestingly, the rav he himself consults seemed sympathetic to the quandary, stating that "when it comes to halakhic questions within Lubavitch, we do not look for *kulas* [leniencies], but when we are asked about people we hope to *mekarev* [bring closer], if I find a *heter* [permissible ruling] to be *mekarev*, that's what I must do." Still, the internal tug-of-war persists in the work of kiruv, if only in the hearts and minds of the outreach workers. As one Chabad emissary put it to me, "I struggle every day whether I am going too far and where to draw the line. But if we don't observe *halakhah*, what are we doing?"[27] He is hardly alone in his daily wrestling with these dilemmas.

Notes

1. David Ellenson, "Traditional Reactions to Modern Jewish Reform: The Paradigm of German Orthodoxy," in *History of Jewish Philosophy*, vol. 2, ed. D. H. Frank and O. Leaman (London, 1997), 733.

2. These themes came to the fore in some of his earliest published essays, such as "Modern Orthodoxy and the Problem of Religious Pluralism: The Case of Rabbi Esriel Hildesheimer," *Tradition* 17 (1979): 74–89, and "The Role of Reform in Selected German-Jewish Orthodox Responsa: A Sociological Analysis," *Hebrew Union College Annual* 52 (1982): 357–80. See also more recently, "Traditional Reactions to Modern Jewish Reform."

3. The grammatically correct Hebrew pronunciation would be *kayruv*, but in Orthodox circles *keyruv* is preferred.

4. Zev Eleff, *Living from Convention to Convention: A History of the NCSY, 1954–1980* (New York, 2009). A brief overview of the history of Orthodox outreach appears in the introduction to a special issue titled "A Review of Kiruv," *Klal Perspectives: A Forum for Discussion of Challenges Facing the Torah Community* 2, no. 1 (2012): i–ii (http://klalperspectives.org/).

5. The overall strategy of Rabbi Schneerson was evident already shortly after he succeeded his father-in-law as the leader of the Lubavitch movement when he declared in a 1951 interview: "Orthodox Jewry up to this point has concentrated on defensive strategies. We were always worried lest we lose positions and strongholds. But we must take the initiative and wage an offensive. This of course takes courage, planning, vision and the will to carry on despite the odds" (quoted from a *Jewish Life* interview in Sue Fishkoff, *The Rebbe's Army: Inside the World of Chabad* [New York, 2003], 112; see also 117, on one of the first sheluchim who was sent to Detroit in 1958). The mission of the sheluchim is described in a forthcoming book on Chabad by Rabbi David Eliezrie of Yorba Linda, Calif., who graciously has shared his understanding of Orthodox outreach over many hours of conversation with me.

6. David Eliezrie, "The Unique Model and Success of Chabad," in *Klal Perspectives*, 18.

7. Ephraim Buchwald, "A New Reality—An Assessment of Contemporary Outreach," in *Klal Perspectives*, 23.

8. For some insight into the impact of Partners in Torah, see Eli Gewirtz and Dena Yellin, eds., *Partners in Torah, Partners in Eternity* (Passaic, N.J., 2009). On Ner LeElef, see www.nerleelef.com/index.htm. On kollelim, see the special issue of *Nitsotsot min ha-ner* devoted to them, 16 (January–March 2004); my thanks to Rabbi Zvi Holland, formerly of the Phoenix Kollel, who graciously took the time to enlighten me about the phenomenon and permitted me to observe kollel classes oriented to community outreach. See also on kollelim, Adam S. Ferziger, *The Emergence of the Community Kollel: A New Model for Addressing Assimilation* (Ramat Gan, 2006).

9. The number was given to me by Rabbi Yitzchok Lowenbraun, head of AJOP. Interview on February 28, 2012.

10. For some candid self-reflection by practitioners about their successes and failures, see *Klal Perspectives*.

11. The motive of the yeshivah world for engaging with Jews whom it once self-consciously shunned is also a fascinating topic for consideration, but it too is not the focus of this essay.

12. This listing is based on conversations with some three dozen kiruv workers, most of whom spoke off the record.

13. Given the many difficulties likely to arise in a synagogue setting, some kiruv workers try to avoid conducting religious services, confining their work to education and social programming.

14. The operative category of Jewish law is *lifne 'iver*—do not place an obstacle in the way of the blind.

15. A similar dilemma arises on fast days: does the kiruv worker inform a group with which he is meeting that it is a fast day—and thereby transform their inadvertent nonobservance into a deliberate act—or keep them ignorant?

16. See Adam S. Ferziger, *Exclusion and Hierarchy: Orthodoxy, Nonobservance and the Emergence of Modern Jewish Identity* (Philadelphia, 2005), for the answers put forth by nineteenth- and early twentieth-century Orthodox rabbis in Europe to many of these predicaments.

17. Moshe Nyuman and Mordechai Becher, *Avotot ahavah: Inyenei kiruv rehokim ba-halakha* (Jerusalem, 2002), and more recently Chaim Avraham Zakutinsky, *Umekarev Beyamin: Iyunim be-she'elot she-mitorerot etsel eleh she-oskim be-kiruv rehokim* (Flushing, N.Y., 2011).

18. We may speculate on whether in the author's view there is a connection between bringing Jews closer to God and hastening "the eternal salvation."

19. "The Laws Regarding the Participation of Public Desecrators of the Sabbath in the Prayer Quorum Being Called to the Torah and Offering the Priestly Benediction," *Minhat Shelomoh*, 2.4.10 (Jerusalem, 1999); the translation is my own.

20. On Ettlinger's conclusions regarding this topic, see Judith Bleich, "Rabbinic Responses to Non-Observance in the Modern Era," in *Jewish Tradition and the Non-Traditional Jew*, ed. J. J. Schacter (New York, 1992), 72–75. Bleich also cites Feinstein's views. On the Lubavitcher Rebbe, see Naftali Loewenthal, "The Baal Shem Tov's Iggeret Ha-Kodesh and Contemporary Habad 'Outreach,'" in *Yashan mi-pene hadash: Mehkarim be-toledot Yehude Mizrah Eropah uve-tarbutam: Shai le-Emanuel Etkes*, ed. A. Rapoport-Robert and D. Asaf (Jerusalem, 2009), 96–97.

21. *Avotot ahavah*, siman bet, p. 10 quotes the words of Rabbi Avraham Danzig, an early nineteenth-century authority, to this effect in his legal compilation *Haye adam*.

22. It is not clear from the letter why this format was employed.

23. The letter is dated 5 Sivan 5756 (May 24, 1996) and is on the letterhead of the NJOP. It was composed in English and signed by Rabbis Ephraim Z. Buchwald and Yitzchak Rosenbaum. Rabbi Buchwald has graciously made it available to me and permitted me to quote from the letter.

24. The entire Hebrew text and translation of this *psak din* of 1956 was published in *The Jewish Observer*, April 1975, 9. For a discussion of how the yeshivah world began to reevaluate its position on teaching in non-Orthodox settings, see Adam S. Ferziger, "From Demonic Deviant to Drowning Brother: Reform Judaism in the Eyes of American Orthodoxy," *Jewish Social Studies* 15, no. 3 (2009): esp. 62–66.

25. "An Interview with HaRav Sholom Kamentsky, Shlita," *Klal Perspectives*, 11. It is not entirely clear from the text where the words of the two rabbis Kamenesky, father and son, begin and end.

26. David Eliezrie, interview by author, December 24, 2012.

27. Ibid.

5

THE TOURO MONUMENT CONTROVERSY

Aniconism vs. Anti-Idolatry in a Mid-Nineteenth-Century American Jewish Religious Dispute

JONATHAN D. SARNA

The Jewish traveler Israel Joseph Benjamin,[1] known as Benjamin II since he followed in the footsteps of the medieval Jewish traveler Benjamin of Tudela, stirred up controversy in 1860 when he condemned a proposal to memorialize the New Orleans Jewish philanthropist Judah Touro with a public statue. "How is it possible that Jews can entertain the wish to carry out an act which is a clear violation of the Ten Commandments . . . ?" he protested. "Let us not carry out a project so decidedly in conflict with our holy religion." Recounting the episode in his popular book of travels, *Drei Jahre in Amerika* (*Three Years in America*), Benjamin cast himself as an Orthodox defender-of-the-faith, courageously waging war against assimilated New Orleans Jews insensitive even to the grossest violations of Jewish law and tradition.[2] The son of one statue supporter, he related, threatened to murder him. A Jewish organization that had promised him a grant of nine hundred dollars to travel to the Orient withdrew all its support. The "*hazan* [cantor] and preacher of the Portuguese synagogue," he claimed, brushed aside his halakhic arguments with a curt "That was in ancient times. Now, however, we live in the nineteenth century." But the intrepid Benjamin, ever the hero of his own stories, struggled onward. "I suffered much and had great losses," he cried, tugging at the heartstrings of his readers. "Nevertheless I had the satisfaction of having acted according to my convictions and of having opposed, not without success, a memorial so public, so enduring and—so unJewish."[3]

On the surface, Benjamin's account reads like a conventional nineteenth-century Jewish account of tradition vs. modernity. It reinforced a typical stereotype about America: that the country was good for Jews politically and economically, but disastrous for them religiously. Though the term had not yet come into widespread use, the implication was clear: America was a *treifene medinah* (an unkosher state).[4]

A more careful reading of Benjamin, however, raises daunting questions concerning his account. Most surprisingly, he reports that it was "the preacher of the Cincinnati Reform congregation," Isaac Mayer Wise, who rushed to his defense, insisting that, except for gravestones, "no other pillar, statue or monument was ever considered lawful in Israel." At the same time, with but one minor exception, he found that "not a single Orthodox rabbi in America took my side." Instead, the two most traditional Jewish newspapers of the day, Isaac Leeser's *Occident* and Samuel Isaacs's *Jewish Messenger,* published articles by James K. Gutheim against him. Benjamin fails to explain this anomaly, implying that in America even the Orthodox spurned major commandments. But given well-known debates over a whole series of reforms—the organ, mixed seating, liturgical reforms, and more—this is hardly persuasive.[5]

Second, a close reading of Benjamin's account makes clear that two different plans were afoot to memorialize Judah Touro. One envisaged "a monument," defined as "a shaft, column or pillar," and the other "a statue (cast in bronze or chiseled of marble)." He conflates the two, implying that both violated the same commandments. Yet contemporaries clearly viewed the two plans as different, even from the perspective of Jewish law. Why were they not different to him?[6]

Finally, the two central protagonists in the debate turn out to have been James K. Gutheim (who defended the proposed memorial) and Isaac Mayer Wise (who condemned it). These men were never otherwise known as bitter ideological opponents, and both are remembered by historians as religious moderates, rather than radicals, and as pioneers of Reform Judaism (though Gutheim, at the time, was still ministering to an Orthodox synagogue).[7] If the central issue in the dispute was "tradition" vs. "modernity," as Benjamin implies, why did these men lead the charge for the respective sides, and not people much further apart on the Jewish religious spectrum?

This article takes a fresh look at the controversy over the Touro Monument, utilizing hitherto overlooked sources and new interpretive frames. Far from being a controversy over tradition versus modernity, as Benjamin imagined it, we shall see that the controversy focused instead around two opposite approaches to the place of "graven images" and the plastic arts in modern Jewish life. One approach, championed by Wise, insisted that Judaism was *aniconic,* opposed to pillars, statues, and monuments of any kind. The other, championed by Gutheim, insisted that Judaism was only *anti-idolic,* meaning that non-idolatrous three-dimensional art was unobjectionable. Since, as Steven Fine has observed, "art has been a litmus test for interpreting the place of the Jew in modern society," both of these positions came laden with different assumptions and implications.[8] Even though the Touro monument was never built and (as we shall see) the Civil War rendered the whole matter moot, the debate that took place in the 1860s prefigured contrasting approaches to questions of Jewish art lasting well into contemporary times.

Judah Touro (1775–1854)—born in Newport, raised in Boston, and for more than fifty years a resident of New Orleans—accumulated a large fortune as a merchant, ship owner, and real estate investor. Eccentric, indecisive, difficult, and peculiar, he stood out in New Orleans for the simplicity of his tastes, his business probity, and his reputation for philanthropy. Late in life, he rededicated himself to Judaism, became a regular attendee at Sabbath services, and decided to leave a substantial portion of his wealth to Jewish institutions.[9]

Touro is remembered as a lifelong bachelor. His siblings predeceased him, and he was described on his gravestone as "the last of his name."[10] Recent evidence suggests, however, that (like many among the New Orleans elite), he carried on a long-term relationship with a free person of color, Ellen Wilson. Under Louisiana law, marriages of "free white persons with free people of color" were forbidden, and Wilson never became his wife. Nevertheless, strong family tradition maintains that Touro fathered Wilson's daughter, Narcissa. She was raised in Boston by Catherine Hays, Touro's beloved cousin. Narcissa subsequently married another Touro relative, Richard Gustavus Forrester of Richmond, the mulatto son of Gustavus Myers. In time, the couple became the progenitors of a distinguished African American clan.[11]

From the perspective of Louisiana law, of course, Touro still had no "forced heirs"—those legally entitled to inherit a portion of his estate.[12] Having made this clear in the first article of his remarkable will, he went on to bequeath more than $500,000—some $12 million in today's money—to philanthropic institutions both Jewish and general across the United States, including orphanages, hospitals, benevolent societies, synagogues, and a fund to help "ameliorate the condition of our unfortunate Jewish brethren in the Holy

Land." He was especially generous to institutions in New Orleans, some fifteen of which received individual bequests. Newspapers throughout the United States reported details of Judah Touro's will in their pages. His may well have been the most generous American will of its time, raising the bar for personal philanthropy in all sections of the country.[13]

Within days of Touro's demise, in January 1854, the New Orleans Board of Assistant Aldermen resolved to erect a monument in his honor. Americans, in those days, proposed far more monuments than they actually erected. The *New Orleans Bee* estimated "a hundred monuments voted to the illustrious dead, which have never to this day left the quarry." The paper nevertheless hoped that in Touro's case "the matter will not end in mere declaration of idle resolves." For pedagogic reasons, and perhaps also with an eye toward improving the city's overall appearance, it called upon the city fathers to place monuments "on every hill-top to remind the rising generation of the virtues and glory of their ancestors."[14]

As an incentive for the city to act, Rezin Davis Shepherd, who had saved Touro's life after he was shot in 1815 during the Battle of New Orleans and who now stood to gain hundreds of thousands of dollars as his principal heir, offered the city up to $300,000 from his benefactor's residual estate (over $7 million in today's money) for street improvements and further embellishments to the Touro Alms House, provided that it change the name of Canal Street to Touro Street and erect a "simple yet substantial cenotaph [empty tomb] . . . at some appropriate place thereon."[15] Some in the city demurred. An editor, recalling "Mr. Touro's hostility to all display," suggested that money allocated for the cenotaph be allocated instead to the budget of the Touro Asylum.[16] An alderman urged Shepherd to consider a "grander object": converting the public buildings in Baton Rouge into "an institution of learning to be called The Touro University," and shifting Louisiana's capital to New Orleans.[17] But Shepherd held his ground, and on March 21, 1854, his offer was unanimously accepted. By January the architect Richard Saltonstall Greenough had furnished a plan for the Touro monument: "A group of figures eight feet in height, representing charity—placed on a pedestal ten feet high—to be wrought in bronze, at a cost of $10,000."[18]

Shepherd (who was not Jewish) also oversaw the creation of a "noble and substantial monument" to Touro at the Old Jewish cemetery of Newport, where he had been laid to rest. The eighteen-and-a-half-foot granite obelisk, erected in 1855, resembled those nearby that memorialized Touro's sister, brother, and parents, all of whom had predeceased him. As if to underscore

Judah's elevated status, however, his monument towered high above all the rest; it remains the tallest monument in the entire cemetery.[19]

For reasons that remain unclear, Richard Saltonstall Greenough's proposed New Orleans monument to Touro became one more that "never left the quarry." The 1857 recession and Shepherd's prolonged legal troubles, unrelated to the Touro estate, may have undone his earlier agreement. Earlier, the city council had decided to restore Canal Street to its original name.[20] So, in 1860, the Jewish community took it upon itself to memorialize Touro, led by George Jonas, the first president of the Touro Infirmary Board of Managers. "As Israelites and American citizens," the new Touro Monument Association declared in proceedings sent out to the Jewish and general press, "we deem it a sacred duty as well as a proud privilege to testify in an enduring form our respect, admiration and gratitude in which we hold the memory of our late benevolent and patriotic fellow citizen, Judah Touro."[21]

What kind of monument the association contemplated soon became a matter of dispute. I. J. Benjamin, who happened to be in New Orleans as part of his journey across America, claimed that the Portuguese congregation, Nefutzoth Yehudah (Dispersed of Judah), which Touro in his last years both built and attended, "wished to set up a statue of Judah Touro." A similar report appeared in the general press, which linked the proposed statue to that of Henry Clay, inaugurated with much fanfare just over a month earlier (April 12, 1860), as the first of a projected series.[22] By contrast, Isaac Hart, the corresponding secretary of the Touro Monument Association, claimed to have "heard only a monument mentioned," and not specifically a statue. A correspondent to the *Occident* agreed, calling the statue "a proposition which had never been broached." In retrospect, it seems that two different proposals were floated, one to erect a statue in Touro's likeness and the other to erect a monument in his memory.[23]

Whatever the case, the Touro Monument Association's proposal set off a firestorm of debate. The traveler I. J. Benjamin, as noted, condemned it on the basis of the divine commandment, "Thou shalt not make for thyself a graven image." Citing both Joseph Karo's *Shulhan Arukh* (*Yoreh Deah* 141:4) and the commentary thereon by Shabetai ben Me'ir ha-Kohen (ShaKh), he insisted, in a "protest" published in the short-lived New Orleans Jewish newspaper *The Corner Stone,* that the project was "decidedly in conflict with our holy religion," and should not go forward.[24]

Isaac Mayer Wise, the architect of American Reform Judaism, agreed. Taking advantage of the opportunity to attack the "two orthodox ministers" who signed their names to the association's proceedings, he quoted an array of sources to prove that monuments, including statues were prohibited to Jews, for "Sacred Scripture prohibits to erect monuments, statues or pillars"; only gravestones were permitted. Even "the idea of erecting a monument by Jews is entirely new," he claimed; "all precedents are missing." Indeed, he insisted that *any* form of three-dimensional art compromised Jewish monotheism in all its distinctiveness. "Monuments set to the departed were the first cause of idolatry," he warned. "What security can be offered that in two or three centuries the monument of Judah Touro will not be worshipped as is now the cross or the images of the saints?" Wise, in this case, employed language more commonly used by his Orthodox antagonists. The Touro Monument Association, he declared, has "no right to break up a sacred law so conscientiously observed by our ancestors and contemporaries; a law which is essential and characteristic of Judaism with its purely spiritual monotheism."[25]

Wise's opposition to the Touro Monument reflected what he had absorbed from the leading German thinkers of his day. The great German philosopher Immanuel Kant in 1790 described the commandment "Thou shalt not make unto thee any graven image" as perhaps the most "sublime passage in the Jewish Book of the Law," and credited it for "the enthusiasm that the Jewish people felt in its civilized period for its religion when it compared itself with other peoples." Seeking to reposition Judaism in the most favorable possible light in the face of this and other modern philosophical challenges, Jewish thinkers, according to Kalman Bland, came to portray Judaism as "fundamentally aniconic, preeminently spiritual, coterminous with ethics, and quintessentially universal." So the liberal German Jewish philosopher Solomon Formstecher described Judaism in 1841 as "the religion of the spirit," and warned that it should consider the plastic arts its "severe foe." In a similar vein, historian Heinrich Graetz wrote in 1846 that sculpture reflected "the artistic act created in Greek paganism, in accord with its sensuous God-Concept." It was, he implied, antithetical to Judaism. Opposition to three-dimensional art, even if it was totally secular, became a marker of Jewish distinctiveness and superiority in German Jewish circles. In attacking the Touro monument, Wise was defending these same critical boundaries, and applying them to the United States.[26]

Personal factors too may have led Wise to weigh in as strongly as he did. He had warmly embraced Benjamin a few weeks earlier, when the latter visited Cincinnati, and had also collected money on his behalf to promote the inveterate traveler's proposed journey to the Orient. He may even have recommended that Benjamin visit New Orleans, knowing that Touro had funded a Hebrew Foreign Mission Society in that city to assist suffering Jews in China. Seeing that New Orleans Jews promised funds to Benjamin and then withdrew them in the face of his "protest," Wise's counterthrust on Benjamin's behalf may well have displayed loyalty to a friend.[27]

Wise no doubt also enjoyed casting his New Orleans opponents as heterodox. Judah Touro's will, after all, had conspicuously omitted from its list of beneficiaries Wise's Bene Jeshurun congregation as well as Har Sinai in Baltimore and Emanu-El in New York—all of them identifiably Reform. Gershom Kursheedt, who drafted the list of Jewish institutions for Touro, was an Orthodox Jew with close ties to the Orthodox Jewish leader Isaac Leeser. While Touro did bequeath funds to Wise's Talmud Yelodim Institute, reputedly "the best Jewish elementary school in all America," Wise was known to believe that most of Touro's money could have been put to better use—such as his dream for a college to prepare rabbis and "perpetuate our national literature." So in addition to everything else, Wise's opposition to the Touro monument provided him with a measure of revenge against those who had excluded him.[28]

The central figure arrayed against Wise and Benjamin in the debate over the monument was James Koppel Gutheim (1817–86). One of comparatively few German-educated Jewish religious leaders in America with an excellent command of English, Gutheim, who immigrated in 1843, was friendly with Leeser (they shared a common Westphalian background and a common teacher, Rabbi Abraham Sutro),[29] and like him moved from business to the rabbinate without ever having been formally ordained. In New Orleans, where he then served as minister of the Portuguese congregation Dispersed of Judah, he was the best paid, most beloved, and most revered Jewish religious leader in town. In 1860 Gutheim still identified as Orthodox, though his liberal tendencies were evident, and his small congregation included many of Touro's closest Jewish friends and acolytes. As the most Jewishly learned among those supporting the Touro monument, it fell to him to defend it.[30]

Gutheim did so in two ways. First, he published an eight-column exposé of Benjamin. He raised questions about his credentials, competence, and character; attacked his "literary and philanthropic pretensions"; and rehearsed for American readers the many criticisms of his earlier work that had appeared in European publications. He concluded that Benjamin was simply a failed businessman who reinvented himself as a traveler as "a very plausible and easy way to make a good subsistence."[31]

Second, and much more importantly, he published a long and learned response to Wise, in an effort to demonstrate that "the Rev I. M. Wise has given a totally perverted interpretation of the law in question and that the erection of a monument for the purpose indicated involves no violation of the law of God." Citing an array of traditional authorities, Gutheim argued that the prohibition against monuments "refers exclusively to monuments created for purposes of worship . . . but monuments of every other description are not interdicted." Far from being idolatrous, the proposed monument, he declared, was "an act of the most genuine gratitude and purest piety . . . in full harmony with the spirit, the principle and practices of Judaism." In a footnote, Gutheim added that while his article focused on the permissibility of a monument, "there can be no grievous wrong in the erection of even a real statue of Judah Touro."[32]

Gutheim's argument challenged the aniconic German Jewish approach to art that Wise had championed. While he agreed that idols were forbidden, secular monuments created for a purpose other than as a direct object of worship were to his mind acceptable, and even desirable. German Jewish thinkers may have believed that by recoiling as far as possible from the plastic arts Jews elevated themselves in the eyes of their neighbors, but Gutheim felt that Jews would be more elevated still by having monuments raised in their own honor. A monument for Judah Touro, he rhapsodized, "would be as effective in eradicating the traces of the yet lingering prejudices against our people as any event that has transpired in modern times. The visitor to the Crescent City [New Orleans] would carry the salutary impression made upon his mind by contemplating the monument of Judah Touro, *the benevolent Jew*, to the furthest ends of the land."[33]

Sephardic Jews, ancestors, in some cases, of members of Gutheim's own Portuguese congregation, had long accepted this more lenient anti-idolic but not anti-iconic attitude toward graven images. Seventeenth-century Dutch Jews permitted their portraits to be painted, and some of them, according to Rochelle Weinstein, "took pride in sculpture gardens, as artist, owners or visitors." Rabbi Saul Levi Morteira of Amsterdam, according to one source, sanctioned the display of paintings and sculptures in Jewish homes, a practice that apparently carried over to sepulchral decoration. Jewish tombstones in both the Netherlands and Curaçao preserve numerous examples of three-dimensional art, including bold reliefs depicting the final day of the deceased.[34]

Whether Gutheim actually knew any of this is doubtful. He did know, however, that non-Jews in New Orleans found the whole controversy quaint. "'The Corner Stone', a Jewish paper published in this city, comes out against the statue, whilst articles for it have appeared in some of our uncircumcised dailies," the correspondent of the *Nashville Advocate* reported impishly from New Orleans. "I notice this controversy as something queer and out of the usual course."[35] To avoid further communal embarrassment, put a stop to the polemical thrusts and parries among Jewish religious leaders, and reassure the public that Jewish law would be strictly upheld, Gutheim urged that the issue be resolved the way Jews had traditionally resolved such controversies: by submitting the question to a higher rabbinic authority. The motion passed the Touro Monument Association, and letters soon went out to four European rabbis: Nathan Marcus Adler, the chief rabbi of England; Zacharias Frankel, director of the Jewish Theological Seminary at Breslau; Samson Raphael Hirsch, rabbi of the Orthodox congregation Adass Jeschurun in Frankfurt-am-Main; and Solomon Judah Loeb Rapoport ("Shir"), chief rabbi of Prague. It was agreed that the decision of these men, described as "good men and true, concerning whose eminent learning and piety there is but one opinion," would be "cheerfully and strictly complied with."[36]

The decision to turn to these luminaries was, in many ways, revealing. All four were the products of central Europe (where the bulk of America's Jews at that time had been religiously formed); boasted rabbinical ordination as well as proven scholarly credentials; opposed the Reform movement; and, in different ways and to different degrees, sought to balance tradition and modernity.[37] Revealingly, the outstanding Orthodox *posek* of the era, Joseph Saul Nathanson of Lemberg, was not consulted; nor was the Reform Jewish leader and scholar Abraham Geiger; nor was any Sephardic luminary, even though Touro was of Sephardic lineage. Instead, the Touro Monument Association looked to prestigious middle-of-the-road figures to advise them, people whose names they knew and whose authority they respected.

Gutheim, "acting president of the Touro Monument Association," addressed the formal letter to each of the "eminent Rabbinical authorities" in June 1860. He explained the association's goal: "To perpetuate the memory of the late honored philanthropist, by erecting a statue (of bronze or marble) or some other monument (a shaft, pillar or column) in honor of the deceased, *provided such action be not in conflict with the laws and usages of Israel*." He then proceeded to pose six interrelated questions to the rabbis, designed to elicit their opinions both on the specific issue—a statue or monument in memory of Touro—and on related issues. He asked about erecting and sponsoring three-dimensional art, subscribing to monuments and statues honoring Jews and non-Jews, and most revealingly, whether a Jew may keep statues in his home or "devote himself to the art of sculpture . . . not made for purposes of idolatry?"[38]

By the time the rabbis replied, in 1861, Louisiana had seceded from the Union, Fort Sumter had fallen, and the first battles of the Civil War were raging. The *Occident* nevertheless devoted front-page coverage to the rab-bis' replies and made three of them available from the original German in full English translation (Rapoport's reply, embedded in a letter to his friend Theophilus Wehle, only addressed one of the questions posed to him and arrived later.)[39] All the replies echoed the aniconic position characteristic of German Jews. "The erection of a statue . . . is, according to Jewish law, pro-hibited in any place and for any object," Hirsch decreed, and the other rabbis basically agreed. Nor did they permit Jews (in Frankel's words) to "keep stat-ues or statuettes of human beings in their houses." Adler and Frankel (unlike Isaac Mayer Wise) had no problem with other kinds of memorial monuments, including shafts, pillars, or columns. But Hirsch was stricter: "The historical usage in Israel, prevailing throughout the whole Jewish past, would declare itself against the erection of a monument in honor of a man." As for whether Jews could themselves pursue the art of sculpture, Adler came down mostly on the negative side ("not lawful . . . in so far as it relates to *human* images, the sun and moon") and Frankel only slightly less so. Hirsch and Rapoport ignored the question completely, perhaps because they considered the answer obvious.[40]

Gutheim remained unbowed. "I had . . . hoped that the eminent rabbis, who were consulted, would descend to the very source of the prohibition and sub-ject the deductions from [the biblical prohibition] to a critical examination," he advised readers of the *Jewish Messenger*. Instead of complying "cheerfully and strictly" with the rabbis' rulings, as he had earlier promised to do, he reiterated his original position ("no grievous wrong in the erection of even a real statue"). He then dramatically announced that a soon-to-be-published "critical exposi-tion" of the issue, by a "much abler champion" than himself, would demonstrate "conclusively, that according to the strictest talmudical construction and in consonance with the most conservative principles of Judaism, there is not the shadow of an objection to the erection of a Monument or Statue."[41]

That "abler champion" turned out to be a well-educated recent immigrant from Dresden named Jonas Bondi (1804–74). A descendant on his mother's side of Rabbi Jonathan Eybeschuetz, Bondi had received an excellent theological and business education in Prague and was a wealthy banker in his hometown until business failure drove him and his family, in 1858, to immigrate to Amer-ica. He brought with him his large rabbinic library, later described as "perhaps the best selected collection of rabbinical literature in the United States."[42] After serving for a year as the (unordained) minister of New York's Congrega-tion Anshe Chesed, he moved into journalism, serving first as associate editor of the *Occident* and, from 1865, as editor of the *Hebrew Leader*.[43]

The controversy over the Touro monument spurred Bondi to undertake a "thorough examination of the original writings and documents" bearing on the question of monuments and statues in Judaism. He focused particularly on whether a statue for a man like Judah Touro, designed not for an idolatrous purpose but in order to memorialize his noble deeds, might be permitted. As he observed, "until now, no government leader in the world would have permitted or suffered Jews to elevate and honor one of their own with a memorial statue, no matter how greatly he had been respected." In the face of this new reality, he wondered whether the aniconic ritual instinct that had led Europe's rabbis to forbid the statue could withstand close halakhic scrutiny. His basic conclusion, "a rejoinder to the opinions of the Rev. Rabbis," appeared in (awkward) English in 1861, quoting the fourteenth-century commentary of Rabbi Nissim of Gerona: "It requires a positive proof of the intention to idolatrize a statue to establish a prohibition of its erection." He promised that a full-scale treatise on the subject would "shortly appear in type."[44]

That promise went unfulfilled.[45] In the interim, Benjamin published *Drei Jahre in Amerika 1859–1862* (1862), giving his version of the controversy, along with the opinions of the European rabbis. The chapter on the Touro Monument stimulated an important exchange in Ludwig Philippson's German Jewish newspaper, the *Allgemeine Zeitung des Judenthums*, concerning Jewish art and its limits. Geskil Saloman, a Danish-born Jewish painter working in Gothenburg, wrote to Philippson expressing significant concern over the implications of the rabbis' opinions for Jewish artists like himself. He wondered aloud whether Jewish art might be viewed differently, recognizing that it could help "preserve among Jews a feeling for our religious ceremonies" and also "secure for them the respect of other faiths."[46]

Perhaps in response to this flicker of European interest in the controversy, Bondi's treatise (written in rabbinic Hebrew) finally began to appear in 1866 in Joseph Kobak's scholarly journal, *Jeschurun: Zeitschrift für die Wissenschaft des Judenthums*, published in Fürth and Bamberg. Since it filled fifty-six closely printed pages, and was continued through three different irregularly published issues, the study only reached its conclusion in 1871. But it was comprehensive—far more comprehensive, indeed, than any previous contribution to the subject. After discussing a full range of rabbinic sources, commentaries, codes, and responsa, Bondi dissented from accepted rabbinic wisdom and instead reached much the same conclusion that Gutheim had several years earlier. So long as a statue did not lead people astray, was not employed for religious purposes, and was purely decorative or secular, it was unobjectionable, he concluded. Judaism, according to his review of the sources, fiercely opposed idolatry but was not otherwise aniconic.[47]

Bondi's learned treatise, while a pathbreaking and highly unusual work of scholarship for a Jew living in New York at that time, made no discernible impact in America. By the time it appeared, the whole controversy was a distant memory. The Battle of New Orleans, the city's occupation during the Civil War ("our intestine difficulties at the present time [are] more likely to destroy statues than to erect any"),[48] and the strains of postwar Reconstruction reshaped the priorities of New Orleans. The Touro monument was never built.

That, however, should not obscure the larger significance of the Touro Monument controversy. The proposal to memorialize Touro, who for a time was the country's most admired philanthropist, led to an important debate concerning three-dimensional art that divided American Jewish leaders on the eve of the Civil War, and then was echoed in Europe. Carried on through the medium of traditional halakhah, with citations to biblical and rabbinic texts, it essentially pitted opposite strategies of integration against one another. The first approach depicted Judaism as aniconic. Under the influence of modern German thought and liberal Protestant aniconism, it opposed three-dimensional art in a bid to elevate Jews and still distinguish them from their neighbors. The second approach depicted Judaism as anti-idolatrous. Under the influence of grand public sculpture and burgeoning secularism, it welcomed three-dimensional art (so long as it was not religious), in a bid to elevate Jews and promote their virtues to their neighbors. Both of these approaches developed in modernity—before then, almost all public statues were religious in character—and both were propounded by thoroughly modern Jews.[49]

In time, the second approach would become normative outside of fervently Orthodox circles,[50] as well-known public statues memorializing Haym Salomon, Uriah P. Levy, Louis Brandeis, and many others demonstrate. What set the two sides apart while the controversy raged, however, were not so much conflicting attitudes toward tradition, as I. J. Benjamin had imagined. They differed instead over how best to define Jewish tradition vis-à-vis contemporary culture, and how best to win for Jews their neighbors' respect.[51]

Notes

1. On Benjamin and his travels, see Oscar Handlin's introduction to I. J. Benjamin, *Three Years in America 1859-1862*, trans. Charles Reznikoff (Philadelphia, 1956), 1:1–36.
2. Tales of Jewish assimilation in New Orleans were commonplace in European Jewish periodicals, revolving in many cases around the antics of Rabbi Albert J. ("Roley") Marks. See Bertram W. Korn, *The Early Jews of New Orleans* (Waltham, Mass., 1969), 202, 237–45.

3. Benjamin, *Three Years in America 1859-1862*, 1:320–33 (quotes 321, 322, 333). The original edition, published in German as *Drei Jahre in Amerika 1859-1862*, was published in Hannover in 1862 and is available on Google Books at http://books.google.com/books?id=LaSSBztFj3IC&printsec=frontcover&dq=Drei+Jahre+in+Amerika:+1859-1862 (accessed January 23, 2014); see 365–82 for the Touro Monument controversy.

4. Arthur Hertzberg, "Treifene Medine: Learned Opposition to Emigration to the United States," *Proceedings of the Eighth World Congress of Jewish Studies, 1981, Panel Sessions, Jewish History* (Jerusalem, 1984), 7–30.

5. Benjamin, *Three Years in America*, 1:323–24; *Israelite*, June 1, 1860, 382. For Gutheim's articles, see *Jewish Messenger*, June 29, 1860, 196; *Occident*, June 22, 1860, 81.

6. Benjamin, *Three Years in America*, 1:325.

7. For convenient biographies, see Gary P. Zola, "Gutheim, James Koppel," *American National Biography Online*, February 2000, www.anb.org/articles/08/08-01796.html (accessed January 23, 2014); and Sefton D. Temkin, "Wise, Isaac Mayer," *American National Biography Online*, February 2000, www.anb.org/articles/08/08-01691.html (accessed January 23, 2014).

8. Steven Fine, *Art and Judaism in the Greco-Roman World: Toward a New Jewish Archaeology* (New York, 2005), 6, 82.

9. Korn, *Early Jews of New Orleans*, provides the most accurate account of Touro's career, and corrects many errors in the standard biography, Leon Huhner, *The Life of Judah Touro* (Philadelphia, 1946).

10. Huhner, *Life of Judah Touro*, 117.

11. The family story is recounted online at Eyes of Glory: An American Story of Faith, Family, and Freedom, www.eyesofglory.com/third-generation/ (accessed January 23, 2014); and in Joshua D. Rothman, *Notorious in the Neighborhood: Sex and Families across the Color Line in Virginia 1787-1861* (Chapel Hill, N.C., 2003), 90. Korn, *Early Jews of New Orleans*, provides some supporting evidence on 89, 292; see also Steve Clark, "Richard Gustavus Forrester," *Richmond Times-Dispatch*, February 10, 2009. For the ban on interracial marriages, see *A Digest of the Civil Laws now in force in the Territory of Orleans with Alterations and Amendments* (New Orleans, 1808), 24. Korn's speculations concerning Touro's executor, Pierre Andre Destrac Cazenave, whom he describes, based on R. G. Dun records, as a "Quadroon," may now be put to rest, based on Linda Epstein, "Paul Andre Destrac Cazenave: Judah Touro's 'Pet' or a Man of Means?" *Louisiana History* 53 (Winter 2012): 5–29. For a general account of the relationships between white New Orleans men and free women of color (*femmes de couleur libres*), see Lawrence N. Powell, *The Accidental City: Improvising New Orleans* (Cambridge, Mass., 2012), 284–93.

12. See U.S. Legal Definitions, http://definitions.uslegal.com/f/forced-heir/ (accessed January 10, 2014).

13. Korn, *Early Jews of New Orleans*, 255–58; for a carefully annotated text of the will, see Morris U. Schappes, *A Documentary History of the Jews in the United States 1654-1875* (New York, 1971), 333–41 (quote on 337). For the story of Touro's bequest to the Jews of the Holy Land, see A. Schischa, "The Saga of 1855: A Study in Depth," in *The Century of Moses Montefiore*, ed. Sonia and V. D. Lipman, 269–346 (Oxford, 1985).

14. *New Orleans Bee*, January 25, 1854, English section.

15. *Philadelphia Inquirer*, February 8, 1854; *New York Evening Post*, February 7, 1854; John Smith Kendall, *History of New Orleans* (Chicago, 1922), 2:678. Kendall claims that a "magnificent cenotaph" to Touro's memory was planned.

16. *New York Sun*, February 3, 1854.

17. *Baton Rouge Daily Advocate*, February 16, 1854.

18. *Charleston Courier*, March 28, 1854; *Augusta Chronicle*, January 17, 1855.

19. *Newport Mercury*, December 1, 1855; see David Mayer Gradwohl, *Like Tablets of the Law Thrown Down: The Colonial Jewish Burying Ground in Newport Rhode Island* (Ames, Ia., 2007), 42–47 (Gradwohl measures the obelisk as seventeen feet tall, perhaps because of settling); and Joshua L. Segal, *The Old Jewish Cemetery of Newport: A History of North America's Oldest Extant Jewish Cemetery* (Nashua, N.H., 2007), 88–98.

20. For Shepherd's legal troubles, which finally reached the Supreme Court, see *Lucas v. Brooks*, 85 US 436 (1873); Korn, *Early Jews of New Orleans*, 85. Without explaining why, the New Orleans City Council restored Canal Street to its original name on April 19, 1855; see *The Laws and General Ordinances of the City of New Orleans* (New Orleans, 1870), 483; and Kendall, *History of New Orleans*, 2:678.

21. *Jewish Messenger*, June 8, 1860, 172; *Occident*, June 7, 1860, 65; *Israelite*, June 1, 1860, 382. On George Jonas, see Irwin Lachoff and Catherine C. Kahn, *The Jewish Community of New Orleans* (Charleston, S.C., 2005), 41.

22. Benjamin, *Three Years in America*, 1:320; *New York Commercial Advertiser*, June 5, 1860; on the Dispersed of Judah congregation, see Korn, *Early Jews of New Orleans*, 248–52.

23. *Occident*, July 5, 1860, 91; July 26, 1860, 108; questions about each proposal were ultimately addressed to European rabbis; see Benjamin, *Three Years in America*, 1:325.

24. The "protest" is reprinted in Benjamin, *Three Years in America*, 1:321–22.

25. *Israelite*, June 1, 1860, 382. The *London Jewish Chronicle* noted that in this case, "the orthodox and the reformers have changed parts" ("Our Communal Weekly Gossip," *London Jewish Chronicle*, July 27, 1860). Surprisingly, David Einhorn's *Sinai* seems to have taken no stand on this controversy.

26. Immanuel Kant, *Critique of the Power of Judgment*, trans. P. Guyer and E. Matthews (Cambridge, 2000), 156. Kalman P. Bland, *The Artless Jew* (Princeton, N.J., 2000), 15–16, 22.

27. For Wise's support of Benjamin, see *Israelite*, June 15, 1860, 398; and Benjamin, *Three Years in America*, 1:313. The story of the Hebrew Foreign Mission Society is recounted in Michael Pollak, *Mandarins, Jews, and Missionaries: The Jewish Experience in the Chinese Empire* (Philadelphia, 1980), 181–87. Joseph Simon insisted that other factors and not the protest underlay the decision to withdraw the promised funds from Benjamin; see *Occident*, July 26, 1860, 108.

28. On the will, see Korn, *Early Jews of New Orleans*, 255; and Schappes, *Documentary History*, 334–41. The comment on Talmud Yelodim is from Benjamin, *Three Years in America*, 313; and Wise's comment on the college is in *Israelite*, June 1, 1860, 382.

29. On Sutro, see Lawrence Grossman, "Isaac Leeser's Mentor: Rabbi Abraham Sutro, 1784–1869," in *Rabbi Joseph H. Lookstein Memorial Volume*, ed. L. Landman, 151–62 (New York, 1980).

30. On Gutheim, see Gary P. Zola, "Gutheim, James Koppel," *American National Biography Online*, February 2000, www.anb.org/articles/08/08-01796.html (accessed January 23, 2014); and Scott Langston, "James K. Gutheim as Southern Reform Rabbi, Community Leader and Symbol," *Southern Jewish History* 5 (2002): 69–102; see Benjamin's description of Dispersed of Judah (Nephutzoth Yehudah) in *Three Years in America*, 317.

31. *Occident*, June 14, 1860, 71–74. Benjamin published a rejoinder in *Occident*, July 5, 1860, 90–91, followed by Isaac Leeser's editorial comment critical of Benjamin; and Max Lilienthal proffered an "impartial report" on the controversy in *Israelite*, July 13, 1860, 14. Salo Baron discusses Moritz Steinschneider's articles that were deeply critical of Benjamin in Salo W. Baron, *History and Jewish Historians* (Philadelphia, 1964), 298–99.

32. *Jewish Messenger*, June 29, 1860, 196; *Occident*, June 22, 1860, 81; see Benjamin's account of Gutheim's views in *Three Years in America*, 1:321.

33. *Jewish Messenger*, June 29, 1860, 196; *Occident*, June 22, 1860, 81.

34. Richard I. Cohen, *Jewish Icons: Art and Society in Modern Europe* (Berkeley, 1998), 33; Rochelle Weinstein, "Stones of Memory: Revelations from a Cemetery in Curaçao," in *Sephardim in the Americas: Studies in Culture and History*, ed. M. A. Cohen and A. J. Peck (Tuscaloosa, Ala., 1993), 81–140, esp. 111; Saul Levi Morteira, *Tratado da verdade de lei de Moises*, ed. H. P. Salomon (Coimbra, Portugal, 1988.), lxi n.19, qtd. in Marc Saperstein, *Your Voice Like a Ram's Horn* (Cincinnati, 1996), 417 n.20 (the responsum is identified as Biblioteca Naçional de Madrid 18292, fols. 132–35), and in Steven Nadler, *Rembrandt's Jews* (Chicago, 2003), 76; Isaac S. Emmanuel, *Precious Stones of the Jews of Curaçao* (New York, 1957), 123–28, esp. 126. Emmanuel (124) notes that in the nineteenth century, Dutch rabbis refused to sanction busts in the Curaçao cemetery and insisted upon their removal.

35. *Nashville Advocate*, as reprinted in *New York Commercial Advertiser*, June 5, 1860.

36. *Jewish Messenger*, June 29, 1860, 196; *Occident*, June 22, 1860, 81.

37. On these themes, see, e.g., on Adler, Steven Singer, "Chief Rabbi Nathan Marcus Adler: Major Problems in His Career" (MA thesis, Yeshiva University, 1974), 143–85. On Frankel, see Michael A. Meyer, *Response to Modernity: A History of the Reform Movement in Judaism* (New York, 1988), 84–89. On Hirsch, see Robert Liberles, "Champion of Orthodoxy: The Emergence of Samson Raphael Hirsch as Religious Leader," *AJS Review* 6 (1981): 43–60. On Rapoport, see Isaac Barzilay, *Shlomo Yehudah Rapoport [Shir] (1790-1867) and His Contemporaries* (Ramat Gan, 1969).

38. Benjamin, *Three Years in America*, 1:324–26; *Occident* 19 (May 1861): 49–50. Hirsch's *Jeschurun* ran a brief article about the planned monument to Touro back in 1855, quoting the *New Orleans Daily Delta*, so the subject may already have been familiar to the European rabbis; see *Jeschurun* 1 (February 1855): 294.

39. Rapoport's Hebrew letter was published in English translation in *Jewish Messenger*, August 9, 1861, 19, and reproduced in Hebrew, in part, in Benjamin, *Three Years in America*, 1:326–27. In the letter, he claims ("if my memory does not deceive me") that Bernard Illowy was among those seeking to prevent the statue from being erected. Illowy only arrived in New Orleans in spring 1861, but he had opposed tombstone images earlier. See Moshe D. Sherman, "Bernard Illowy and Nineteenth Century American Orthodoxy" (PhD diss., Yeshiva University, 1991), 217–18. For other evidence of Illowy's uncompromising Orthodoxy and European reputation, see David Ellenson, "A Jewish Legal Decision by Rabbi Bernard Illowy of New Orleans and its Discussion in Nineteenth Century Europe," *American Jewish History* (December 1979): 174–95.

40. *Occident* 19 (May 1861): 49–58; Benjamin, *Three Years in America*, 1:326–33; for Rapoport's letter in English, see *Jewish Messenger*, August 9, 1861, 19.

41. *Jewish Messenger*, May 17, 1861, 148.

42. *American Israelite*, September 15, 1876, 7.

43. Bertram W. Korn, "Jonas Bondi," *Encyclopaedia Judaica* 2nd ed. (Detroit, 2007), 4:58; "Jonas Bondi," *Universal Jewish Encyclopedia*, ed. I. Landman (New York, 1940), 2:451; Moshe Davis, *The Emergence of Conservative Judaism* (Philadelphia, 1963), 332–33; Guido Kisch, *In Search of Freedom: A History of American Jews from Czechoslovakia* (London, 1939), 89–90, 302–3; *Jewish Messenger*, March 13, 1874, 6.

44. *Jewish Messenger*, May 17, 1861, 146; Jonas Bondi, "Ma'amar: Yonati mehagve hasela," in *Jeschurun*, ed. Kobak (1866), 5:48 (my translation). Bondi's translation from Rabbi Nissim (*Ran*) seems to be based on Bavli Avodah Zarah Rif 19a and is taken somewhat out of context. This text plays a far more minor role in his *Jeschurun* article discussed below.

45. The *Jewish Messenger* had printed Joshua Falk's learned Hebrew commentary on Pirke Avot (*Sefer Avne Yehoshua*) in 1860, and Bondi's book may have been slated to appear from the same press. The Civil War and Bondi's financial difficulties likely precluded that from happening; see Yosef Goldman with Ari Kinsberg, *Hebrew Printing in America 1735-1926: A History and Annotated Bibliography* (Brooklyn, 2006), items 41, 688, 1015.

46. *Allgemeine Zeitung des Judenthums*, February 17, 1863, 113–16; February 24, 1863, 125–30; Fredric Bedoire and Robert Tanner, *The Jewish Contribution to Modern Architecture 1830-1930* (New York, 2004), 459–66; Ezra Mendelsohn, *Painting A People: Maurycy Gottlieb and Jewish Art* (Hanover, 2002), 66–67. Saloman noted that in his day, portraits of Jews, including rabbis, had become commonplace—notwithstanding doubts that had once been expressed. See on this theme Richard I. Cohen, "Representations of the Jewish Body in Modern Times—Forms of Hero Worship," in *Representation in Religion: Studies in Honor of Moshe Barasch*, ed. J. Assmann and A. I. Baumgarten, 237–76 (Leiden, Netherlands, 2001).

47. Jonas Bondi, "Ma'amar," (1866), 5:46–86; (1868), 6:105–14; (1871), 7:81–87. Note that the European editor dissented from Bondi's conclusions and warned readers not to issue halakhic rulings based on them.

48. *Jewish Messenger*, September 19, 1862, 92.

49. For a parallel controversy in France, also involving modernized Jews, see the 1862–64 debate over the statue to the eminent composer Fromental Halévy; *Jewish Messenger*, September 19, 1862, 92; Ruth Jordan, *Fromental Halevy: His Life and Music, 1799–1862* (New York, 1996), 209.

50. Zev Eleff has pointed out to me that Abraham Danzig (1748–1820) and Naphtali Tzvi Judah Berlin (1817–93) likewise ruled leniently on the question of portraying human features, perhaps following the ruling of Yom Tov ben Avraham Asevilli, the RITVA (1250–1330); see Ritva on Avoda Zara 43b; Abraham Danzig, *Hokhmat adam, hilkhot avodat kokhavim* 69:6; and Naphtali Berlin, *Ha'amek she'elah*, Yitro 57:3. All three insisted, in effect, that Judaism was anti-idolatrous and not aniconic.

51. As a coda, in 1876, following two years of widowerhood, Isaac M. Wise married Selma, the daughter of Jonas Bondi. Bondi's books soon became part of the Hebrew Union College library. Wise in 1899 overcame his earlier objections and sat for a bust modeled from life by the eminent Jewish sculptor Moses Jacob Ezekiel. See James G. Heller, *Isaac M. Wise: His Life, Work and Thought* (New York, 1965), 426–29; Adolph S. Oko, "Jewish Book Collections in the United States," *American Jewish Year Book* 45 (1944): 74; David Philipson, "Moses Jacob Ezekiel," *Publications of the American Jewish Historical Society* 28 (1922): 45–46.

6

REVERSE ENGINEERING THE TWENTIETH-CENTURY BAR/BAT MITZVAH

ISA ARON

In his essay "Judaism Resurgent" David Ellenson notes a paradox in contemporary Jewish life: "The twin trends of renewed ethnic-religious expression and pride, on the one hand, and the ever-growing attenuation of such attachments, on the other."[1] In this essay I focus on what is, to me, a particularly piquant example of this paradox, the increased importance of the bar/bat mitzvah ceremony in the life of American Jews. Over the centuries bar mitzvah changed from a modest ritual celebrating the point in a male's life when he becomes obligated to fulfill the full range of mitzvot into an elaborate ritual in which observing mitzvot is less important than connecting to family and expressing one's Jewish identity. This type of evolution is not unusual in religious life; over time, many rituals stray far from their original significance. But I will argue that the contemporary bar/bat mitzvah is different from most contemporary traditions because, rather than evolving organically, it was reinvented or reengineered by groups of rabbis and educators whose goal was to increase participation in synagogue life. This revised set of standards and expectations has had a deleterious effect on both Jewish education and synagogue life. If one wants, as I do, to undo some of this damage, one needs to understand both the forces that led to the distortion and the forces that might lead to the acceptance of a newer reverse-engineered bar/bat mitzvah, which would have greater meaning for twenty-first-century American Jews.

I begin this essay with a brief review of the history of bar mitzvah, and explore the interplay between folk and elite that led to its current manifestation, in which the interplay between modernity and traditionalism (or, perhaps, a faux traditionalism) is evident. Though it is neither possible nor desirable to restore this ritual to a (mythical) pristine form, it is important to consider the unanticipated and unfortunate consequences of the twentieth-century redesign. I describe one effort to modify both the ritual and the preparation so that they conform to values that both folk and elite can endorse. In the final section I consider the forms of resistance synagogues are likely to encounter as they attempt this reverse engineering, along with some possible strategies they might employ to help it proceed more smoothly.

A Very Brief History of Bar Mitzvah

What we think of today as the bar mitzvah ceremony derives from a series of isolated rituals and practices, some of which date back to late antiquity. Historian Ivan Marcus argues, however, that "there is no evidence to support the idea that each dot on the graph represents anything more than an isolated case."[2] After reviewing the historical references to bar mitzvah, Marcus offers the following summary:

> The evidence . . . points to the German Empire where bar mitzvah rites developed well into modern times and from there spread to Eastern Europe. . . . [We do not] know when the rite is taken for granted in the New World and in different Jewish communities in Muslim lands, where it was not all that important before. At some point, apparently no earlier than the eighteenth or maybe even the nineteenth century, or even later, modern Jews adapted an elaborate bar mitzvah rite in nearly all of these places.[3]

American studies professor Jenna Joselit picks up the story from there. In the process of transplantation from the Old World to the New, this rite of passage assumed a brand-new centrality and immediacy. Taking a meaningful, if restrained, religious event and transforming it into something larger (and quite different from) the sum of its parts, immigrant Jews invented the "fancified" bar mitzvah.[4]

While this "fancification" was most evident in the lavish parties that followed the service, the service itself demanded more of the thirteen-year-old than it had in previous eras. To prepare boys for this ceremony, numerous after-school programs whose sole aim was to prepare boys for this ceremony, called by their critics "bar mitzvah factories," arose before the First World War. Volumes of "bar mitzvah *drashas* [talks]" were published, so that boys whose Jewish education was minimal could sound sufficiently learned and eloquent.[5]

Because of the dearth of research on American b'nai mitzvah we do not know whether observance of this life-cycle event waxed, waned, or held steady over the past 125 years. Despite early attempts by Reform rabbis to abolish the bar mitzvah in favor of confirmation, by 1960 more than 96 percent of American Reform congregations had reintroduced the ceremony.[6] The bat mitzvah, first introduced in 1922, was slow to take root, but is now the equivalent of the bar mitzvah and is common in all denominations except the Orthodox.

This brings us back to the Ellenson quotation at the beginning of this essay. Over the course of the twentieth century, the rate of intermarriage among American Jews grew, and the rate of synagogue affiliation declined, along with the rate of *Shabbat* (Sabbath) and holiday observance. But, at least anecdotally, it seems that b'nai mitzvah observances are as popular in the twenty-first century as they were in the twentieth.[7] And although there are many things we don't know about the development of the bar/bat mitzvah ceremony in twentieth-century America, it seems clear that it grew from the recitation of a few blessings, and perhaps a Torah reading, to a more extensive performance that included reading Torah and Haftarah, giving an original *devar torah* (short speech on the Torah portion), and, in many cases, leading parts of the service.

A Cornerstone of the Folk Religion

Why have subsequent generations of American Jews held onto the tradition of bar mitzvah so steadfastly? And why has the ceremony itself (rather than just the party) become more elaborate, even among Jews who observe few other Jewish rituals? A persuasive explanation is offered by sociologist Stuart Schoenfeld, who relies on political scientist Charles Liebman's distinction between folk and elite.[8] The elite, who include rabbis, cantors, educators, scholars, and particularly active lay leaders, "are responsible for conserving and adapting the sacred tradition. When the emphasis of authority was thought to lie primarily on the side of tradition, the religious elite . . . were able to claim the legitimacy to define religious belief and practice and to channel change within a process which they could usually control."[9] Folk beliefs and practices, on the other hand, "emerge from the needs of daily life," and, at times, prevailed, despite the disapproval of the elite. "In traditional Judaism the religious elite would sometimes campaign vigorously against folk beliefs and practices which they found subversive, but they would also accommodate others into their view of what was permissible, or deal with deviant beliefs and practices simply by overlooking them."[10]

Even when both folk and elite celebrate the same holiday or life-cycle event, there can be (and often is) a wide disparity between the ways each group thinks about that practice. This is especially true of the bar/bat mitzvah, which, for the elite, marks a child's entry into a life of mitzvot; to the folk, it signifies something much different. As Schoenfeld writes: "Instead of being a ceremony acknowledging the full participation of the adolescent in sacred rituals, bar mitzvah appears to have become a ritual of discontinuity, the last time the boy was obligated to present himself as a participant in his father's world. It became a ritual in which traditional commitments were affirmed and then ignored."[11]

I would argue that bar/bat mitzvah became a cornerstone of the folk religion because it was a once-in-a-lifetime event whose core values were identified by the folk as family and community, rather than religious observance. As Liebman notes, "One does not have to believe with Emile Durkheim . . . that all religion is the celebration and ritualization of communal ties, to observe that this is the major function of Jewish folk religion in America."[12]

But if the folk see bar/bat mitzvah as signifying commitment to family and community rather than to ritual mitzvot, how did the ceremony expand from a brief aliyah to the Torah to an elaborate performance, requiring months, if not years, of preparation? Archival documents unearthed by Schoenfeld tell at least one version of the story. In the first half of the twentieth century, he reports, "far fewer than one-half of American Jewish families were synagogue members. Organized Jewish schools enrolled only a minority of school-aged children and many received tutoring only before their bar mitzvahs."[13] In a rare concerted effort among a broad range of Jewish institutions, the Conservative, Reform, and Reconstructionist movements and the Bureaus of Jewish Education in at least eleven major metropolitan areas banded together to require several years of supplementary schooling as a precondition for celebrating a bar mitzvah at a synagogue.

A 1937 editorial in *The Reconstructionist* suggested a strategic approach: "In order that these rites may not represent merely the attainment of certain ages, but also the accomplishment of certain minimum education, it would be necessary for the national organizations, such as the United Synagogue of America and the Union of American Hebrew Congregations, to set up for their respective constituents standard requirements for *bar mizvah* [*sic*] and for Confirmation."[14]

In a similar vein the Chicago Board of Jewish Education (BJE) mandated in 1938 that congregations affiliated with the BJE require all boys to have "a minimum of three years' attendance at a daily Hebrew School of recognized standing, or evidence of the candidate's fitness, to be determined by the Board of Jewish Education through examinations."[15]

While Schoenfeld focuses his attention on the success of the elite in increasing synagogue affiliation and religious school enrollment, I would argue that the elite also succeeded in changing the nature of the bar mitzvah itself. They redefined bar mitzvah on their own terms and created an expectation that one did not become bar mitzvah unless this change of status was sanctified in a ceremony held in a synagogue and led by a rabbi and a cantor.

Paraphrasing British scholar Eric Hobsbawm, one might say that the elite reinvented the bar mitzvah. He defines an "invented tradition" as a "set of practices, normally governed by overtly or tacitly accepted rules and of a ritual or symbolic nature, which seek to inculcate certain values and norms of behavior by repetition, which automatically implies continuity with the past. . . . In short, they are responses to novel situations which take the form of reference to old situations."[16]

Although not a wholly invented tradition, bar mitzvah was reinvented, or, perhaps more precisely, reengineered, by the rabbis and educators who made Jewish education a prerequisite for its celebration. It does not take very long to learn to recite the *berakhot* (blessings) before and after an aliyah to the Torah. What, then, would justify the requirement that children attend religious school for three years? From the perspective of the elite, and, undoubtedly, some of the folk as well, the rationale was an enriched Jewish education, leading to an appreciation of and commitment to Jewish living. But if the analyses of Joselit, Schoenfeld, and Liebman are correct, this aim would not have been sufficient to convince many of the folk, who would have wanted more concrete proof of the utility of a Jewish education. Competent (or even excellent) performance of a series of difficult synagogue skills would offer one such demonstration.

Hobsbawm notes that the invention of a tradition typically coincides with rapid social change and the desire of the inventors to impart a new vision or a new set of values. This is precisely what happened with the reengineering of the bar mitzvah in twentieth-century America. Jews of eastern European extraction were moving out of the first and second areas of settlement into the suburbs, leaving behind their Jewish neighborhoods and social institutions. Increasing the competencies to be demonstrated at a boy's bar mitzvah helped convince people of the value of synagogue membership and Jewish education.

The Unanticipated Consequences

At first, the elite must have considered the reconfigured bar mitzvah as a triumph. While their effort to link bar mitzvah celebration to attendance in religious school was more successful in some Jewish communities than in others (for example, the synagogues and schools of New York City failed to reach such an agreement), it was, overall, remarkably effective. The percentage of school-aged children enrolled in supplementary schools went from 25 to 30 percent before World War II to 53 percent in 1963.[17] Data of this sort cannot demonstrate causality, and it is likely that a number of factors—including the Holocaust, the founding of the State of Israel, and increased social and economic mobility—accounted, in part, for the increase in enrollment. Nonetheless, it seems equally likely that the policy that required several years of study in a synagogue school in order to obtain clergy officiation at b'nai mitzvah played a key role.

But although the elite were able to assert their authority and increase their synagogue budgets, the folk also benefited, and continue to benefit, from the bargain. Linked to religious school attendance, bar mitzvah came to be seen as a graduation ceremony. And while a minority of congregations has been able to retain their middle school and high school students by offering attractive programs that match adolescent needs and interests, most religious schools experience a steep decline in enrollment starting at age thirteen. A 2006–7 census of supplementary schools throughout the United States found drop-out rates ranging from 35 percent in eighth grade and 55 percent by ninth grade, to 80–85 percent by eleventh and twelfth grade.[18] Moreover, most congregations allow children from certain families to circumvent the requirements that were established in the 1950s. It is possible for a child to prepare for a bar/bat mitzvah through private tutoring, without having had any formal Jewish schooling. Over the decades, parents have lobbied to reduce the number of days of attendance at religious school from three days a week to two days in the Conservative movement, and from two days to one in the Reform movement. Today, an increasing number of families are bypassing the synagogue entirely. One need only Google "bar mitzvah preparation" to locate any number of entrepreneurs who will tutor a child and officiate at a private service for less than the price of an annual synagogue membership. Finally, when parents associate synagogue membership with the celebration of b'nai mitzvah, they see no need to retain their membership in subsequent years. Thus, surveys of membership in Reform congregations consistently find that the distribution of families with children peaks when the youngest child reaches the age of thirteen.[19]

Ultimately, both folk and elite lost a great deal from this Faustian bargain. Hebrew education in supplementary schools has been reduced to decoding (sounding out letters without any comprehension), a skill many students fail to master no matter how many years they study.[20] And a ritual that should have, at its core, an affirmation of mitzvot, has devolved, instead, into a demonstration of the child's prowess. To the folk, the ability of a thirteen-year-old to chant Torah and Haftarah, deliver a *devar torah*, and lead parts of the service is proof of how special both she and her parents are. To the elite, the same proficiencies attest to how special the synagogue and school are. How many times has one heard, from both clergy and congregants, "Our congregation does the *best* b'nai mitzvah!" Eighth graders, already stressed out by academic and extracurricular pressures, now face an additional pressure to perform (flawlessly) rituals whose significance may elude them.

Reverse Engineering the Bar/Bat Mitzvah

To connect b'nai mitzvah ceremonies to values that all Jews—both folk and elite—can endorse; to imbue the ceremony, and preparation for it, with meaning; and to rescue Hebrew education from the travesty of pure decoding, we need to reverse-engineer the twentieth-century bar mitzvah. In July 2012, the Union for Reform Judaism's Campaign for Youth Engagement and Hebrew Union College's Rhea Hirsch School of Education joined forces to experiment with this process. We called our project the B'nai Mitzvah Revolution (BMR), and we described its goals on our website (www.bnaimitzvahrevolution.org) as follows:

- We aim to empower synagogues to return depth and meaning to Jewish learning and reduce the staggering rates of post–b'nai mitzvah dropout. We believe that a root cause of these challenges is the perception that b'nai mitzvah celebrations are like graduation ceremonies.
- We share with many synagogues a growing unease about the way b'nai mitzvah are celebrated, and the fact that b'nai mitzvah

preparation has, in many cases, supplanted other goals of synagogue educational endeavors.

- In many synagogues b'nai mitzvah observances are standard-
  ized, taking into account neither the differences among thirteen-
  year-olds, in terms of maturity and interest, nor the differences
  between families, in their motivations and Jewish identification.
  Because these ceremonies are centered on the individual child's
  performance of a ritual that she or he may not be able to fully
  understand or appreciate, current methods of b'nai mitzvah
  preparation are inefficient, wasting much instructional time in
  the religious school. Anecdotal evidence suggests that they often
  prove counterproductive as well, driving children and their families away from the synagogue and Jewish community, rather than
  strengthening their involvement. Thus, the opportunity for bar/
  bat mitzvah to usher in a new phase of involvement in the Jewish
  community is missed.

Response to this effort has been very strong. Thirty-nine congregations
applied to join the pilot group (fourteen were chosen); more than seventy
have joined a less-intensive group called the Active Learning Network. In 2013
we began working with a small number of from Conservative, Reconstructionist, and independent congregations as well.

The congregations in the pilot cohort vary in their size (from 245 to more
than 2,800 member units), location, and vision of how they would like to
change the bar/bat mitzvah ritual. Some are satisfied with the traditional service and its requirements. They have focused their efforts on helping parents
and children understand the values behind the ceremony and the meaning of
the rituals they will be leading. Others are eager to experiment with the rituals themselves. The changes they are exploring include offering b'nai mitzvah
opportunities to demonstrate their understanding of the Torah portion (or
Jewish values and traditions that are important to them) through the arts;
ways of making the service more of a communal event; and holding the service
or ceremony at a site where the child has done ongoing volunteer work.

All of the congregations are approaching these changes with caution.
Mindful of the fact that b'nai mitzvah customs are deeply rooted in American Jewish culture, the lay and professional planning teams are proceeding
slowly, often starting with a few families who seem most open to becoming
more actively involved and experimenting with new approaches.

However careful BMR congregations are in laying the groundwork, they are not so naïve as to assume that it will be easy to institute these changes. An elite group of leaders (and I include here the lay members of the planning team) attempting to reshape a long-standing folk tradition is bound to face resistance. We have found it useful to think about both the sources of, and possible antidotes to, resistance through four different organizational schemata, known to those familiar with the work of organizational theorists Lee Bolman and Terrence Deal as the four frames.[21] Each frame enables its viewers to see organizations differently, and each offers different approaches to the issues that accompany change.

The Political Frame

Theorists who view organizations through the political frame begin by noting the enduring differences among stakeholders and the battles over scarce resources that ensue because of these differences. Based on Schoenfeld's analysis, I would predict that the major cleavage in BMR congregations would be between the folk and elite. The folk are likely to resist any changes that take the focus away from the child and the family. On the other hand, some, though not all, clergy members will have difficulty compromising what they believe to be appropriate standards. And both staff and clergy will be concerned about the effects of their changes on the synagogue's budget. By requiring several years of synagogue membership and religious school attendance before b'nai mitzvah, the synagogues of the 1940s and 1950s not only championed the cause of Jewish education; they secured their own financial future. Imagine the situation of a congregation that decided that it is unnecessary to spend four years learning to decode Hebrew. The elite (including key lay leaders) would undoubtedly see this as an opportunity for students to spend more time exploring Jewish content more deeply. But some of the folk, especially those who were themselves raised believing that the purpose of Jewish schooling was b'nai mitzvah preparation, might lobby for a further reduction in the days of religious school, or simply withdraw their children from the school until they were ready to start learning how to decode. Some synagogues could end up losing hundreds of thousands of dollars.

When enduring differences persist, there is no way of resolving them completely, which is why theorists operating within the political frame advocate negotiation. Since the use of b'nai mitzvah as a bargaining chip in an earlier era was what led to the situation we are in today, I am leery of negotiation as a tactic. Instead, I look to the three other frames, which point to ways in which the differences might be bridged.

The Structural Frame

The structural frame calls attention to division of labor, lines of authority, and communication. When one looks at synagogue life within the structural frame it is striking how often synagogue programs and functions (from worship to education to community building) are planned and implemented discretely, with little relationship to one another. A former synagogue president describes it in the following way:

> The congregation . . . is well intended. Everyone wants to make the school better, do more outreach, be more responsive to new members, to kind of have more of a warm, fuzzy feeling about themselves. Everybody wants that, and you can set up a committee to try to implement it. You have all these ideas, but does it have follow through? Does it become the culture? Is the congregation imbued with that attitude? Does it become holistic or just [include] individual activities?[22]

This segmentation stems from the fact that most synagogues are underfunded and understaffed, and that it seems inefficient to have several professional or lay leaders collaborate on a program when one will do. Another reason is that many synagogue leaders have become accustomed to having their own spheres of influence, unencumbered by the need to cooperate or compromise.

Perhaps no arena of synagogue life is more segmented than that of bar mitzvah preparation. The child learns Hebrew in the religious school; studies further with a tutor; meets individually with one or more members of the clergy. Too often information that one person has (about the child and the parents) is not transmitted to the others. The parents, in the meantime, must work with the synagogue administrator, the caterer, and any number of committees. One synagogue that tried to rationalize the process of b'nai mitzvah preparation identified more than twenty discrete tasks, from selecting a date through assigning various honors. It is no wonder, then, that both b'nai mitzvah candidates and their families fail to grasp the deeper meaning of this rite of passage.

The division of labor that interferes with a holistic approach to b'nai mitzvah preparation will only be overcome when synagogue staff members rethink their roles and make sure that there is one main point of contact for each family. This will undoubtedly require a reconsideration of staff responsibilities in the synagogue as a whole, which, while difficult, will make the congregation less functional and more visionary.[23]

The Human Resource Frame

The human resource frame examines the way members of an organization interact with one another. Are staff members or congregants treated in a perfunctory or impersonal manner? Conversely, are they nurtured and empowered? Do congregants expect to find friends at the synagogue? Do they feel a sense of community? Once this question is asked it is difficult to avoid the realization that "community" is an ambiguous term. I have argued that the folk see family and community as the core values of b'nai mitzvah. But families who don't regularly attend Shabbat morning services do not have a genuine community on the occasion of the child's bar/bat mitzvah. The invited guests (many of whom are not congregants or, if they are congregants, do not attend regularly on Shabbat) tend to overshadow the "regulars," who, in most Reform synagogues, and some Conservative ones, are few in number. As one rabbi put it: "Every Saturday morning there are 50 cars or 100 cars parked in the parking lot. But every Saturday morning it's a different 50 or 100 cars, depending on that week's bar mitzvah."[24]

A vicious cycle is created when both the family and those congregants who attend on Shabbat morning perceive the service as a family-only affair, which makes the "regulars" uncomfortable, and even less likely to attend. To deal with this problem, a growing number of congregations have created Shabbat morning minyanim (prayer quorums) for the regulars, leaving the "bar mitzvah" service entirely privatized. In order to make b'nai mitzvah truly communal celebrations, synagogues will need to work hard to create genuine communities among both parents and children in the congregation. Reform congregations, in particular, may need to acknowledge that this might not happen on Shabbat morning, and will need to think about how a sense of community can be developed at other times, in other ways.

An even greater human resource problem is posed by the demands placed on candidates for b'nai mitzvah. For children who attend a day school or who attend Shabbat services on a regular basis, or for those children who have a flair for languages and performance, the tasks may not be onerous. But what of children unused to prayer, unable to decode fluently, or uncomfortable performing before a crowd? How much harm is done when parents nag their children to "practice your Torah portion!" As one congregation wrote in its

BMR application: "Students squeeze their b'nai mitzvah preparation into hectic lives with multiple commitments. Many see it as a burden. The bar/bat mitzvah is out of context for our students, as the synagogue skills they obtain are not in their experience until a couple of months before their 'day.'" How stressful is it that, as a writer for the Huffington Post put it, "For this boy, not really yet a man, success, however measured, is the only option."[25]

Congregations in the BMR seek to change the parameters of "one size fits all" b'nai mitzvah by tailoring the demands for performance to the interests and abilities of the child. But they can expect resistance from family members who see the child's performance as a measure of the parents' success in raising their child. They can even expect resistance from the children themselves.

The only way to counter resistance through the human resource frame is to engage people in an ongoing conversation and to keep reminding parents, children, and the entire community that the bar/bat mitzvah ceremony signifies an understanding and embrace of core Jewish values, not an achievement test. This change will certainly take time.

The Symbolic/Cultural Frame

The symbolic frame teaches us that the participants in an organization are not solely rational. They are influenced as much (or more) by symbols, myths, and stories as by logical argument. Members of a synagogue's BMR team might be able to convince parents intellectually that up to the mid-twentieth century, b'nai mitzvah were much more modest; still, in their heart of hearts, many would feel that a *real* bar or bat mitzvah is the one they, or their nephew, or their neighbor's daughter celebrated. Following Edgar Schein, the cultural/symbolic frame makes us aware of the contradictions between our stated norms and the deeper-seated tacit assumptions that contradict them.[26] For example, no matter how much they talk about wanting their children to be part of a community, the moment parents are most likely to cherish is that part of the service in which they speak personally to their child.

The antidotes to these deeply held expectations and stories are new expectations and new stories; and these will take time to develop and spread. BMR congregations are already starting to tell these stories—of the girl with learning disabilities who couldn't give a speech, but could develop a study sheet that engaged the entire congregation in a discussion of her Torah portion; of the boy who spent a year working at an organization called Tree People and celebrated his bar mitzvah at their site; of the group of children who studied together about Israel and then served as tour guides for their families' trips to Israel.

The perspectives of the structural, human resource, and symbolic frames offer some hope that we can reverse engineer b'nai mitzvah. If synagogue leaders use the tools of the structural frame to facilitate teamwork and communication; if thinking through the human resource frame reminds them to attend to real, rather than idealized, children, families, and communities; and if they exploit the symbolic frame to their advantage, sharing stories of inspiring new approaches; then we may be able to bridge the divide between the folk and the elite and restore b'nai mitzvah ceremonies to their rightful place as beginnings, rather than endings.

Notes

1. David Ellenson, "Judaism Resurgent," *After Emancipation: Jewish Religious Responses to Modernity* (Cincinnati, 2004), 44.
2. Ivan Marcus, *The Jewish Life Cycle: Rites of Passage from Biblical to Modern Times* (Seattle, 2004), 85.
3. Ibid., 105.
4. Jenna Joselit, *The Wonders of America: Reinventing Jewish Culture, 1880-1950* (New York, 1994), 90.
5. Ibid. 91.
6. Michael A. Meyer, *Response to Modernity: A History of the Reform Movement in Judaism* (New York, 1988), 374.
7. Stuart Schoenfeld, personal communication, January 2, 2013.
8. Charles Leibman, *The Ambivalent American Jew: Politics, Religion and Family in American Jewish Life* (Philadelphia, 1963).
9. Stuart Schoenfeld, "Some Aspects of the Social Significance of Bar/Bat Mitzvah Celebrations," in *Essays in the Social Scientific Study of Judaism and Jewish Society*, ed. Simcha Fishbane and Jack Lightstone (New York, 1994), 278.
10. Ibid., 278.
11. Stuart Schoenfeld, "Folk Judaism, Elite Judaism and the Role of the Bar Mitzvah in the Development of the Synagogue and Jewish School in America," *Contemporary Jewry* 9 (1987): 79.
12. Liebman, *Ambivalent American Jew*, 67.
13. Schoenfeld, "Folk Judaism, Elite Judaism," 71.
14. Cited in ibid., 72.
15. Ibid.
16. Eric Hobsbawm, "Introduction: Inventing Traditions," *The Invention of Tradition*, ed. E. Hobsbawm and T. Ranger (Cambridge, 1983/2012), 1-2.
17. Schoenfeld, "Folk Judaism, Elite Judaism," 77.
18. Jack Wertheimer, *A Census of Jewish Supplementary Schools in the United States 2006-2007* (New York, 2008), 10.
19. In the Conservative movement there is also a drop in membership after the bar/bat mitzvah of the youngest child, but it is not as dramatic as it is in the Reform

movement (26 percent in the Conservative movement, as opposed to well over 35 percent in the Reform movement. See Steven M. Cohen, "Members and Motives: Who Joins American Jewish Congregations and Why," www.huc.edu/faculty/faculty/pubs/StevenCohen/MembersAndMotives.pdf, 5 (accessed March 1, 2014). See alsoLawrence A. Hoffman, Steven M. Cohen, Ron Miller, Jonathon Ament, www.bjpa.org/Publications/details.cfm?PublicationID=14164 (accessed March 1, 2014).

20. Lifsa Schachter, "Why Bonnie and Ronnie Can't 'Read' (the Siddur)," *Journal of Jewish Education* 76 (2010): 74–91.

21. Lee Bolman and Terrence Deal, *Reframing Organizations* (San Francisco: Jossey Bass, 2008).

22. Isa Aron, Steven M. Cohen, Lawrence Hoffman, and Ari Y. Kelman, *Sacred Strategies: Transforming Congregations from Functional to Visionary* (Herndon, Va., 2010), 3.

23. Ibid, chap. 2.

24. Isa Aron, Steven M. Cohen, Lawrence Hoffman and Ari Y. Kelman, "Functional and Visionary Congregations," *CCAR Journal*, Winter 2009, 10.

25. William Grassie, "The Neuroscience of the Bar Mitzvah," *Huffington Post*, December 10, 2011. www.huffingtonpost.com/william-grassie/neuroscience-of-the-bar-mitzvah_b_1126955.html (accessed January 13, 2014).

26. Edgar Schein, "What Is Corporate Culture Anyway?" *The Corporate Culture Survival Guide* (San Francisco, 1999), 15–26.

7

"AND IT NOT BE STILLED"

The Legacy of Debbie Friedman

DEBORAH E. LIPSTADT

When Debbie Friedman died in January 2011 the cantorial soloist at a Canadian Reform congregation posted a statement on the official blog of the Reform movement: "It is impossible to overstate Debbie's importance to our prayer, to our sense of spirituality, to our music, and to our Jewish lives. . . . She changed the way that congregations sing."[1] The World Union for Progressive Judaism, the international organization of Reform Judaism, credited Friedman with having changed the nature of worship in Reform synagogues: "While Reform worship was once characterized by organs and choirs, Debbie taught us to sing as communities and congregations. . . . [S]he opened our hearts and souls to the joy of communal song."[2] This praise was echoed by rabbis, cantors, and members of the laity. The *New York Times* described her as "one of the brightest stars of the Jewish music world," noting that she was credited with having given "ancient liturgy broad appeal to late-20th-century worshippers."[3] The *Wall Street Journal* blog put it even more forcefully: "The woman who changed the sound of the synagogue has died."[4]

But dissenting voices were also heard. Writing on a faculty e-mail list, a Jewish studies professor and aficionado of *hazanut,* cantorial art, declared that she "turned shul into camp, and hazanut into campy, burying the marvelous riches of Reform Sacred Music under a heap of corny, shmaltzy, sing-along crap." Then, in a comment that shocked many of his colleagues, added: "A dubious legacy. May she and her mediocre music rest in peace."[5]

While his comments were singularly insensitive, those who had been following Friedman's career since the 1970s were familiar with such sentiments.

When Friedman's music first emerged on the scene in the late 1960s rabbis and cantors dismissed it as a passing fad worthy, at the most, of camp. Jerry Kaye, director of a Reform summer camp and one of the first Jewish professionals to recognize the potential in her work, recalls playing Friedman's earliest songs for some rabbis. They dismissed the music as inappropriate for their synagogues. By contrast, the campers loved it.[6] As her popularity grew and younger members of Reform congregations began to demand the inclusion in the service of "Debbie songs," many of which were liturgical settings, the skepticism, particularly among cantors, morphed into outright hostility.[7]

There was something striking about the strength and persistence of the reaction to this genre of music. Writing in the early 1990s, Samuel Adler, who taught both at Eastman School of Music and at Julliard and was the son of a Reform cantor, declared that synagogues had "surrendered to the spirit of populism" and "genuine banality," as new liturgical music that was "fueled by ignorance [and] misinformation" replaced traditional liturgy. He bemoaned the fact that contemporary synagogue music had "fallen largely into the hands of the 'new traditional composers' who write in a popular style that is pseudo-Jewish, pseudo-pop-American, and pseudo-Israeli."[8] A few years before Friedman's death, a cantor, addressing the Reform movement's American Conference of Cantors, called for educating congregants musically so that "they can be part of a music that's *not* Debbie Friedman." Sadly, he noted, that was "where they are at the moment."[9]

Students at the Hebrew Union College (HUC) School of Sacred Music (SSM) often felt caught between their professors' preference for classical liturgical music and their own preference for more contemporary genres, particularly Friedman's. Some instructors at the school telegraphed the message that this music was unworthy of Jewish liturgical tradition. Jeff Klepper, who was influenced by Friedman to write new settings for the liturgy and then went on to cantorial school, recalled that he felt tension at the school over this influence.[10]

What was it about this woman's music that aroused such opposition? Was the opposition rooted in her work per se, or did the synagogue hierarchy feel threatened by something else? And, given the depth of that initial opposition, how did she move from the outer reaches of the periphery of organized synagogue life to its center when in 2007 she joined the faculty of the SSM? HUC president David Ellenson's invitation to her was issued, not insignificantly, with the enthusiastic support of the director of the SSM, Professor Bruce Ruben, himself a trained cantor who initially felt threatened by the demands for the inclusion of her work in the service.[11] Some considered her faculty appointment to have "confirmed her place in American Jewish musical history" and in Reform worship. Others consider the seminal moment to have occurred in 1996 when Union of American Hebrew Congregations (UAHC) president Alexander Schindler asked that Friedman provide the music for his retirement service. This decision, ethnomusicologist Mark Kligman observes, did not go unnoticed by Reform cantors.[12]

There are a number of contexts within which to analyze this sea change in attitudes toward Debbie Friedman. The history of innovation in Jewish worship is, of course, rife with altercations. In his study of the 1817 introduction of the organ into the Hamburg synagogue, Ellenson illustrates how severe the opposition could be. Orthodox critics attacked the organ as something that would destroy hazanut and constitute a "perversion of Jewish worship." The Hatam Sofer, Rabbi Moshe Sofer of Pressburg, convinced that innovation was forbidden by the Torah, verbally eviscerated the organ supporters, calling them the "wicked of the earth [rish'e arets]." In response, the defenders argued that the use of instruments, rather than constituting a threat to hazanut, would result in "uplift of the soul [hit'orerut ha-nefesh]."[13] While the debate over the organ concerned a halakhic (legal) matter, the opposition to Friedman's music was stylistic. Yet the reaction to her was often so virulent that one must ask whether, in fact, it might have been about something more than just a new musical style.

One must set the debate over introducing contemporary folk music into Reform worship into a larger zeitgeist, already evident in North American churches.[14] Some of the impetus for change to the Catholic mass came from the Second Vatican Council (1962–65), which itself introduced alterations to the service. Communion was received by hand rather than by mouth. The priest faced the congregation during the mass, not the "tabernacle," and mass was recited in the local vernacular. Some priests, emboldened by this spirit of innovation, went a step further. Celebrating Vatican II's pronouncement that "Mother Church earnestly desires that all the faithful should be led to fully conscious, and active participation in liturgical celebrations," they instituted folk masses, replacing the organ with the guitar and traditional music with contemporary selections. Many of these masses became wildly popular.[15] The Anglican Church faced a similar "assault" on its highly developed choral tradition. Age-old musical compositions were jettisoned, replaced by more contemporary songs. Regarding this debate about the relative value of "contemporary" versus "classical" liturgical music, one faculty member at Yale's

Institute of Sacred Music attributed it all to a matter of "taste." In response, the scholar of religion Martin Marty wondered whether it was not something more profound.[16]

Those demanding change came out of the Vietnam protest generation. Starting with the Berkeley Free Speech movement in the mid-1960s and the rising opposition to the Vietnam war, attacks on the country's political and cultural "establishment" became commonplace. The establishment, young activists posited, represented all that was obscurantist, while change was good and innovative. In the Reform movement, nothing represented the establishment more than the synagogue hierarchy. Everything about the synagogue reinforced this message. Rabbis and cantors stood on pulpits situated high above the congregation. They used a "somewhat stilted [speaking] manner and stylized speech patterns." This "formal style" often became a "frozen style."[17] The liturgy, both the English and the few remnants of Hebrew that remained, were intoned by the rabbi and sung by the cantor and choir. The music, while beautiful, was not designed for congregational participation. Except for a few key moments, the "people" were passive. This was deliberate. In the nineteenth century, Reform Judaism reduced "lay involvement in the liturgy. The masses were noisy, individualistic, and unappreciative of the higher artistry that characterized western aesthetics."[18] And so it remained for well over a century.

In the 1960s things were different in Reform youth groups and camps. The liturgy and music were participatory. Most of it, however, was not Jewish. UAHC songbooks were filled with songs by Woody Guthrie, Bob Dylan, Joan Baez, and Peter, Paul, and Mary. Participants considered the messages of these songs—for example, "This land is your land; this land is my land" or "Love between my brothers and my sisters"—to be intrinsically Jewish.[19] They had no access to contemporary Jewish songs that expressed these sentiments. Debbie Friedman, a product of this youth movement who had "grown up with Peter, Paul, and Mary," replicated what she heard on their records and quickly began to set Jewish liturgical texts to music, in this way merging contemporary musical style with traditional texts. It is striking that, having just taught herself to play guitar and to compose, she began by writing an entire service, *Sing unto God.*[20] She approached the teacher of the honor choir at the high school from which she graduated and convinced her to let her cut a record of the service using the choir.[21] Thanks to the record and the proliferation of cassette tapes, knowledge of the service spread throughout North America. Young Reform Jews returned from youth group conclaves and camp asking and then, in the spirit of the times, *demanding* that Friedman's music be included in the liturgy. (Some of the songs from that initial service are today considered classics in the Reform movement.)

The Conservative movement experienced a similar form of "protest" against the formal service. Young people formed independent minyanim and *havurot* (participatory communities). Group members gave the *divre Torah* (short exegetical sermons), led the service, and chanted from the Torah. These groups emphasized singing, much of it "neo-Hasidic," and fellowship. They yearned, in the words of Cantor Benjie-Ellen Schiller, for a "populist version of traditional authenticity." The music they relied on was "simpler, thoroughly democratic in its singability, largely Hebrew, and playable on guitar."[22] These minyanim tended to be ritually liberal and were in the forefront of according full participatory rights to women. The leaders of Ezrat Nashim, the group that first protested women's limited role in the Conservative service, came from these minyanim.[23] It is notable that in the Conservative and Reform movements, the demands for change came from the young people who were products of the movements' camps and youth groups. They wanted worship that, as Lawrence Hoffman put it, "belong[ed] to the people." They wanted to be part *of*, not observers *at*, the service.[24]

But it was not just an anti-establishment protest that propelled the calls for change. As a wave of rising ethnic identity became manifest in the United States, the melting pot was no longer the ideal. America had by the late 1960s become a "hospitable place for the recovery of one's cultural roots."[25] Many American Jews, particularly baby boomers, embraced more overt expressions of their Jewish identity. This expression of enhanced Jewish identity was buttressed, if not propelled forward, by euphoria about Israel's 1967 military victory. Many American Jews adopted Naomi Shemer's "Yerushalayim shel zahav" (Jerusalem of Gold) as a quasi-communal anthem despite the fact that most of them did not understand any of its words other than the title. Nurit Hirsh's "Ba-shanah ha-ba'ah" (Next Year) and her setting for "Oseh Shalom" (May [God] Make Peace) became ubiquitous. Rabbi Daniel Freelander, who wrote music together with Klepper and went on to become a vice president of the UAHC, recalled the time: "Our people wanted to hear Hebrew and they wanted to sing Hebrew, so Hebrew becomes a real crucial piece." The 1965 UAHC songbook contained almost no Hebrew songs. Hebrew songs that were included were transliterated in Ashkenazic pronunciation. By the late 1960s Sephardic transliteration had replaced Ashkenazic. American folk tunes and African American spirituals, which had dominated previous songbooks, were largely replaced with songs by Shlomo Carlebach, songs heard at the Israeli Hasidic Song Festival, and compositions by Friedman and other contemporary young songwriters, including Freelander and Klepper. As Freelander observed, "this pro-ethnic and pro-Israel stuff, combined with the anti-authority stuff of the late '60s, created the stage for radical change."[26]

Some rabbis recognized that this music could bring young people into the synagogue, so they were more open toward including it in the service.[27] Of course, they could afford to be more forthcoming, as their status was unaffected. No one was demanding that, in lieu of the rabbi, laypeople deliver the sermon.[28] But such was not the case for cantors and choir leaders. They felt that this new body of music pushed them to what they contended was the "lowest common [musical] denominator." They feared that the majesty and sophistication of Jewish music was being "repressed, and suppressed." Their high level of training seemed to be irrelevant. On a more personal level, they were being asked to do something—play guitar, lead a congregation in song, sing in an accessible key—that was outside their area of expertise. This was a genre of music for which they had no training, and therefore appropriately felt ill equipped to perform. They had been trained as operatic soloists. The aesthetics of Friedman's music was diametrically opposed to what cantors had been trained to sing.[29] The situation was further complicated by the fact that this Sturm und Drang came precisely when the American Conference of Cantors was working to enhance cantors' professional status. The HUC program was changed from an undergraduate to a graduate degree. Increasingly, the training required of cantorial students was much more closely on par with that of rabbis. They had to have as much Hebrew language training as rabbinical students and were required to spend a year studying in Israel, as rabbinical students had long been required to do.

It is possible that this increased professionalization of the cantorial school helped cement the already existing rancor toward Friedman and her type of music. One former SSM student recalled that some instructors complained about Friedman's music even when the song in question was not by her. When that fact was pointed out to them, they waved off the correction by attributing the song to "Friedman's influence." Merri Lovinger Arian, an instructor at the SSM, believes that Friedman "took the hit for all of her contemporary songwriting colleagues."[30] Friedman was a particularly easy target. One of the first people to write songs for the Reform movement's youth groups that were liturgical, participatory, and playable on guitar was Michael Isaacson. Unlike Isaacson, who had studied music composition as an undergraduate and eventually received graduate degrees from Julliard and Eastman School of Music, Friedman was untrained. She could not read music, had no voice training, did not finish college, and initially possessed no deep-seated knowledge of *nusah*, Jewish texts, or tradition.[31] Cantors dismissed what they unfairly described as her "happy clappy" tunes and saw her as the "anti-cantor."[32] One cantor at a major New York Reform temple considered her "*Haman ha-rasha*," the evil Haman of the Book of Esther.[33] Another, declaring himself a "*nusah* policeman," deprecated her for ignoring it. In response, Friedman argued that, while she respected *nusah* and its importance in Jewish tradition, "if you don't have Jews coming in the doors [of the synagogue] what good is [protection] of nusah?" She was exceptionally sensitive about the attacks on her. "Who is my music hurting? I don't want to compete with anybody. I'm not a great lover of organ music, but I am a great lover of nusah. How is writing in our own musical vernacular not an acceptable or legitimate expression of our culture?"[34] In analyzing the hostility toward her one cannot ignore the fact that she was a woman. While there is no way of ascertaining whether the opposition would have been different had she been male, eventually she rather reluctantly acknowledged that she thought it would have been.[35]

Ironically, none of those who complained about the absence of "Jewish roots" in her music acknowledged that Jewish liturgical music is replete with tunes that are rooted in churches and folk songs. Music historian A. Z. Idelsohn traces the roots of the melody for "Ma'oz tsur," the quintessential Hanukkah song, to a chorale by Martin Luther. Others trace it further back, to a German folk song that Luther adapted.[36] Nor did the critics note that the towering nineteenth-century hero of cantorial composition, Louis Lewandowski, choirmaster of Berlin's Neue Synagoge, did *not* include traditional Jewish melodies or nusah in much of the music he created. "What he did in the nineteenth century," ethnomusicologist Mark Kligman has observed, "is as revolutionary as what Friedman did in the twentieth."[37]

How then do we explain the changed attitude toward Friedman? Part of the explanation is generational. Those young people who were such fans of her work had, by the 1990s, become the lay and professional leaders of the movement. Many of them had been deeply touched by her songs and credited their religious Weltanschauung to her work. But something else had happened as well. Her music had grown more textured and was more deeply in conversation with the tradition. Her work was increasingly becoming a "musical midrash," a commentary on the text in which the word and the melody often worked together. Such was the case in one of her signature pieces, "Lekhi lakh." When I asked her about it she said, "When God told Abraham *lech lecha*, [go forth] Sarah went as well. Sarah was Abraham's partner. So God must have said to her—using the feminine case—*lekhi lakh*."[38]

This metamorphosis was enhanced by the learning partners she sought. In the late 1980s she co-led teachers' seminars on liturgy with two experts in Jewish education, Rabbi Stuart Kelman and Dr. Gail Dorph. Kelman and Dorph had developed ideas from Abraham Joshua Heschel's notions of empathy and expression. They taught that prayer can best be understood as a response by the liturgist to the deepest of human needs, challenges, and wonderments, the same needs, challenges, and wonderments we face today. Friedman increasingly moved to adapting and expanding on the text and to giving her "audience" room to apply it to their lives.[39] This is what she did with many interpretations of liturgy. For example, Arian observes, her *tefilat ha-derekh,* the prayer for travel, constitutes a contemporary setting that spoke not just to someone who was about to travel, but also to someone who was facing a life-cycle transition, a moment fraught with possibility and foreboding.[40] She broadened the way in which this and so many other prayers could be experienced. Throughout her life she sought out learning partners from across the spectrum. She studied *nusah* with a Conservative cantor. She cowrote with Drora Setel and Tamara Cohen, both of whom were pursuing higher degrees in Jewish studies. She had an Orthodox *hevruta* (learning partner), Joe Septimus, with whom she studied Talmud on a weekly basis for close to a decade, and after joining the HUC faculty she sat in on classes, including those on traditional hazanut.

"And the women." In her Jewish world women were not silent appendages. They journeyed *with* Abraham. They danced to Miriam's song. They were "Mothers in Israel" who, like the biblical Deborah, fought for justice.[41] In these and so many of her other songs, she wove together Hebrew and English, turning her compositions into educational tools. Through her music liberal Jews learned the names of the Jewish months.[42] They began to put their children to sleep not just with bedtime stories, but with the Sh'ma and the Angel Blessing.[43] Nowhere was personal midrash more evident than in her signature composition, "Mi Shebeirach," which was based on the traditional prayer for healing. In it she defines *refuah shelemah* not as complete healing, but as finding the courage, despite the pain, "to make our lives a blessing." She was prompted to write it, not, as many people assume, by her own illness, but by the ability of other people who, despite their pain, were able to persevere.[44] The prayer was not about "healing in the conventional sense, but about finding wholeness despite one's pain."[45] Using it as a lynchpin, Friedman developed the concept of a healing service. Today such services are routinely held in Reform and Conservative congregations. An equally revolutionary act, one that has had a profound impact on liberal Jews, was her writing of songs that allowed one to turn to God for help. No longer was the God of the Reform movement only the God of social justice. This was a God to whom one could implore: "Don't hide your face from me. I'm asking for your help." This was a God to whom one could pour out one's heart and say, "Oh hear me now."[46]

At bottom, however, there is an intangible element here, one that cannot be measured or scientifically analyzed. It shaped Debbie Friedman's career, her life, and the impact she had on countless people. She had a singular ability to turn an audience into a congregation. She had more than charisma. She was able to connect with an audience in a unique fashion. As Kligman observes, she blurred "the boundary between prayer and song. . . . For Friedman, praying in a synagogue or singing on stage both have the goal of connecting with and uplifting the audience." She was able to tap into the needs of a broad swath of the congregation, because "she had her finger on the pulse of *amkha*, the people."[47] It was and remains rare to find anyone else who can duplicate the transcendent, almost prayer-like, atmosphere she created when she sang with her audience. Simply put, it was not just the music or the midrash. It was the woman, her talents, and the force of her unique personality.

She was able to do this even with those who were skeptical—if not hostile—to her. Steven Dress, a Conservative cantor, recalled her appearance before the national convention of Conservative cantors in the mid-1990s: "One-third of the assembly didn't applaud when she was introduced," a singular lack of *derekh erets*, common decency.[48] Dresser admitted to sharing the sentiments of his reticent fellow cantors. But, he recalled, "The diminutive woman with the powerful, uplifting voice and quiet respect for Jewish tradition won him over." She did more than just that. He considered her appearance at that convention as "a turning point in my growth as a hazan and in my personal growth."[49] At the service marking the naming of the SSM in her memory a large group of cantors, spanning both the Reform and Conservative movements, some of whom were once her fiercest critics, sang her compositions as part of the choir.

One wonders if she spent too much of her increasingly limited energies worrying about being accepted by cantors and about justifying her approach to Jewish liturgy.[50] The once reluctant Dresser may have expressed this most forcefully—even more bluntly than how Friedman would have—when he noted that he used one of her English songs in services. "So it's not rooted in nusah. So what?"[51]

Composers now create formal settings for her songs.[52] This development is not surprising. Mahler, Brahms, Bartok, and a host of other great composers regularly took familiar folk tunes of their day and incorporated them into their compositions.[53] Some of the new settings are quite stunning.[54] This may well be the greatest validation and vindication—though she hardly needed either—of Debbie Friedman and her work. Friedman would probably have been pleased with some of these compositions. But at the end of the day, she would have wanted her music to stay primarily in the mouths of the "people." She said as much in 2007 when she accepted the Alexander M. Schindler Distinguished Leadership Award for Jewish Leadership in front of five thousand attendees at the Reform movement's biennial assembly. There she declared: "Alex [Schindler] had a vision of community. He had a vision that we would sing together. You are that community. You are that song. . . . It is for you . . . [and] it is because of you that I write these songs."[55]

Debbie Friedman may be gone but, to paraphrase her setting of Psalm 30, her soul still sings to us. And may it not be stilled.[56]

Notes

The essay title comes from Debbie Friedman, "Mourning into Dancing," adapted from Psalm 30, on the compact disc *One People* (Los Angeles: Jewish Music Group, 2006).

1. Dawn Bernstein, "She Changed the Way We Pray," RJ.org blog, January 13, 2011, http://blogs.rj.org/blog/2011/01/13/she_changed_the_way_we_pray/ (accessed January 13, 2014).
2. Sue Fishkoff, "Singer-Songwriter Debbie Friedman, Inspiration to Thousands, Dies at 59," *Jewish Telegraphic Agency,* January 10, 2011, www.jta.org/news/article/2011/01/10/2742484/a-song-for-debbie-friedman (accessed December 28, 2012).
3. Margalit Fox, "Debbie Friedman, Singer of Jewish Music, Dies at 59" *New York Times,* January 11, 2011, www.nytimes.com/2011/01/11/arts/music/11friedman.html (accessed December 27, 2013).
4. Charles Passy, "How Debbie Friedman Changed the Sound of the Synagogue," *Wall Street Journal Speakeasy,* January 10, 2011, http://blogs.wsj.com/speakeasy/2011/01/10/how-debbie-friedman-changed-the-sound-of-the-synagogue/ (accessed December 29, 2012).
5. Though he later apologized for his words, he stressed in an e-mail to me that "the apology was for the offense caused, not the insult." Given that he stands by his insult, I quote it here. *JFR: The Jewish Faculty Roundtable: An E-mail Collation on Campus Jewish Issues,* January 11, 2011, e-mail to author, January 14, 2011. See also Allan

Nadler, "Not Dead Yet: The Remarkable Renaissance of Cantorial Music," *Jewish Ideas Daily*, December 25, 2012, www.jewishideasdaily.com/5624/features/not-dead-yet/ (accessed January 13, 2014).

6. Interview with Jerry Kaye, December 29, 2012.

7. During the years 1972–74 I served as director of Northeast Federation of Temple Youth, an arm of the Reform movement's youth organization NFTY. I watched the growth of both the popularity of Friedman's music and the resentment toward it by many cantors.

8. Samuel Adler, "Sacred Music in a Secular Age," in *Sacred Sound and Social Change: Liturgical Music in Jewish and Christian Experience*, ed. L. Hoffmann and J. R. Walton (Notre Dame, Ind., 1992), 294, 296.

9. Judah Cohen, *The Making of a Reform Cantor* (Bloomington, Ind., 2009), 219.

10. Klepper was invested as a cantor in 1980. The students mentioned in Cohen's book were at the school in the early 2000s. Both spoke of Friedman and that genre of music as being deprecated. Jeff Klepper in *A Journey of Spirit*, dir. Ann Coppel, DVD (Seattle, 2006). Cohen, *The Making of a Reform Cantor*, 219.

11. Interview with Bruce Ruben, December 28, 2012. It must be noted that the invitation came from HUC's president and the head of the SSM. It was not voted upon by the faculty, as is the norm for a tenured position.

12. Fishkoff, "Singer-Songwriter Debbie Friedman," 1. Interview with Mark Kligman, December 27, 2012. One cannot, of course, ignore the fact that the HUC School of Sacred Music was named after her. However, since there is serious question whether that would have happened if not for her untimely death, I choose not to cite it as a marker of the transition.

13. David Ellenson, *After Emancipation: Jewish Religious Responses to Modernity* (Cincinnati, 2004), 127–31. Letter of David Ellenson, February 14, 2011. (Since this letter was to someone who had vigorously opposed the naming of the school the recipient's name was blacked out.)

14. Interview with Judith Clurman, December 28, 2012.

15. Vatican II, *Sacrosanctum concilium* (Constitution on the Sacred Liturgy, December 4, 1963), no. 32, www.vatican.va/archive/hist_councils/ii_vatican_council/documents/vat-ii_const_19631204_sacrosanctum-concilium_en.html (accessed January 2, 2013). For examples of "Folk Mass" music see www.folkmass.us/audio-selections.html (accessed December 28, 2012); Julie Byrne, "Roman Catholics and the American Mainstream in the Twentieth Century," *National Humanities Center*, http://nationalhumanitiescenter.org/tserve/twenty/tkeyinfo/tmainstr.htm (accessed December 30, 2012); Keith F. Pecklers, "Roman Catholic Liturgical Renewal Forty-Five Years after Sacrosanctum Concilium: An Assessment," Yale Institute of Sacred Music, *Colloquium Journal* 5 (Autumn 2008): 1–9, www.yale.edu/ism/colloq_journal/vol5/pecklers1.html (accessed December 29, 2012). Interview with Mark Jordan, January 3, 2013.

16. Martin Marty, "The Future of Classical Music in the Church," Yale Institute of Sacred Music, *Colloquium Journal* 5 (Autumn 2008): 63–68, www.yale.edu/ism/colloq_journal/vol5/marty1.html (accessed December 29, 2012). This issue seems to have once again reared its head in American Protestant churches; see Amy O'Leary, "Building Congregations around Art Galleries and Cafes as Spirituality Wanes," *New York Times*, December 30, 2012, www.nytimes.com/2012/12/30/us/

new-churches-focus-on-building-a-community-life.html?src=me&ref=general (accessed January 13, 2014).

17. Lawrence Hoffman, *The Art of Public Prayer* (Washington, D.C., 1988), 197–210.

18. Ibid., 222.

19. Interview with Jeff Klepper, as cited in Kligman, "Contemporary Jewish Music in America," *American Jewish Yearbook* 101 (2001): 116.

20. Debbie Friedman, *Sing unto God*, lyrics adapted from Ps. 96, 98, and 149, on *The Best of Debbie Friedman*, recording (New York, 1972).

21. "Debbie Friedman—My Music My Story Part 1," Jewishtvnetwork.com, uploaded by DFPICKS, January 13, 2011, www.youtube.com/watch?v=M_G9vFzrU6Q (accessed January 14, 2014). One of the other influences on Friedman was Michael Isaacson, who created some of the first Jewish camp songs. Michael Isaacson, "Music on the Balanced Bimah," paper presented at The Milken Archive—Jewish Theological Seminary Conference, "Only in America: Jewish Music in a Land of Freedom," November 10, 2003, www.michaelisaacson.com/writingpdfs/MusicontheBalancedBimah.pdf (accessed December 31, 2012). Interview with Elka Abrahamson, January 3, 2013.

22. Benjie-Ellen Schiller, "The Hymnal as an Index of Musical Change in Reform Synagogues," in Hoffman and Walton, *Sacred Sound and Social Change*, 207.

23. Paula Hyman, "Statement," Jewish Women and the Feminist Revolution, *Jewish Women's Archive*, http://jwa.org/feminism/_html/JWA039.htm (accessed December 26, 2012). See also Jewish Women's Archive, "Ezrat Nashim Presents Manifesto for Women's Equality to Conservative Rabbis, March 14, 1972," http://jwa.org/thisweek/mar/14/1972/ezrat-nashim (accessed December 30, 2012).

24. Lawrence Hoffman, "Music Tradition and Tension," 35, cited in Kligman, "Contemporary Jewish Music in America," 120.

25. Kligman, "Contemporary Jewish Music In America," 104.

26. Interview with Daniel Freelander, cited in ibid., 117.

27. The first time I heard Debbie Friedman's music performed with a full choir was in 1973 at Temple Israel in Boston, a bastion of Reform worship in that city. Rabbi Roland Gittelsohn invited Friedman to perform her entire service with a youth choir from the congregation. The hall was packed.

28. Isaacson, "Music on the Balanced Bimah," 4.

29. Interview with Bruce Ruben, December 26, 2012. Interview with Merri Lovinger Arian. January 3, 2013

30. Interview with Arian.

31. *Nusah* is the various modes in which the prayers are sung. There is a different *nusah* for morning and evening prayers, Shabbat and holidays, weddings and funerals.

32. Interview with Kligman.

33. Richard Botton in *A Journey of Spirit* (documentary), dir. Ann Coppel (Ann Coppel Productions, 2003).

34. Susan Josephs, "Queen of Souls," *Baltimore Jewish Times*, January 19, 1996, 47.

35. Botton, *A Journey of Spirit*.

36. A. Z. Idelsohn, *Jewish Music and Its Historical Development* (New York, 1992), 171, 174. Interview with Angela Buchdahl, January 1, 2013.

37. Interview with Kligman.

38. Debbie Friedman & Savina Teubal, "L'chi Lach," adapted from Gen. 12:1–2, on *And You Shall Be a Blessing*, compact disc (San Diego, 1989).

39. Interview with Stuart Kelman and Gail Dorph, January 1, 2013.
40. Debbie Friedman, "T'filat Haderech," adapted from traditional text, 1, https: //myspace.com/debbiefriedmanmusic/music/song/t-filat-haderech-53766193-58154656989 (accessed February 14, 2014). Interview with Arian.
41. Debbie Friedman, "Miriam's Song," on *And You Shall Be a Blessing*, compact disc (San Diego, 1989). Debbie Friedman and Tamara Ruth Cohen, "Devorah's Song," based on Judges 4:12, on *The Water in the Well*, compact disc (San Diego, 2000).
42. Debbie Friedman and Tamara Ruth Cohen, "Birkat HaLevanah," adapted from Exod. 12:2, on *Debbie Friedman at Carnagie Hall*, compact disc (San Diego, 1999).
43. Debbie Friedman, "Sh'ma and V'ahavta," lyrics adapted from Deut. 6:4–9, 1971, on *In the Beginning*, compact disc (San Diego, 2004). Debbie Friedman, "The Angel's Blessings," adapted from nighttime *Sh'ma*, on *Songs of the Spirit: Debbie Friedman Anthology*, compact disc (New York, 2005).
44. Debbie Friedman and Drorah Setel, "Mi Shebeirach," 1989, on *And You Shall Be a Blessing*, compact disc (San Diego, 1997). For background on this, see "Debbie Friedman—My Music My Story, Part 2," Jewishtvnetwork.com, uploaded by DFPICKS, January 13, 2011, www.youtube.com/watch?v=zQurNX_8tn4 (accessed February 13, 2014).
45. Debbie Friedman, "Mi Shebeirach: An Introduction," in *R'fuah Sh'leimah: Songs of Jewish Healing*, ed. M. Lovinger Arian (New York, 2002), 54–55. Interview with Arian.
46. Debbie Friedman, "Al Tasteir (Don't Hide Your Face)," adapted from Ps. 23, on *Renewal of Spirit*, compact disc (San Diego, 1997). Debbie Friedman, *Light These Lights*, compact disc (New York, 2011).
47. Interview with Kligman; interview with Arian.
48. Mishnah Avot 4:15; bPes 112a.
49. Fishkoff, "Singer-Songwriter Debbie Friedman," 1.
50. This one of the dominant themes of Ann Coppel's documentary film about Friedman, *A Journey of Spirit.*
51. Fishkoff, "Singer-Songwriter Debbie Friedman," 1.
52. See "Highlights of Dedication of Debbie Friedman School of Sacred Music," December 7, 2011, uploaded by webmaster1875, January 3, 2012, www.youtube.com/watch?v=vdlcgglWLg0, Oseh Shalom at 3:55; Shalom Aleichem at 10:14 (accessed January 14, 2014).
53. Interview with Ruben. Interview with Clurman.
54. See, for example, the arrangement of Friedman's "V'ahavta," to which Eleanor Epstein has added a Hebrew textual overlay: "And You Shall Love/ V'ahavta"—URJ Biennial Choir rehearsal, uploaded by Pat Myers, December 14, 2011, www.youtube.com/watch?feature=player_detailpage&v=-UshncUO0yo (accessed January 14, 2014).
55. "Debbie Friedman Tribute—2011 URJ Biennial," uploaded by urjweb, December 15, 2011, at 5:50, www.youtube.com/watch?feature=player_detailpage&v=-7A7t0t8qfE (accessed January 1, 2013)
56. Debbie Friedman, "Mourning into Dancing."

8

FROM THE RHINE VALLEY TO JEZREEL VALLEY

Innovative Versions of the Mourners' Kaddish in the Kibbutz Movement

DALIA MARX

Someone of our generation who loses a parent or a close friend—
suffers from two kinds of orphanhood, one through the loss of a
dear one, and the second . . . because he has lost the forms of speech,
the cherished expression and the spiritual heritage, through which
his forebears used to convey their mourning . . . one orphanhood is
the loss of a person, the second, the loss of tradition.

Uriel Tal, "Kaddish Yatom"

One can hardly imagine a prayer that evokes stronger emotional responses
among Jews than the Mourners' Kaddish. Some draw consolation from its theology, many more are compelled and soothed by its familiarity and repeti-
tiveness, still others are alienated by its theological message. Yet few remain
indifferent to the Kaddish, and even the fiercest atheists among my acquain-
tances tremble at the sound of the words "Yitgadal ve-yitkadash shemeh
raba." One reaction to the Kaddish is that of the German Jewish poet Heinrich Heine, who converted to Christianity. When he reflected on his own
impending death, he wrote in his poem "Gedächtnisfeier" (commemoration):
"Keinen Kadosch wird man sagen, / Nichts gesagt und nichts gesungen / Wird
an meinen Sterbetagen" (No Kaddish will be recited / Nothing will be said or
sung / on my dying days).[1] Indeed, the Kaddish represents much more than its

literal meaning; it has come to be a powerful symbol, regardless of its original function and regardless of the wording or theology the prayer manifests.

After a brief description of the existential context that transformed an ancient prayer into a ritualized theological response to catastrophe that became the mourners' prayer, I will turn to contemporary Israeli literary liturgical responses to this traditional prayer. I believe that the journey between two valleys, from the medieval Rhine to the contemporary Jezreel valley, may serve as a useful test case for liturgical innovations and may reveal a complex multifaceted Jewish religiosity.

The Kaddish prayer is mentioned by name for the first time in Geonic sources,[2] but it is probably much older. Some scholars, such as Ismar Elbogen, date it to the Second Temple period.[3] Originally, the Kaddish had no connection to death or grief. Joseph Heinemann has argued that it originated in the *Bet ha-midrash* (House of Study), not the synagogue and that its original historical and cultural context was as the concluding prayer after a sermon or Torah study.[4] Unlike most other Jewish prayers, there are at least five different versions of it, and it serves different liturgical functions.[5] Yet the best known of all the Kaddish versions was the last to develop—*Kaddish yatom* (the Orphans' Kaddish, or, as it is better known in English, the Mourners' Kaddish).

The Kaddish as a mourners' prayer should be considered contextually within the variety of mourning and memorial liturgical and ritual innovations that followed the Crusader persecutions, beginning in 1096 in Ashkenaz. The devastation resulting from these cruel pogroms, brought upon the established and learned communities of the Rhineland, resulted in tremendous religious creativity.[6] Among the innovations that served as responses to the persecutions were the *Yizkor* (communal service for the dead),[7] the *Yahrzeit* (a commemoration of the death anniversary), lighting candles for the deceased, a variety of lamentation hymns and the prayer *Av ha-rahamim*, a general requiem for martyrs.[8]

The first known explicit connection between the Kaddish and mourning was made in the minor tractate *Sofrim*, dating to the eighth century.[9] However, at this stage, it was recited by the cantor and not the mourners, and there is no reason to assume that there was a specific version of the Kaddish designated for the mourners. There is a reference to the requirement for a boy to recite the Kaddish in the literature of the school of Rashi, dated from the eleventh to the mid-thirtieth centuries,[10] but the explicit requirement for a mourner to say the Kaddish on behalf of his dead father did not appear until the thirteenth century in *Or zaru'a*, a legal compendium composed by Rabbi Yitshak ben Moshe of Vienna, who wrote: "It is our custom here, in the land of Canaan [Bohemia], as well as it is the custom of the inhabitants of Rhineland, for an orphan to rise and recite the Kaddish after worshippers have finished reciting *En Kelohenu*. In France, however, I observed that they did not insist that the one who recites the Kaddish would be an orphan child or a child who has a father and mother. Our custom seems more reasonable, on account of the story of Rabbi Akiva" (*Shabbat*, 50). Following this, Rabbi Yitzhak cites an aggadic story of Rabbi Akiva, whose training of an orphan boy to recite the Kaddish was instrumental in saving his father from the sufferings of hell. This story appears in many versions, some of them older than the one in *Or Zaru'a*, although this is the first time the Kaddish is specifically mentioned as a means for a child to rescue his dead father from the torments of the *gehinom* world of the dead.[11] The popular theological notion that a son's actions can benefit his deceased father appears already in Amoraic literature, but it was largely ignored.[12] Israel Ta-Shema argued that the concept gained popularity in the Geonic period, but even then it was not unanimously accepted.[13] And as mentioned in *Or Zaru'a*, there was a parallel custom to let a child recite the Kaddish, regardless of whether he was an orphan or has parents, in order to accustom him to lead the congregation.[14]

As an outcome of the Crusades, including the existence of many children who were orphans, it became the task of the survivors to recite a special version of the Kaddish—the Mourners' Kaddish. The belief that a son can benefit his deceased father merged with the custom of allowing a child to recite the Kaddish. Consequently, the child symbolically took the place of his father in the congregation.

The Kaddish seemed suitable for this purpose since it deals with the sanctification of the name of God and establishing God's kingdom on earth. In a catastrophic time, when the situation is uncertain and unstable, the desire for just rule and for the presence of God's hand in the world may be felt as especially necessary. And there is more to the Kaddish than a response to the situation of the persecuted Ashkenazic communities. Death, in and of itself, is a highly traumatic experience for the survivors of the deceased, and probably every culture creates coping devices and means to deal with it. In our case, the unnatural death of so many Jews, including mass suicides and the killing of children by their own parents in order to avoid forced conversions,[15] required a special religious response. And indeed their deaths were considered

Kiddush hashem (martyrdom, and literally, [death for] the sanctification of the Name). According to this view, God's presence in the world increases through the martyrs. This was a way of finding consolation and giving meaning to the unprecedented martyrdom,[16] as the Kaddish reiterates the desire for the magnification of the Divine name in the wounded world:

Magnified and sanctified be His Great Name	יִתְגַּדַּל וְיִתְקַדַּשׁ שְׁמֵהּ רַבָּא
in the world that He created according to His will.	בְּעָלְמָא דִּי בְרָא כִרְעוּתֵהּ
And may He Establish His Kingdom . . .	וְיַמְלִיךְ מַלְכוּתֵהּ . . .

As mentioned, the traumatic events in medieval Ashkenaz gave rise to the creation of the Mourners' Kaddish, the obligation of which was not only on orphans, but also on other immediate relatives: parents, spouses, and siblings. Consequently, far from its denotative meaning and from its original use, the Kaddish became fixed in the Jewish consciousness as the prayer of mourners.

The Mourners' Kaddish in Israel

The historian and thinker Uriel Tal (1926–84) notes a connection between the alienation of the members of the nation as a nation and the status of the individual mourner in isolation. Tal begins his article on the Mourners' Kaddish with the heart-wrenching words quoted in the epigraph for this article. People "of our generation" experience alienation and loneliness not only as a result of the loss of someone beloved, but they are also separated from their heritage and cannot turn to it for support when facing a personal tragedy. "Our silence" (as a result of the lack of a vocabulary of grief), Tal writes, "is deafening."[17]

This situation in Israel can partly be explained by the polarization with regard to religion between the "religious" (namely Orthodox and ultra-Orthodox) and the so-called "secular,"[18] with a minority of non-Orthodox religious communities in between. This polarization makes the mere entrance into a synagogue (any synagogue) a political act. Many Israelis shy away from any expression of Jewish religiosity, since they connect it with rejection of modernity, disrespect for democratic values, and religious coercion and corruption.[19] This being said, it seems that Israelis do turn to religious ceremonies when it comes to lifecycle events (and to a lesser extent, annual holy day observances), especially when facing death. Unlike other life ceremonies that can be planned, death, in most cases, requires a quick response. Death generally finds the grieving family unprepared, no matter how predictable the death may have been. The chaotic nature of death causes many people to seek the security of structure and prescribed protocol.

It is interesting that the very need that created the Mourners' Kaddish in the first place in medieval Germany is by and large operative in an entirely different context in modern Israel. Secular Israelis turn to traditional funeral forms and especially to the recitation of the Kaddish. Among other responsible factors might be the fact that funerals are dominated by an Orthodox religious institution, since religious life in Israel is regulated through the Orthodox Chief Rabbinate. A ceremony that is meant to be a meaningful rite of passage turns out to be awkward and exclusive, and in many cases funerals feel alien and alienating. Private funerals in private cemeteries are possible but very expensive, and most Israelis are insufficiently informed about them.

There is a discrepancy between the dependence upon the Kaddish and the fact that people do not understand its theology or even its simple meaning and pronunciation. The journalist Benny Ziffer wrote about the embarrassing situation in which a son,[20] who had just lost a parent, received a laminated card with the words of the Kaddish on it from the burial society person and was helpless in dealing with it:

[The son looks] like someone who must decipher for the first time in his life a hieroglyphic inscription. He begins to mumble the words and to stumble over every possible Aramaic obstacle, . . . every word on the cardboard looks like a train of meaningless letters, whose cars piercingly bump into each other. Only toward the end, when the Kaddish comes closer to Hebrew, the ashamed man, who failed the reading of the fundamental test, finds consolation with the sentence: "May the One who makes peace in His lofty heavens . . . "[21] which every Israeli, even the most secular, remembers from the song Yigal Bashan sang at the first Chassidic Song Festival in 1969.[22]

Ziffer, "a completely secular person," as he refers to himself, understands the Kaddish as a "great poetic text that everyone should know" and calls upon Israelis to learn the Kaddish in order to understand it and to be able to recite it properly when needed.[23]

The vast majority of the Jewish prayers are in Hebrew, the Israeli vernacular (albeit formulated in an older and loftier linguistic register). Israelis can read them without the need for translation. The Kaddish, however, is composed in Aramaic, a foreign language. Linguistically, Aramaic is indeed the closest language to Hebrew, but the words of the Kaddish sound foreign to the Israeli ear, so that the natural sense of alienation (caused by death itself) increases due to the alienation from the text.[24] There was some experimentation with reciting the Kaddish in Hebrew but, as far as I know, it never worked in the long run. People longed for the mantra-like rhythm of the undecipherable words, treating them as a chant. When it comes to language and religiosity, the Kaddish puts Israelis in the same place as their siblings in the Diaspora.[25]

The Kaddish is chanted, along with the memorial prayer *El male rahamim*, at every official memorial ceremony for the Holocaust or Israeli Fallen Soldiers and Victims of Terrorism on Remembrance Days. It is usually a moving moment at these ceremonies, but unlike other elements, these two prayers are a fixed part of the service, recited by a military cantor, not by those in attendance.

As an example of liturgical reactions to the Kaddish, I will turn to a discussion of the ways in which this prayer has been dealt with in the Kibbutz Movement. I will confine myself to texts that were composed for actual liturgical use, and will not deal with poems or other means of expression. It is my contention that by composing and using new versions of the Kaddish, with a drastically changed theology, the kibbutz members took ownership of their religiosity and control of their mourning.

The Kaddish Prayer in the Kibbutz Movement

One of the main arenas in which Israeli ritual creativity has taken place is the Kibbutz Movement, which used to be the vanguard of the socialist, secular State of Israel in its early years. Some of the more creative expressions of Israeli spirituality nested within the gates of the kibbutzim. The kibbutzim took charge of the social and cultural life of their members. To this day, some of the most interesting and groundbreaking Israeli ritual innovations have strong roots in the kibbutzim. Treatment of mourning and grief is no exception to this rule.[26]

I will outline now three somewhat blended yet distinct stages of the uses of the Kaddish in kibbutz funerals and memorial events in general: spontaneity and silence; creative adaptations of the prayer; and retreat to tradition.

Spontaneity and Silence

The early kibbutz funerals were not marked by formal structure. Most of the members were young, and were not generally related to one another by family. The kibbutz project began, for the most part, with a total rejection of religious ritual and religious symbols,[27] yet members were soon engaged in spontaneous experimentation with rituals of grief. Nehama Zitser tells of the death of Yitshak Turner, a young man of the Ha-shomer movement in 1915. She describes the despair and helplessness of his young friends. At a certain moment one member got up and began to hum the *Hora* to himself. Gradually he raised his voice and eventually got up on his feet and began dancing. Little by little, all the members joined him, singing and dancing. He encouraged them, saying: "Hey, hey, friends, Turner didn't want tears, he wanted life and growth." They ceased dancing at dawn, when they had to go to work.[28]

Still, many funerals were marked by silence, no prayers or eulogies being delivered.[29] The following poem by Shalom Yosef Shapira (1904–90) may illustrate the "Temple of Silence" that the kibbutz members created:

When a person dies	אדם כי ימות..., ש. שפירא
When a person[30] dies in the Jezreel Valley The sheaves will be silent. The Jezreel Valley is Holy of Holies And no one weeps in the Holy of Holies.	אָדָם כִּי יָמוּת בְּעֵמֶק-יִזְרְעֶאל תִּדֹּמְנָה שִׁבֳּלִים. קֹדֶשׁ קָדָשִׁים הוּא עֵמֶק-יִזְרְעֶאל וְאֵין בּוֹכִים בְּקֹדֶשׁ הַקֳּדָשִׁים.
When night descends upon the Jezreel Valley The stars will shimmer; They are the memorial lights in the Jezreel Valley for those for whom there is no "Kaddish."[31]	וּבְרֶדֶת הַלַּיְלָה עַל עֵמֶק-יִזְרְעֶאל יִזְדַּעְזְעוּ כוֹכָבִים; נֵרוֹת-נְשָׁמָה הֵם בְּעֵמֶק-יִזְרְעֶאל לְאֵלֶּה שֶׁאֵין לָהֶם "קַדִּישׁ". "

This fierce poem proposes an alternative religiosity—instead of Jerusalem and its (lost) Temple, the Jezreel valley is portrayed as the Holy of Holies, which requires restraint and self-discipline. No one is allowed to cry in the presence of the Sanctum Sanctorum. But the heavens and the stars in the sky lend themselves to serving as memorial candles for those for whom the Kaddish is not recited.

The composer Yehudah Sharet (1901–79) of Kibbutz Yagur, in a letter from the 1920s, recalled the funeral of a young man called Shuster who was killed in a work accident. He wrote: "No sob, no moan, no scream—a bleak orphanage, this is what our funerals will look like. The stillness of the mother and the lack of motherly crying, and nothing more. . . . It was as if the silence were a testimony to our uprootedness."[32] But the silence was also a deliberate choice. Aharon David Gordon (1856-1922), a spiritual leader of the pioneer Zionist movement, left the following will: "This is what I would do, and this is how I wish others would treat me [when I die]: those who wish to honor me shall honor me with silence. For at least one year, no one shall talk about me nor write a single word about me."[33] Silence was perceived as the proper response to the cruelty of death. But there were other nonverbal responses. The anthropologist Nissan Rubin notes two separate stages: the 1910s, which were marked with song and dance, and the 1920s–50s, "a period of silence."[34]

One may suggest that the lack of words of prayer in the kibbutz funerals was not a mere result of the so-called "secular" nature of the socialist settlements but also due to the fact that the young members felt that they could not allow themselves to sink into paralyzing grief in the face of the death of many young people (due to disease, conflict with Arabs, accidents, and suicide).[35] In a way, this was a renunciation of the self for the sake of self-discipline. The pioneers could not allow themselves to cease from their demanding daily routine and to be engulfed by sorrow.

Literary Creativity

The issue of death and mourning became more central in the 1960s when the founders of the kibbutzim began to pass away.[36] Gradually, the silence at the funerals became unbearable. In the early sixties, Yitshak Tabenkin (1888-1971), one of the founders of the Kibbutz Movement, said in a private conversation that the poets and thinkers of the Kibbutz Movement should be approached in order to find poetic expression of "our love of life" in a new version of the Kaddish.[37] Soon enough, some new versions of the Kaddish were composed. I will present here four examples that represent diverse literary styles.

Shortly after Tabenkin's call, Zvi She'er (1904–87), an educator who also worked in Kibbutz Yagur's plants, composed the first known alternative version of the Kaddish.[38] According to some testimonies, he did so as a response to the unbearable silence at the graveside. Yagur's Kaddish, as it is usually referred to, is still read in funerals at Yagur and in some other kibbutzim.[39]

Magnified be the person who holds on to his hopes from the morning of his life until his very last day.
Whose heart is not tainted and whose ways are upright,
And who never despairs in his quest for redemption.

In whose heart is both the world's suffering and its joys,
who is its radiance both manifest and hidden.

Hope will not end with him
And the way of the upright will not perish.

May the glory of humankind be forever blessed.

Magnified, indeed, be the Hebrew person on his land
And sanctified be the one who lives with the memory of the life that has been taken away.

Life has ended, sealed in the soil of Yagur, in its toil, in the hearts of its members.

May his memory abide with us as a blessing.

יִתְגַּדַּל הָאָדָם הַשּׁוֹמֵר תּוֹחַלְתּוֹ
מִבֹּקֶר חַיָּיו עַד יוֹמוֹ הָאַחֲרוֹן.
אֲשֶׁר לִבּוֹ לֹא סָג וְיָשָׁר מַעֲשֵׂהוּ,
וּמִגְּאֻלָּה לֹא נוֹאָשׁ.

אֲשֶׁר בְּלִבּוֹ סֵבֶל הָעוֹלָם וְשִׂמְחָתוֹ,
שֶׁהוּא זִיו בְּגִילּוּיוֹ וְסִתְרוֹ.

לֹא תִתּוֹם עִמּוֹ תִּקְוָה
וְדֶרֶךְ יְשָׁרִים לֹא תֹאבֵד.

יְבוֹרַךְ יְקָר הָאָדָם לָעַד.

יִתְגַּדַּל הָאָדָם הָעִבְרִי עַל אַדְמָתוֹ
וְיִתְקַדֵּשׁ הֶחָי בְּזִכְרוֹן הַחַיִּים
שֶׁנִּפְקָדוּ.

תַּמּוּ חַיִּים חֲתוּמִים בְּאַדְמַת יָגוּר,
בַּעֲמָלָהּ, בְּלֵב חֲבֵרֶיהָ.

יְהִי זִכְרוֹ לִבְרָכָה בְּתוֹכֵנוּ.

She'er quotes the well-known opening words of the traditional Kaddish but changed its original meaning dramatically. Instead of praising God and God's future kingdom, it praises the individual in the specific context of his "kingdom ," the kibbutz. The phrase ziv ha'olam (the world's radiance), which is one of the attributes of God, s applied here to the deceased. It is important to note that the phrase Yitgadal ve'yitkadash shem ha'adam ("May the name of person be magnified and sanctified") was coined half a century earlier by the writer Yosef Haim Brenner (1881–1921), who used it to end an article he wrote in 1905, in the aftermath of the Russian Revolution.[40]

This text exalts the individual within the fabric of the communal life, an action that is entirely missing from the traditional Kaddish, which does not refer to the deceased at all. The glory and the sanctification of God, the center of the traditional text, are completely missing from this one, which eliminates any reference to the Divine.

There are some similarities among the different versions of the Kaddish used by the kibbutzim: all of them begin with the traditional word yitgadal; all of them are dedicated to the memory of the individual in the framework of the kibbutz; all of them wish for the memory to be for a blessing; and all of them are formulated in the male singular voice but are modified when the deceased is a female. But each emphasizes different elements.

The following text was composed by the poet Eli Alon (born in 1935) from Kibbutz Ein Shemer.

Kaddish for the People of Ein Shemer   קדיש לאנשי עין-שמר

Magnified and sanctified be the person in his life and in his death	יִתְגַדַל וְיִתְקַדַש הָאָדָם בְּחַיָיו וּבְמוֹתוֹ

Magnified and sanctified be the person in his life
and in his death
In his happiness, in his suffering and in his toil.
Blessed and praised be our kibbutz through those
who love it
And gave it their strength without restraint
And their reward—meaning to their lives and
their labor.
And when a life well lived should end—the
memory of their deeds will not be lost.
For the way of the upright will never perish
because the aspirations of their deeds may
remain forever.
May the seed that they sowed sprout forth,
the tree bear fruit, and the home flourish, bustling with life
and multiplying generations.
The soil of Ein Shemer gathers you in today with
sadness and love to its breast.
Let the clods of earth be sweet to you.
May your life and your deeds be bound up in the
bond of our lives
For consolation and for hope.

יִתְגַדַל וְיִתְקַדַש הָאָדָם בְּחַיָיו וּבְמוֹתוֹ
בְּשִׂמְחָתוֹ, בְּסִבְלוֹ וּבַעֲמָלוֹ
יִתְבָּרַךְ וְיִשְׁתַּבַּח קִבּוּצֵנוּ בְּאוֹהֲבָיו
אֲשֶׁר נָתְנוּ מֵחֵילָם לְלֹא חָסָךְ
וּגְמוּלָם - טַעַם חַיֵּיהֶם וַעֲמָלָם.
וְאִם תַּמּוּ חַיִים שֶׁל טַעַם - לֹא
יִפָּקֵד זֵכֶר פָּעֳלָם.
כִּי דֶרֶךְ יְשָׁרִים לֹא תֹּאבַד
וְתוֹחֶלֶת מַעֲשֵׂיהֶם תַּעֲמֹד לָעַד.
יִנְבֹּט הַזֶרַע אֲשֶׁר זָרְעוּ,
הָעֵץ יַעֲשֶׂה פְּרִי, הַבַּיִת יִשְׂגְּשֶׂג,
יֶהֱמֶה חַיִּים וְיִרְבֶּה דוֹרוֹת.
אַדְמַת עֵין-שֶׁמֶר אוֹסֶפֶת אוֹתְךָ
הַיּוֹם בְּעֶצֶב וּבְאַהֲבָה אֶל חֵיקָהּ.
יִמְתְּקוּ לְךָ רִגְבֵי עֲפָרָהּ.
יִהְיוּ חַיֶיךָ וּמַעֲשֶׂיךָ צְרוּרִים בִּצְרוֹר
חַיֵּינוּ לְנֶחָמָה וּלְתִקְוָה.

In this version, even more than in Yagur's Kaddish, there is an emphasis on the kibbutz communal life and on the meaningful choices that the deceased made as a kibbutz member. Whereas the Kaddish of Yagur emphasizes the living, this version places the deceased at the center, saying that the fruits of his deeds will last long and that he and his deeds will not be forgotten. Alon cites not only the Kaddish, but also the mourning prayer El male rahamim, giving it a completely new meaning. Instead of asking God that the soul of the deceased may be "bound up in the bonds of life," referring to the life in the World to Come, it promises that the deeds of the deceased will be "bound up in the bonds of our lives," that is, they will continue to be present and to impact the community long after he is gone. Similarly, the sentence "For the way of the upright will never perish" is an adaptation of a biblical verse (Hosea 14:10), which speaks about the upright walking in the ways of God, in which the righteous are allowed to step.

The following text was composed by Shalom Smid, a member of Kibbutz Negba, which belongs to Hakibbutz Ha-Artzi, a left-wing group and the most antireligious of the Kibbutz Movement:

The Kaddish of the Kibbutzim   קדיש הקיבוצים

Magnified be the name of the person,
    Extolled be the labors of his life
and blessed through our memory
    for the sum of his deeds
through his days in the world
    And for the actions which he did not
    manage to complete.
For dreams that were spun and were then
    no more
And for precious virtues and even human
    weaknesses that have faded away
through the foggy mists of time.

May the person's memory be radiant and
    the reflections of his life be like the
    brilliance of the firmament in our hearts—
Let his name endure as long as the sun
    shines (Ps. 72:17).[41]
What remains of the person[42] is the memory
beyond the limits of time.
His name shall not be covered by darkness.
The imperative of life's continuity will
    bring relief to our inmost pain.[43]
The march of time will be compassionate.
And we shall cherish the fruits of his life
    for many a day.
Magnified and sanctified.

יִתְגַּדַּל שֵׁם הָאָדָם, יִתְעַלֶּה פּוֹעַל־חַיָּיו,
וְיִתְבָּרֵךְ בְּזִכְרוֹנֵנוּ עַל צְרוֹר מַעֲלָלָיו
בִּימֵי חֶלְדּוֹ וְעַל הַמַּעַשׂ שֶׁלֹּא הִסְפִּיק
לְהַשְׁלִימוֹ
עַל הַחֲלוֹמוֹת שֶׁנִּיטְווּ וְנָמוֹגּוּ
וְעֲלֵי סְגוּלוֹת יָקָר וְאָף חוּלְשׁוֹת־אֱנוֹש
שֶׁנָּגוֹזוּ,
מִבַּעַד הַדּוֹק הָעַרְפִלִּי שֶׁל הַזְּמָן.

יַזְהִיר זֵכֶר הָאָדָם וְהֵד חַיָּיו בְּזוֹהַר
הָרָקִיעַ בְּלִבֵּנוּ—
"וּשְׁמוֹ לִפְנֵי שֶׁמֶשׁ יָנּוֹן" (תהלים עב, יז),
כִּי מֻתָּר הָאָדָם הוּא הַזִּכָּרוֹן
מֵעֵבֶר לִמְחִצּוֹת הַזְּמָן.
לֹא בַחֹשֶׁךְ שְׁמוֹ יְכֻסֶּה.
צַו הֶמְשֵׁךְ הַחַיִּים יַצְמִיחַ פָּרְקָן לְכָאבֵנוּ
הַמְּשֻׁקָּע.
הַזְּמָן בְּמַהֲלָכוֹ יְרַחֵם.
וְנִנְצוֹר אֶת כָּל פִּרְחֵי חַיָּיו לְיָמִים רַבִּים.
יִתְגַּדַּל וְיִתְקַדָּש.

This text emphasizes the pain and loss in the face of death. Its first half speaks of the human fate to leave this world without accomplishing our aspirations and realizing our dreams, the second part is dedicated to consolation of the mourners and hopes for the future. Unlike She'er's text, here the Zionist aspect and the kibbutz ideology are not stressed. In fact, they are referred to only indirectly. Instead, it reflects doleful reflection on the finite nature of human life; it stresses the memory and the consolation of the mourners.

Another version, composed by Oved Sadeh (literally: the worker of the field, 1925–2008) from Kibbutz Beir Keshet, follows more closely the structure of the traditional Kaddish. However, it employs a completely different set of images:

Magnified and sanctified	יִתְגַּדַּל וְיִתְקַדַּשׁ
be the clod that crushed	הָרֶגֶב שֶׁקָּרַס
as the plow split	בְּפַלַּח מַחֲרֵשָׁה
the hard soil	הָאֲדָמָה הַקָּשָׁה
Glorified and extolled—be the leaf	יִתְהַדַּר וְיִתְעַלֶּה - הֶעָלֶה
that sprouted and greened, reddened—and fell.	שֶׁלִּבְלֵב, וְהוֹרִיק הֶאְדִּים–וְנָשַׁר.
Acclaimed and lauded	יִתְרוֹמֵם וְיִתְנַשֵּׂא
be the one who carries the burden	הַנּוֹשֵׂא בַּמַּשָּׂא
and when his path collapsed[44]	וּבְכְרֹעַ דַּרְכּוֹ
my path too collapsed.	גַּם דַּרְכִּי נִרְמְסָה.
Blessed and praised	יִתְבָּרֵךְ וְיִשְׁתַּבַּח
be the voice of the singular one[45]	קוֹל הַיָּחִיד
along with the voice of the many.	עִם קוֹל הָרַבִּים.
Magnified and sanctified	יִתְגַּדַּל וְיִתְקַדַּשׁ
Be the individual in his uniqueness.	הַיָּחִיד בְּיִחוּדוֹ.[46]

Sadeh's version is a carefully crafted text: it rhymes and has a meter. The imagery is clearly based on the farming cycle. Unlike the other kibbutz versions, here it is the clod of earth that is "magnified and sanctified," and indeed, this text is deeply grounded in the agricultural kibbutz experience. And yet it stresses the individual. Only toward the end does it mention the community, and even then it is done in order to stress individual uniqueness.

All the above-cited texts make use of the traditional Kaddish, especially of its opening words, which profoundly resonate the expression of mourning, regardless of their denotation. Yet it drastically changes the content, not only in that it shifts the focus from the heavenly kingdom to the earth (in the most tangible sense of the word), from the Divine to the human, and from the metaphysical to the concrete and visceral. God is completely taken out of the picture. Although each composer has his literary, ideological, and cultural agenda, it seems that they cite one another, having created a subgenre of liturgical expression in which one can identify slightly different emphases.

The writers of these texts (and of similar ones) made a conscious choice in keeping the connotative expression of the Kaddish while supplying ideologically appropriate content. In their texts, these writers made bold statements; they showed that they own the spiritual property, as it were, of the Jewish tradition, yet they choose to use it in an informed way that is adequate to their faith and way of life.

In order to compare the data from the studies of Kalekin-Fishman and Klingman, Rubin, and Shua from the eighties with the situation today, I wrote to those in charge of the cultural life or of mourning committees on the kibbutzim. I inquired about the recitation of the Kaddish prayer and about changing trends in burial rituals within their communities. I have received responses from about forty kibbutzim, and they reveal a very diverse picture. Generally speaking, the number of kibbutzim in which the traditional Kaddish is recited is more or less the same as those in which a special kibbutz Kaddish is in use. In many kibbutzim both are recited. Typically, the traditional text is read by a family member and the kibbutz Kaddish by a "reader" from the community. Some of the people I have spoken with stressed that both men and women recite the Kaddish. About half of the kibbutzim that recite only the traditional Kaddish invite a rabbi or a religious person from a neighboring town or settlement to conduct the funeral, a situation that was almost never seen in the kibbutzim in the past. In many cases, the Orthodox burial leader acts as mara d'atra, the local authority, and dictates the nature of the ceremony. In some kibbutzim, especially those affiliated with the Ha-Kibbutz Ha-Artzi movement, no Kaddish is recited. In general, however, the number of kibbutzim in which Kaddish is recited, or at least in which its recitation is a legitimate option, is much larger than in the 1980s, and needless to say, it is much more frequent than in the past. Many kibbutzim stress the autonomy of family to make the choices regarding the nature of the burial ceremony; a committee member visits the family and shares possible texts and practices, and the family makes the actual decisions. Central kibbutz protocol regarding funerals and mourning gives way to choices made by each family.

Retreat to Traditionalism

Nissan Rubin writes: "As long as the ideological fervor was strong, secular formulations of ritual could be preserved. With the waning of ideological fervor, some of the secular elements of mourning customs disappeared and more traditional content was reinstated."[47] This trend—along with absorption into the kibbutzim of people uncommitted to kibbutz values and clusters of nonmembers, economic as well as cultural privatization, and the centrality of the nuclear family—all these brought about the retreat (or "withdrawal," as some kibbutz members refer to it) to traditionalism.

This process does not mean, for the most part, that the kibbutzim are becoming more traditional or embracing Orthodoxy. It is rather an indication of the weakening of the ownership the kibbutzim took of their cultural life and of the secular religiosity they created. Authoritative figures, "those who know how," mostly from outside the community, manage significant parts of the cultural life.

In some kibbutzim there have been functioning traditional synagogues for many decades. Most were rather marginal and intended to address the needs of members' parents. In the last decade, many kibbutzim have built new synagogues. Some of these institutions are models of inventiveness and creativity,[48] while others are adopting Orthodox formulae, often under the guidance (or supervision) of Orthodox rabbis. Lately, in some secular kibbutzim separate dancing takes place during Simhat Torah, and needless to say, the women, placed behind the mehitsah (separation wall), are not allowed to dance with the Torah scroll.[49] The existence of more and more Orthodox synagogues in the secular kibbutzim is a symptom of a broader phenomenon: a decrease of self-confidence in the social and communal way, the ebbing of mutual social and economic care, and the privatization of most of the kibbutzim have caused a decline in the quality of cultural life. Religious formulae that present themselves as confident and efficacious find their way into the feeble fabric of kibbutz life.[50]

The treatment of the Kaddish is no exception to the rule. While the "Kibbutz Kaddishim" are still recited at funerals in many kibbutzim, some choose to add the traditional Kaddish and sometimes also the burial prayer, El male rahamin. In some cases these traditional prayers have even replaced the Kibbutz Kaddishim entirely. The submission to forms of traditionalism and its authoritative agents often occurs without dealing with it or even understanding it. Paradoxically, one can say that the retreat to tradition reflects a diminished commitment to vibrant Jewish activity.

We may, in conclusion, point to three, albeit somewhat blurred, stages in the treatment of mourning prayers in the kibbutzim. In the first years, spontaneous reactions but mostly utter silence were deemed a proper response to death. Later, new versions of mourning readings, based on the traditional Kaddish but reflecting the kibbutz's ideological worldview, were created. In the third phase we are witnessing a return to tradition, not necessarily as an informed religious choice but rather as an adaptation of ready-made formulae, which are deemed "authentic."[51]

This was a journey from the Rhine Valley, where the Mourners' Kaddish became a device for coping with trauma, to the Jezreel Valley, almost a thousand years later, where Israeli Jews struggle with it, recite it, and even innovate within it in order to cope with human finitude and with their beliefs and fears.[52] It seems that even when Jews walk through the Valley of Death, they may draw consolation and strength from the sources, and that is true for religious as well as secular, and even devotedly atheist Jews.

Notes

1. Heinrich Heine, *Sämtliche Schriften* (Munich, 1975), 1:113. See also David Telsner, *The Kaddish: Its History and Significance* (Jerusalem 1995); Leon Wieseltier, *Kaddish* (New York, 1998), 271–72. All translations are mine.
2. Tractate Sofrim specifies this prayer among other parts of the service that cannot be fulfilled without a quorum of ten worshipers (Sofrim 10:6). It also says: "After the Mussaf (the Additional service) it is customary for the cantor to go behind the synagogue's door, or to the corner of the synagogue, where he joins the mourners and their relatives to offer a blessing. He then recites Kaddish" (Sofrim 19:9). The first text of the Kaddish appears in Seder Rav Amram Gaon (ninth century in Babylon). Regarding the Kaddish prayer in general, see the following: Ismar Elbogen, *Jewish Liturgy: A Comprehensive History*, trans. R. P. Scheindlin (Philadelphia, 1993), 80–84; Lawrence A. Hoffman, ed., Minhag Ami/*My People's Prayer Book: Traditional Prayers, Modern Commentaries*, vol. 6 (Woodstock, Vt., 2002); Stefan C. Reif, *Judaism and Hebrew Prayer: New Perspectives on Jewish Liturgical History* (Cambridge, 1993), 207–10, 219–20; David de Sola Pool, *The Old Jewish-Aramaic Prayer, the Kaddish* (New York, 1964); Telsner, *The Kaddish*; Wieseltier, *Kaddish*.

3. Elbogen, *Jewish Liturgy*, 81–83. Some scholars have indicated the similarities between the Lord's Prayer (Matthew, 6:9–13) and the Kaddish. See Baruch Graubard, "The Kaddish Prayer," *The Lord's Prayer and Jewish Liturgy*, ed. J. Petuchowski and M. Brocke, 59–72 (New York, 1978).

4. Joseph Heinemann, *Prayer in the Talmud: Forms and Patterns*, trans. R. Sarason (Berlin, 1977), 251–75.

5. The different formulations are the Scholar's Kaddish, recited after studying the Torah; the Full Kaddish, recited at the end of the service; the so-called "Half Kaddish," which divides different rubrics of the service; the Mourners' Kaddish; and the Burial Kaddish, recited at funerals and at the end of the study of a Talmud tractate. Significantly, only this last form of the Kaddish mentions the resurrection of the dead.

6. "The Crusades provoked the first major attempt to exterminate an entire Jewry in Europe. It failed but it left many, many mourners in its wake" (Wieseltier, Kaddish, 81). For reference, see: Ivan Marcus, *The Jewish Life Cycle: Rites of Passage* (Seattle, 2004), 227–44.

7. Solomon Freehof, "Hazkarat neshamot," *Hebrew Union College Annual* 36 (1965): 179–89.

8. Marcus, *Life Cycle*, 228–31. One should add to this list a multitude of local memorial customs, many of which are not observed today. See, for example, Gabriel Sivan, "The Hymns of the Isles," *Judaism* 39 (1990): 326–37.

9. See Heinemann, *Prayer in the Talmud*, 251–75.

10. There are numerous mentions of the Kaddish in Mahzor Vitry (composed by Rabbi Simha ben Emanuel of Vitry, a disciple of Rashi), the prototype of the Franco-German religious practice. In most places, it says that the cantor recites the Kaddish, but in others it specifies that a child (na'ar) does it. See, for example, paragraphs 157, 193, 312, and 356.

11. For an exploration of the versions of the tale, see Myron Bialik Lerner, "The Tale of the Tanna and The Dead Man: Its Literary and Halakhic Versions" [in Hebrew], Asupot 2 (1988): 29–70; Telsner, *The Kaddish*, 68–76; Wieseltier, *Kaddish*, 126–31.

12. "A son can bring merit זֹכֶה to his father, a father cannot bring merit to his son" (*bSan* 104a).

13. Israel Ta-Shema: "Some Notes on the Origins of the Kaddish" [in Hebrew], *Tarbiz* 53 (1984): 559–68.

14. Siddur Rashi, 216. See Ta-Shema, "Some Notes."

15. See for example: Shlomo Eidelberg, trans. and ed., *The Jews and the Crusaders: The Hebrew Chronicles of the First and Second Crusades* (Madison, Wisc., 1987); Robert Chazan, *God, Humanity, and History: The Hebrew First-Crusade Narratives* (Berkeley, Calif., 2000); Jeremy Cohen, *Sanctifying the Name of God: Jewish Martyrs and Jewish Memories of the First Crusade* (Philadelphia, 2004).

16. The idea of God's sanctification through Israel appears in Ezek. 20:41: *v'nikdashti vakhem l'einei ha-goyim* ("and I shall be sanctified through you in the sight of the nations") and *bi-kerovai ekadesh* ("Through them that are nigh unto Me I will be sanctified," Lev. 10:3). See the commentary to these verses.

17. Uriel Tal, Kaddish, 35.

18. This is a problematic term because it refers to a social affiliation more than to a theological conviction. I am using it here because this is the accepted term in the Israeli public sphere.

19. See Haim Cohn, "Religious Freedom and Religious Coercion in the State of Israel," *Israel among the Nations: International and Comparative Law Perspectives on Israel's 50th Anniversary*, ed. A. E. Kellermann, K. Siehr, T. Einhorn, 79–110 (The Hague, 1998). It should be noted that "Secular" Israelis do seek spirituality, and many turn to Eastern practices or to forms of noninstitutionalized religiosity; see below.

20. Ziffer uses a male reference since he refers to "normal" funerals, namely, Orthodox, where only males are allowed to recite the Kaddish.

21. Only the concluding sentence (and probably the last to be added) of the Kaddish is in Hebrew.

22. Benny Ziffer, "Learn the Kaddish!," in *Siddur ishi*, ed. H. Yovel [in Hebrew] (Tel Aviv, 2009), 73.

23. Ibid., 74.

24. Dan Meller, an atheist activist of Humanistic Judaism, wrote a fierce accusation against the use of the Aramaic language for the Kaddish, calling it deceptive and manipulative of people experiencing personal tragedies. See Dan Meller, "Kadish," on Hofesh: Freedom from Religion website [in Hebrew], www.hofesh.org.il/articles/kadish.html (accessed March 2, 2014).

25. Dalia Marx, "When *L'shon HaKodesh* Is Also the Vernacular: The Development of Israeli Reform Liturgy," *CCAR Journal* 56, no. 4 (2009): 31–62.

26. For general information regarding mourning in the non-Orthodox kibbutzim, see Devorah Kalekin-Fishman, "Bereavement and Mourning in Non-religious Kibbutzim," *Death Studies: Education, Counseling, Care, Law, Ethics* 12, no. 3 (1988): 253–70; Nissan Rubin, *New Rituals, Old Societies: Invented Rituals in Contemporary Israel* (Boston, 2009), 92–109; Rubin, *Death Customs in a Non-Religious Kibbutz*, Israeli Judaism, ed. S. Deshen, C. S. Liebman, and M. Shokeid, 323–34 (New Jersey, 1995).

27. Avraham Azili, *The Attitude of Ha-shomer Ha-tsa'ir to Religion and Tradition* (1920–1948) [in Hebrew] (Givat Havivah, 1984), 10–17.

28. Muki Tzur, Ta'ir Zvulun, and Hanina Porat, eds., *The Beginning of the Kibbutz* [in Hebrew] (Tel Aviv, 1981), 124. For more examples, see Rubin, "Death Customs," 327–29.

29. Rubin, "Death Customs," 330.

30. The Hebrew word *adam*, which is grammatically male, refers to the human being in general.

31. Printed in *Yalkut avlut*, ed. Zvi Shua and Arye Ben-Gurion [in Hebrew] (Beit Hashita, 1990), 144. The poem was set to music by Moshe Rapaport.

32. Shua and Ben-Gurion, *Yalkut*, 128.

33. *Sippura shel Degania* [in Hebrew] (Tel-Aviv, 1962), 123.

34. Rubin, "Death Customs," 330. It seems, though, that there is no clear division between these periods and, to some extent, they coincided.

35. Muki Tzur, *Lelo ktonet pasim* [in Hebrew] (Tel Aviv, 1976), 33.

36. Rubin, "Death Customs," 325.

37. Shua and Ben-Gurion, *Yalkut*, 145.

38. A testimony to the legendary status of this Kaddish is the variety of stories about the circumstances of its creation. According to one, it was already composed in 1948 as a response to the death of Yehoshua Globerman, a commander in the Haganah organization and the first soldier to be killed in the 1948 war (Shua and Ben-Gurion, Yalkut, 147). But according the Yagur archives, it was composed in the sixties. (I thank Rabbi Gadi Raviv of Yagur for the information).

39. The Yagur Kaddish is recited by the reader while the traditional Kaddish is recited at Yagur, if the family chooses it, by the family itself.

40. Yosef Haim Brenner, "Letters to Russia" [in Hebrew], Ktavim 3 (1985): 103.

41. The phrase shemesh yinon (Ps. 72:17, which I translated as "endure as long as the sun shines") was understood by the rabbis as referring to the Messiah (bPes 54a; bSan 98b).

42. The phrase motar ha-adam refers in Ecclesiastes (3:19) to the question whether the human being is preferable to the beast.

43. The phrase yatsm'iah purkan is a paraphrase of a sentence included in the Sepharadic version of the Kaddish: Yatsmah purkane vi-karev meshihe (May he bring salvation and draw the Messiah near).

44. Bikhro'a literally means "when knelt down."

45. Or "the singular voice" or "the voice of the individual" or "the voice of the one."

46. Shua and Ben-Gurion, Yalkut, 149.

47. Rubin, "Death Customs," 323.

48. For example, the synagogue instituted and led by Buja (Binyamin) Yogev in Kibbutz Beit Ha'emek. And see Naamah Azulay, "'A House of Prayer for All Nations': Unorthodox Prayer Houses for Nonreligious Israeli Jews," in Between Tradition and Modernity, ed. L. Remennick and A. Prashizky, 22–41 (Bar Ilan, 2008); Rachel Werczberger, "The Jewish Renewal Movement in Israeli Secular Society," Contemporary Jewry 31, no. 2 (2011): 107–28.

49. For example, in Kibbutz Mazuva the woman cantor, who served the local congregation for many years, was not allowed to officiate during the High Holidays of 5972 (1986).

50. I thank the sociologist Dr. Nir Resisi, who shared this analysis with me. When an Orthodox synagogue was established in Degania, "the mother of the kevutsot," I wrote its members an open letter, which was published in the press. I concluded with the plea: "You, the sons and daughters of the Kibbutz movement, breathed new life into Judaism by adding content and richness to our holidays, and you even created new ones. When you reach out to Judaism, don't approach it submissively and with feelings of inadequacy. Approach it securely, with engagement and ownership. Approach it with the happiness that comes with the performance of a commandment" (Ynet, June 8, 2008).

51. In order to fully appreciate the role and status of the Kaddish in Israel, one should examine theological treatment of this prayer. See David and Verete, The Kaddish Prayer. For musical innovation, see Hanan Yovel, A Personal Siddur [in Hebrew] (Tel Aviv, 2009), 70–75. For graphic artistic depictions of this prayer, see especially the series of silk screens by the Moshe Gershuny, each of which depicts a word from the Kaddish and creative commentaries. And, finally, for poems citing the Kaddish, see David and Verete, The Kaddish Prayer; Eli Alon,

"On the Secular Kaddish," *Hazrimah hadu-sitrit shel ha-ivrit*, ed. Z. Luz, 144–54 [in Hebrew] (Tel Aviv, 2011).

52. In the future, I hope to deal with special Kaddish versions written for the remembrance of the Holocaust.

9

NEW WATERS IN AN OLD VESSEL

A History of Mikveh in Modern Judaism

MICHAEL A. MEYER

The interaction of tradition and innovation, rather than replacement of the first by the second, has been a characteristic of Judaism in modern times. For David Ellenson, displaying evidence of their lack of separation has long marked his work, leading him to explore both the role of modernity in Jewish Orthodoxy and the persistence of tradition in Reform Judaism. It is the purpose of this essay to follow a similar path by examining, through a specific instance, how a particular tradition, having been abandoned by a segment of modern Jewry, can in response to intellectually and aesthetically induced vicissitudes, regain vitality—can pour new waters into old vessels.

In recent centuries non-Orthodox Jews have rejected or reinterpreted both rites and doctrines, seeking to adapt their religious lives to modern tenets and values. They have thereby reimagined Judaism, stretching out its protean possibilities. But pulling at the cord does not mean that all of the threads are torn. In summarizing a different metaphor by Walter Benjamin on this point, Hannah Arendt wrote of his conviction "that although the living is subject to the ruin of the time, the process of decay is at the same time a process of crystallization, that in the depth of the sea, into which sinks and is dissolved what once was alive, some things 'suffer a sea-change' and survive in new crystallized forms and shapes that remain immune to the elements."[1] One might add: they remain immune at least for a while. A rite abandoned may in the course of time be revisited by a generation that seeks out a once hallowed form in order to fill it with a new content that mixes easily, or only after effort, with the substance that had previously filled the vessel.

Within a religious context successful innovation cannot be separated from the tradition with which it interacts. However radical, however subjectively based, it must seek legitimation by linking itself to ideas or practices that are rooted in the past.[2] This process assumes particular interest when there is a sharp dichotomy between a traditional practice and the new meanings that are ascribed to it. In modern Judaism I know of no institution that has undergone so unexpected a revival and at the same time so fundamental a shift in meaning as ritual immersion in a mikveh.[3] Although a considerable literature on new uses of mikveh, as well as the aesthetics and ethics surrounding them, has sprung up in the last two decades, there has yet to be a broad-ranging historical treatment of the subject that reaches back to the nineteenth century and forward into the present. This article attempts to fill that lacuna. Focusing in particular on the Reform movement in the United States, it will also discuss the varying attitudes to immersion (*tevilah*) in modern Orthodoxy, in Conservative Judaism, and in Progressive Judaism in Israel. Its objective will be to illustrate the resilience of a long neglected tradition that, reinterpreted, has been able, at least for some modern Jews, to absorb the most contemporary sensibilities.[4]

The public discourse on mikveh within the Reform movement goes back to the year 1845, when the Jewish community of Bingen sent a question to the conference of non-Orthodox rabbis meeting in Frankfurt am Main.[5] The community's governing board explained that lack of rain had required using the same water repeatedly during the summer. Bathing in it had become like bathing in a puddle of stagnant rainwater crawling with worms. As a result, three quarters of the local Jewish women, who should have been using the mikveh upon completion of their monthly menstrual cycle, were not doing so, especially the younger ones. The community's leaders were well aware that failure to observe the commandment of family purity (*tohorat ha-mishpahah*) according to Jewish law incurs the severe penalty of *karet*, divine punishment by untimely death. Consequently they were requesting permission from the assembled rabbis to allow use of the newly built bathhouse on the banks of the Rhine although the water pumped into it was technically drawn water (*mayim she'uvim*), instead of *mayim hayim*, the rainwater required by the halakhah.

The rabbis' very serious discussion of the subject is remarkable, refuting the misconception that the Reform movement was opposed to mikveh from the very start.[6] The most conservative among them opposed acceptance of the request, being unwilling to break with a Talmudic interpretation even if there was no explicit biblical basis for it. The radical Rabbi Samuel Holdheim argued that purity laws were anchored in the ancient Temple cult and deserved to be abandoned in the modern age. However, the large majority was not only sympathetic to the Bingen request but spoke up in favor of mikveh. Gotthold Salomon, preacher at the Reform Hamburg Temple, argued that since so many women were neglecting mikveh entirely, it would be better to go against a rabbinic prohibition than to allow the practice to be neglected altogether. One after another, the leading rabbis, Abraham Geiger and David Einhorn among them, argued for the symbolic value of mikveh and indicated their desire to make observance more palatable. Rabbi Abraham Adler proposed that the outer cleansing symbolically represents an inner moral cleansing and went on to suggest that the assembly urgently recommend the immersion of the woman completing her menstrual cycle (*tevilat nidah*) as a religious practice. At bottom, the discussion was less about the halakhic permissibility of easing a stringency (*hakalah*) than about the effect of the experience on those who underwent it. One of the rabbis spoke explicitly of the *Wohlgefühl*, the sense of well-being, that the women visiting an attractive mikveh would experience. In its focus on the subjective aspect of immersion, the Frankfurt meeting laid down a theme that would follow discussion of the issue down to the present.

When the subject of mikveh appeared again in the Reform movement it was not in connection with women's monthly cycle but rather with conversion. The issue of whether both circumcision and immersion should be required of proselytes arose as early as the first meeting of Reform rabbis in the United States, held in Philadelphia in 1869. Although circumcision (*milah*) was the main topic, ritual immersion was also part of the discussion. Whereas milah divided the group, no one present argued against tevilah. The radical David Einhorn cited the position of Rabbi Joshua in the Babylonian Talmud, who maintained that a proselyte who has immersed but not been circumcised was nonetheless a legitimate proselyte.[7] This was a position that Abraham Geiger, in commenting on the Philadelphia conference, fully endorsed.[8] And it seems at the time likewise to have been the position of Einhorn's rival, Rabbi Isaac Mayer Wise.[9] The Reform movement collectively took mikveh seriously once more, this time again in Germany, when at the synod held in Augsburg in 1871 the gathered rabbis and laymen voted unanimously that, in contradiction to the *Shulhan Arukh*, two women—and not two men—should serve as witnesses at the mikveh ritual for female converts.[10]

But then a major shift in attitude occurred. Especially in the United States, the Reform movement increasingly fostered a Judaism that sought to liberate itself from the physical aspects of religion and to focus its attention almost exclusively on worship in the synagogue. Classical Reform Judaism rejected body-related observances as distractions from the true purpose of religion, which was exaltation of the spirit through prayer and commitment to moral deeds. This attitude was notably reflected in the Pittsburgh Platform of 1885 and in the discussions on conversion held by the Central Conference of American Rabbis shortly after its formation. In 1892 the CCAR passed a resolution stating that conversion to Judaism could be effected "without any initiatory rite, ceremony or observance whatever."[11] Some Reform rabbis continued to value tevilah in connection with conversion, notably Bernhard Felsenthal, who believed that for the prospective convert it was a meaningful symbolic act that would prevent "the historical thread from being torn in two in revolutionary fashion."[12] But the majority now favored tenet over tradition: conversion was an act of mind and spirit alone, the verbal rejection of the old faith and the affirmation of the new. Purification of the heart no longer required purification of the body. The resolution of 1892 was incorporated into the manuals for Reform rabbis beginning in 1928 and continued in effect so that, at least in Reform circles, conversions done with neither milah nor tevilah could not be considered illegitimate.[13] It remains the official position even down to the present when it no longer represents the standard practice.

Until well after the Second World War the Reform objection to tevilah remained essentially unchanged. In some circles it gained in virulence, spurred by the influx of eastern European Jews whose *mikva'ot* were no less hygienically and aesthetically repulsive than the mikveh in Bingen. In fact, shortly before the First World War, the New York City Board of Health had noted that as many as three hundred people used a mikveh before the water was changed.[14] Immigrants had discovered bathtubs, which many greatly preferred to the ritually specified but aesthetically unappealing mikveh.[15] At a time when the Reform movement was mostly composed of upwardly mobile German Jews, whose rabbis sought to "raise" Judaism from the imagined primitivism of the immigrants' Orthodoxy, use of the filthy mikveh served as a potent symbol of differentiation. When Orthodox Jews were raising money to build a mikveh in Cincinnati in 1888, the city's recently ordained Classical Reform rabbi, David Philipson, branded it "another face of barbarism" and exploded in his diary: "Oh! The shame of it." With his views unchanged more that forty years later when a similar effort was undertaken, he now wrote to a local newspaper that the mikveh is "entirely foreign to our modern interpretation of Jewish faith and practice."[16] From here it would be a long road to the recovery of mikveh within Reform Judaism.[17] But by the time it was ready for a shift in attitude, Reform could point to parallel quests for new meanings in both modern Orthodoxy and Conservative Judaism.

For Orthodox Jews, the laws of ritual separation (nidah) and mikveh are obligatory. They always have been and remain still, first and foremost, divine commandments. In fact, halakhic literature finds them weightier than even public prayer in the synagogue.[18] Not surprisingly, therefore, Orthodox works on the subject usually focus on the legal requirements and the objective benefits. Thus, for example, in a sixteenth-century Yiddish-language manual for Jewish women in Poland, Rabbi Benjamin Slonik tells his female readers exactly how they are to behave, noting that before going into the water they should pray for pious children, and upon emerging from the mikveh they should make sure that they see first a scholar so that their children will likewise become scholars.[19] A popular nineteenth-century work dwells in precise detail on the divine punishment that a Jewish woman will incur if she fails to observe the laws of ritual purity.[20] And a frequently reprinted late twentieth-century manual issued in America by the Orthodox Union notes that mikveh belongs to the category of Jewish laws (hukim) "for which there is no apparent reason."[21] Recent years have produced an unprecedented outpouring of Orthodox works on the laws of mikveh, no fewer than thirty between 1999 and 2008. These publications, written by men, may, as one commentator suggests, have appeared for the personal reason that halakhic analysis of this topic "speaks to the soul."[22] But whatever the motivation, they are all based on exegesis, without reference to individual experience. Nonetheless, there is also an Orthodox literature that dwells on the subjective dimension of separation between husband and wife during menstruation and the immersion that marks its conclusion. One of the most popular books that does so is Rabbi Norman Lamm's A Hedge of Roses, which affirms the moral value of "family purity," declaring it the "joyous Jewish affirmation of life and the abhorrence of death and suffering" and touting that mikveh "offers the possibility of a magnificent beginning for human life in love with life."[23]

Once Orthodox women began to write of family purity in relation to mikveh, they too had to acknowledge that the practice was rooted in divine commandment, but added—as the men writing on the subject could not—their own specific experiences. Their writing, like that of Jewish women in liberal Jewish circles, had been affected by a significant shift in American feminism. Whereas first-wave feminists tended to focus on the quest to attain equality with men and thus minimized the significance of biological difference, a later wave, which appeared in the 1960s and thereafter came under the influence of Carol Gilligan, dwelt unabashedly on the particular physical qualities of womanhood and the experiential possibilities that it offered.[24] Despite all of the Orthodox stress on modesty, a new cultural climate also allowed and even encouraged the discussion of topics that previously had been relegated to the private space between mother and daughter. Instead of feeling tied to bodies that hindered them from achievements available to men—bodies that in Jewish tradition were governed by laws enforced by men—some observant Jewish women began to see mikveh as a rite that united body and spirit, that was productive of a form of empowerment, and that enabled them symbolically to express the agency that they were increasingly taking for their lives.[25]

Blu Greenberg, long a leading figure among Orthodox Jewish feminists, gave expression as early as 1981 to "an insider's view" of nidah and mikveh, seeking to defend them at a time when the laws of nidah were neglected even by "many who consider themselves Orthodox." It was difficult to overcome the negativity that feminism attributed to the notion of women at any time being impure.[26] As an Orthodox woman, Greenberg affirmed that her foremost reason for observing nidah and mikveh was because they were divine commandments. But to this motivation she added her own feelings: the sense that she was doing what Jewish women have done in the past, the generation of "a different sense of self, a feeling of self-autonomy," and the attachment of "some measure of holiness to a primal urge."[27] Performance of a "woman's mitzvah" could provide entry to a sacred world otherwise dominated by the multiple mitzvot required of men. No doubt these factors have played a role in increasing observance of nidah and mikveh in recent years, though even among the Orthodox there exists great variation regarding the severity of separation during the required twelve days preceding immersion.[28]

For Conservative Jews, whose movement, though officially halakhic, has been increasingly moving away from strict observance, the commandedness of mikveh plays less of a role and meta-halakhic considerations loom larger. Whereas for the Orthodox, subjective meanings are pluses or even rationalizations, for Conservative Judaism the individual factor is what matters most. Like Reform Jews, the vast majority of its members do not observe rituals unless they find personal meaning in them. Yet because Conservative Judaism is more oriented toward tradition than is Reform it possesses a greater inherent attachment to mikveh and the desire to integrate its observance within a flexible halakhah.

The lengthy platform of the Conservative movement, issued in 1988, contains only a brief restrained reference to our subject among other women's rituals: "In recent days, the discussion of the role of women has rekindled interest in some quarters in areas as diverse as *tohorat ha-mishpahah* (the system of family purity) revolving around the use of the *mikveh* (ritual bath), the creation of naming ceremonies for girls and special women's observances of *Rosh Hodesh*."[29] The Conservative movement's standard work on Jewish practice, published a decade earlier, had been far more explicit and directive, devoting two chapters to the stringent observance of the laws of family purity; its more recent guide is likewise descriptive of Orthodox practice.[30] And as early as 1966 Jewish Theological Seminary professor Dov Zlotnick had proposed that "at a time when morals have broken down, when restraint is out of fashion, we should try in some way to make *taharat ha-mishpahah* relevant."[31] Yet monthly use of the mikveh by eligible Conservative-affiliated women has been estimated to be under 10 percent.[32]

What has driven discussion of the subject to the forefront within Conservative Judaism more recently, aside from general cultural factors, has been the ordination of Conservative women rabbis beginning in 1985. Could they take upon themselves the mitzvot previously limited to men, for example *tefilin*, while neglecting one assigned specifically to women? By the 1990s the subject of mikveh was getting considerable attention in the media of Conservative Judaism. Two Conservative women rabbis, both feminists and both observers of the laws of family purity, have played the leading roles. Unlike their Orthodox counterparts, one of them notes that "we do not assume we will observe; we must be convinced to observe." Whereas Orthodox women may complement their adherence to halakhah with personal reasons, for Conservative women the reasons themselves are the "*raisons d'etre* for observance."[33] They are determined to seek their own personal significance within the tradition.

In 2006 Rabbis Susan Grossman and Miriam Berkowitz, along with Rabbi Avram Reisner, submitted responsa to the Rabbinical Assembly's Committee on Jewish Law and Standards, all of which were accepted by a large majority of the committee as legitimate options. While remaining within the tradition to a high degree, the responsa did differ from accepted halakhic theory and practice. The two women rabbis wished to be less strict with regard to physical contact during the period of abstention and chose to reframe the entire subject, substituting for the language of purity and impurity the language of holiness—*kedushat ha-mishpahah* in place of *tohorat ha-mishpahah*. Though generally all three respondents were in agreement, they disagreed with regard to the length of the abstention following menstruation, Berkowitz choosing to retain the full twelve days, but Grossman and Reisner allowing resumption of relations after seven.[34]

By the time the subject was taken up by the Conservative rabbis, interest in mikveh had spread within the movement. Students at the Jewish Theological Seminary were increasingly observing mikveh, and within a period of a few months, beginning in 2001, mikveh received attention in three popular Conservative magazines.[35] One of the writers claimed that Conservative synagogues had built ten new mikva'ot during the previous ten years. For the most part, however, the Conservative mikveh, unlike its Orthodox counterpart, was used with less regularity, serving especially for one-time occasions such as conversion or preceding a wedding.[36] This fundamental shift in relating to mikveh was even more characteristic of the Reform movement.

As late as 1962 a report of the CCAR Committee on the Unaffiliated reiterated that neither circumcision nor ritual bath was required of a potential convert.[37] But that was the last official affirmation of the earlier position. The first indication of a different attitude appeared in an article published in the *Central Conference of American Rabbis Journal* in 1984 but which referred back to an experience of 1967. Rabbi Alan Sokobin of the Reform congregation in Sylvania, Ohio, reported that shortly after the Six-Day War a woman who was seeking conversion and planning to live in Israel underwent immersion under his direction. Her experience overwhelmed not only the woman herself but also Rabbi Sokobin: "What happened at the *mikveh* was one of the more moving and emotionally constructive moments in my life and rabbinate. . . . I witnessed, as never before, a religious experience." Sokobin wrote that he then came to realize that "she, in essence, had to be reborn as a Jew. . . . She had to be baptized out of her Catholicism and into Judaism." Thereafter, Rabbi Sokobin became one of the first twentieth-century Reform rabbis not merely to suggest but to require immersion of all Jews-by-choice.[38] Four years later another rabbi associated with the Reform movement, Herbert Weiner, called for the use of mikveh before conversion, principally because he believed— with too high a measure of optimism—that it would supply a larger measure of legitimacy in Orthodox circles in Israel, but also because at least some of those who participated in the ritual would derive spiritual elevation from the experience.[39]

In the following years the increasing number of converts entering Reform Judaism forced greater attention to the subject. In a 1977 Reform responsum, Rabbi Walter Jacob remarked that tevilah was being encouraged or required for conversion by a number of Reform rabbis and suggested that if it possesses meaning for the community or the individual it should be encouraged, adding that it would make it a bit more difficult for traditionalists to challenge Reform conversions.[40] In the spirit of now taking mikveh more seriously, the Reform rabbinate a year later officially changed its stand. While it did not, and has not since, *required* mikveh preceding conversion, the CCAR Committee on Conversion in 1978, after noting the 1893 decision, adopted the following statement that was subsequently printed both in its guide to the Jewish life cycle and its rabbi's manual: "Nevertheless Reform Judaism recognizes that there are social, psychological, and religious values associated with the traditional initiatory rituals, and it is recommended that the rabbi acquaint prospective *gerim* with the halachic background and rationale for *berit milah, hatafat dam berit* [taking a drop of blood from an already circumcised male convert], and *tevilah*, and offer them the opportunity, if they so desire, to observe these additional rites."[41]

As this new Reform attention to mikveh focused especially upon conversions, its dominant motif came to be the change in status that immersion would bring about. Basing himself on rabbinic texts, Walter Jacob had written that the symbolic purification of mikveh changed the status of the individual involved and added that this symbolism was meaningful to many modern converts in making the transition to Judaism.[42] Shortly thereafter, Professor Michael Chernick of the Hebrew Union College–Jewish Institute of Religion in New York published an article that dwelt on this very point. Downgrading the element of ritual purity, Chernick argued that the basis for mikveh was most fundamentally a change of status, one that for converts "reinforces the sense of new beginnings and changed identity."[43]

By the following decade sentiment in favor of mikveh in the Reform movement had become more intense. In 1995 Rabbi Elyse Goldstein testified to fellow rabbis of the transformative power that mikveh exercised in her own life.[44] A year later a responsum by Rabbi Joan Friedman not only went into great detail on the specifications for a proper mikveh but enumerated "compelling reasons why American Reform Jews should adopt or retain the practice of mikveh for conversion." According to Friedman, the prospective convert's use of the mikveh creates continuity with the Jewish tradition and people, establishes solidarity with Progressive Jews in Israel who insist upon it, and serves as "an important statement of our dedication to *kelal yisrael*, the unity of the Jewish people."[45]

As in Conservative Judaism, so too in Reform, the subject of mikveh eventually broke into the movement's popular media. *Reform Judaism Magazine*, which is distributed to every Reform family, featured affirmative articles in 1995, 1996, 1999, and again in 2008.[46] The official Reform religious school CHAI curriculum now included teaching about mikveh and noted that the practice of tevilah is required for converts "by many, if not most Reform and Reconstructionist rabbis."[47] On the ground, temples began to build mikva'ot on their premises: in West Bloomfield, Michigan, in Scottsdale, Arizona, and in Newtown, Pennsylvania, where its senior rabbi, Elliot Strom, devoted his Rosh Hashanah sermon in 1998 to the subject. In Toronto, where, as in the rest of Canada, Reform converts are required to immerse, a mikveh was built in the basement of the Reform Leo Baeck Day School, and there is a plan afoot to construct one under Reform auspices in Brooklyn.[48] In part, the motivation has been unpleasant experiences at Orthodox mikva'ot, but it has also been a desire to take control. As the Reform movement had earlier begun training its own *mohalim* to bring Jewish boys ritually into the community, so it now sought to bring converts into Judaism under its own auspices. In addition, it was the notion that mikveh belonged to those ritual practices, such as the wearing of head coverings and prayer shawls and the observance of *selihot* and *tashlikh* services, that would tie Reform Judaism more closely to tradition. It now became entirely appropriate that at the biennial conference of the Union for Reform Judaism, held in 2007, there should be a workshop, entitled "Taking the 'Ik' Out of Mikvah." It drew about eighty people, who concluded with a devotional hand-washing ritual symbolizing immersion in the mikveh.[49] Five years later, in 2012, the Central Conference of American Rabbis, meeting in Boston, followed with an evening devoted to a performance of *The Mikveh Monologues*. Produced by Mayyim Hayyim, a popular nondenominational mikveh in Newton, Massachusetts, the keynote program drew more than 250 attendees, a slight majority of them women.[50]

The meanings that Reform Jews now attributed to mikveh varied greatly. When Rabbi Richard Levy suggested, perhaps impishly, that the new platform which, as CCAR president, he was proposing for the Reform movement should include the recommendation of mikveh use "for periodic experiences of purification," the resonance was overwhelmingly negative.[51] Very few Reform Jewish women had chosen then, or have since, to adopt the monthly regimen of nidah and mikveh. The association with impurity set it too strongly against feminist ideology. Yet feminism has played a role in one form of reappropriation: reimagining mikveh as "a wholly female experience," a ritual that women do not take over from men, like kippah and talit, but which is uniquely theirs and connects them with women past and present.[52] While this reinterpretation cut the link to the menstrual cycle, mikveh could be connected to other specifically female celebrations such as *rosh hodesh*, the beginning of a new month, or with appropriate liturgy could serve as a powerful restorative ceremony for the dominantly female trauma of rape.[53] Thus tevilah was separated from nidah, and, for some writers, it had also lost the necessity of connection with the physical mikveh. The experience could be created, at least imperfectly, even in a bathtub or with a pitcher of water.[54]

Even as immersion became a rite that allowed women to express their femininity, it became at the same time more acceptable for liberal Jewish men. Mayyim Hayyim instituted a men's initiative, and it has been estimated that one-fifth of the visitors there are men; in San Raphael, California, Reform congregation Rodef Shalom scheduled a "Men's Mikvah" early on a Sunday morning before the High Holidays.[55]

In Israel interest in mikveh outside Orthodox circles has found expression in the publication of a paperback Hebrew volume devoted to the subject. Edited by four women rabbis affiliated with Progressive Judaism and published by an establishment publisher, *Parashat ha-mayim* explores the subject from many angles.[56] Due to the Chief Rabbinate's insistence that prospective brides immerse and bring a note from a recognized mikveh attendant confirming their menstrual status before an Orthodox rabbi will conduct their weddings, mikveh among non-Orthodox Jews is associated with religious coercion.[57] Moreover, in government-controlled mikva'ot prospective Reform and Conservative converts have been either refused entry or treated very badly. As there is currently only one non-Orthodox mikveh in Israel, at the Conservative Kibbutz Hanaton in the Galilee, nearly all Reform and Conservative immersions take place in open bodies of water; for Israelis the place, the mikveh itself, is less important than the act, the tevilah. At the two Reform kibbutzim in the southern desert, immersion is commonly practiced by a portion of the members in preparation for the High Holidays or for marriage.

However, in Israel, as also in America, a variety of nontraditional occasions for mikveh use have come to the fore. Unique to Israel is immersion of the young man or woman about to enter army service. Becoming more widespread in both countries are occasions that may be divided into celebratory and restorative. The celebratory occasions include b'nai mitzvah, menarche, marriage, significant life anniversaries, recovery from accident, illness, or an operation (among women, often mastectomy or hysterectomy), and receipt of an academic degree. For these occasions and also, following Sephardic tradition, especially before a wedding, the immersion often takes place in a party-like atmosphere among close friends and family, sometimes also accompanied by a joyous liturgy composed especially for the event. The restorative, solemn types of occasion embrace mourning for a loved one, rape, infidelity, divorce, and miscarriage. In both America and Israel it has also become more common for Conservative and Reform rabbinical students, mostly but not only women, to immerse before their ordination as a form of consecration to their new sacred role.

Looking back on the development mikveh has undergone in Reform Judaism, especially in recent decades, one finds perhaps the outstanding example of a Jewish custom that has gone from neglect and even revulsion to enthusiastic affirmation within expanding circles of the same movement. Although the practice has not personally touched the great majority of non-Orthodox, its increased popularity within the context of a Reform Judaism seeking to reattach itself more securely to tradition, speaks to the possibility of finding innovative meanings in an ancient ritual. For those Reform Jews who value mikveh, it has come to represent an acknowledgment of the close tie between body and spirit that an earlier Reform Judaism chose to deny.[58] In keeping with the individualism both of liberal religion and of contemporary society, its observance is not an act of obedience to Jewish law, but rather the quest for an experience that creates a personal religious moment.[59] In the words of Rabbi Elliot Strom, the Reform rediscovery of mikveh has been "a 'kissing' of old and new—like the 'kissing' of rain and tapwater in the *mikveh.*"[60] Or in the words of the editors of *Parashat ha-mayim,* the once despised mikveh has become a *keli ruhani,* a spiritual vessel.[61]

Notes

1. Walter Benjamin, *Illuminations,* ed. with an introduction by Hannah Arendt, trans. H. Zohn (New York, 1969), 51.
2. I have dealt with this subject in general terms in my brief article "Tradition and Modernity Reconsidered," in *The Uses of Tradition: Jewish Continuity in the Modern Era,* ed. J. Wertheimer (New York, 1992), 465–69.
3. I have preferred the spelling *mikveh* over *mikvah.* Both vocalizations can be found in the Bible. For a discussion, see Philologus, "Mikveh Mysteries, Solved," *Forward,* January 18, 2008. Unfortunately, the expression *tohorat ha-mishpahah* is frequently miswritten as *taharat ha-mishpahah.* I have chosen not to alter the spelling or italicization in citations.
4. One contemporary woman, admitting that she keeps neither the dietary laws nor the Sabbath, nonetheless observes "the mitzvah of immersion because it is the only one that seems truly relevant to me. All the others seem outdated" (Varda Polak-Sahm, *The House of Secrets: The Hidden World of the Mikveh,* trans. A. Hartstein Pace [Boston, 2009], 111).
5. "Zuschrift aus Bingen, einige religiöse Anfragen enthaltend," in *Protokolle und Aktenstücke der zweiten Rabbiner-Versammlung abgehalten zu Frankfurt am Main* (Frankfurt am Main, 1845), 219–21.

6. Ibid., 180–89.

7. *The New World of Reform, Containing the Proceedings of the Conference of Reform Rabbis Held in Philadelphia in November 1869*, trans. S. D. Temkin (Bridgeport, Conn., 1974), 73.

8. Geiger wrote that it was incumbent upon the rabbi to make the prospective convert familiar with "the elevated meaning of circumcision; should he decide in favor of it, well and good; if not, let him take the ritual bath and therewith he becomes a Jew" (Abraham Geiger, "Die Versammlung zu Philadelphia," *Jüdische Zeitschrift für Wissenschaft und Leben* 8 [1870]: 27).

9. Wise recalled that early in his American career he had denied an accusation made against him that he had ridiculed the ritual bath, claiming that he "certainly never made sport of religious customs." At the Philadelphia conference Einhorn asserted that Wise in principle agreed with him regarding mikveh in conjunction with the acceptance of proselytes. But when he reported for the CCAR committee dealing with proselytes in 1892, Wise noted that neither the circumcision nor the immersion of proselytes was ordained in the Bible, that both were post-Mishnaic, and that they were to be seen merely as customs rather than canon law. See Isaac Mayer Wise, *Reminiscences*, trans. and ed. D. Philipson (Cincinnati, 1901), 161; *Central Conference of American Rabbis Year Book (CCARYB)* 3 (1893): 93–94.

10. *Verhandlungen der zweiten israelitischen Synode zu Augsburg* (Berlin, 1873), 210–11.

11. *CCARYB* 3 (1893): 94.

12. B[ernhard] Felsenthal, *Zur Proselytenfrage im Judenthum* (Chicago, 1878), 36. Still in 1892 a minority within the CCAR continued to favor the retention of at least tevilah for prospective converts. See *CCARYB* 3 (1893): 73.

13. Central Conference of American Rabbis, *Rabbi's Manual* (Cincinnati, 1952), 153–54.

14. Joshua Hoffman, "The Institution of the *Mikvah* in America," in *Total Immersion: A Mikvah Anthology*, ed. Rivkah Slonim (Northvale, N.J., 1996), 79–80.

15. Herman Wouk, *This Is My God* (New York, 1959), 157. However, Wouk claims as early as 1959 that new ritual pools were being built in many cities, "handsomely tiled, with something like beauty parlors in their anterooms" (158).

16. David Philipson Diary, January 2, 1888, Manuscript Collection 35, American Jewish Archives, Cincinnati; Aaron Rakeffet-Rothkoff, *The Silver Era in American Orthodoxy: Rabbi Eliezer Silver and His Generation* (Jerusalem, 1981), 86.

17. None of 461 Reform rabbis and only 62 of 247 Conservative rabbis surveyed in the early 1950s required converts to undergo ritual immersion. See David Max Eichhorn, "Conversions to Judaism by Reform and Conservative Rabbis," *Jewish Social Studies* 16 (1954): 309.

18. In his paean to the mikveh and guide to its discreet construction within the home, David Miller includes an illustration of a scale. The lighter pan containing an entire synagogue and a kaftan-clad Jew standing in front of it holding a Torah is shown to be outweighed by the religiously heavier mikveh on the scale's opposite pan. See Rabbi David Miller, *The Secret of the Jew: His Life—His Family*, 12th revised edition (Oakland, Calif., 1938), 221.

19. Edward Fram, *My Dear Daughter: Rabbi Benjamin Slonik and the Education of Jewish Women in Sixteenth-Century Poland* (Cincinnati, 2007), 192–98.

20. S[eligmann] B[aer] Bamberger, *Die jüdischen Frauenpflichten*, 2nd ed. (Satoraljaujhely, 1907).

21. Aryeh Kaplan, *Waters of Eden: The Mystery of the Mikvah*, rev. ed. (New York, 1982), 8. Kaplan nonetheless goes on to enumerate a list of benefits provided by nidah and

mikveh, including keeping couples from becoming bored with sex, lowering the divorce rate, and nullification of the ego. He derives spiritual benefits not from personal experience, but from midrashic and mystical Jewish texts, all created by men.

22. Hillel Goldberg, "The Efflorescence of *Mikveh* Studies," *Tradition* 43, no. 3 (2010): 79.

23. Norman Lamm, *A Hedge of Roses: Jewish Insights into Marriage and Married Life* (New York, 1966), 89. The book was reissued in 1980.

24. Gilligan argued the case for separate gender identities, with men aiming at abstract ideals while women sought to cultivate relationships. See Carol Gilligan, *In a Different Voice: Psychological Theory and Women's Development* (Cambridge, Mass., 1982).

25. See, for example, Polak-Sahm, *The House of Secrets*, 96. But a survey of Orthodox women who practiced mikveh also revealed some who regarded it as oppression and others for whom it was an entirely neutral experience. See Naomi Marmon Grumet, "The Voices of *Mikvah* Observance," *To Be a Jewish Woman* 4 (2007): 53–56.

26. See Rachel Adler, "*Tumah* and *Taharah—Mikveh*," in *The Jewish Catalog*, ed. R. Siegel and M. and S. Strassfeld (Philadelphia, 1973), 167–71.

27. Blu Greenberg, "In Defense of the 'Daughters of Israel': Observations on Niddah and Mikveh," *On Women and Judaism: A View from Tradition* (Philadelphia, 1981), 105–23. See also her article "Integrating Mikveh and Modernity," *Sh'ma* 11, no. 205 (January 9, 1981): 37–38, where she suggests a number of reforms including the observance of nidah and mikveh by unmarried sexual partners. Very different in tone is Chana Weisberg's approach to the subject. Avoiding the personal, she dwells on theological meanings, based largely on texts. See her *The Feminine Soul: A Mystical Journey Exploring the Essence of Feminine Spirituality* (Toronto, 2001), 70–104. The most intimate personal account of her experience with mikveh by an Orthodox woman of which I am aware is the preface by Rivkah Slonim to her *Total Immersion*, xiii–xvii.

28. Susan Weidman Schneider, *Jewish and Female: Choices and Changes in Our Lives Today* (New York, 1984), 206; Naomi Marmon, "Reflections on Contemporary *Mikveh* Practice," *Women and Water: Menstruation in Jewish Life and Law*, ed. Rahel R. Wasserfall (Hanover, N.H., 1999), 234; Grumet, "The Voices of *Mikvah* Observance," 56. Radical innovation exists even within the Orthodox community. With the intent of diminishing the gender specific in the mikveh experience, one Orthodox woman has expressed a preference for husband and wife performing the monthly ritual together in an open body of water. See Haviva Ner-David, "Reclaiming *Nidah* and *Mikveh* through Ideological and Practical Interpretation," in *The Passionate Torah: Sex and Judaism*, ed. D. Ruttenberg (New York, 2009), 131–33.

29. *Emet Ve-Emunah: Statement of Principles of Conservative Judaism* (New York, 1988), 47.

30. Isaac Klein, *A Guide to Jewish Religious Practice* (New York, 1979), 509–22; Martin S. Cohen and Michael Katz, eds., *The Observant Life: The Wisdom of Conservative Judaism for Contemporary Jews* (New York, 2012), 273–75.

31. Dov Zlotnick, "Today's *Met Mitzvah*" [originally delivered as a sermon in 1966], in Slonim, *Total Immersion*, 110.

32. Miriam C. Berkowitz, *Taking the Plunge: A Practical and Spiritual Guide to the* Mikveh, 2nd rev. ed. (Jerusalem, 2009), 112. Naomi Malka, who is in charge of the mikveh at Conservative Adas Israel in Washington, D.C., estimates monthly use at Conservative mikva'ot nationally at less than 5 percent, but notes that the percentage is significantly higher at the Adas Israel mikveh thanks to education and outreach. Naomi Malka to Lauren Strauss, private correspondence, November 1, 2012.

33. Susan Grossman, "Feminism, Midrash and Mikveh," *Conservative Judaism* 44, no. 2 (1992): 12.

34. "Mikveh and the Sanctity of Family Relations," Rabbinical Assembly website, www. rabbinicalassembly.org/sites/default/files/public/halakhah/teshuvot/20052010/ mikveh_introduction.pdf (accessed January 23, 2014).

35. Johanna R. Ginsberg, "Dipping into Tradition: The Mikveh Makes a Comeback," *Jewish Theological Seminary Magazine* 10, no. 3 (Spring 2001): 12–13, 19–21; Diana Stevens, "The Growth of the Mikveh Movement," *The United Synagogue Review* (Fall 2001): 17–19; "Two Mikveh Midrashim," *Women's League Outlook* 73, no. 1 (2002): 15.

36. The website for the Conservative mikveh in Wilmette, Illinois, lists monthly use last among the reasons given for which the mikveh, that has "welcomed thousands," is used; http://bhcbe.org/jewish-life/mikvah/ (accessed January 23, 2014). However, at one Conservative congregation a core group participated in a "mikveh club." See Ginsberg, "Dipping into Tradition," 12.

37. Report submitted by Rabbi Joshua O. Haberman, *CCARYB* 72 (1962): 134.

38. Alan Mayor Sokobin, "*Mikveh*: A Personal Remembrance," *Journal of Reform Judaism* (Fall 1984): 50–51. Another Reform rabbi, Henry A. Zoob, recalled similar experiences with converts in the early or mid-seventies. See Union for Reform Judaism, http:// urj.org/archives/torah/ten/eilu/archives/v8w1/ (accessed January 23, 2014).

39. Herbert Weiner, "Conversion: Is Reform Judaism So Right?," *Dimensions in American Judaism* 5, no. 2 (1971): 4–7.

40. "The *Mikveh* and Reform Converts" (December 1977), in Walter Jacob, *Contemporary American Reform Responsa* (New York, 1987), 76.

41. *Gates of Mitzvah: A Guide to the Jewish Life Cycle*, ed. Simeon J. Maslin (New York, 1979), 146; *Rabbi's Manual*, ed. David Polish (New York, 1988), 232. The manual added a paragraph explaining mikveh procedure and noting the permissibility of substituting a natural body of water or a swimming pool "especially when the local *mikveh* is not made available to Reform converts" (233). It also added new prayers for the rabbi and the convert to recite as part of the tevilah ceremony (210–12). The "Guidelines for Rabbis Working with Prospective Gerim," adopted by the CCAR in June 2001, affirm the 1978 resolution and recommend that the rabbi, not the prospective convert, decide on the initiatory rituals. See "Guidelines for Rabbis Working with Prospective Gerim," CCAR: Central Conference of American Rabbis, www. ccarnet.org/rabbis-communities/professional-resources/guidelines-for-rabbis-working-with-prospective-gerim (accessed January 16, 2014).

42. Jacob, "The Mikveh and Reform Converts," 78.

43. Michael Chernick, "*Mikveh*: A Medium for Change of Status," *Journal of Reform Judaism* (Spring 1988): 61–64, esp. 63 and 64 n.4.

44. Elyse Goldstein, "The Mikvah as Spiritual Therapy, *CCAR Journal: A Reform Jewish Quarterly* (Winter/Spring 1995): 33–37.

45. "A 'Proper' Reform Mikveh," CCAR: Central Conference of American Rabbis, www. ccarnet.org/responsa/nyp-no-5756-6/ (accessed January 17, 2014).

46. Beth M. Gilbert, "A Mikveh in Michigan," *Reform Judaism Magazine*, Summer 1995, 68; Jane Solomon [pseud.], "Entering the Mikveh," *Reform Judaism Magazine*, Spring 1996, 29–32; Elliot M. Strom, "A *Mikveh* of Our Own," *Reform Judaism Magazine*, Summer 1999, 79–80; Sue Fishkoff, "Reimagining the Mikveh," *Reform Judaism Magazine*, Fall 2008, 10, 12, 19.

47. *CHAI: Learning for Jewish Life*, Level 5, Lesson 4: "Conversion: Becoming a Part of the Jewish Community" (New York, 2004), 284.

48. Information regarding the plan for a mikveh at Beth Elohim in Park Slope, Brooklyn, received in personal communication from Sara Luria, November 7, 2012.

49. My thanks to Rabbi Sue Ann Wasserman for providing me with material regarding this event.

50. Personal communications from Brian Zimmerman and Deborah Bravo, November 5, 2012, and November 27, 2012. Established in 2004, according to its blog for April 2012, Mayyim Hayyim could by then boast ten thousand immersions.

51. Richard N. Levy, "Ten Principles for Reform Judaism," *Reform Judaism Magazine*, Winter 1998, 15, and the following responses. But family purity has become a meaningful concept for at least a few Reform rabbis. See, for example, Pauline Bebe, "Contemporary Reflection," *The Torah: A Women's Commentary*, ed. T. Cohn Eskenazi and A. L. Weiss (New York, 2007), 652–53; and D. L. Eger, "*Taharat HaMishpachah*: A Renewed Look at the Concept of Family Purity," *CCAR Journal: A Reform Jewish Quarterly* (Fall 2005): 78–83.

52. Elyse M. Goldstein, "Take Back the Waters: A Feminist Re-Appropriation of Mikvah," *Lilith* 15 (Summer 1986): 15–16; Goldstein, in *Half the Kingdom: Seven Jewish Feminists*, ed. F. Zuckerman (Montreal, 1992), 82–83.

53. For the latter, see especially Laura Levitt and Sue Ann Wasserman, "Mikvah Ceremony for Laura (1989)," in *Four Centuries of Jewish Women's Spirituality: A Sourcebook*, ed. E. M. Umansky and D. Ashton (Boston, 1992), 321–26.

54. Emphasis on the act rather than the nature of the body of water receives unusual expression in a Conservative rabbi's suggestion that "if you cannot go to a *mikveh*, you may want to create a water experience in your own bath." See Nina Beth Cardin, *Tears of Sorrow, Seeds of Hope: A Jewish Spiritual Companion for Infertility and Pregnancy Loss*, 2nd ed. (Woodstock, Vt., 2007), 35. A volume devoted to Jewish girls arriving at puberty suggests that they perform a monthly ritual in their bathtubs. See Penina Adelman, Ali Feldman and Shulamit Reinharz, *The JGirl's Guide: The Young Woman's Handbook for Coming of Age* (Woodstock, Vt., 2005), 106–7. Even more distant from the actual mikveh is the suggestion that women celebrating Rosh Hodesh together in a group "take the concept of *mikveh*" and, using any available water, symbolically enact their own "informal *mikveh*." See Penina V. Adelman, *Miriam's Well: Rituals for Jewish Women Around the Year* (Fresh Meadows, N.Y., 1986), 114.

55. "Men," Mayyim Hayyim, www.mayyimhayyim.org/Using-the-Mikveh/Men (accessed January 17, 2014); *Jewish Telegraphic Agency*, June 19, 2006; "Monthly Calendar," Congregation Rolof Sholom, www.rodefsholom.org/general/monthly-calendar (accessed January 17, 2014). For an example of mikveh as a religious experience inclusive of men, see Jay Michaelson, *God in Your Body: Kabbalah, Mindfulness and Embodied Spiritual Practice* (Woodstock, Vt., 2007), 145–153. It has, however, been noted that there are those who say that men's use of the mikveh "detracts from one of the few rituals that are expressly tied to women's own experience." See Schneider, *Jewish and Female*, 212.

56. Alona Lisitsa, Dalia Marx, Maya Leibovich, and Tamar Duvdevani, *Parashat ha-mayim: Tevilah ke-hizdamnut le-tsemihah, le-hitaharut u-le-ripui* (Tel Aviv, 2011).

57. Ibid., 28, 133. This is true even at Ivria, a luxurious spa in Givat Shmuel, which subordinates tevilah as the last among its services. See "About Ivria," Ivria Spa, www.ivria.co.il/en/about.php (accessed January 17, 2014).

58. Undoubtedly New Age thinking has played a role at least for some who have redis-
    covered mikveh. See, for example, the Hebrew essay by Simcha Daniel Burstein in
    Lesitsa et al., *Parashat ha-mayim*, 184–89.
59. See, for example, Vanessa L. Ochs, *Inventing Jewish Ritual* (Philadelphia, 2007), 48–50.
    For some recently surveyed Orthodox women, the subjective experience is likewise
    paramount. See, for example, Polak-Salm, *The House of Secrets*, 100.
60. Strom, "A Mikveh of Our Own," 80.
61. Lesitsa et al., *Parashat ha-mayim*, 31. The Hebrew word *keli* can also be defined as an
    instrument, thereby adding a second appropriate meaning.

10

GERMAN JEWRY AND DUTCH JEWRY

Two Separate Paths to Modernity

STEVEN M. LOWENSTEIN

Throughout his career David Ellenson has been exploring the sociology of developments in Jewish religion and culture and especially the process we generally refer to as modernization. His work covers several countries including Germany, Israel, and the United States and has occasionally touched on other countries, including the Netherlands. In this preliminary study, I would like to explore this modernization process through the comparison of Jewry in two neighboring countries. The parallels and surprising differences help highlight anew the complexities of the modernization process and the impossibility of extrapolating from one country to another. I am happy to honor a longtime friend and colleague in this small way.

The analysis in this article will concentrate on a number of specific and mainly quantitative indications of modernization and integration in German and Dutch Jewry. Among these are religious reform, economic advancement, falling birth rates, neighborhood integration, conversion, and intermarriage. In virtually all these traits, Dutch Jewry differed considerably from German Jewry. Despite the seeming head start of Jewry in the Netherlands in the early modern period, most of the differences in the twentieth century showed Dutch Jews as more traditional than their German counterparts.

In the early modern period the Jewish communities of the Netherlands seemed to be pioneers in moving toward a more modern way of life. With relatively free political conditions, the influence of a more secularly educated Sephardic community, and a society in which free-wheeling commerce found a respectable place, the Jews of the Netherlands seemed to have started out ahead in the process of integrating into general society compared to other northern European Jews. And yet by the end of the nineteenth century and the beginning of the twentieth century, Jewry in the Netherlands seemed less modern, less socially integrated, and less economically successful than their brethren across their eastern border. Although they were clearly *Westjuden* rather than *Ostjuden*, and were certainly quite different from the traditional community of a century earlier, many of their characteristics seemed to be in between those of Jews in Germany and those in eastern Europe.

Both German Jews and Dutch Jews began as part of the same West Ashkenazic cultural continuum. They had similar liturgy, synagogue chants, spoken Yiddish dialects, and holiday customs. Although Jews in the Netherlands absorbed more influences from eastern Europe than did Jews in Germany,[1] their customs were for the most part clearly western European. In some ways they were even further from eastern European practice than German Jews. For instance whereas eastern European Jews waited six hours after eating meat before eating dairy products, and German Jews generally waited three hours, Dutch Jews waited only one hour or 72 minutes.[2] Rabbis moved freely among Germany, eastern Europe, and the Netherlands, and Hebrew and Yiddish books printed in Amsterdam were read throughout the Ashkenazic world.

Political emancipation came to the Jews of the Netherlands much earlier and with less societal dislocation than in Germany. Jews in seventeenth- and eighteenth-century Netherlands did not have equal rights, as some have wrongly imagined, but the political and social limitations on their daily life were far less than in Germany. Whereas most states in Germany limited the numbers of Jewish residents, restricted the Jews to a few occupations, and often did not permit Jews to marry without permission, the Dutch Republic had far fewer restrictions. This may be one of the reasons that Ashkenazic Jews flocked to the Netherlands in the late seventeenth and eighteenth century.[3] Sephardic ("Portuguese") Jews were the founders of modern Jewish life in the Netherlands and remained the majority probably until the end of the seventeenth century. Although the Sephardic percentage of the Jewish population in the Netherlands declined steadily until it reached about 5 percent in the early twentieth century, the place of Sephardim in the Dutch Jewish self-perception far outpaced the actual numbers. As a symbol of the Sephardic cultural presence, the great Portuguese synagogue (*esnoga*) in the center of the old Jewish quarter continued as an impressive monument. There were some Sephardic influences on Dutch Ashkenazic Jewry, such as the pronunciation of "ayin" (as *ng,* for instance in mangariv) or the use of a few Portuguese words and Sephardic culinary items. The Sephardic influence on German Jewry was much subtle than in the Netherlands and focused more on cultural models and historical memories than on concrete remnants of actual Sephardic populations, except in parts of northwest Germany.[4] Escapees from Spain and Portugal did help found a number of Jewish communities in northwest Germany, notably Hamburg and Altona, and although they had some influence on the first Reform Temple in Hamburg, their influence soon waned. Only one small Sephardic house of worship survived into twentieth century Hamburg, while all the others closed down in the nineteenth century or were taken over by Ashkenazim.

In the early nineteenth century, the Jews made up 2 percent of the Dutch population, compared to barely 1 percent in Germany. Outside the Catholic south there were few parts of the Netherlands with under 1 percent Jews and, in 1795, the twenty thousand Jews of Amsterdam were the largest Jewish community in western Europe and made up 10 percent of the city's population. The acquisition of equal political status in the various German states was a long drawn-out process, beginning with Christian von Dohm's theoretical statement in 1781,[5] and ending with the granting of complete legal equality in 1871.[6] Along the way there was seemingly endless discussion and a long period when the various states granted limited and conditional rights dependent on the Jews showing that they were worthy of full equality and ready to become fully German. Though not without its own controversies or expectation of Jewish integration into the majority society and culture, political emancipation of the Dutch Jews was relatively rapid and with few strings attached. First introduced in the wake of the French revolution by the Batavian republic in 1796 and reaffirmed by the Dutch government after the fall of Napoleon in 1814, legal equality was virtually unlimited. That this did not necessarily mean social acceptance or integration will become clear later in this article. But the basic idea that Jews were full citizens was hardly challenged until the 1930s. Although anti-Jewish statements and actions certainly occurred in the Netherlands throughout the nineteenth and early twentieth centuries, political anti-Semitism played virtually no role until the founding of the Nationaal-Socialistische Beweging (NSB) in 1931–32.[7] The important role of political anti-Semitism in Germany from the late 1870s on is too well known to need repetition here. One might therefore expect Jewish integration to have been more thoroughgoing in post-emancipation Dutch society, but this was not the case.

Although Germany is generally viewed as the birthplace of Jewish religious reform, it was Amsterdam that had the first community that made modernizing liturgical changes—Adath Yeshurun or Die neie Kille. In his study of *Melitz Yosher* (1808–9), the Hebrew pamphlet justifying the innovations of the neie Kille, David Ellenson has shown that some of the changes, mainly instituting increased decorum, were the forerunners of later changes in German Jewry.[8] Despite this seeming head start, religious innovation in Dutch Jewry was far slower than in Germany. The relative "lack of progress" in Dutch Jewry was already noticed by the German Jewish press by the 1840s.[9] The militant attack on the Reform rabbinic conferences of the 1840s in Germany found much impetus from the efforts of the Lehren brothers, Amsterdam bankers who helped organize and bankroll the protests. Even relatively moderate innovations such as the introduction of a male choir aroused fierce opposition in parts of Dutch Jewry and led to a split in the Jewish community in Groningen in 1851 and the founding of a breakaway synagogue without a choir.[10] The introduction of Dutch vernacular sermons in the synagogue was delayed in many Netherlands synagogues because German-born rabbis refused to speak anything but German. In the synagogue of Leeuwarden in Friesland, Chief Rabbi Baruch Bendit Dusnus (1811–86) continued to preach in Yiddish until his death, a phenomenon that had disappeared in Germany decades earlier.[11] Eventually Dutch synagogues, like German synagogues, were marked by a great deal of decorum and formality, with rabbis wearing clerical robes and laymen wearing top hats (*hoge hoeden*).[12] The Netherland Orthodox rabbinic seminary was transformed into an institution on the German model, with rabbis receiving a secular education and a modicum of modern scholarly training under the leadership of Polish-born but German-trained chief rabbi Josef Hirsch Duenner (1833–1911), who headed the seminary beginning in 1862. The highly centralized structure of organized Dutch religious life modeled on the Napoleonic French example was certainly typical of modernized western Jewish communities,[13] but it had the effect of impeding religious innovation. With the seminary, a centralized Jewish communal structure, and provincial chief rabbis, the Dutch Jewish community retained an official Orthodox monopoly until the 1920s. All efforts to found Liberal synagogues or other institutions were unsuccessful until then,[14] and the institutional establishment of Dutch Liberal Judaism had to await the arrival of the German Jewish refugees in the 1930s.

The fact that virtually all Dutch synagogues remained Orthodox in their ritual did not preclude the decline of traditional religious practice among many Jews in the Netherlands. But the pattern of nontraditional Jews in the Netherlands did not follow the German (and American) Jewish patterns of liberal denominationalism. Instead, it seemed to be somewhat between the patterns of eastern Europe, where non-Orthodox Jews became secularized and rejected religion altogether, and those of the British Empire, where the majority of Jews rarely attended synagogue but when they did they preferred Orthodox synagogues to liberal ones. Although our evidence on the relative percentage of Jews living Orthodox lives in the Netherlands is more vague than that available for Germany, the estimates are similar for both countries.[15] In both countries it was estimated that, around 1900, 15 percent of the Jews remained traditionally observant.[16] Many Dutch Jews, as indeed many German Jews, who no longer strictly observed the Sabbath, still marked Friday night with a family meal, a white tablecloth, and other festive trappings. Other Dutch Jews, even those who became secularist socialists, retained various types of ethnic identification with the Jewish people.

The economic rise of German Jewry in the second half of the nineteenth century was rapid and dramatic. The German Jews became an overwhelmingly middle-class community, with an average income noticeably higher than the average for the German population. Jews played prominent roles in banking, the textile industry, department stores, wholesale trade, and the free professions. Many of the Jewish poor immigrated to America. The rise in economic status was accompanied by a massive urbanization as small-town German Jews sought opportunity in the larger cities. The shrinking Jewish population in the small towns was less prosperous than urban Jewry but often made a decent living in the dry goods and cattle businesses.

Economic development in the Netherlands went through periods of advance and stagnation. Unlike the German case, the great age of Dutch prosperity took place in the past (the "Golden Age" of the seventeenth century) and was followed by a period of decline. The Dutch economy modernized and became more prosperous during the nineteenth century, but the growth came in fits and starts and often lagged behind that of neighboring countries like Germany and Belgium. Many Dutch Jews became prominent in banking, the diamond industry, textile manufacturing, and department stores, but their influence was not as great as that of Jews in Germany (and it certainly was less of a source of discussion and opposition). The occupational census of 1930, for instance, shows that Jews were overrepresented in commerce and the free professions but much less so than were the Jews in Germany. The 1933 German census counted more than five thousand Jewish physicians and more than three thousand Jewish lawyers, respectively 10.9 percent and 16.3 percent of the total in a country where Jews were a mere 0.8 percent of the population.

By contrast, in the Netherlands the census of 1930 counted only 149 Jewish physicians, 68 Jewish dentists and 141 lawyers (respectively 4.1 percent, 4.5 percent, and 5.0 percent of the total).[17] Dutch Jews were most heavily over-represented in the diamond industry, especially as workers. The relationship between urban and rural Jews in the Netherlands also differed from that in Germany. The Amsterdam Jewish community had contained close to half the country's Jewish population in the eighteenth century, and its percentage increased only slightly over time. There was a tendency toward migration from smaller towns to larger cities among Jews in the Netherlands, but it was not as overwhelming as in Germany, where the Jewish population started out overwhelmingly rural.[18] The remaining rural Jewish population in the Netherlands did bear many similarities to surviving rural Jewry in Germany, especially northwestern and southern Germany, in the predominance of shop-keepers and cattle dealers or butchers.

In a way seemingly unique among western European Jews, Dutch Jewry continued to have a large and noticeable native-born proletariat until the early twentieth century. This was most noticeable in Amsterdam where the old Jewish quarter remained a slum area and where as much as one quarter of the Jewish population worked in the diamond industry, mainly as gem cutters.[19] The Jewish diamond cutters were a relatively well paid and heavily unionized part of the Amsterdam working class. In other western European cities, such as Berlin, Paris, or London, where there were poor Jews working in industry, the poor were overwhelmingly recent eastern European immigrants. In the Netherlands this does not seem to have been the case. Many Dutch-born Jews, including some of Sephardic backgrounds, worked in industry or lived in the slums of the old Jewish quarter. There certainly was a wave of eastern European Jewish immigration to the Netherlands beginning in the 1880s, but it is much harder to measure the numbers of "*Ostjuden*" in the Netherlands compared to eastern European Jews in Germany. Many Jews stopped in Amsterdam on their way to further migration to the United States and other countries. More generous Dutch naturalization practices meant that many immigrants became Dutch citizens and were no longer counted separately. The figures from the 1941 Dutch census stated that 84.3 percent of "full Jews" were Dutch nationals, 10.3 percent were German nationals, and only 5.4 percent were of other (mainly eastern European or stateless) nationalities. An unpublished German report based on this census said that 15.1 percent of Jews in the Netherlands were born abroad; 8,257 had arrived before January 30, 1933, and 15,992 after the Nazis took power in Germany. The vast majority of those arriving after 1933 came from Germany or Austria. Some 3,509 foreign Jews had acquired Dutch citizenship, most of them of German origin, but perhaps 800–900 of eastern European origin.[20] According to one report, the eastern European Jewish community in Amsterdam numbered only 600 families in 1931.[21] The German census of 1933 counted 19.8 percent of the Jewish population as holding foreign citizenship and 14.7 percent as being born abroad, mainly in eastern Europe.[22] This was a considerably higher percentage of eastern European immigrants than that found in the Netherlands.

The relationship between urban and rural Jewry (in the Netherlands, spoken in terms of "Mokum" [Amsterdam] and "Mediene" [the provinces]) was somewhat different between Germany and the Netherlands. The predominance of Berlin Jewry in Germany developed progressively from small beginnings and was never as total as the predominance of Amsterdam Jewry in the Netherlands. There was some similarity between the image of rural Jewry as the site of a more traditional lifestyle than in the secular metropolis in both countries,[23] but there were differences as well. While Berlin, too, had pockets of traditionalism, it was not the center of the centralized Orthodox establishment that Amsterdam was. Amsterdam was the site of the Nederlands Israelitisch Seminarium, the Nederlands Israelitisch Kerkgenootschap, and most of the Dutch Jewish press. Its synagogues were run on strictly Orthodox lines throughout the nineteenth century, and kosher food and other traditional necessities were easily available. It was also the center of a relatively segregated Jewish ethnic life to a degree much beyond that of Berlin or any major German city.

Both German and Dutch urban Jewish communities exhibited a degree of voluntary residential segregation far greater than the segregation among the Christian denominations. But the degree of segregation in Amsterdam far exceeded that of German cities. In Germany in the late nineteenth and early twentieth centuries, the index of dissimilarity between Jews and the general population ranged between 35 and 45 percent.[24] This meant that 35 to 45 percent of the Jewish population would have to relocate in order to duplicate the general population's residential pattern. An analysis of the Amsterdam census of 1920 shows a Jewish index of dissimilarity of 61.9 percent between the Ashkenazic Jews and the total population. By the time of the Nazi census of 1941 the index had declined to the still very high 54.6 percent. In both censuses there were a number of districts with a Jewish majority and, in 1920, 3 of 99 districts were over 90 percent Jewish, 4 others between 70 and 90 percent,

1 more between 50 and 70 percent, and 5 between 30 and 50 percent Jewish. Jews made up just under 10 percent of the overall population of the city in 1920. The original Jewish district in the eastern part of central Amsterdam continued to be known officially as the Jodenbuurt. From this mainly slum area, the Jewish population spread out first to the east in the Plantage area, then to the southeast in the Transvaalbuurt, and finally to the south to the modern and middle class Rivierenbuurt (where many German Jewish refugees also settled in the 1930s). In 1941 some 13,750 Jews lived in the old Jewish quarter or Plantage area (districts 9–10), 11,100 in the Transvaalbuurt (district 38), and 24,400 in the Rivierenbuurt (districts 27, 31–33). Together, these seven districts had 57.4 percent of Amsterdam's Jewish population, 13.1 percent of the overall city population, and 8.1 percent of the non-Jewish population.[25]

The residential segregation of the Jews was part of a larger pattern of segmentation (*verzuiling*) in the society of the Netherlands. Before World War II, Dutch society was divided into four main segments or pillars: Protestant, Catholic, liberal, and socialist. Each group had its own political parties, newspapers, youth movements, hospitals, and social networks. There was relatively little social mixing between the groups, although they worked together in their occupations and official duties. All were equal citizens before the law, but there was little expectation that they would mix socially or give up their distinctive views and lifestyles. Although the Jews were too small a group to form their own separate segment, this pattern of communal life put less pressure on the Jews to give up their distinctiveness totally. They could keep a degree of their own uniqueness without being thought of as "un-Dutch." In general Jews felt most comfortable with fellow citizens of the liberal and socialist "pillars." Although a rudimentary division also existed in Germany between Protestant, Catholic, and socialist subcultures, it was never accepted as natural as it was in the Netherlands. Jews in the Netherlands certainly did adapt to the general population in terms of language, dress and forms of socialization, but they did so more slowly than in other western countries.

The segmentation of Dutch society is probably one of the factors explaining the lesser degree of intermarriage and conversion in the Netherlands as compared to Germany. Both phenomena gradually increased in the Netherlands as in Germany, but here too Dutch Jewry lagged behind. The intermarriage rate in Amsterdam was 5.0 percent between 1898 and 1908, 10.8 percent between 1913 and 1917, and 13.2 percent between 1926 and 1927. This contrasts with overall rates for Germany of 7.9 percent in 1901–4, 12.0 percent in 1910–11, and 21.3 percent in 1927.[26] German Jewry was marked by sharp regional differences in intermarriage rates, with 1926/27 figures ranging from 28.8 percent in Hamburg and 24.5 percent in Berlin to 14.0 percent in Frankfurt and 10.3 percent in the former grand duchy of Hessen. Less is known about regional differences in intermarriage in the Netherlands since there are few figures from outside Amsterdam. The 1941 census of the occupied Netherlands gives much indirect evidence based on the relative number of "full Jews" as compared to "half Jews" and "quarter Jews," the latter being the offspring of mixed marriages in the previous generations. Overall, 87.4 percent of persons of Jewish origin counted in the census were full Jews, as against 9.1 percent half Jews and 3.6 percent quarter Jews. The percentage of persons of mixed origin was lowest in Amsterdam, where half Jews were only 6.2 percent and quarter Jews 1.7 percent of those counted (see table 1). The second- and third-largest Jewish communities—the Hague and Rotterdam—had considerably higher percentages of partially Jewish persons. Most other parts of the country had figures in between those of the three largest cities. Nazi officials were quite surprised at the results of the Dutch census of 1941, which showed a much smaller percentage of persons of mixed origin than had the German census of 1939 (see table 2) (12.6 percent in the Netherlands as against 25.4 percent in Greater Germany).

Until the beginning of the twentieth century, only a tiny part of the population in either the Netherlands or Germany failed to register as a member of a religious denomination. Thereafter, the number of those without a denomination increased rapidly especially in the Netherlands. In the 1920 Netherlands census, 7.8 percent of the population declared itself as being without religion, and this increased to 14.42 percent by 1930. By contrast, only 1.8 percent of the population in the 1925 German census declared itself without religion, which increased only to 3.7 percent by 1933.[27] Being religiously unaffiliated seems to have been more acceptable and widespread in the Netherlands than in Germany in the early twentieth century. This tendency away from formal religious affiliation also became ever more common among Jews who left the Jewish communal fold. The numbers of Jews converting to Christianity declined sharply in Germany after the 1896–1905 period,[28] but the numbers disaffiliating from the Jewish community continued to grow. The evidence of the Nazi censuses of 1939 in Germany and 1941 in the Netherlands shows that the decision of ex-Jews to become unaffiliated rather than Christian was even more common in the Netherlands than in Germany. In "Greater Germany" some 33,132 (10 percent) of the 330,539 persons registered as "un-mixed" Jews by race were not registered as members of the Jewish religious community. Of these, 24,163 were members of a Christian denomination, and 8,969 (27.1 percent) were in one of the nonaffiliated categories.[29] In the Dutch figures the percentage of "full Jews" who were not registered with a Jewish community was virtually the same as in Germany (10.3 percent). But of the 14,486 Dutch "full Jews" not registered with the Jewish community, only 1,915 were listed as Christian, and 12,571 (86.8 percent) were listed as without religious affiliation. Even among half and quarter Jews registered, about 60 percent were registered as without affiliation.[30]

In other demographic characteristics Dutch Jews resembled German and other Western European Jews but sometimes seemed to have somewhat more traditional characteristics. They share the pattern of late marriage with German Jews and with other western European Christians and Jews, in contradistinction to what we at least assume was a traditional Jewish pattern of early marriage. In early nineteenth-century Germany, Jewish late marriage was exacerbated by government marriage laws that pushed Jewish marriage ages to unusually high numbers, especially in southern Germany.[31] Even after the repeal of restrictions on Jewish marriage, German Jews tended to marry later than Christians. In 1925 the median age of marriage among German Jewish men was about thirty, and for women about twenty-six. Statistics from Amsterdam in the early twentieth century show little difference in marriage age of Jews and non-Jews. For example, 37.2 percent of Jewish men who married in 1909–11 and 47.1 percent of Jewish women had not yet reached their twenty-fifth birthday. Comparative figures for non-Jews were 33.9 percent and 51.1 percent.[32]

Another nontraditional demographic characteristic, which, unlike late marriage, developed fairly swiftly in the late nineteenth century, was the decline of both mortality and fertility. The latter at least seems to go hand in hand with an abandonment of traditional religious attitudes toward family planning. The sharp decline in birthrates occurred in both German and Dutch Jewry earlier than among non-Jews. However, in the Netherlands, where non-Jewish fertility declined more slowly than in Germany, Jewish birthrates remained higher than they were in Germany.

In Germany, Jewish birthrates declined earlier than those of non-Jews and declined in a fairly uniform way all over the land. In Prussia, for instance, the crude Jewish birth rate declined from 32.26 per thousand in 1875–79 to 16.55 per thousand in 1905–9.[33] The overall birth rate in the Netherlands continued to be high long after the decline of the general birth rate in Germany despite a rapidly declining death rate.[34] In 1900–1903 the Jewish birthrate per thousand in Amsterdam ranged between 23.55 and 25.23, compared to 31.52 to 33.15 for Protestants and 33.33 to 35.44 for Catholics. The Jewish rate was still considerably higher than the rate among German Jews: in the same decade it was 16.55 in Prussia, 18.1 in Bavaria, 18.66 in Hesse-Darmstadt, and 15.2 in Hamburg.[35]

In most of the social characteristics outlined in this article, Jews in Germany and the Netherlands differed in ways that reflected the general differences between Dutch and German society. Some writers on Dutch Jewry writing in Dutch, beginning with Sigmund Seeligmann in 1923,[36] have postulated the existence of a uniquely Dutch Jewish type (positively valued), which they called Species Hollandia Judaica, characterized by a high degree of adaptation to their Dutch homeland and a distance from the Jews of other countries. The original idea behind this ideal type was that Dutch Jews were better integrated into their country than Jews in other countries. Many of the traits described in this article give a contrary picture, showing a Dutch Jewish community retaining quite a bit of social separateness. Other images associated with the Species Hollandia Judaica, like formality (top hats, decorous religious services, a high degree of patriotism), would seem to apply to many other western European Jews, most especially German Jews. In a long article in the Dutch Jewish newspaper *Nieuw Israelietisch Weekblad* for Hanukkah 1965, Jozeph Michman criticizes the idea of the "Species," especially Seeligmann's claim that Dutch Jews were never cut off from general culture and did not need emancipation to become equal members of society. He sees elements tying Dutch Jewry to world Jewry (like the presence of foreign-born rabbis or the importance of Zionism) as well as specifically Dutch Jewish characteristics. But he sees the specifically Dutch characteristics as no different from the acculturation of Jews to the local and national culture in other Western countries. The special characteristics of Dutch Jewry do not make it sui generis, but simply put it along a continuum of forms of Jewish integration influenced by specific local political, social, cultural, and economic conditions. Further research will be needed to see to what extent Dutch Jewry itself had a uniform character and to what extent it varied internally from province to province and town to town. What is clear from the Dutch example is that the German model of Jewish modernization is not the only model and that each country and region had its own way of balancing the various forces of modernization and tradition, integration and separate identity.[37]

Table 1. Full Jews and Partial Jews in the Dutch Census of 1941 by Region

	Full Jews	Half Jews	Quarter Jews	Total
Amsterdam	79,497 (92.1%)	5,359 (6.2%)	1,435 (1.7%)	86,291
Overijssel	4,286 (89.9%)	315 (6.6%)	167 (3.5%)	4,768
Drenthe	1,394 (88.7%)	73 (4.6%)	104 (6.6%)	1,571
Gelderland	6,537 (88.0%)	638 (8.6%)	255 (3.4%)	7,430
Groningen	4,816 (85.8%)	25 (7.5%)	373 (6.6%)	5,614
Limburg	1,340 (85.6%)	175 (11.2%)	50 (5.2%)	1,565
Friesland	854 (85.1%)	83 (8.3%)	67 (6.7%)	1,004
Hague	13,862 (80.6%)	2,272 (13.2%)	1,058 (6.2%)	17,192
North Holland outside Amsterdam	7,305 (80.4%)	1,300 (14.3%)	485 (5.3%)	9,090
Nord Brabant	2,231 (80.1%)	367 (13.2%)	188 (6.7%)	2,786
Utrecht	3,796 (79.9%)	640 (13.5%)	313 (6.6%)	4,749
Rotterdam	8,368 (76.0%)	1,871 (17.0%)	767 (7.0%)	11,006
South Holland outside the Hague and Rotterdam	2,613 (73.5%)	624 (17.6%)	318 (8.9%)	3,555
Zeeland	157 (61.3%)	57 (22.2%)	42 (16.4%)	256
TOTAL*	137,056 (87.4%)	14,199 (9.1%)	5,622 (3.6%)	156,877

Table 2. Full Jews, Half Jews, and Quarter Jews in Germany and the Netherlands

	Full Jews	Half Jews	Quarter Jews
Greater Germany (1939)	330,539 (74.6%)	71,126 (16.1%)	41,456 (9.4%)
Germany within 1933 borders (1939)	233,094 (73.5%)	51,756 (16.3%)	32,478 (10.2%)
Netherlands (1941)	137,056 (87.4%)	14,199 (9.1%)	5,622 (3.6%)

Notes

1. They said *challe* rather than *berches* or *datscher* for Sabbath bread, did not use illustrated Torah binders (wimpels), and used the pronouns *maan, daan, zaan* like Polish Jews instead of *mayn, dayn, zayn* like German Jews.
2. Other western rather than eastern traits were to be found in the liturgy and liturgical music, the basic premodern Yiddish dialects, and many shared foods and proverbs. See, for instance, Hartog Beem, *Jerosche: Jiddische spreekwoorden en zegswijzen uit het nederlandse taalgebied* 2nd ed. (Amstelveen, 1998), 11–15, where it is remarked that the Yiddish dialect of the Netherlands resembled that of northwestern Germany. Like German Jews, Dutch Jews said *oren* (to pray) and *shalet* (a Sabbath food) as against eastern European Yiddish *davenen* and *cholnt*.
3. Despite the widespread impression that Sephardic Jews were dominant in Dutch Jewry, Ashkenazic Jews became the majority by the eighteenth century. In the 1930 census of the Netherlands, there were 106,723 Ashkenazic Jews and only 5,194 Portuguese (Sephardic) Jews
4. See for instance Ismar Schorsch, "The Myth of Sephardic Supremacy," *Yearbook of the Leo Baeck Institute* 34 (1989): 47–66.
5. Christian Wilhelm von Dohm, *Über die bürgerliche Verbesserung der Juden* (Berlin-Stettin, 1781).
6. For a summary of the German process of emancipation of the Jews, see Ernst Hamburger, "One Hundred Years of Emancipation," *Leo Baeck Institute Yearbook* 14 (1969): 3–66.
7. And even the NSB admitted Jewish members until about 1937.
8. David Ellenson, "Emancipation and the Directions of Modern Judaism: The Lessons of *Melitz Yosher*," reprinted in in Ellenson, *After Emancipation: Jewish Religious Response to Modernity* (Cincinnati, 2004), 99–120.
9. Thomas Kollatz, "Fascination and Discomfort: The Ambivalent Picture of the Netherlands in the German Jewish Press in the 1830s and 1840s," *Studia Rosenthaliana* 32, no. 1 (1998): 43–66; Judith Frishman, "Gij, Vromen, zijt Nederlanders! Gij, onverschilligen, zijt Israelieten! Religious Reform and Its Opposition in the Mid-Nineteenth Century in the Netherlands," *Studia Rosenthaliana* 30, no. 1 (1996): 137–50.
10. Stefan van der Poel, *Joodse Stadjers; de joodse gemeenschap in de stad Groningen, 1796–1945* (Groningen, 2004), chap. 4.
11. Tehilah van Luit, *Mediene Remnants: Yiddish Sources in the Netherlands Outside of Amsterdam* (Leiden, 2009), xvii–xxii, discusses survivals of Yiddish in the nineteenth-century Netherlands, including in sermons. It mentions Hartog Beem's information on Rabbi Dusnus's use of Yiddish in sermons until the 1880s but states this must be based on oral testimony since there is no written record of the sermons. There is little evidence of rabbis in nineteenth-century Germany purposely using Yiddish in their sermons, but there is evidence of the inability of many older rabbis to speak proper German in the second quarter of the nineteenth century (see, e.g., Steven Lowenstein, "The 1840s and the Creation of the German-Jewish Religious Reform Movement," in *The Mechanics of Change: Essays in the Social History of German Jewry* (Atlanta, 1992), 85–131, esp. nn. 30, 32. Aron Hirsch Heymann's memoirs recall in detail the Yiddish or Yiddish mixed with German sermons of Rabbis Jakob Joseph Oettinger (1780–1860) and E. Rosenstein in Berlin in the 1830s and 1840s (Monika Richarz, *Jüdisches Leben in Deutschland: Selbstzeugnisse zur Sozialgeschichte 1780–1871*

[Stuttgart, 1976], 224–26). I know of no discussion of Yiddish sermons in Germany in the second half of the nineteenth century.

12. The early nineteenth-century Dutch Jewish leadership often adopted Christian terminology for Jewish institutions parallel to those favored by German Jewish leaders of the time. In Germany rabbis were often referred to as *Prediger* (preachers) or *Geistliche* (clergy), Passover was called Ostern (Easter), and even the term *Kirche* (church) was sometimes applied to Jewish religious institutions. Such extremes tended to disappear in Germany by the late nineteenth century. It is curious that they continued in generally traditional Dutch Jewry, and that the term *Kerkgenootschap* (church community) was used by the Orthodox Jewish leadership throughout the twentieth century and even today with seemingly little discomfort.

13. A systematic comparison of the communal structure of German and Dutch Jewry goes beyond the scope of this article. However, a few comparative observations are in order. Both countries shared the general concept of an officially recognized community in each town that administered Jewish institutions in that locality, but the details varied over time and place. In both countries, the government intervened at times to regulate the administrative structure of the religious communities and in some cases provided subsidies for some of their activities. In Germany, which underwent unification only in 1871, the individual states continued to have differing regulations on religion. Some (mainly smaller) states like Baden and Württemberg had centralized consistories and district rabbinates, while some like Prussia recognized no structure above the local community. In the Netherlands a central structure was in place throughout the country, with most of its administrators located in Amsterdam. Attempts in Germany to create umbrella organizations that united all German Jewry were based on the voluntary adherence by individual communities and were limited in their influence. Nationwide organizations were created mainly as a response to anti-Semitic challenges (the Central Verein in 1893 and the Reichsvertretung der deutschen Juden in 1933) and generally did not interfere in the operation of the individual religious communities. The German situation was also complicated by the existence of rival ideological organizations (Orthodox, Liberal, and Zionist) that competed for control of the local communities and resisted the aims of rival groups to gain dominance. Ideologically contested elections for local Jewish communal administrations, which were common in Germany, do not seem to have been prominent in the pre–World War II Netherlands.

14. The attempt by Isaac Löb Chronik, a radical reform rabbi who later moved to the United States, to found a Liberal Jewish community was repulsed by Orthodox violence in 1859. See Frishman, Gij Vromen zijt Nederlanders," 147–49; Chaya Brasz, "Dutch Jewry and Its Undesired German Rabbinate," *Leo Baeck Institute Year Book* 57 (2012). The master's thesis of Lisbeth Schimmel, "Towards a Future of Sincerity and Harmony: Dutch Jews and the Appeal of Reform Judaism" (University of Utrecht, 2007), deals with the delayed beginnings of Reform Judaism in the Netherlands in detail.

15. In Germany ideological elections for community leadership give us one clue as to the relative strengths of the religious parties, as does information on the affiliations of rabbis hired in various communities. Such evidence seems absent in the Netherlands.

16. Chaya Brasz, "Dutch Jewry and Its Undesired German Rabbinate," *Leo Baeck Institute Year Book* 57 (2012): 83.

17. Volkstellingen 1795–1971, www.volkstellingen.nl/nl/volkstelling/imageview/ BRT193007S3/index.html (accessed February 10, 2014), beroepentelling, 673–77.

18. The percentage of Jews in the Netherlands in cities of more than a hundred thousand inhabitants increased from 55.83 percent in 1849 to 76.65 percent in 1920, while the percentage in towns with fewer than twenty thousand fell from 30.91 percent to 11.63 percent (E. Broekman, "De Verspreiding der Joden over Nederland," reprinted in *De Vrijdagavond*, April 9, 16, 23, 30, and May 7, 1926, table VIII). By comparison, the approximate percentage of Jews in Germany in cities of more than a hundred thousand went from 7.7 percent in 1852 to 66.8 percent in 1925, while those in towns with fewer than twenty thousand fell from 83.8 to 20.8 percent.

19. "Berufsgliederung der jüdischen und nichtjüdischen Bevölkerung Amsterdams," *Zeitschrift für Demographie und Statistik der Juden* (hereafter ZDSJ), September 1911, 136, shows 26.77 percent of Jews and 2.95 percent of non-Jews employed in the diamond industry. The Dutch occupational census of 1930 counted 3.483 Jewish men (55.4 percent) and 491 Jewish women (76.3 percent) in the diamond industry out of a total of 6,276 and 643 respectively in all of the country . Jews were 87 of 132 of the owners of diamond firms.

20. Document 491, Rapport over Joden in Nederland met statistieken (6 tabellen) over de aantalen Nederlandse Joden en Joden afkomstig uit andere Europese landen in 1941, Centrum voor Holocaust en genocide studies, www.archieven.nl/nl/zoeke n?mivast=0&mizig=262&miadt=966&milang=nl&mizk_alle=rapport%20joden%20 statistieken%201941&miview=lst (accessed March 3, 2014).

21. Leo Fuks, "East European Jews in the Netherlands," in *Aspects of Jewish Life in the Netherlands: A Selection from the Writings of Leo Fuks*, ed. Renate G. Fuks-Mansfeld (Assen, 1995), 206.

22. *Statistisches Reichsamt, Volkszählung: Die Bevölkerung des Deutschen Reichs nach den Ergebnissen der Volkszählung 1933* (Berlin, 1936), 5:49.

23. Jozeph Michman,"Centrum en Periferie: Amsterdam's omstreden positie als centrum van joods Nederland," *Studia Rosenthaliana* 19, no. 2 (1985): 203–20. Michman quotes a humorous limerick illustrating one view of the contrast of rural and urban Jews: "Een parnes, een slager in Meppel / Had een zoon, een student genaamd Seppel. / Als Seppel leefde in Amsterdam / At hij broodjes met ham, / Maar in Meppel droeg Seppel een keppel" (A Jewish leader, a butcher in Meppel [a small town] / had a son, a student named Seppel / When Seppel lived in Amsterdam / he ate sandwiches of ham / but Seppel wore a kippa in Meppel).

24. Steven M. Lowenstein, "Jewish Residential Concentration in Post-Emancipation, Germany," *Leo Baeck Institute Year Book* 28 (1983): 471–95, esp. 482, 485, 491.

25. "De bevolking van elke buurtcombinatie bij de volkstelling van 1930 naar kerkelijke gezindte en het geslacht," from *De Bevolking van Amsterdam, deel II. De uitkomsten der tienjaarlijksche volkstellingen van 1830 to 1930* (Amsterdam, 1934), Downloaded from www.amsterdamhistorie.nl/buurtcombinaties_1930.religie.xls (accessed January 18, 2014). Data on neighborhood composition by religion in 1941 can be found at www.amsterdamhistorie.nl/de joodsche bevolking in de verschillende wijken der Gemeente (Mei 1941), table 78 1941, www.amsterdamhistorie.nl/bestanden/ religie/joden1941.xls (accessed February 10, 2014).

26. *Zeitschrift für Demographie und Statistik der Juden*, October 1930, 54.

27. *Statistik des deutschen Reichs*, Band 401, II: *Die Bevölkerung des deutschen Reich nach den Egebnisse der Volkszählung 1925, Teil II Textliche Darstellung der Ergebnisse*, 601–3. *Statistisches Reichsamt, Volkszählung* 3 (1933): 5.

28. *Statistisches Reichsamt, Volkszählung* 5 (1933): 8.

29. Those three categories were Gottgläubig, Glaubenslos or ohne Angabe.

30. According to Jozeph Michman, one half of the baptized Jews in the Netherlands in 1941 were German nationals. See Jozeph Michman, "Ideological Historiography," in *Dutch Jews as Perceived by Themselves and by Others*, ed. Chaya Brasz and Yosef Kaplan, Proceedings of the Eighth International Symposium on the History of the Jews in the Netherlands (Leiden, 2000), 211.

31. Between 1836 and 1845 the average age of Jews marrying for the first time in a sample of Mittelfranken (Bavarian) towns was 34.8 for men and 31.1 for women (Steven Lowenstein "Voluntary and Involuntary Limitation of Fertility in Nineteenth-Century Bavarian Jewry," in Lowenstein, *The Mechanics of Change*, 71). For a broader discussion of Jewish marriage age in Germany and elsewhere, see Steven Lowenstein, "Ashkenazic Jewry and the European Marriage Pattern: A Preliminary Survey of Jewish Marriage Age," *Jewish History* 8, no. 1–2 (1994): 155–75.

32. Recalculated figures from "Amsterdam: Das Alter der jüdischen eheschliessenden Personen in den Jahren 1909, 1910, 1911," *ZDSJ*, June 1914, 94.

33. Heinrich Silbergleit, *Die Bevölkerungs- und Berufsverhältnisse der Juden im Deutschen Reich*, vol. 1, *Freistaat Preussen* (Berlin, 1930), 14*–15*.

34. Michael Wintle, *An Economic and Social History of the Netherlands, 1800–1920: Demographic, Economic and Social Transition* (Cambridge, 2004). 7–38.

35. "Die jüdische Bevölkerung in Amsterdam," *ZDSJ*, July 1906, 98.

36. Seeligmann was himself a German-born Jew.

37. This is part of the argument of Todd Endelman, "The Englishness of Jewish Modernity in England," in *Toward Modernity: The European Jewish Model*, ed. Jacob Katz, 225–46 (New Brunswick, N.J., 1986).

11

ZIONISM, AMERICAN JEWRY, AND THE "NEGATION OF DIASPORA"

ARNOLD EISEN

Introducing a set of his collected essays called "The Dialectics of Modern Jewish Religion and Identity," David Ellenson makes the point, that "Judaism, like all religions . . . is fundamentally a history of interpretations. Each generation in the chain of tradition links itself in multiple ways to the past and, in so doing, opens various portals to the future."[1] The same holds true for any tradition, whether religious, artistic, literary, scientific, or ideological; Zionism too, therefore, should be viewed as a tradition, ever subject to diverse offshoots and surprising interpretations. The Zionist tradition is complicated by the fact that it began and continues both as *challenge* to inherited forms of the tradition we call Judaism and as claim to be the *authentic continuation* of that tradition.

Ellenson's work on the intersection of Judaism and Zionism, against the background of the encounter with modern societies, cultures, and politics, has focused in part on sermons about Zion and Zionism delivered by American rabbis in the 1940s and on the place of Israel in liberal Jewish liturgies in North America.[2] Both pieces demonstrate that American Jews—or at least their rabbis and liturgies—have tended to present Zionism "in religious and moralistic terms," downplaying or even rejecting ethnic, national, and secular elements. In summarizing his view, Ellenson has observed: "Universalism informs and animates this vision of the Jewish State, a vision that is highly consonant with the American and Diasporan context that inspired it."[3] The liberal rabbis examined by Ellenson, we might say, had adapted Judaism in ways that made it consonant in their eyes with the utterly new conditions they faced in America—and then adapted Zionism to suit that new form of Judaism.

"Modernity" has of course called forth many other adaptations of Judaism in the course of the past few centuries—and many other forms of Zionism. Some Israeli Zionist thinkers, at the polar opposite of the ideological spectrum from liberal American rabbis and liturgies, have engaged—and continue to engage—in the practice known in Zionist thinking as "shelilat ha-golah," negation of the Diaspora. My focus in this essay will be one such thinker, the novelist and essayist A. B. Yehoshua, whose work has often been dismissed by critics because of its stridency and overtly polemical character. I shall argue that, far from being idiosyncratic, Yehoshua's attack on Diaspora carries forward a polemic at the heart of the school of thought known as political Zionism. Moreover, on the matter of Diaspora negation, more than any other, virtually all Zionist theorists and activists have agreed in one way or another—from the very start of the movement almost until the present day, and no matter whether those theorists and activists were religious or secular, socialist or revisionist—that *galut* (exile) and *golah* (a word connoting both exile and Diaspora in Zionist usage) must be opposed, contemned, denied legitimacy, and speedily brought to an end, in short, "negated." Diaspora Jews, according to standard Zionist analysis, were and are doomed to suffer assimilation or anti-Semitism, or both. Indeed, Zionists of all streams have not only agreed on this matter but have repeatedly remarked on that agreement. In recent years, Zionist thinkers and intellectuals across a broad spectrum have attacked American Jewry for its preference for the universal over the particular, its apparent pursuit of personal meaning at the expense of collective Jewish needs, and its lack of sustained attention to the forces undermining Diaspora existence.

In this essay, I will reflect on the reasons for that critique, which in many corners of Zionist ideology continues unabated. I shall examine the dilemmas that Diaspora (especially American) Jewry have posed for Zionist (especially Israeli) theorists and polemicists, and I shall argue that the opprobrium in which the Diaspora has long been held in Zionist thought points to problems for Diaspora and Israeli existence alike. The issue merits careful scrutiny, I believe, despite the exaggeration and oversimplification that often characterize Zionist statements on this matter. I believe that extreme statements, such as those offered by Yehoshua, bring to the surface viewpoints that are more widely—and sometimes more subtly—held. When spokespeople for nearly half the Jewish world routinely charge that the "hyphenated identity" of the other half lacks both authenticity and viability,[4] this challenge—directed most often at Diaspora existence in America—deserves a serious hearing. I find the challenge both profound and troubling. American Jews, I believe, ignore it at our peril.

A. B. Yehoshua's Negation of Diaspora

A. B. Yehoshua, long a critic of Diaspora Jewry, presented his most recent critique of American Jews at a banquet celebrating the hundredth anniversary of the American Jewish Committee. In its early years, that venerable organization was proudly anti-Zionist, a stance that began to change in the early years of Israeli statehood when the AJC's president, Jacob Blaustein, reached a historic modus vivendi with David Ben-Gurion that clearly defined the respective authority of Israeli and Diaspora leaders.[5] In recent decades the AJC has devoted significant resources both to defending Israel in the court of world opinion and to improving relations between Israeli Jews and the Diaspora. Despite that organizational history, or perhaps because of it, Yehoshua declared before the AJC in 2006 that "Judaism outside Israel has no future." If you "do not live in Israel . . . your Jewish identity has no meaning at all." Yehoshua then made two further claims: only the State of Israel could ensure the survival of the Jewish people, and only inside Israel could an individual Jewish life be full, authentic, or genuine. Diaspora Jews were play-acting Judaism, Yehoshua said pointedly. Only Israelis could be Jews for real.[6]

Responding days later to the furor his remarks had caused, Yehoshua published a clarification in which he claimed (disingenuously, I think) that he "did not talk about 'the negation of the Diaspora.'" The Jewish Diaspora has existed for 2,500 years, he wrote, and will continue: "We know its cost, and we are aware of its accomplishments." In fact, "it is Israel and not the Diaspora that could be a passing episode in Jewish history, and this is the source of my compulsion to reiterate the old and plain truth that apparently needs to be repeated again and again." That remarkable admission was followed by return to the issues of survival (possible only in Israel) and identity (authentic or whole only in Israel). Other participants at the AJC conclave, Yehoshua charged, had failed to address the overwhelming reality of anti-Semitism in modern Jewish history. Israelis understood that Jewish survival could not be taken for granted and that Diaspora Jews had seriously compromised their own survival as Jews through assimilation. Judaism in the Diaspora was like a garment that one puts on and takes off at will. For Israelis, Judaism was not garment but skin—inescapable, not an attribute of the self but simply who one *is*. Perhaps his American Jewish hosts had treated him with such courtesy, even though he had offended them, Yeshoshua concluded that "because deep down, they felt that I was speaking the simple truth."[7]

We can restate the three points that constitute that alleged truth—all of them standard in Zionist theory—as follows:

1. *Survival.* There is no future for Jewish communities outside Israel. Only the State of Israel can ensure the survival of the Jewish people.
2. *Collective Identity.* Jewish life outside Israel has no meaning; it is based on delusion. The twin threats of assimilation and anti-Semitism cannot be avoided.
3. *Personal Authenticity.* Jewish life in the Diaspora lacks integrity: it is "neurotic"; only in Israel can a Jew be whole or complete.[8]

I will take up these issues in turn.

Survival: "No Other Place"

The brevity of this essay requires me to stipulate (rather than argue) that Yehoshua was correct in claiming that the concept of exile barely figures in modern Diaspora Jewish thought,[9] and—still more telling—that only political Zionism among modern Jewish intellectual and social movements has made the demonstration and analysis of anti-Semitism (always coupled with assimilation in the modern Jewish lexicon) a central, or even *the* central, strand in its view of the Jewish condition.[10] Herzl's *Der Judenstaat* focused on "Jew-hatred" from start to finish. Ahad Ha'am, too—though he wrote far more about the predicament and possibilities of Judaism in an increasingly secular age than he did about anti-Semitism—took the disabilities of Diaspora, including persecution, utterly for granted. In a key essay on "negation of the Diaspora," he wondered at Diaspora Jews' failure to "negate Diaspora" *objectively*, by leaving it, despite widespread agreement among them ("*subjective* negation") that the Diaspora was not good for Jewish bodies or Jewish souls.[11] Every Zionist essay or tract on the subject that I can recall makes similar claims about the dangers facing Diaspora Jews, including works by major Orthodox religious Zionists.[12] Many focus at length on anti-Semitism. By contrast, for all that "defense organizations" have been a major feature of Diaspora Jewish life for 150 years, and despite the fact that American Jews continue to profess anxiety about the prospect of significant anti-Semitism in their lifetime and notwithstanding major contributions to the understanding of anti-Semitism made by Diaspora scholars,[13] few Diaspora Jewish thinkers have engaged in parallel discussions of anti-Semitism or accorded it major importance in their writings.

This is the context for Yehoshua's claim—perhaps articulated most famously in Zionist literature by the Biblical scholar Yehezkel Kaufmann and the philosopher Ya'akov Klatzkin—that the Diaspora has no future.[14] It is impossible to evaluate that sweeping claim here; two further stipulations must suffice.

First, Diaspora existence remains uncertain nearly seventy years after the end of the Holocaust, threatened not only by overt anti-Semitism but by subtler forms of denigration and exclusion that have undermined Jewish communities throughout the modern era and have frequently led Jews to minimize their distinctiveness from the larger society. Anti-Semitism is often a goad to assimilation as well as a danger in its own right.[15] The severity of the problem cannot be denied.

Second, a final stipulation: anti-Semitism has been successfully contained for the time being in contemporary North America and persists only at relatively low levels. Assimilation threatens continuity, but to some degree it too has been successfully combated. Jewish communities can and do thrive, and individual Jews have attained a high degree of integration, achievement, wealth, status, influence, and even power. It is therefore unconvincing to conflate the immense variety of Diaspora political situations to the single category of *golah* or *galut*—as even the respected Israeli political scientist Shlomo Avineri did when, in the heat of the Pollard affair, he charged that American Jewry was no different from Iranian Jewry.[16]

Kaufmann's magisterial survey of Jewish history, *Golah ve-nekhar*, makes the case more persuasively that only religion had kept the Jews apart during their long bout with Diaspora wandering and persecution, a safeguard that could not continue to operate in the modern, highly secularized West.[17] One finds similar arguments in the course of the spirited debate that David Ben-Gurion conducted during the 1950s and early 1960s with leading Israeli intellectuals about the direction of their new State. The two sides disagreed on many things—but *not* on whether the State had rendered the Diaspora irrelevant to the future course of Jewish history (all agreed that it had) or if communities outside Israel could long endure (they could not).[18] Gershom Scholem, a member of that group who quarreled frequently with Ben-Gurion, famously argued that the Jews had "reentered history" with the return to their homeland—a Ben-Gurion–like claim that assumed, as Yehoshua does—that Diaspora history was not and is not history in the true sense of the word. Diaspora Jews, now that Israel had again become a state, stood outside of the only Jewish action that really mattered.[19]

Scholem's assertion reminds us that Zionism, from the very outset, differed fundamentally from all other modern nationalist movements when it came to the relation between center and periphery.[20] Only Zionism needed to uproot the members of the nation en masse from every actual place that they had called home over the past two millennia except one—Palestine—in order to build the national home. Other national movements sought to liberate their peoples while leaving them largely in place, and so, unlike Zionism, they could tolerate the presence outside the homeland of a significant percentage of the nation's members. They had no need to "negate" their diasporas or will the disappearance of other population centers of their people. It bears noting that until recently, proponents of the Zionist Center have also had to contend with a Diaspora much larger than the population living in what they consider the only real home Jews should have. Zionists have had to do battle with the Jewish history that they denigrated as not really being history in the true sense of the word. For it could not be denied that for at least nineteen hundred years, Zion had been an object of special concern and longing to Jews, but not an actual *address* for the vast majority of the Jewish people. Jews had rarely attempted to settle there. Zionist thinkers—many of whom *had* left Diaspora homes to settle in Palestine, or attempted to do so—were driven all the more to highlight the miseries of Diaspora Jewish history over the centuries, to argue that the situation for Diaspora Jewry could only grow worse in the modern period (as it, in fact, did), or to claim that "true history" required agency and initiative that were precluded beyond the bounds of a sovereign State.

Yehoshua, as we have seen, is alert to one final weakness of the "survival" argument: namely, that the so-called "secure refuge" for world Jewry does not always seem secure. Israel's survival is far from assured. Its enemies are real, and the threat they pose remains potent more than sixty years after the declaration of statehood. This threat, combined with the affluence and apparent security of the American Diaspora, strengthens the attraction of the latter and undermines the Zionist claim that Israel and only Israel can ensure its own future and that of Jews everywhere. Avraham Burg—son of a prominent Israeli leader of Ben-Gurion's generation, a former speaker of the Knesset, and head of the Jewish Agency for Israel—recently made precisely these points in a controversial post-Zionist polemic.[21]

It is worth noting, in light of several recent essays on the subject, that Yehoshua (to my knowledge at least) does not claim that Diaspora Jews actually *weaken* Israel by not joining the ranks of Israelis. Nor does he explore the increasingly vexed question of whether the Law of Return that guarantees automatic citizenship to Diaspora Jews (and to no one else) should be amended, now that most Diaspora Jews do not face overt persecution. Some Israeli thinkers have seen a conflict between the Law of Return and the State's commitment to democracy and human rights. Others have contended that the Israeli polity is weakened by the need to serve as "the State of the Jewish people" no matter where the members of that people reside. I think we can expect debate over the validity of the "survival" theme to continue and intensify in the years to come.[22]

Collective Identity: "Slavery In the Midst of Freedom"

Assimilation, unlike anti-Semitism, *has* been a major theme in modern Jewish communal debate. The locus classicus of the subject in Zionist discourse is Ahad Ha'am's polemical essay "Slavery in the Midst of Freedom" (1891).[23] Western Jews are accused of "moral slavery" manifested in bending over backward to proclaim loyalty to *la patrie* and in pleading the Jews' case in terms of threats to the general good, even when survival itself was at stake. Worse, Ahad Ha'am asserted, these same Jews were guilty of "intellectual slavery" evident in the "famous gospel of the mission of Israel among the nations." That claim to ethical preeminence could not be taken seriously, Ahad Ha'am wrote, given Jewish bourgeois comfort (there could be no mission without suffering) and widespread assimilation (every mission requires distinction from those the missionaries seek to save).[24]

Ahad Ha'am believed that, with religion fading as a source of Jewish belief and motivation, Judaism had to be transformed from faith to culture. This transformation could only occur in the Center, that is, in and through the life that a small nucleus of Jews would build for themselves upon the Land of Israel and within the framework of the reborn Hebrew language. The influence of that Center could and would radiate outward to the Diaspora, which would be nourished from the Center, and thus given the resources needed for survival. *Absent* the Center, Jews and Judaism had no future; *outside* the Center, no creative Jewish life could flourish independently. The Center would permit a greatly attenuated form of Diaspora existence. (Ahad Ha'am respected traditional forms of Jewish faith, but apparently he expected that they would soon wither away.[25] He did not expect the majority of world Jewry to flock to Palestine—and was not sanguine about their prospects in Diaspora).

Historians have noted that this argument by secular spiritual and political Zionists is built on longstanding Haskalah critiques of Orthodox backwardness and irrelevance in the modern age, even as Zionists joined with Orthodox thinkers in dismissing non-Orthodox forms of Diaspora Judaism as illegitimate and not viable.[26] Religious Zionists, of course, could not dismiss Orthodoxy as inauthentic or attack the framework of Jewish law. But they could and did argue that Jewish *life* in the Diaspora—on which the survival of Judaism depended—was under siege.[27] Acceptance of the "yoke of the kingdom of Heaven," as philosopher Yeshayahu Leibowitz wrote time and again, depended on freedom from "the yoke of the Gentiles."[28] Renewed statehood offered greatly expanded opportunities for fulfillment of God's Commandments, particularly (but not exclusively) those that the Halakhah termed "dependent on [residence in] the [Holy] Land."

Rabbi Abraham Isaac Kook—the leading theoretician of religious Zionism in the twentieth century and still unrivaled in his influence on that movement—contrasted the stunted nature of Jewish life in the Diaspora to the possibilities of a more expansive Jewish life, culture, society, and politics made possible by return to the soil of the Land of Israel and the unique spiritual qualities of the Hebrew language. That return constituted a giant leap in the progress of the Jewish people and the entire world toward messianic redemption.[29] Rabbi David Hartman has made similar arguments (without Kook's mystical language or messianic assumptions), emphasizing the greatly expanded opportunities for "covenantal fulfillment" possible in the reborn State. Israelis should seize hold of their tradition and apply it to such areas as health care, foreign policy, treatment of Arabs, and a host of other problems over which Diaspora Jews—always small minorities—could not exercise control. It is one thing to voice prophetic critique from the sidelines. Israelis, exercising majority power, experience the "joy" that comes with renewed "responsibility."[30]

Secular Zionists, claiming explicitly or implicitly that traditional religious belief and practice cannot be maintained in the modern world, have nonetheless made frequent appeal, explicit and implicit, to religious texts, rituals, and imagery when criticizing the Diaspora and urging return to Zion. Yehoshua's charges echo those of Ben-Gurion and other Zionist theorists in this regard.[31] Three features of the Jewish religious tradition figure prominently in Zionist argument about Diaspora assimilation:

1. Exile, in traditional Jewish sources, is never anything but punishment. From the very first passages of Torah onwards, exile represents the quintessential punishment: a *metaphysical* state of alienation, the human condition, the way the world has been since

Adam and Eve's expulsion from the Garden; and a *political* condition, marked by lack of a homeland, minority status in other peoples' lands, and the powerlessness and persecution that result from that status. Exile cannot be positive or neutral. It is wholly negative.

2. One cannot imagine redemption except as the polar opposite of exile; *galut* is the mirror image of *ge'ulah*. The tales of homelessness and wandering that dominate the Book of Genesis are countered by the laws and narratives of homecoming to the Land of Israel ("*the Land*") in the pages of Deuteronomy. Rabbinic writings too look forward to the end of Jewish life outside the Land. The Messiah's coming will mean "ingathering of the exiles."[32]

3. The rabbis in fact assumed a two-fold task: they had to fashion a Judaism that would allow Jews to live as Jews—that is, with a significant degree of distinctiveness, obedient to God's law—wherever they were. At the same time, however, they worked to make sure that Jews regarded every place that Jews lived under foreign rule, including the Land of Israel, not as home but as "somewhere else," as exile. The Messiah and only the Messiah would right the wrongs of history and take Jews home.

Yehoshua, like many Zionist writers before and since, has appropriated as well as rebelled against this religious heritage. His dual task, we might say, precisely mirrored that of the rabbis to opposite ends. Zionist theorists have taken part in the return to Zion for which the rabbis waited, and have consistently urged the dismantling of the Diaspora that the rabbis maintained but could never entirely affirm as good or positive. Jews, according to the rabbis, were meant to come home to Zion, led there by the Messiah. Zionists refused to wait for the Messiah and (except for the religious among them) rejected much of Jewish law and Jewish faith. Ironically, they have won a hearing for their views—including the refusal to wait for Messiah—by deploying some of the most powerful imagery stored up in Jewish tradition, including that of the Messiah.

Diaspora Jews, as David Ellenson's studies remind us, encounter this imagery of return every time they open a traditional text or observe a religious ritual. Since the creation of the State of Israel, no Diaspora Jew can entirely avoid the Zionist claims associated with the powerful images of, and prayers for, return and ingathering. Yet the great bulk of Diaspora Jews have continued to live where they do while continuing to pray for the "ingathering of exiles from the four corners of the earth." They thereby reinforce both the Zionist argument that they should come home to Zion and the expectation, honed over many centuries, that Jews who say these prayers will remain outside Zion, in need of ingathering. Jewish faith, now as ever, offers a connection to ultimate meaning and to God that is not dependent on residence in the Holy Land.

Faith often trumps nationalism in the minds and hearts of believers, for all that the two are intimately connected. Nonreligious Zionists such as Klatzkin, Ahad Ha'am, or Yehoshua have presumed or called for the imminent demise of faith and have made the case for a Judaism based primarily on culture (Ahad Ha'am) or on land and language (Klatzkin and Yehoshua). Diaspora Jews, if they regard themselves as religious to any degree, can and do claim legitimacy for remaining in Diaspora on the basis of three millennia of history and tradition. Secular Diaspora Jews have to make the more difficult case that their Jewish culture, too, has staying power, authenticity, and legitimacy. Orthodox Jews in Diaspora are pulled in both directions, exhibiting the highest rate of aliyah and involvement in Israel of any denomination, as well as the highest degree of what we might call "Diaspora staying power," achieved through a combination of tribal exclusivism, ritual observance, and resistance to assimilation.[33]

Yehoshua has raised almost all these profound issues about the alleged "intellectual and moral slavery" of Diaspora Jews and Judaism in his remarks—and has given none of them the careful scrutiny they deserve.

Personal Authenticity: A Self "Without any Foreign Admixture"

I turn now to Yehoshua's final claim: that personal Jewish identity in Diaspora is not and cannot be authentic or complete. A Jew in Israel is *really* a Jew, a Jew in his or her *essence*, *fundamentally* and *forever* a Jew. A Jew in the Diaspora assumes Jewishness as one trait among others, can slough it off at will like a piece of clothing, and therefore is essentially *not a Jew at all* but rather an American—which is to say a Gentile. The traditional resonance and power of this argument are obvious. So too is its prominence in Zionist ideology. Consider this statement by Ben-Gurion to the scholar Simon Rawidowicz, who not only chose to remain in the Diaspora but defended the necessity of the Diaspora in a major study entitled "Babylonia and Jerusalem": "The Jew in the Golah, even a Jew like you who lives an entirely Jewish life, is not able to be a complete Jew, and no Jewish community in the Golah is able to live a complete Jewish life. Only in the State of Israel is a full Jewish life possible. Only here will a Jewish culture worthy of that name flourish."[34]

Ahad Ha'am asked in an important essay entitled *Ha-musar ha-le'umi*, "The National Morality" (1899; regrettably the essay has never been translated into

English),[35] what it could mean to be a Jew in the strictly nationalist sense, that is, as a matter of culture rather than religion. The nationalist Jew, in the absence of religious faith, would have to submit to a distinctive moral standard, morality being "perhaps more than any other area of culture a national possession."[36] A true Jew—a "kosher nationalist" in Ahad Ha'am's term—should be able in all situations to answer the question: "What are the obligations which the true national morality, without any foreign admixture, imposes upon us in our relation to ourselves and to others?"[37] Ahad Ha'am was not sure what that would look like, but he was confident—as was Yehoshua a century later—that nonreligious Jews outside the Land and its language could not achieve it.

It seems to me that Zionists who wish to prosecute this claim must argue persuasively that authentic selfhood—linked to the notion of "genuine" cultural creativity—is not only a coherent and worthwhile objective, but that it can be found only in the nation's geographic center. This claim, common among Zionist theorists, is patently problematic on a number of counts. I leave aside the well-known question of whether Philip Roth and Saul Bellow should be counted as "Jewish writers" or "American writers." The matter rests on notions of culture, authorship, creativity, and, of course, *Judaism* that are too complex for treatment here. Let us rather stipulate that there is truth to both sides of the contemporary debate about whether creativity can and does occur at "the center" or on "the periphery."[38] Much excellent Jewish writing in the past century—by which I mean, at a minimum, writing by Jews who focus on Jewish themes and display extensive Jewish knowledge and even commitment—has transpired outside the Land of Israel and in languages other than Hebrew.

Consider Yehoshua's concept of Judaism as a cultural identity consisting primarily or entirely of two elements: land and language. Both are enormously important to Israeli Jews of all stripes; both are central to historical Judaism; and neither is of more than minor importance to the bulk of Diaspora Jews. Note, however, that Yehoshua himself at times sees the limits of his own definition of Judaism: "Jewish values" creep inexorably into the defense he penned in *Haaretz*. He praises Jews who care deeply about social justice and compassion. It is hard to assert credibly that Israelis who know nothing of Jewish tradition are, by dint of where they live and what language they speak, "more Jewish" than Diaspora Jews fluent in that tradition and committed to its practice. The either/or that Yehoshua posits seems patently unsupportable. He would have done better, I think, to speak of the *potential* open to a large percentage of Israelis, by virtue of where they live and the language in which they speak and dream, for *substantive appreciation of and participation in a* culture shaped more significantly by the Jewish past. This cultural advantage over Diaspora cannot be denied.

The notion of a Jew "without any foreign admixture" is patently problematic. Would Maimonides without Aristotle or Islamic philosophy, if such a thing were possible, be "more Jewish" or more valuable on this account than Maimonides, as we have him, bearing those cultural influences? Should Israeli Jews remain ignorant of Shakespeare, or know his work only in Hebrew translation? Should Yehoshua refrain from the influence of Kafka or Joyce?

Yehoshua seems to me on stronger ground when he suggests that the core idea of covenant has made Jews unique among the nations by making them *both a people and a religious group*. In the ancient world this pairing was common; during the Middle Ages, the tension could often be managed because Jews lived among Christians or Muslims whose tribal or national existence was inseparable from their faith. In the modern world, however, Jews were granted emancipation on the assumption that Judaism would remain only a religious creed with few lingering ritual practices to set them apart. Judaism would shed its national character. Napoleon made this explicit when he called together the "assembly of notables" and "Sanhedrin." The Jews "signed on" to that agreement. But, as Yehoshua correctly points out, they have not always honored it. The national character of their faith remained even when Jews fully accepted new national identities as Americans or Frenchmen. When that religious faith weakened, Jews often clung to national loyalties stronger than those allowed for or captured in twentieth-century notions of "ethnicity" and "cultural pluralism."

The result, Yehoshua argues forcefully (if simplistically), is a *neurosis* from which Diaspora Jews cannot escape.[39] Their selfhood is either senseless or split. Only "normalization" through secular Zionism can solve the problem, hence the name of his 1980 collection of essays, *Bi-zekhut ha-normaliyut* ("The Case for Normality," a title poorly rendered in English as "Between Right and Right.").[40] The claim for neurosis is overblown and unprovable, but the line of analysis is not entirely mistaken. As the American Reform Jewish leader Julian Morgenstern put it in an essay from the 1940s: "Nation, people, religion—what are we?"[41] I have argued that Jewish discussion of "chosenness" in America over the past century has repeatedly served as a way to air and answer that question.

Yehoshua—closely echoing Kaufmann and other Zionist theorists—argues that a people chosen by God from among the nations *cannot be normal*. Religion must be sacrificed along with Diaspora if Jews are finally to lead healthy lives and fit into the world. Yehoshua recognizes that the strictures he applies to religious Judaism apply no less to Ahad Ha'am's argument on behalf of a unique national Jewish *morality*. Normality means being like every other people. This can of course include aspiring to greatness, as nearly every people does—and deceiving oneself about how great one actually is. Yehoshua imputes a fatal blindness to Jews "too busy with mythology and theology instead of history, and therefore the warnings voiced by Jabotinsky and his colleagues in the early twentieth century—'Eliminate the Diaspora, or the Diaspora will surely eliminate you'—fell on deaf ears." But Yehoshua also accuses Israelis of hiding from social responsibilities by focusing on what he scornfully calls "spiritual pursuits." There are more important things to worry about than "the study of text and the mining of memories and some occasional communal involvement." Such activities, we note, are just as available outside Israel as they are inside it, another mark against them in Yehoshua's eyes. Jews retreat to synagogue life and affect religious forms in order to preserve collective identity, but avoid facing up to the evils of the Jewish situation, and other evils too. If Judaism is a matter of religion or culture, it is "not by chance [that] more than half a million Israelis now live outside of Israel . . . what's the problem with taking the Israeli kids and exiling the whole family to some foreign high-tech mecca? After all, the core of the identity is eternal and accessible anywhere."[42]

The author's frustration is palpable. Religion trumps nationalism—and so endangers both the Diaspora and Israel. One suspects that, at least in part, this aspect of Yehoshua's Zionist "case" against the Diaspora rarely receives the honest consideration it deserves because the matter is so politically sensitive, touching issues of dual loyalty and Diaspora support for Israel. If so, silence on the matter confirms Yehoshua's claims. Assimilation, he would say, is not only a matter of mimicking the other to the point of disappearance, but of looking away from matters crucial to the assertion and flowering of the self. And Israelis are not wholly immune to the curse.

Conclusion

I find discussions about Zionism that flow through predictable ideological channels less valuable than reflections that treat the choice for Israel or the Diaspora as differing existential *bets*—neither without great risks on the better future for oneself, one's family, and the extended family of Jews. Ehud Luz has articulated this choice beautifully in his book on competing currents in Zionist thought;[43] it echoes too from the powerful (and highly personal) conclusion to Gershom Scholem's classic essay "The Messianic Idea in Judaism."[44] I wonder whether a meeting of the minds between Israeli and Diaspora Zionists could be conceived precisely here, at the existential point concerning assimilation where they may seem most divided. Can we imagine a kind of Jewish religious thought in both Israel and the Diaspora that affirms the sanctification of time as well as of space? That sees possibilities for covenantal fulfillment in both modes, Israeli and Diaspora? That takes due note of the expanded responsibilities that come with sovereignty? That does not dispute the centrality of Israel in contemporary Jewish history, but also does not detract from the importance of Diaspora achievement? Few American Jews, after all, accept the militant "Diasporism" brilliantly articulated by Philip Roth in *Operation Shylock*, and few outside the small circle of fervently anti-Zionist, ultra-Orthodox Jews accept the argument, advanced energetically by the scholars Daniel and Jonathan Boyarin, that the future of Judaism—and of Jews—demands rejection of power in a sovereign state in favor of the cultural and moral advantages of powerlessness in a liberal Diaspora.[45]

The leadership of Israeli and American Jewries has long developed a mutual respect that goes beyond a modus vivendi and functional coexistence. There seems to be real appreciation of the Other despite deep-seated ideological differences about the better setting for Jewish selves, Jewish culture, and Jewish faith, and despite occasional outbursts that undermine the peace. Yet it is my experience that even among these leaders—and certainly among the rank and file—there is widespread ignorance about the social and existential reality of one another's lives. Many American Jews know little about Israeli society, even if they recognize the fragility of their own community's achievement and fear an outbreak of anti-Semitism. Many Israeli Jews know little about American Jewry, even as they worry about Israel's ability to survive external threat and internal division. Significant numbers on both sides seem aware that the North American Diaspora is unique when compared with others past or present—a modern Jewish reality no less unprecedented, perhaps, than a modern, sovereign, as yet premessianic Jewish state in the Land of Israel.

There is a great need for frank and probing discussion of the sort Yehoshua attempted to initiate, no less than for the careful and perceptive historical analysis of American reception of Zionism that David Ellenson among others has supplied. One hopes that more examples of both will soon be forthcoming.

Notes

1. David Ellenson, *Between Tradition and Culture: The Dialectics of Modern Jewish Religion and Identity* (Atlanta, 1994), xi.

2. Ibid., 131–52, 153–78.

3. Ibid., 178.

4. See Berel Lang, "Hyphenated-Jews and the Anxiety of Identity," *Jewish Social Studies* 12 (2005): 1–15; Arnold Eisen, "Jews, Judaism, and the Problem of Hyphenated Identity in America," in *Ambivalent Jew: Charles Liebman in Memoriam*, ed. Stuart Cohen and Bernard Susser, 89–106 (New York, 2007).

5. See Naomi W. Cohen, *Not Free to Desist: The American Jewish Committee, 1906–1966* (Philadelphia, 1972), 311–15.

6. *The A. B. Yehoshua Controversy: An Israel-Diaspora Dialogue on Jewishness, Israeliness, and Identity* (New York, 2006). Not all of these quotations appear in the edited transcript of Yehoshua's remarks distributed by the AJC. A number of those present at the speech quoted this passage in their responses. See, for example, Uri Dan, "Speak for Yourself, A. B. Yehoshua," *Jerusalem Post*, May 10, 2006; and Hillel Halkin. "More Right than Wrong," *Jerusalem Post*, May 11, 2006 (both were reprinted with permission in *The A. B. Yehoshua Controversy*).

7. A. B. Yehoshua, "The Meaning of Homeland," *Haaretz Magazine*, May 13, 2006 (reprinted with permission in *The A .B. Yehoshua Controversy*).

8. Perusal of Israeli reaction to Yehoshua's remarks to the AJC reveal, that his view of Diaspora in all these particulars was widely shared in Israel. He had been tactless, some respondents complained, but he was not wrong. Americans by contrast were generally outraged.

9. Gershon Shaked, *There Is No Other Place* [in Hebrew] (Tel Aviv, 1983).

10. Ruth R. Wisse, *Jews and Power* (New York, 2007). Wisse has cogently declared this lacuna a fundamental failing of modern Jewish thought. See also A. B. Yehoshua, "An Attempt to Identify the Root Cause of Antisemitism," *Azure* 32 (2008): 48–79.

11. Ahad Ha'am, "The Negation of the Diaspora," in *The Zionist Idea: A Historical Analysis and Reader*, ed. Arthur Hertzberg, 270–77 (Philadelphia, 1997).

12. See, for example, Eliezer Don-Yehiya, "The Negation of Galut in Religious Zionism," *Modern Judaism* 12, no. 2 (1992): 129–55.

13. See, for example, Larry Witham, "U.S. Jews See Anti-Semitism as Biggest Threat, Study Finds: Few Call Religious Observance Important to Their Identity," *Washington Times*, June 2, 1999.

14. Yehezkel Kaufmann, *Golah ve-nehkar*, vol. 2 [in Hebrew] (Tel Aviv, 1962), 402; Jacob Klatzkin, *Tehumim* [in Hebrew] (Jerusalem, 1928), 45–54.

15. Cf. Arnold M. Eisen, *Rethinking Modern Judaism: Ritual, Commandment, Community* (Chicago, 1998), chap. 4.

16. Shlomo Avineri, "Letter to an American Friend: Soured Promise," *Jerusalem Post*, March 10, 1987, www.jonathanpollard.org/7890/031087.htm (accessed August 25, 2009).

17. Kaufmann, *Golah*, 1:205–7.

18. For more on Ben Gurion's debate with the intellectuals, see Michael Keren, "Ben Gurion and the Intellectuals: Power, Knowledge, and Charisma," *Forum on the Jewish People* 57/58, (1985–86): 7–15; David Ohana, *Messianism and Statehood* [in Hebrew] (Beer Sheva, 2003).

19. Gershom Scholem, *The Messianic Idea in Judaism: And Other Essays on Jewish Spirituality* (New York, 1971), 35–36; Gershom Scholem, *On Jews and Judaism in Crisis: Selected Essays* (New York, 1976), 244–60.

20. Anthony D. Smith, *The Ethnic Origins of Nations* (Oxford, 1986).

21. See Ari Shavit, "Leaving the Zionist Ghetto: Interview with Avraham Burg," *Haaretz*, June 8, 2007. For a more complete expression of Burg's views see Avraham Burg, *Defeating Hitler* [in Hebrew] (Tel Aviv, 2007). See also Allan Arkush, "From Diaspora Nationalism to Radical Diasporism," *Modern Judaism* 29 (2009): 326–27.

22. See Eliezer Schweid, *Medinah yehudit-democratit: Ma'amar filosofi-politi histori*, pamphlet (Jerusalem, 2007); Ruth Gavison *Yisrael ke-medinah yehudit ve-demokratit: metahim ve-sikuyim* (Jerusalem, 1999); and Chaim Gans, *A Just Zionism* (Oxford, 2008).

23. Ahad Ha'am, "Slavery in Freedom," in *Selected Essays of Ahad Ha'am*, ed. Leon Simon (New York, 1970), 171–94.

24. Ahad Ha'am. *Complete Writings* [in Hebrew] (Tel Aviv, 1965), 159–64. See also Arnold Eisen, *Galut: Modern Jewish Reflection on Homelessness and Homecoming* (Bloomington, Ind., 1986), 73–74.

25. Steven J. Zipperstein, *Elusive Prophet: Ahad Ha'am and the Origins of Zionism* (Berkeley, Calif., 1993), chap. 5.

26. See Alan Mintz, *Banished from Their Father's Table: Loss of Faith and Hebrew Autobiography* (Bloomington, Ind., 1989).

27. Don-Yehiya, "The Negation of Galut in Religious Zionism."

28. See, for example, Yeshayahu Leibowitz, *Judaism, the Jewish People, and the State of Israel* [in Hebrew] (Jerusalem, 1976), 121.

29. For a good introduction to Kook's work in English, see Abraham Isaac Kook, *The Lights of Penitence, The Moral Principles, Lights of Holiness, Essays, Letters, and Poems*, ed. and trans. B. Z. Bokser (New York, 1978).

30. David Hartman, *Joy and Responsibility: Israel, Modernity and the Renewal of Judaism* (Jerusalem, 1978), 6–7.

31. See Eisen, *Galut*, chaps. 1–3.

32. See the introductory chapter to Lawrence A. Hoffman, ed., *The Land of Israel: Jewish Perspectives* (Notre Dame, Ind., 1986).

33. Steven Bayme, "On Gabriel Sheffer's 'Loyalty and Criticism in the Relations between World Jewry and Israel,'" *Israel Studies* 17, no. 2 (2012): 111–19.

34. David N. Myers, *Between Jew and Arab: The Lost Voice of Simon Rawidowicz* (Waltham, Mass., 2008), 85.

35. See also Eisen, *Galut*, 131–33.

36. Ha'am, *Complete Writings*, 159–64.

37. Ibid., 313–20.

38. Homi K. Bhabha, "Cultural Diversity and Cultural Differences," in *The Post-Colonial Studies Reader*, ed. B. Ashecroft, G. Griffiths, and H. Tiffin (New York, 1995), 156.

39. A. B. Yehoshua, "Exile as a Neurotic Condition," in *Diaspora: Exile and the Jewish Condition*, ed. É. Levine, (New York, 1983), 15–35.

40. A. B. Yehoshua. *Bi-zekhut ha-normaliyut* (Jerusalem, 1988), published in translation as *Between Right and Right* (Garden City, N.Y., 1981).

41. Julian Morgenstern. "Nation, People, Religion: What Are We?," address delivered at the inauguration of the sixty-ninth academic year of the Hebrew Union College (Cincinnati, 1943).

42. A. B. Yehoshua, "The Meaning of Homeland," *Haaretz Magazine*, May 13, 2006, reprinted with permission in *The A. B. Yehoshua Controversy*, 7–10.

43. Ehud Luz, *Wrestling with an Angel: Power, Mortality, and Jewish Identity*, trans. M. Swirsky (New Haven, Conn., 2003).

44. Scholem, *Messianic Idea in Judaism*, 35–36.

45. Daniel Boyarin with Jonathan Boyarin, "Diaspora: Generation and the Ground of Jewish Identity" Critical Inquiry 19, no. 4 (1993): 693–725. For a more expanded development of this argument, see Daniel Boyarin and Jonathan Boyarin, *Powers of Diaspora: Two Essays on the Relevance of Jewish Culture* (Minneapolis, 2002).

12

TRADITIONAL EXEMPLARS IN A TIME OF CRISIS

MICHAEL MARMUR

Abraham Joshua Heschel published a series of eight articles titled "Personalities in Jewish History" in the Berlin *Jüdisches Gemeindeblatt* in 1936.[1] The pieces were written at a time of unparalleled concern in the Jewish community. The Nuremberg laws had been passed only a few months earlier. The eight articles appeared over six months, starting February 23, 1936, some two weeks before the German reoccupation of the Rhineland, and ending August 16, 1936, the precise date of the closing ceremony of the Berlin Olympic Games.

In this article I will offer a brief description of the content of these eight pieces and their context. In discussing the polemical, pedagogical, and political purposes of Heschel's presentation of the lives of these Sages in these articles and later in his career, I shall compare them with other modern representations of these ancient rabbis, especially in the State of Israel in the early twenty-first century. These reflections are offered in friendship as a tribute to David Ellenson, with whom I have explored Heschel's earliest writings,[2] and who is constantly engaged as a scholar, thinker, teacher, and leader with the question of what tradition might mean in a contemporary key.

Heschel was twenty-nine years old in the year these articles were published. Born in Warsaw, he had arrived in Berlin in 1927 after a period of study in Vilna. By the mid-1930s he had already achieved a certain standing in the German Jewish community, having completed his doctorate at the university and his studies at the Hochschule. He was a published Yiddish poet and a known intellectual, well regarded yet perhaps not in the first rank of spiritual leaders of the German Jewish community. To judge from these articles, Heschel had achieved a high level of mastery of the German language.

A year earlier his biographical monograph on Maimonides had been published, and his doctoral dissertation on prophecy appeared that year. The two modes of writing for which he was to become famous in subsequent decades, theological reflection and social commentary, had not yet come to expression. The most widely distributed Jewish publication in Germany at that time, the *Gemeindeblatt* of the Berlin Jewish community, provided a major platform from which Heschel could address a Jewish public that was divided into factions and ideological movements but united by concern and a strong sense of foreboding.

Eight Sketches

The subjects of these vignettes are some of the great Rabbinical heroes of the Tannaitic period—Rabbis Johanan ben Zakkai, Gamaliel II, Akiva, Simeon ben Gamaliel II, Elisha ben Avuyah, Meir, Judah "the Prince," and Hiyya.

Rabbi Johanan ben Zakkai is described as heir to a prophetic tradition, and lauded for his capacity to identify spiritual priorities even at a time of enormous social upheaval. His approach of "insightful humility" was predicated on his conviction that military resistance to the force of imperial power was futile and that "only peace could avert total disaster." His worldview is contrasted with that of hotheads, revolutionaries, and extremists. He promulgated "the myth of erudition" and placed study at the heart of Judaism. More than any other contribution to the Jews of his day and to posterity he "showed how an ultimate political catastrophe could be transformed into moral and spiritual recovery."

Whereas Heschel's Johanan ben Zakkai may be credited with promulgating the ethos of study, he is not the person who created the institutions capable of maintaining and promoting it. This distinction is reserved for Rabban Gamaliel II: "This iron patriarch ran a powerful organization. Only centralization and the creation of a legislative institution, the standing and worth of which would be generally recognized, could save the teaching and the nation from disintegration. He carried out his intention with relentless courage. He managed to obtain legislative power for the decisions of the Sanhedrin, the center of Jewish self-government of which he was the head."

"Of greatest importance were the attempts by Rabban Gamaliel to overcome the anarchy that arose as a result of the party struggles." Despite his remarkable organizational achievements and his success in establishing prayer as a fixed institution, the article describes the overthrow of Gamaliel by his contemporaries.

In Rabbi Akiva the ideology of the Oral Torah reaches its apogee. In contrast to the other figures to whom articles were devoted, Heschel returned to Akiva later in life: in the 1960s Rabbi Akiva and Rabbi Ishmael are the two central protagonists of *Torah min ha-shamayim*. In the 1936 article, the midrash according to which Moses sits in the class of Akiva is employed to place the latter on the same plane as the former. Rabbi Akiva's "pioneering idea was the assumption that the Oral Teaching was inherent in the Bible. His virtuosity in the art of exposition enabled him to discover the one in the other. To some extent he changed the status of the Bible: the stark words thawed, joined the flow and produced unimagined content: erratic traditions side by side with explicit meaning."

Heschel credits Akiva with making great strides in the systematization of that approach to learning which Johanan ben Zakkai had preached and Gamaliel defended. When it comes to the political aspect of Akiva's life and its their direct link with the circumstances of his death, Heschel chooses to present this as the result of an effulgent enthusiasm:

> He combined in himself analytical sharpness of mind with a systematic view of the world, methodical virtuosity with congenial originality, learning with depth, theoretical productivity with pedagogic activity, mighty common sense with a holy life style. He was an incomparably attractive person. No other master was capable of gathering such crowds of disciples around him.
>
> This enthusiastic life took a tragic turn when Rabbi Akiva turned his mystical way of life into a political game. He had participated as a spokesman in a delegation to Rome and went on official business to Babylonia. When Bar Kochba emerged, Rabbi Akiva applied to him the verse in the Bible, "A star will rise in Jacob," joined the uprising with messianic enthusiasm and, as it seems, undertook other journeys in order to win the masses for Bar Kochba. After the collapse, he became a victim of Roman vengeance.

Rabbi Simeon ben Gamaliel II is presented as a man in profound disagreement with the Akivan worldview. In this sense, the article on this Sage presents an approach that is associated with Rabbi Ishmael in Heschel's later work. Simeon ben Gamaliel II is called to respond to a wave of what might be termed *anomie*: "The collapse of the resistance was not followed by a collapse of faith, but by an avalanche of resignation that disastrously swept through the Jewish world. Enthusiastic faith was transformed into contempt for the world, valor turned into a fury of despair. The Jews lost their relationship to reality."

Under the influence of Rabbi Ishmael, Rabbi Simeon ben Gamaliel placed the practical needs of the people above spiritual abstractions, and "the primary value of life" contrasted with "life-denying ideologies." Preferring knowledge to acuity and community spirit to the vice of intellectual narcissism (which Heschel identifies in this article with Rabbi Meir), Rabbi Simeon ben Gamaliel is presented as a counterbalance to some tendencies inherent in an Akivan position taken to extremes.

In the fifth article Heschel provides a portrait of Elisha ben Avuyah. He is also described as an opponent of Rabbi Akiva, both on personal and ideological grounds. While the Akivan camp "had forbidden anything dealing with Greek" and some of his followers refused to teach their talented sons a trade, Elisha ben Avuyah immersed himself in Greek culture and criticized the fact that students in the House of Study were not trained in professions.

In this article a process of decline is charted. Philosophical speculations sparked by the prevalence of evil and injustice in the world lead him to the verge of Gnosticism, combined in Heschel's account with a devotion to pleasure and the enjoyment of the senses. Over time, "the apostate turned into an enemy."

Rabbi Meir makes an appearance both in the treatment of Rabbi Simeon ben Gamliel, and in a major supporting role in the tragic tale of Elisha ben Avuyah. Heschel's sixth article is devoted to this complex Sage. Many of the characteristics well known from Rabbinic sources associated with Meir's biography, such as his expertise as a scribe, his illustrious wife, Beruryah, and the death of his sons are mentioned in this vignette. Heschel stresses Rabbi Meir's imaginative capacity, which is able to produce fables and parables, but also to engender a method bordering on casuistry. His conflict with the Patriarch is portrayed as a struggle between scholarly freedom and institutional conformism.[3] Rabbi Meir leaves the Holy Land, and his genius is under-acknowledged as a result of his polemical clashes. The article ends by citing Rabbi Meir's version of the Torah in which the Biblical phrase *Ve-hineh tov me'od* is rendered *Ve-hineh tov mavet*.[4] In Rabbi Meir's reading, death itself is good.

Whereas the portrait of Rabbi Meir is sketched in somber shades, the image of Rabbi Judah the Prince is bathed in gold. His was "a golden appearance in the history of the Jews." In this piece Heschel describes a man of aristocratic bearing, possessing "the most constructive head and the boldest heart of the Talmudic age," whose "character and way of life" grounded his authority and assured his fame even more than his deeds.

Heschel suggests that ambivalence and duality are central to understanding his essence. Aloof yet sensitive, austere yet bold, Rabbi Judah is described as possessing a princely bearing. Even his monumental redaction of the Mishnah is outshone by his capacity to have it accepted around the Jewish world. Tellingly, Heschel compares this achievement to the ultimate failure of Maimonides to see his codex accepted. Rabbi Judah the Prince earned the "holy authority" necessary to effect lasting change.

One might have expected this series of Tannaim to run from Johanan, the symbol of its inception, to Judah, the embodiment of its apogee. In fact, Heschel chose to end the series with Rabbi Hiyya, and throughout the article he presents this less-renowned figure as an alternative hero. Rabbi Hiyya holds no official position in the community, and he is portrayed as having a complex relationship with Rabbi Judah the Prince. Though seeking no political authority, "the power of his prayer was said to supersede that of 'the Prince.'"

Significantly, Rabbi Hiyya is not a native of the Land of Israel. He is portrayed as an émigré scholar, modest where Judah was haughty, connected to the common people while Judah looked upon them with disdain. Whereas Rabbi Judah the Prince "collected the most important teachings," Rabbi Hiyya "stored the neglected material." It is with this figure that Heschel brings his collection of vignettes to a close.

Persecution and the Presentation of Tradition

These articles should not be read as historical essays. The sources upon which the essays are based are not referenced,[5] and there is no discussion of the methodological challenges of adducing accurate historical data from them. They make no contribution to the debate about the possibility of Rabbinic biography. He had made some reference to the inadequacy of scientific textual scholarship in "Die Prophetie," his 1934 doctoral dissertation.[6] Later in his career Heschel did make significant comments on the attempt by scholars to limit the significance of ancient sources to a question of their scientific verification and literal accuracy, referring to the scientific study of the Bible rather than to Rabbinic literature.[7] In his great work on the theology of the Rabbis he was also to show an awareness of, and sensitivity to, contemporary scholarly debates on the complexities associated with Rabbinic biography.[8] Here, though, the issue is beside the point. What matters is the presentation of the lives of men living in a period of great duress, called upon to show resilience and creativity.

Each one of the articles contains some passages with clear parallels to the actual life situation of its readers. "Mystical speculations, apocalyptic visions and messianic exaltations dominated the spirit of the age" in Rabbi Johanan ben Zakkai's days. The Judaism of Rabbi Akiva's era "found itself at a cultural turning point." Rabbi Simeon ben Gamaliel's era was characterized not by "a collapse of faith but by an avalanche of resignation."[9] This same term, "resignation," appears in the discussion of Elisha ben Avuyah, in which Heschel comments that "the shattering of faith is not new in Judaism" and is a theme harking back to Job. The belief in an individual deity leads to a faith in appropriate reward for piety. When this reward fails to come, *Resignation* may follow.

The eighth article opens with a paragraph whose resonances could hardly have been lost on his readers: "The Jews in Palestine, the people and the scholars, lived in fear that the Torah might be lost to them. The land was slipping away from them. The leaders had been killed and safety of existence denied. They were, to a large extent, refugees, emigrants and martyrs. Their children could not be taught and the places of instruction for judges could hardly be maintained. Disaster hung over them."

Along with references to dark times "in those days and in our time," the emphases to be found in these pieces reflect something of the preoccupations of the Jewish community in Nazi Germany. One recurrent term is *authority*. It is absent from the descriptions of Rabban Johanan ben Zakkai and of Elisha ben Avuyah, but Rabban Gamaliel II is described as an "iron patriarch" who "ran a powerful regime. Only centralization . . . could save the teaching and the nation from disintegration." In a somewhat chilling comment, he comments that the "authority of the patriarchate was established with merciless discipline."

Rabbi Akiva's genius is understood against the backdrop of a crisis of authority. The paradigm that had allowed for a gulf separating the written and oral law and relied on the authority of the Sanhedrin was no longer viable "at a time of total uncertainty." Consequently, Rabbi Akiva's spiritual and conceptual revolution was crucial in equipping Rabbinic Judaism with the theological weight and flexibility necessary to cope with a new reality. As a result of this and other groundbreaking changes he initiated, "Rabbi Akiva, who held no official position, enjoyed equally both uncontested authority in learned circles and popularity among the people."

Nowhere is the term *Autorität* as prominent as in the description of Rabbi Judah the Prince. The combination of intellectual, spiritual, personal, and political dimensions gave him the holy authority necessary to promulgate epoch-making changes in Judaism. Lest the reader think that the acquisition of authority is an ultimate good, the articles close with an account of Rabbi Hiyya, who "kept away . . . from every leadership position" and "did not strive for authority."

Before the publication of these articles, the closest Heschel had come to reflection on contemporary events had been in his 1935 *Maimonides*, in which he reflected on the life of his subject in a way that would have seemed particularly resonant to his Jewish readers under Nazi rule. Here is his description of Jewish life in Spain under the Almohades: "A shadow lay across the lives of the Jews. From the gloom of frightened minds rose a distrust of Providence and an intimation of disaster. . . . Despair lured minds into the most daring and insidious subtleties. The force of circumstances overpowered the suppressed and afflicted pseudo-converts, shattering their last bit of courage."[10]

While Heschel is usually read as an explicit writer, sharing his views and insights with a wide audience, there is ample evidence that strategies of hinting, known to him from his extensive knowledge of the Jewish esoteric tradition and employed during his years living under the Nazi regime, stayed with him throughout his life.[11]

Having already mentioned Maimonides and our Tannaim, the presence of suggestive writing strategies in Heschel's work can be shown with reference to another figure from Jewish history. In 1937 Heschel wrote a monograph on Isaac Abrabanel (1437–1508).[12] In the last sentences of the piece, Heschel notes that many of the prominent leaders of Spanish Jewry were sent into exile. He then notes that had they remained they would have been implicated in the conquest and murder of hundreds of thousands in Haiti and elsewhere. In fact, writes Heschel to his Jewish readers in Germany circa 1937, the Jews could not have known what grace their banishment had provided them. Here, too, it stretches credulity to believe that these words could have been written or read without an acute sense of contemporary woes.

It can be argued convincingly that Heschel's arrival in the United States heralded a new voice in his writing and speaking, one in which the explicit was more dominant than the allusive. However, the art of hinting never deserted Heschel. In a 1967 interview Heschel was asked if there is a specifically Jewish mode of coping with suffering.[13] In response, he read and translated from the conclusion to his monograph on Abrabanel, written thirty years earlier.

I argued above that Heschel's brief articles should not be read as historical essays. They do not pretend to add scholarly insights. Indeed, they are popular articles written for a readership under unprecedented pressure. Nonetheless, the historical character of this writing is significant. The message that emerges from these pieces read together is that at another period of drama and crisis the Jewish people found the spiritual resources necessary to prevail. In this sense, the historicity of the pieces is significant—this is not an exercise in literary analysis. Rather, it is an expression of the faith that *Netsah Yisra'el*, the eternal spirit of Israel, will prevail.

It is most significant that more than one exemplar is chosen to embody this eternal spirit, Rather than one archetype of heroic resistance, a range of approaches is modeled. The message is not that the radicals or the pacifists or the intellectuals or the Zionists or any one faction in the panoply of Jewish responses can find a mandate in tradition. They all can claim such a mandate, including those on the verge of resignation.

If diversity is one message of these portraits, another is the power of the individual to effect change. Throughout his life Heschel remained convinced of this, in opposition to intellectual trends that emphasized impersonal processes, economic factors, and other structural explanations. In contrast, he emphasized the primacy of the individual and highlighted particular persons through whom broad conceptions were explored and developed. A list of such men populating Heschel's pantheon would include the early biblical prophets, Rabbi Akiva and Rabbi Ishmael, Saadiah Gaon, Abrabanel, Solomon ibn Gabirol, Maimonides, and later figures such as the Baal Shem Tov and Menahem Mendel of Kotsk. This emphasis expressed more than an interest in the philosophies of these leaders. Heschel's understanding of their personalities played a central role in his approach.

Some twenty years after the appearance of these articles Heschel declared his emphasis on the individual and his resistance to the zeitgeist: "Much has been spoken and written in our midst about nation and society, about the community and its institutions. But the individual has been lost sight of. . . . The time has arrived to pay heed to the forgotten individual. Judaism is a personal problem."[14]

If that statement is a celebration of all individuals, particular figures were presented as symbolic exemplars. In a 1946 essay called "The Eastern European Era" Heschel declared: "If Isaiah were to rise from his grave and were to enter the home of a Jew, the two would easily understand one another."[15] In 1951 we find a prescriptive statement rather than a description: "Our way of life must remain to some degree intelligible to Isaiah and Rabbi Johanan ben Zakkai, to Maimonides and the Baal Shem."[16] In an unpublished talk to Hebrew

Union College students in Cincinnati in the early 1950s, Heschel expresses his fear of what he calls spiritual assimilation and asks if he and his generation would really be understandable to Johanan ben Zakkai.[17] Later, in a speech in 1965, Heschel places responsibility for the Jewish future on the current generation: "We are either the last Jews or those who will hand over the entire past to generations to come." He defines a Jew as "a witness to the transcendence and presence of God; a person in whose life Abraham would feel at home, a person for whom Rabbi Akiva would feel deep affinity, a person of whom the Jewish martyrs of all ages would not be ashamed."[18]

Something of Heschel's conception of Jewish tradition is revealed in these comments. In its authentic expression, the Judaism of every generation keeps faith with the essence of that which precedes it. This fidelity is expressed using the criterion of intelligibility: a Jew is enjoined to ask not if the Judaism of her day is identical in every detail to that of previous years, but rather if its essential thrust would be comprehensible to the giants of the past. Looking to the future, Heschel is concerned that the encounter with the forces of enlightenment and modernity, inevitable and exciting as it may be, will bring this chain of intelligibility into doubt.[19]

Fathers of the Universe

In 1962 Heschel published the first volume of his monumental work on Rabbinic theology, *Torah min ha-shamayim be-aspeklaryah shel ha-dorot*. In that work, and most particularly in this first volume, two worldviews are presented: those of Rabbi Akiva and Rabbi Ishmael.

Some contemporary scholars are highly dubious and somewhat dismissive regarding the historical method Heschel employed in *Torah min ha-shamayim*.[20] Questions of historical method and methodological credulity are beyond the ambit of this article, but it is interesting to note that in his three-volume work Heschel does use some biographical details as a backdrop to his primary goal: a spiritual portrait of the two opinions epitomized by Akiva and Ishmael as they play out throughout Jewish history. So, for example, Heschel acknowledges that according to most sources, both men suffered a martyr's death. He is at pains to argue that, despite their common fate, the two Sages had quite different approaches to martyrdom.[21]

The Ishmael–Akiva dichotomy is presented as an echo of earlier tensions and a precursor of tensions yet to come. Rabbi Akiva's views are linked with apocalyptic literature and Rabbi Ishmael's with the classical prophetic tradition.[22] Akiva's perspective is heavenly while Ishmael's is of this world. Akiva is an ideologue of martyrdom; Ishmael prefers to live to serve God another day. Akiva finds meaning in the crowns on the letters; Ishmael believes the text was written in the language of human beings. In the wake of these *Avot Olam*, these fathers of the universe of normative Jewish discourse, the subsequent great debates of Judaism take shape. Heschel summarizes his approach in the posthumously published third volume in which he asserts that the "changes and disagreements of subsequent generations have their roots in the systems of these two 'Fathers of the Universe.'"[23]

We can only speculate about the reasons for Rabbi Ishmael's noninclusion in the list of biographical vignettes back in the 1930s. However, the essence of the Ishmaelian position is presented in the portrait of Rabbi Simeon ben Gamaliel: "Rabbi Akiva saw in every idiom of the Torah a subject for interpretation. Rabbi Simeon ben Gamaliel, on the other hand (similar to Rabbi Ishmael), thought that the Torah uses hyperbole not to be taken literally. Rabbi Akiva and his school favored dialectic discussion over pure accumulation of knowledge. Rabbi Simeon ben Gamaliel preferred knowledge to astuteness."

The kernel of the thesis of *Torah min ha-shamayim*, or at least aspects thereof, is to be found in these biographical sketches, even though the presentation of two "fathers of the universe" is not to be found.

Crises Ancient and Modern

Emigration, spiritual entrenchment, political resistance, despair—these are the responses rehearsed in these short articles, and they reflect the debate being waged among Heschel's readers in 1936 Germany.[24]

Heschel's recourse to the Tannaim was by no means unique. Marcus Lehmann's historical novel *Akiba* had been reprinted in 1920 and 1930.[25] In 1929 a religious youth movement had been established in Palestine, and it bore the name B'nei Akiva, the sons of Akiva. In the very same year that Heschel published his articles, the man who was to become his colleague, Louis Finkelstein, published his *Akiba: Scholar, Saint and Martyr.*

In the introduction to that work, Finkelstein made the argument for the particular relevance of Rabbi Akiva to contemporary concerns, asserting that "in our own generation special interest attaches to Akiba as one of the builders of civilization."[26] In Finkelstein's version, Rabbi Akiva is portrayed struggling with questions which constitute a modern agenda: "The problems of international peace, universal education, the status of woman, the rights of laborers, the prerogatives of hierarchy, the removal of superstition from religion, and the advancement of pure scholarship are still unsolved."[27] Yehudah Mirsky has recently compared Finkelstein's Akiva with Heschel's Akiva and reached the striking conclusion that the two presentations are almost diametrically opposite.[28]

Only three years later, Milton Steinberg published *As a Driven Leaf*. This retelling of the Elisha ben Avuyah traditions has become a classic of American Judaism. In Jonathan Steinberg's formulation, his father's work "combines a rigorous logical theology and popular fiction in a unique and evidently successful amalgam. The romantic plot and the descriptive images . . . reveal a theological discomfort, a terrible and painful attempt to link tradition with its obligations to the twentieth century and its freedoms."[29]

It is remarkable to note that in contemporary Israel these Tannaitic figures continue to exercise significant attention. To cite one example from among the figures discussed by Heschel in the 1936 articles, Dalia Marx has catalogued the vast range of roles played by Rabbi Johanan ben Zakkai in modern Israeli discourse.[30]

While it is a commonplace that the Bible has played a more central role in the formation of an Israeli national myth than have the Sages, it is interesting to note that recently the Tannaim have been enjoying a resurgence of popularity, beyond even their potency as symbols of martyrdom. In the early twenty-first century, the Sages of the period of the Mishnah feature in the list of Israeli bestsellers. Starting in 2007 Rabbi Binyamin Lau published a series of works titled *The Sages*, in which the period of the Second Temple leading to the Talmud is covered in the main through portraits of Sages. These works have been very well received by a wide reading audience. Lau is keenly aware of the political overtones of his subject in the light of contemporary debates about power, sovereignty, and religious authority. Hence, Rabbi Johanan ben Zakkai's contribution to Jewish history is described as crucial: "It would be impossible to imagine Jewish life today without his bold legislative enactments, which preserved the memory of the Temple while allowing Judaism to persevere in its absence. Controversy about his political views continues to reverberate in our own day, but it in no way detracts from the greatness of this leader, who navigated Jewish life at a crucial moment in our people's history."[31]

Lau does not find it necessary to leave the contemporary resonances of his work to the imagination of his readers. Sections at the end of some chapters are designed to bring home the contemporary relevance of the Sage under discussion. Rabbi Johanan's revolution in Torah study leads to a comparison of Lithuanian and Sephardi approaches to learning in our day. Rabban Gamaliel's example serves as an introduction to a homily according to which "we each have the potential to become a figure of authority, capable of deciding among a multiplicity of voices."[32]

All of the Sages described in Heschel's articles are treated by Lau, occasionally with a quite different emphasis. Both agree, for example, that Rabbi Hiyya's democratic and popular approach differed sharply from the elitism of Rabbi Judah the Prince. However, in Heschel's account "his relationship to Rabbi Judah the Prince was very problematic" since "the prince devoted himself decidedly little to collegiality." This is far from the description to be found in Lau's work, in which Rabbi Hiyya knows how to "read" the Patriarch.[33]

Given the fact that Binyamin Lau is a leading voice of what may be described as the moderate wing of modern Orthodoxy in Israel, it is not surprising that of all the Sages it is Rabbi Akiva whose legacy occupies him the most. Indeed, he deliberately stays away from a discussion of the apostasy of Elisha ben Avuyah, saying that it is not his concern in that work. Rabbi Akiva features in two chapters designed to elicit contemporary parallels. While the first relates to the culture of Torah study as part of contemporary Israeli leisure culture, the second takes on the political legacy of those who see themselves as heirs of Akiva's activism. He asserts that "Rabbi Akiva was responsible for introducing the notion that nationalism is an inherent component of religious identity" and traces the reemergence of this notion, notably in the thought of Rav Kook.[34]

In his introduction to the volume including his treatment of Rabbi Akiva, Lau recounts an anecdote that is meant to describe the dual legacy of that Sage as experienced by an Israeli of Lau's political and religious hue. He is on his way from his home to his congregation to teach a class on Rabbi Akiva's nationalism. En route, "I found myself growing increasingly angry with Rabbi Akiva for leading the entire nation to war and ruin." At that moment, in the rebuilt Jerusalem, he is reminded of the verses in the eighth chapter of the Book of Zechariah in which the prophet sees the streets full once again with playing children: "This was the same scene that Rabbi Akiva envisioned when he rejoiced at the sight of foxes scurrying through the ruins of the Holy of Holies."[35]

Heschel had cited the same source, but in 1936 Berlin it was evidence of the "pathos of a martyr," not the prescience of a visionary. Nonetheless, Lau ultimately rejects the Maimonidean notion that Akiva's messianic conviction was unanimously shared: "It became clear to me that many Sages did not support Rabbi Akiva's nationalistic vision of his aspirations for sovereign freedom."[36]

This article does not allow for a systematic comparison between the presentations of the Sages in these different periods of contemporary Jewish history. The following reflection by Lau on the resonance of his subject matter will have to suffice: "Over the course of my work on . . . this book, I found myself thinking about the relationship between tradition and change. It became clear to me that the internal tensions which dominated the *bet midrash* . . . at Yavneh are particularly relevant in our times. Contemporary Judaism—driven between movements that resist all innovation . . . and those that regard the notion of change itself as inherently sacred—can learn a great deal from the debates of Yavneh. Perhaps in attempting to understand the past, we can be wiser in the present, thereby benefitting generations to come."[37]

One of the best-selling novels in Israel in 2012 was Yochi Brandes's *Akiva's Orchard*, an ingenious reworking of many Rabbinic traditions concerning Rabbi Akiva and his contemporaries. The author (who makes special mention of Lau's work in her acknowledgments) suggests that Rabbi Akiva is exposed in the Pardes, the mysterious orchard from which he alone emerged unscathed, not to mystical secrets, but rather to the fate of the Jewish people. He and his associates learn what is to befall the Jews in the coming millennia. Both Akiva's nationalism and his creation of a portable Torah are read as responses to this blood-soaked epiphany.

For Brandes and Lau, the Sages of old are seen through the prism of contemporary debates about sovereignty, history, authority, and identity.

Solace, Challenge, and Fidelity

In the spring of 1936, in the midst of radical uncertainty, the Sages of the Mishnah are presented as exemplars of a multifaceted tradition. They do not offer the guarantee of a happy ending to the current chapter, but they are cited as evidence that the story continues. Emigration, resistance, resignation, internal organization, defiance, despair, elitism, populism—all these responses and more are epitomized in these characters.

These were not the only articles Heschel published in the *Gemeindeblatt* that year. On September 16, in the High Holy Day edition, he contributed an extraordinary article on repentance, titled "The Marranos of Today." In this important piece, Abraham Joshua Heschel edged toward his mature voice of cultural critique. Harking back to the image of the pseudo-converts he had mentioned in his *Maimonides*, he argued that the Jews of his day were in the grip of a cultural and spiritual malaise to match their political plight. The year 1933 had seemed to offer some illumination, "an awakening to God and of the community,"[38] but instead, Jews had become inverted Marranos, forced to acknowledge their Jewish identity on the outside but estranged from its essence.

His appeal to the figures of old was not solely intended to provide solace. It was also a call for lives to be lived in Jewish terms, in the spirit of Rabbi Judah the Prince, whose "life played out in a totally Jewish way: he had the style of a Jewish prince." Succor and support are matched with critique and challenge. Neither Judah nor others in his line were devoid of a secular education—to live in a totally Jewish way did not imply insularity. Hence we learn that Rabbi Simeon ben Gamaliel II "had received an education in his father's house and was also interested in physiological and botanical studies. This energy and the talent for statecraft that he had inherited from his father enabled him to lead the restoration of Palestinian Jewry."

In 1948 Heschel wrote a blistering essay in Hebrew, translated as "To Save a Soul." It is a powerful reflection on the aftermath of the Holocaust years, in which a section is devoted to memory: "Just as an individual's memory determines the nature of his personality, so the collective memory determines the destiny of nations. How bitter are the lives of those who do not know who their ancestors were . . . At times they are gripped by horror, feeling as if they were blinded, and they wander aimlessly in deep darkness upon a volcano . . . The power of collective memory is one of the characteristics of Israel . . . It is incumbent upon us to remember those events that occurred to our ancestors, events through which the spirit of God established residence in the history of our people."[39]

In Heschel's view, to believe is to remember, and in this sense Heschel's articles may be read as expressions of faith. Beyond the functions of comforting and discomforting his readers, these historical sketches also call to mind the link between faith in God and fidelity to the history of the Jewish people. In these reserved and recondite pieces, Heschel offers his beleaguered readers something of the comfort provided by precedent, and the pride to be gleaned from a sense of peoplehood.

Heschel never tired of portraying exemplars. His two books on the Kotsker Rebbe occupied him until his very last days. In America of the 1970s, just as in Germany of the 1930s, he saw his role as telling the stories of these heroic yet complex figures. How are we to explain the relationship between this kind of writing and the other Heschel, campaigning for change and undermining orthodoxies? The answer may be found in a famous statement, with which we bring this brief examination to a close. In it, Abraham Joshua Heschel points to a link between modernity and tradition, between harbingers of the new and exemplars of long-standing values: "The authentic individual is neither an end nor a beginning but a link between ages, both memory and expectation. Every moment is a new beginning within a continuum of history. It is fallacious to segregate a moment and not to sense its involvement in both past and future. Humbly the past defers to the future, but it refuses to be discarded. Only he who is an heir is qualified to be a pioneer."[40]

Notes

1. Dow Marmur translated these pieces, and Marcel Marcus helped prepare them for publication. This combined Marmur-Marcus translation, as yet unpublished, is quoted from throughout this article. It is our hope to publish these translations with commentary and explanation at a later date.

2. David Ellenson and Michael Marmur, "Heschel and the Roots of Kavanah," in *New Essays in American History*, ed. Pamela S. Nadell, Jonathan D. Sarna, and Lance J. Sussman (Cincinnati, 2010), 345–66.

3. Marcel Marcus has commented that of all the portraits, Rabbi Meir's seems to be the most critical. His suggestion is that it is Rabbi Meir's resistance to authority at a time of crisis to which Heschel objects.

4. Genesis Rabbah, 9.8.

5. This is extremely rare in Heschel's work. He is usually scrupulous in providing referential pointers to the source material. It is to be assumed that the exception in this case is related to the size and nature of the pieces. For an excellent recent survey of changing attitudes to the question of Rabbinic biography, see David Levine, "Ha'im bi'ografyah talmudit adayin efsharit?," *Mada'ei Hayahadut* 46 (2009): 41–64. Among the representations of the Sages in historical works of this and earlier eras, particular mention should be made of Heinrich Graetz's *Geschichte der Juden*, the relevant volume of which appeared first in 1853; Isaac Hirsch Weiss's *Dor dor ve-dorshav* (from 1871); Wilhelm Bacher's *Die Agada der Tannaïten* (from 1882); and Aharon Hyman's *Toldot Tannaim ve-Amoraim* (1910). The *Sefer agadah* of Bialik and Ravnitzky (published 1908–11) offered a presentation of the Sages that gleaned much from the biographical or quasi-biographical sources which were also used by Heschel in his pieces.

6. See Heschel, "Die Prophetie" (PhD diss., Polish Academy of Sciences, 1936), 151–52, where he decries the tendency of nineteenth-century scholarship to explain away what it saw as the primitive irrational layer of Biblical thinking.

7. See Abraham Joshua Heschel, *God in Search of Man: A Philosophy of Judaism* (New York, 1955), 258; and Heschel, "Protestant Renewal: A Jewish View," in *The Insecurity of Freedom: Essays in Applied Religion* (New York, 1966), 171–72.

8. See Abraham Joshua Heschel, *Torah min ha-shamayim be-aspeklaryah shel ha-dorot*, vol. 1 (London, 1962), especially xxxvii–xxxix.

9. The term employed is "eine Lawine der Resignation."

10. Abraham Joshua Heschel, *Maimonides* [1935], trans. Joachim Neugroschel (New York, 1982), 6–7.

11. Time and again in his work on prophesy in the Middle Ages we find references to discretion and absence of full disclosure. His Maimonides had a prophetic urge, but

there is only circumstantial evidence: nothing is ever stated explicitly. "The hearts of the Sages are the burial grounds of secrets," and Maimonides would reveal a little in order to conceal more. For the English translation of this essay, see "Did Maimonides Believe that He Had Attained the Rank of Prophet" [1945], in Abraham J. Heschel, *Prophetic Inspiration After the Prophets: Maimonides and Other Medieval Authorities* (Hoboken, N.J., 1996), esp. 70.

12. Abraham Joshua Heschel, *Don Jizchak Abravanel* (Berlin, 1937).

13. "The People of the Covenant," *Ararat* 30 (1967): 73.

14. Abraham Joshua Heschel, "The Individual Jew and His Obligations" (1957), in *The Insecurity of Freedom*, 190–91. See also Abraham Joshua Heschel, *Who Is Man* (Stanford, Calif., 1965), 34, 35, 59.

15. Abraham Joshua Heschel, "The Eastern European Era in Jewish History," *YIVO Annual of Jewish Social Science* 1 (1946): 101.

16. Abraham Joshua Heschel, *Moral Grandeur and Spiritual Audacity*, ed. Susannah Heschel (New York, 1996), 9. See also Abraham Joshua Heschel, "To Save a Soul" in *Moral Grandeur and Spiritual Audacity*, 64.

17. A recording is in the American Jewish Archives. See Abraham Joshua Heschel, "A Time for Renewal" (1972), in *Moral Grandeur and Spiritual Audacity*, 47, which invokes Rabbi Akiva.

18. Abraham Joshua Heschel, "Existence and Celebration" [1965], in *Moral Grandeur and Spiritual Audacity*, 27, 32.

19. See Einat Ramon, "Avodah ve-sanvarei ha-ne'orut be-hagut Avraham Yehoshua Heschel," *Daat* 71 (2011): 105–31.

20. See Azzan Yadin, *Scripture as Logos: Rabbi Ishmael and the Origins of Midrash* (Philadelphia, 2004), esp. introduction and pp. 93–94.

21. See Abraham Joshua Heschel, *Torah min ha-shamayim be-aspeklaryah shel ha-dorot*, vol. 1 (London, 1962), 115.

22. Ibid., 1:242–56.

23. Abraham Joshua Heschel, *Torah min ha-shamayim be-aspeklaryah shel ha-dorot*, vol. 3 (New York, 1995), 22. *Torah min ha-shamayim* is not a biographical work in the conventional sense. The closest the book comes to a presentation of historical details relating to the two main characters of the book is in 1:xxxvii–xl. In that chapter and elsewhere in the book there are a number of historical sources for the lives of these Sages. Most of these works were published after the 1936 articles were composed. Of the earlier works, it is interesting to note that he relied much more heavily on Wilhelm Bacher than he did on Isaac Hirsch Weiss. For references to Bacher's works in the first volume of *Torah min ha-shamayim*, see for example pp. vi, xii, 6,10,11,20,68, 114, 120, 121, 146, 188, 206, 212, 215 and 264. For Weiss's *Dor dor ve-dorshav*, see p.9.

24. See, for example, Marion A. Kaplan, *Between Dignity and Despair: Jewish Life in Nazi Germany* (Oxford, 1998). It is interesting to note that on p.70 Kaplan observes that the mood in relation to the option of emigration underwent a significant change between 1935 and 1937.

25. Marcus Lehmann, *Akiba: Historische Erzählung aus der Zeit der letzten Kämpfe der Juden gegen die römische Weltmacht. Nach talmudischen und römischen Quellen* (Frankfurt am Main, 1920).

26. Louis Finkelstein, *Akiba: Scholar, Saint and Martyr* (New York, 1936), ix.

27. Ibid., x–xi.

28. Yehudah Mirsky: "Rabbi Akiva: Liberal, Existentialist, Navi . . . ," *Daat* 71 (2011): 93–104.
29. Jonathan Steinberg, "Milton Steinberg, American Rabbi—Thoughts on His Centenary," *Jewish Quarterly Review* 95, no. 3 (2005): 588.
30. Dalia Marx: "Mitos atik be-sherut ha-hoveh . . . ," *Akdamot* 24 (2010): 156–76.
31. Binyamin Lau, *The Sages: Character, Context and Creativity*, vol. 2, *From Yavneh to the Bar Kochba Revolt*, trans. Ilana Kurshan (Jerusalem, 2011), 21.
32. *The Sages*, 2:186.
33. Binyamin Lau, *Hakhamim* (Tel Aviv, 2008), 3:332.
34. Ibid., 2:375–377.
35. Ibid., 2:x–xi.
36. Ibid., 2:xvii.
37. Ibid., 2:xvii.
38. Heschel, "The Meaning of Repentance," in *Moral Grandeur and Spiritual Audacity*, 69.
39. Heschel, "To Save a Soul," in *Moral Grandeur and Spiritual Audacity*, 64.
40. Heschel, *Who Is Man?*, 99.

13

BETWEEN A ROCK AND A HARD PLACE

Rav J. B. Soloveitchik's Perspective on Gender

RACHEL ADLER

Joseph Baer Soloveitchik (1903–93), known to his followers simply as the Rav, was a man caught between tradition and modernity. This was especially true concerning two controversial areas: secular learning and gender relations. He grew up a veritable prince of the Torah, the intellectual heir of his father and of his grandfather R. Hayim Soloveitchik, the Brisker Rav, who had created a new analytical methodology for the study of Talmud and halakhah. But whereas his grandfather had vehemently opposed secular education, J. B. Soloveitchik went to Berlin and got his doctorate at the university.[1] And whereas the previous generations of his family had arranged matches for their sons and daughters within a learned elite, Soloveitchik fell in love with and married Tonya Lewitt, who was not from an aristocratic family, but had a doctorate in educational psychology from the University of Jena.[2]

Soloveitchik's educational policies profoundly affected the classical gender oppositions of Orthodox Judaism. When, under his leadership, the Maimonides School was founded in Boston in 1937, the Rav decreed that in its high school, girls would learn Talmud rigorously alongside the boys.[3] The Rav also inaugurated the study of Talmud at Stern College for Women.[4] Rabbi Norman Lamm relates in his eulogy for the Rav that Soloveitchik taught and treated his daughters just as he taught and treated his son.[5]

Why did the Rav make these changes in women's education? Widely different opinions exist.[6] Presumably the decisions were made in the usual environment for difficult or revolutionary decisions: between a rock and a hard place. Clearly, Soloveitchik felt impelled to advance Jewish women's equality in some way, and that way was education. But offering girls and women a process of Jewish intellectual development comparable to that of men undermined a common rationale for hierarchalizing gender: that since women were inferior because of their ignorance of Torah, they should serve their husbands but could never be their equals. Now that rationale was gone.

Soloveitchik and the Question of Gender

Why then should women not be equal in every way? Soloveitchik does not appear to think they should be, but his thinking on gender is not consistent. How Soloveitchik thought about gender is the question I wish to pursue in this essay. The main sources I will be using are *The Lonely Man of Faith*, which began as a lecture but was converted into an article by the Rav himself, and the collection *Family Redeemed,* whose construction I will discuss later.[7] This is an area of Rav Soloveitchik's thought in which his devotion to tradition and his deviations from it are both unresolved and inconsistently reasoned. The Rav wrestles with binary gender roles and essences, but he never definitively rejects them. His egalitarianism in higher Jewish education was pathbreaking for American Orthodoxy, and distinctively modern. Yet, as I hope to demonstrate, although the Rav needed and wanted gender equality at some level, theologically he could not completely relinquish binary gender constructions. His failure to deal both theoretically and practically with the new challenges to older gender patterns was a failure shared by all of the Judaisms of his time. Susannah Heschel writes in 1983:

> To an extent, the conflict emerging between feminism and Judaism today parallels the conflict between Jews and Western culture that began to take shape with the Emancipation of Jews in Europe two hundred years ago. Just as none of the great ideological movements of the Modern period . . . seemed able, ultimately, to incorporate and accept Jews and Judaism, so, too, none of the religious movements of modern Judaism seems capable of coming to terms with women and feminism. And just as Jews became the crucible of modern political thoughts, so, too, feminism is the crucible for modern Judaism. Today's confrontation with feminism exposes the failure of Jewish religious movements to cope with modernity's challenges to theology and to respond effectively to them.[8]

Soloveitchik's *Lonely Man of Faith*

The Soloveitchik work that seems to address the relationships of women as well as men to Judaism in the modern world is a lecture turned into an essay by Rav Soloveitchik himself, perhaps with the assistance of Tonya Soloveitchik, *The Lonely Man of Faith*. Its first unusual feature is that the essay is prefaced by a dedication reading, "To Tonya, a woman of great courage, sublime dignity, total commitment and uncompromising truthfulness." To my knowledge, no other essay in the Orthodox journal *Tradition* is dedicated to a woman. Tonya's personal attributes, as we shall see, represent a perfect amalgam between the majestic and the covenantal modes.

The Lonely Man of Faith uses the two creation accounts in Genesis 1 to 3 to establish typologies depicting two different masculine personalities. Adam 1 is "Majestic Man." He looks at the universe and asks, "What is it for?" "What can it be made to do?" As God has willed, he and his female counterpart are to "increase and multiply and fill the earth and conquer it." (Gen. 1:28). He is, or presumably, they are, to be creators who exploit the natural world and invent technology to enhance human well-being and dignity. Soloveitchik's concern here is not with man dominating woman but with the impact of the divine command of human dominion over the world that, by defining Adam 1 characterologically, seems to limit him and his consort spiritually.[9]

Interestingly, Soloveitchik does not reference *b. Yevamot* 65b, which establishes women's lack of obligation to procreate by linking the mitzvah with domination.[10] Apparently, he does not want to get entangled here in a battle over obligation and domination. His concern, instead, is intimacy. Adam 1 and presumably the unnamed Mrs. Adam 1 are capable only of I–it relations. This set of spouses has never known aloneness because they were created together, but they have never known intimacy either. Professor Shira Wolosky, who offers a feminist reading of *The Lonely Man of Faith*, writes of Adam 1: "This Adam's very selfhood is shaped through instrumental social relations."[11] She argues that Adam 1 represents society as "a community of interests forged by the indomitable desire for success and triumph" (LM, 43), and thus exposes the deep alienation and isolation implicit in social contract theory.

In contrast, Adam 2, the Lonely Man of Faith, is no utilitarian. He is receptive, contemplative, intuitive, even mystical. Wolosky observes that Soloveitchik endows him with some characteristics often associated with the feminine. She writes that "it is women who have historically undertaken self-limitation as making room for others through a long sociology of nurturing, care, and, indeed, sacrifice."[12] Here it is Adam 2 who finds his companion by sacrificing part of himself (LM, 38). God puts an overpowering sleep upon him, during which his rib is extracted and Eve is created. Adam of Genesis 2 is the first mother.

For Soloveitchik, Adam 2, Eve, and God constitute the first covenantal community. This is an odd origin for community, as women are often regarded as quintessentially individuals and are said to be unable halakhically to constitute a community even with other women.[13] As a member of this first community, Eve must be regarded as an independent moral subject. However, as two individuals speaking experientially in private codes, Adam 2 and Eve would never have coalesced into a community were it not for God. According to Soloveitchik, "Without the covenantal experience of the prophetic or prayerful colloquy, Adam *absconditus* would have persisted in his he-role and Eve *abscondita* in her she-role, unknown to and distant from each other" (LM, 65). As Wolosky remarks, "Such interiority has seldom been ascribed to or even permitted to women."[14]

Soloveitchik's analysis here seems to suggest that conventional gender roles impede people from being genuine with one another and with God. They also appear to be external rather than essential. Experiencing covenantal community overrides or strips away these roles. Roles put aside, "they [Adam and Eve] reveal themselves to one another in sympathy and love" in the context of their shared purpose (LM, 66). They become friends, "an existential, in-depth relation between two individuals" (LM, 66). This sort of friendship between men and women is unprecedented in classical Jewish texts. And yet, although this passage is full of ideas that cry out for further elucidation, nowhere else does Rav Soloveitchik display any interest in the impact of covenantal community on Eve or on gender.

For the man of faith, the covenantal community, while redemptive, is fragile and sporadic. He oscillates dialectically between majesty and power and covenantal humility, and this oscillation both intensifies his loneliness and renders complete redemption unattainable (LM, 75–76). The modern world appears to Soloveitchik to belong almost entirely to Majestic Man. There is no place for the man of faith, much less for his gender-free existential relationship with his Eve.

Soloveitchik the Lecturer

We have said that *The Lonely Man of Faith* began as a lecture. Rav Soloveitchik produced hundreds of lectures, rather than books. Brought up to believe that he must save Jewish learning in an age when modernity threatened it,

Soloveitchik was the hope and pride of his father, who was, perhaps for this very reason, strict and stingy with praise. His grandfather the Brisker Rav so embarrassed him by rising before him in reverence to his learning when Soloveitchik was still an adolescent, that he would hastily leave the *beis-medresh* via the window when his grandfather appeared.[15] Perhaps these huge expectations, warring with what Soloveitchik saw as the needs of a modern Judaism, fueled the anxiety and perfectionism that so curtailed his written output. Instead, he gave lecture upon lecture, prepared and thought through, and preserved on tape.

Lecture is a genre of its own. As an oral genre, lecture is perfectly suited to handing on traditions and stories. It showcases a speaker's ability to teach, to explain, to stimulate people to follow the laying out of quandaries and struggles and to become excited about their resolution. Lecture can be a dramatic way for a thinker to explore ideas, think out loud in the presence of an audience; consequently, the form is tolerant of conflicts and contradictions. Moreover, lectures are tailored to particular audiences; they are contextual. What the Rav would say to his Talmud students at Yeshiva University might have differed from what he would say at a large public lecture like the Yahrzeit lectures for Rebbitzin Tonya Soloveitchik or the annual *derashah* on *teshuvah*, which differed yet again from what he might present to a secular university audience.

It is clear that the Rav's sounding board, critic, and consultant for his lecture writing was his wife, Tonya, and he was quite public about his reliance on her. In his Teshuvah Derashah in September 1968, after her death in 1967, he confides to his audience, "A few days ago, I was writing this annual sermon on repentance [teshuvah derashah]. I always used to talk about it with my wife; she would help me develop and polish my ideas. Again this year, while I was writing this lecture, I wanted to ask her: 'Could you please help me? Should I shorten this idea? Should I expand on this point? Should I express this concept or another one?' I asked my wife, but there was no response. If there was a reply, it was lost in the rustling of the trees and did not reach me."[16] The dependence the Rav expresses upon Tonya suggests that she was his first editor.

The Problem with Family Redeemed

I want to compare *The Lonely Man of Faith* to the essays in *Family Redeemed*, a volume assembled after the Rav's death from a selection of his public lectures. As I will demonstrate, the thinking in *Family Redeemed* is much more consistent with centrist or right-wing Orthodox gender roles than *The Lonely Man of Faith*.

In the articles contained in *Family Redeemed*, the Rav appears paradoxically both to proclaim the equality of women and men and to limit women's actions in the world by means of essentialistic binary gender ideologies.

How can we understand the position the Rav appears to take in *Family Redeemed*? Possibly the essays in *Family Redeemed* indicate the Rav's withdrawal from modernity. But possibly they indicate instead how those disciples who constructed this volume are reshaping his legacy, an apprehension eloquently voiced by Dr. Norman Lamm in his eulogy for Rav Soloveitchik: "We must guard against any revisionism, to misinterpret the Rav's work. . . . He was who he was, and he was not a simple man. We must accept him on his terms as a highly complicated, profound and broad minded personality."[17] It makes sense, then, to begin with an account of how the contents of *Family Redeemed* were constructed, before I proceed to comparisons with *The Lonely Man of Faith*.

The editors of *Family Redeemed* tell us that "the manuscripts, all undated, were used by the Rav in presenting his public lectures, and in some cases, tapes of these presentations are available."[18] However, just for example, the description of the contents of the essay "Adam and Eve" is as follows: "'Adam and Eve' was presented as a lecture at Stern College for Women, Yeshiva University, on December 22, 1971. The chapter here also includes material on natural man taken from a short manuscript titled, 'Psukei Bereshit: Man as a Natural Being Within the Universe and as a Unique Being Opposed to the Universe.' The section on the respective sins of Adam and Eve was taken from another manuscript concerning marriage."[19]

In other words, what Shatz and Wolowelsky, as the editors of this volume, are offering us is an amalgam of three Solovetchik manuscripts, two of them undated. This policy of combining texts presumes that Rav Soloveitchik's ideas were consistent over time, and hence can be combined to form a coherent and consistent whole. A man whose thinking Hillel Goldberg described as "stamped by elemental conflicts so powerful that they would recur over and over in variation, mutation, or repetition of the original form, but never in any clear pattern of development" would seem to be a dubious candidate for this kind of treatment, but the editors express no qualms.[20] Moreover, Shatz and Wolowelsky are not forthcoming about the nature of the editing necessary to produce these essays. Did they rewrite? Did they interpolate transitions and bridges? They do not indicate in the published text where the additions or corrections are their own. Moreover, how did the editors happen to choose these particular Soloveitchik lectures to reproduce as essays? Shatz and Wolowelsky chose lectures dated from 1959 to 1971. Why this particular time period? Were there other lectures that were candidates for publication but were rejected? If so, on what grounds?

When Dr. Haym Soloveitchik went to court in 1999 in an attempt to retrieve his father's legacy, he contended that there had been over 1,800 tapes on Talmud and halakhah that the Rav had delivered between 1978 and his death in 1993. Many of these tapes went missing. Concerning the whole body of J. B. Soloveitchik's taped lectures, Professor Samuel Heilman is quoted as saying, "The lectures were intellectually transformative, the epitome of the encounter between Jewish learning and modern intellect. People who have never heard of that encounter . . . don't know what committed modern Orthodoxy sounds like."[21] The Rav himself confided in a talk to the faculty of the Wurzweiler School of Social Work at Yeshiva University on March 13, 1974: "My students are my products as far as *lomdus* [learning] is concerned. They follow my methods of learning. However, there is some reservation in their minds regarding my philosophical viewpoint. They consider me excellent in lomdus. However, when it comes to my philosophical experiential viewpoint, I am somehow persona non grata. My ideas are too radical for them."[22] Yet it is difficult to detect any distinctive Modern Orthodox theology, much less any radical ideas in the offerings in *Family Redeemed*.

In most of the essays of *Family Redeemed*, Rav Soloveitchik appears to posit an essentialist and binary notion of manhood and womanhood that is ahistorical and premodern. For example, in the glued-together pieces that constitute the essay "Adam and Eve," Soloveitchik posits conflicting notions about gender. He insists that Eve, like Adam, has I-awareness.[23] She is not just an instrument for Adam's use, but has an inner life of her own and is "not the shadow of man, but an independent persona" (FR, 22). At the same time, Soloveitchik maintains that men and women differ "spiritually and personality-wise" and that "the two sex-personalities sin differently" (FR, 22). The man's sin is overreaching and grasping for omnipotent power, while the woman is characterized as passive, receptive, and pleasure seeking (FR, 23).

The idea that personalities are gender specific and that men are active and power seeking while women are passive and indulgent is an instance of essentialism, the belief that there are gender essences that transcend history and culture and remain consistent whether we are talking of a Ndembu midwife (a kind of medico/spiritual professional) or Catherine the Great, Empress of Russia (a personality neither passive nor uninterested in power). Soloveitchik is a maker of typologies, and his types characteristically exist in binary oppositions. About this phenomenon the feminist theorist Elizabeth Grosz explains: "When the system of boundaries or divisions operates by means of the construction of binaries or pairs of opposed terms, these terms are not only mutually exclusive, but also mutually exhaustive. They divide the spectrum into one term and its opposite with no possibility of a term which is neither one nor the other or which is both . . . . Dichotomies are inherently non-reversible, non-reciprocal hierarchies, and thus describe systems of domination."[24]

What Soloveitchik seemed originally to be aiming at is difference, a term derived from Saussurean linguistics in which each of the two or more terms have existences autonomous from the other. Each exists in its own right. Each term is defined by what it is not. This has been used as a metaphor for defining the relation between the sexes without making one the norm and the other its opposite. The notion of difference also accommodates additional terms unlike the binary dichotomy.[25] Theologically, Soloveitchik affirms in the essay, "Marriage": "There is no doubt that in the eyes of the Halakhah, man and woman enjoy an equal status and have the same worth as far as their *humanitas* is concerned" (FR, 71). Yet he needs the binary of man and woman to justify the gender roles into which they are placed. In "Adam and Eve," Eve's punishment for the primal sin is that "she pays the price of self-limitation and self-withdrawal from the vastness of spiritual personalism into the straits of naturalness. She exchanges her yearning for the vast and infinite for a nature-encompassed and restricted life. She ends up as a mother attached to her husband and children. The woman yields to the dictates of nature and surrenders her dreams and visions of the infinite" (FR, 26).

Soloveitchik finds this female pattern in the personage of the Shekhinah. She is "Deity imprisoned in finitude" (FR, 26). "Little wonder," Soloveitchik remarks, "that we experience the immanence of God in the whole of the cosmos as the suffering, bearing, tending, and nourishing Mother, with whom natural necessity interferes, and who is bound by indissoluble ties to an unalterable order of things and events" (FR, 26). The anthropologist Clifford Geertz would identify this as a "model *for* reality," that is, "a template for producing reality."[26] If the Shekhinah is shackled to "an unalterable order of things," how can an ordinary woman not sacrifice her own life dreams, goals, freedom, and safety to satisfy husband and children? This portrait of God/She as a self-sacrificing drudge serving her children rather than being revered by them is rather nightmarish.

About the material in *Family Redeemed*, David Hartman complains that Soloveitchik "seems in these quotations to accept the moral truth of male/female equality—and then (the apologetic turn) to assert that Judaism upholds this equality albeit in a novel way that those unfamiliar with the tradition's theological underpinnings might misperceive. Viewed through Soloveitchik's corrective philosophical lens, traditional halakhah stands in no need of change: it already embodies the inspiration of gender equality."[27]

It is barely possible to imagine Soloveitchik educating young women in Talmud out of concern for their equality with men and then demanding that they relinquish all spiritual and intellectual pursuits in order to bear, nurture, and suffer as is "natural" for them. It seems more like a recipe for revolution. Surely someone is bound to notice that the great philosopher has depicted an entire cosmos and a Deity, as well, that both reinforce the inevitability and inalterability of masculine privilege.

The kind of gender economy Soloveitchik envisions has some of the trappings of modern partnership marriage but devolves into essentialized roles that demand at once too little and too much of mothers. These problems are exemplified in the models of parenting delineated in the essay "Parenthood: Natural and Redeemed": "In the natural community, the woman is involved in her motherhood-destiny; father is a distant figure who stands on the periphery. In the covenantal community the father moves to the center where mother has been all along, and both together take on a new commitment, universal in substance: to teach, to train the child to hear the faint echoes which keep on tapping at our gates and which disturb the complacent, comfortable, gracious society" (FR, 114).

This covenantal model is based on Abraham and Sarah as model parenting partners. Both are imagined as teachers and, as the passage above suggests, covenantal teachers must convey a countercultural message. In this endeavor fathers and mothers have complimentary missions defined by their essential gender characteristics. Fathers are to teach rigorously and intellectually the knowledge and method of Jewish tradition. Mothers are to teach experientially, "through osmosis, through a tear or a smile, through dreamy eyes and soft melody, through the silence at twilight and the recital of *Shema*" (FR, 115).

Of this mother personality, inarticulate and intuitive, a radical transformation is demanded in times of crisis "when man, notwithstanding his great intellectual prowess finds himself entranced and is about to fail in the implementation of his fatherhood commitment" (FR, 116). At such times, "the mother . . . assumes the role of her husband's keeper, his guardian, and teacher. In the covenantal community, motherhood is a more powerful spiritual force than fatherhood. The shy, modest, reserved mother turns into an active personality whenever critical action is called for" (FR, 116). Women are, apparently, concealed superwomen committed to self-sacrifice (FR, 113).[28] In ordinary situations, they are to repress their gifts, their initiative, their learning, and their ego investments. In crisis situations, they must throw on their capes and save everyone. Then, conveniently, "the instant she completes her task, when the crisis is over, she returns quickly to her tent, draws down the curtain of anonymity and disappears" (FR, 119).

This is Soloveitchik's justification for not saying "God of Sarah, God of Rebecca, God of Rachel, God of Leah" even though, as he acknowledges, "they had an equal share in *Borei Olam*, the Creator of the world" (FR, 120) It is the "tragic destiny" of woman, Soloveitchik maintains in this essay, to "act her part with love and devotion in a dim corner of the stage and then [to] leave softly by a side door without applause" (FR, 119–120).

Are the manufactured articles in *Family Redeemed* an accurate representation of Soloveitchik's thought? This question cannot be answered without further research into the provenance of the source manuscripts and tapes, the process of their assembly into articles, and the possible existence of conflicting theologies of gender among Soloveitchik's oeuvre. The information currently available does suggest that Soloveitchik's delicate negotiations with modernity seem to break down on the issue of gender and the need for gender justice. The hints of Eve's autonomy and integrity in *The Lonely Man of Faith* are compromised in the essays on family. Neither do the functions allotted to Jewish women in the essays on family seem logically coherent with Soloveitchik's encouragement of sophisticated higher Jewish education and secular education for women. However, only with the cultivation of all her intellectual gifts and the fullest understanding of Jewish tradition and its imperatives, combined with constant admonitions to sacrifice, to deny her own needs and gifts, can a woman be groomed to be her husband's "*chaverah li'-de'agah,* [the] person in whom one can confide both in times of crisis when distress strikes and in times of glory when one feels happy and content," as Soloveitchik puts it in another essay.[29] Without admonitions and a lifelong praxis of self-effacement, this handily modernized woman might entertain her own visions, seek her own portion in the Torah. That is the Orthodox women's revolution we are beginning to see in the works of Tamar Ross, Tova Hartman, Haviva Ner-David and others.[30]

Notes

1. For biographical information see Shulamith Soloveitchik Meiselman, *The Soloveitchik Heritage: A Daughter's Memoir* (Hoboken, N.J., 1995); Aaron Rakeffet-Rothkoff, *The Rav: The World of Rabbi Joseph B. Soloveitchik*, 2 vols., ed. J. Epstein (Hoboken, N.J., 1999); Hillel Goldberg, *Between Berlin and Slobodka: Jewish Transition Figures from Eastern Europe* (Hoboken, N.J., 1989), 89–113.
2. Meiselman, *The Soloveitchik Heritage*, 147.
3. Rakeffet-Rothkoff, *The Rav*, 1:35; Simcha Krauss, "The Rav: On Zionism, Universalism and Feminism," *Tradition* 34, no. 2 (2000): 35.
4. Krauss, "The Rav," 35.
5. Norman Lamm, "A Eulogy for the Rav," *Tradition* 28, no. 1 (1993): 4–17.
6. For example, Mayer Twersky, "A Glimpse of the Rav," *Tradition* 30, no. 4 (1996): 96–99, denies that this was a modernist decision.
7. Joseph B. Soloveitchik, "The Lonely Man of Faith," *Tradition* 7, no. 2 (1965): 5–67, reprinted as *The Lonely Man of Faith* (New York, 1992). Subsequent citations to *The Lonely Man of Faith* (New York, 1992) will appear in the text as (LM, page number). Joseph B. Soloveitchik, *Family Redeemed: Essays on Family Relationships*, ed. D. Shatz and J. Wolowelsky (Jersey City, N.J., 2000).
8. Susannah Heschel, introduction to *On Being a Jewish Feminist*, ed. Susannah Heschel (New York, 1983), xxiii.
9. Shira Wolosky, "The Lonely Woman of Faith," *Judaism* 52, nos. 1–2 (2003): 3–18.
10. The Mishnah at *b. Yevamot* 65b establishes by majority opinion that women have no obligation to procreate. In the Gemara, R. Ile'a says in the name of R. El'azar b. R. Shimon, quoting Gen. 1:28, "It is the nature of a man to conquer but not the nature of a woman." To this attempt to justify the mitzvah as exclusively male, the Gemara objects that the plural in Gen. 1:28 signifies two, but R. Nachman b. Yitzchak notes that the Masoretic text spells the disputed verb without a vav, allowing it to be read as a singular *vekivshah*—you, masculine—conquer her or it, rather than the plural *vekivshuhah*—you, masculine and feminine—conquer her or it. Because its Masoretic voweling is plural, the rabbis do not contest the word's plurality as scripture. Its missing vav functions for them merely as *remez*, an exegetical hint that the word could also be read as *kibshah*, "[you, masculine, singular] master her/it." It can be inferred that the rabbis are not satisfied with this proof because another prooftext is proposed that restates the commandment of increasing and multiplying in the singular (Gen. 35:11). However, that it is not the first statement of the obligation weakens this second proof. Ultimately, argument, rather than prooftext, is conclusive in establishing the law.
11. Wolosky, "The Lonely Woman of Faith," 6.
12. Ibid., 12.
13. Saul Berman, "The Status of Women in Halakhic Judaism," in *The Jewish Woman*, ed. E. Koltun (New York, 1976), 121–22.
14. Wolosky, "The Lonely Woman of Faith," 9.
15. Rakeffet-Rothkoff, *The Rav*, 1:24–25, 202–3; 2:168, 217; Goldberg, *Between Berlin and Slobodka*, 94.
16. Rakeffet-Rothkoff, *The Rav*, 2:11–12.
17. Lamm, "A Eulogy for the Rav," 13.
18. Shatz and Wolowelsky, in *Family Redeemed*, ix.

19. Ibid.
20. Goldberg, *Between Berlin and Slobodka*, 96.
21. Samuel G. Freedman, "Modern Orthodox Jews Have a Hero but Not All His Words," *New York Times*, May 22, 1999.
22. Rakeffet-Rothkoff, *The Rav*, excerpt 21.08: "Religious Immaturity," vol. 2: 240.
23. Soloveitchik, *Family Redeemed*, 21. Subsquent citations to *Family Redeemed* will appear in the text as (FR, page number).
24. Elizabeth Grosz, *Sexual Subversions: Three French Feminists* (Crow's Nest, Australia, 1989), xvi.
25. Ibid., xvii.
26. Clifford Geertz, "Religion as a Cultural System," *The Interpretation of Cultures* (New York, 1973), 93, 95.
27. David Hartman with Charlie Buckholtz, "Feminism and Apologetics," *God Who Hates Lies: Confronting and Rethinking Jewish Tradition* (Woodstock, Vt., 2011), 75.
28. In this essay Hannah is the exemplar of mothers' sacrifice, but it is a pervasive theme in this volume.
29. Soloveitchik, "Adam and Eve," *Family Redeemed*, 27.
30. Tamar Ross, *Expanding the Palace of Torah* (Waltham, Mass., 2004). Tova Hartman, *Feminism Encounters Traditional Judaism* (Waltham, Mass., 2008). Haviva Ner-David, *Life on the Fringes* (Needham, Mass., 2000).

14

THE TENDENCY OF STORIES AND THE ETHICS OF LIFE'S ENDINGS

WILLIAM CUTTER

Narratives—especially those uninhibited by didactic goals—seem particularly well suited to the more flexible definitions of right and wrong that character-ize our time. They can serve as vehicles for empathy and for examining mul-tiple points of view, a kind of heuristic play with opposing possibilities and alternative outcomes. Reading stories is an excellent way to grasp the context in which particular ethical dilemmas are embedded and to ask questions that take professional behavior beyond the right or wrong of a specific action.[1]

The honoree for this volume, Professor David Ellenson, is partial to aspects of narrative thinking. He has devoted his career to exploring contem-porary applications of classic values and to an ethical *aggiornamento*, and he has become prominent because of his grasp of a modernizing halakhah and responsa literature. In my view, his early essay on covenantal approaches to bioethics was influenced by an aspect of "narrative thinking."[2]

"Narrative thinking" (thinking like a writer and thinking like an inter-preter of stories), though understood in different ways by different people, can serve several separate functions, ranging from thinking about specific ethical dilemmas to seeking broader horizons and more general implications of ethical behavior.[3] Some have referred to this broader perspective as "soft" ethics. But surely we think first of ethical deliberation in specific cases, cases in which narratives may offer tools that enrich analysis of a particular case at hand. Some believe that narratives may accommodate the technology that makes certain ethical perspectives obsolete. Beyond technology is the addi-tional fact that our very understanding of ourselves is changing, and new understandings of community, culture, and individual obligation are as revolutionary as the technical apparatus we use to begin life or to monitor the end of life. More storytelling seems to be a helpful response.

It is true, as one critic noted, that "life is endlessly, heart stoppingly, fragile and unknowable."[4] And because of that unknowability, halakhic formalism as a guide for bioethics is not serving our current generation of non-Orthodox Jews. While narrative thinking is not a perfect antidote to halakhic limitations or to life's fragility, I understand it as a partner to more commonly employed methodologies for addressing the larger ethical questions of our time: the end of life and its beginnings; the complexity of working with research subjects; the assessment of how we distribute services and goods; and the need to encourage human attention to the most fragile citizens among us. It is also a partner to more restricted questions of right and wrong. A fuller understanding of how narratives function may enrich the thinking of any of the schools of non-halakhic ethical thought, which we might call formalist, principlist, or covenantalist.[5]

"Narrative" has become a stylish word in "general" popular culture, and it seems to appear with increasing frequency in our intellectual discourse. One's bookshelves are likely to be filled with the "stories" of experience with life and death.[6] In the medical world, narrative is frequently used to help professionals understand patient needs and their own responses; but narrative presumably helps ethicists respond to the uncomfortable pressures of change in our medical environments by inviting flexibility and deeper understanding of the ramifications of the solutions and strategies we might devise in particular situations. Narratives, it is sometimes argued, fill in the details of a rich specificity.[7] When it comes to the more global issues of health care for society—perhaps "mega issues" would be an appropriate term—narrative has become the road to greater sensitivity about the often-ignored problems in the American health care delivery system.[8]

The increased use of narrative in public life may be at least partly the result of modernity's antinomianism, but it has turned out to produce surprising new perspectives on history, anthropology, and law. It has added what I consider to be a new version of theology, a development that I will cite in a later paragraph. Furthermore, there is a narrative that undergirds almost every discussion about medical care in America—the American story about our independence and enfranchisement, and the "can do" spirit that has been identified in the land since de Tocqueville. This spirit and these attitudes have influenced much of the recent conversation about how to handle difficulties of illness and the complexities of decisions we must make about end of life, distribution of services, medical insurance, reproductive health, and family responsibility. On a less global scale, it is precisely the narratives of individuals that drive a lot of our discourse. Other narratives about health delivery—as in the narrative about the superiority of the American health care system—seem to have led us astray and helped us ignore some of the unappealing dark truths about the American health care system.[9]

Upon completing a draft of this essay, I encountered Marcia Angell, retired editor of the *New England Journal of Medicine*, who wrote in the *New York Review of Books* of her belief that the Death with Dignity Act (which failed to pass in Massachusetts) would eventually surface again, declaring that "the issue will not go away. Most people know someone who has died a miserable, protracted death."[10] So, invoking a version of narrative to make her argument (the personal experience of people), and grounded in a view of personal rights that characterizes the grand American narrative, Dr. Angell anticipates a more enlightened result the next time the Death with Dignity Act is on the Massachusetts ballot. But narrative is not only about demonstrating the "truth" of one side of an experience, as I hope to demonstrate, and the task of narration is more complex than simply trumping a deliberation with one point of view that is overdetermined by personal experience. Indeed, with regard to the libertarian impulse to permit voluntary ending of a life, there will be individuals with the experience of a "counter narrative": an anticipated death that was delayed; another bar mitzvah attended; a family reconciliation; a chance for heroic sharing among family members who care for a loved one with newly discovered spirit and cooperation. In regard to specific moral action, as well as in regard to the American sense of enfranchisement, even the devil can quote narrative thinking.[11]

Narrative thinking will not necessarily lead to lenient conclusions in specific situations, but it might help people be more aware of the inclinations they bring to the table where ethics are considered. It certainly exposes an ethical deliberation to the implications of a decision for a particular subject. Immersing oneself in stories that touch on health and healing can serve to open up discourse among individuals who need to consider ethical issues—both on the level of specific action and in regard to more global questions.

Narrative Texts—The Four Kinds

Jewish tradition is rich in narrative in many forms—from aggadah to hasidic stories, from personal diaries to exemplifications of moral situations—but until recent decades we have not exploited general literary theory that might help account for various narrative genres. My interest in this paper turns toward stories that are useful for Jewish bioethics, but I am equally interested in narrative strategies in a more generalized sense. Certainly, questions about the nature of "aggadah" will be part of this discussion—but only a part.[12] At this point I introduce two narratives about death and dying from distinct literary traditions. Each narrative, though entirely different in genre, serves one or more of four aspects of narrative: (1) stories as didactic in which the outcome of a story or the concluding lines of a narrative seem to make a case for certain ethical behavior; (2) stories as contributing to an individual patient's (or doctor's) self-understanding and to the understanding of ethical "decisors" about their subject—the patient; (3) stories as comprising structural elements that can guide ethical discourse or enrich the moral life of all the parties in an ethical situation; and (4) "story" as the foundation for our fundamental understanding of the culture that gives rise to law. Most proponents of narrative approaches to medical dilemmas argue that stories are one way (and to different degrees) of relieving the flatness and summary description of a situation, that narrative (in the words of Geoffrey Hartman) invites a "sympathetic absorption of each person's words and demeanor, so that no one is too quickly classified, shunted into diagnostic flatness."[13] In a more dramatic characterization of the value of narrative, psychiatrist Bradley Lewis seeks a "trope of narrative multiplicity"—where each simplicity loses the violence of totalitarian control.[14] These views—or views like these—have recently found interest among young Jewish commentators such as Barry Wimpfheimer, Jonathan Crane, and Adam Zachary Newton, who have joined others who bridge classic hermeneutic study with narrative, including Laurie Zoloth, Louis Newman, and Rachel Adler.[15] Many of these thinkers have been influenced by Robert Cover's legendary essay "Nomos and Narrative" for its theoretical speculation that all law grows out of some sort of cultural story.[16] It is perhaps because of the late Professor Cover's work that we have been able to link the theoretical relationship between law and culture to particular activities and particular ethical conundrums.

Before I address more fully the suggestions about "richness and flatness," I will discuss the one form of narrative that is the most prone to a sort of flatness: the aggadic passage about the death of Rabbi Judah the Prince to be found in the Talmud, bKet. 104a:

> On the day when Rabbi [Judah] died, the rabbis decreed a public fast and offered prayers for heavenly mercy. They, furthermore, announced that whoever said that Rabbi was dead would be stabbed

with a sword. Rabbi's handmaid ascended the roof and prayed: "The immortals desire Rabbi to join them and the mortals desire Rabbi to remain with them; may it be the will of God that the mortals may overpower the immortals." When however, she saw how often he resorted to the privy, painfully taking off his tefillin and putting them on again, she prayed: "May it be the will of God that the immortals may overpower the mortals." As the Rabbis continued their prayers for heavenly mercy, she took up a jar and threw it down from the roof to the ground. At that moment they ceased praying and the soul of Rabbi departed to its eternal rest.

This aggadic passage has often been understood as what Joseph Heinemann called an "ethical-didactic" tale, although I suggest that the passage need not be limited to its more obvious, flat, didactic function.[17] The story also contains some telltale formal components that may serve as guideposts to complex ethical deliberations.

Less didactic and more suited to considering the formalist virtues of narrative is the well-known story "The Death of Ivan Ilyich" by Leo Tolstoy. This unit, from chapter 7 of the short story (in all editions), illustrates a part of the wily way narrative can serve a discussion about virtue and can illustrate features of narrative consciousness, as it reflects the cultural context in which characters' behaviors are determined. It is a story that can be read by medical practitioners for its promptings of our own values and ethical tendencies, and it can be used by ethicists as a way of "feeling themselves into" the experience of illness. It has been understood by patients themselves as an opportunity for self-recognition. In this story, generations of readers might note the behavior of patients, servants, doctors, friends, and family as they circulate around the ill patient.

> How it happened it is impossible to say because it came about step by step, unnoticed, but in the third month of Ivan Ilyich's illness, his wife, his daughter, his son, his acquaintances, the doctors, the servants and above all himself were aware that the whole interest he had for other people was whether he would soon vacate his place, and at last release the living from the discomfort caused by his presence and he himself be released from his sufferings. . . .
>
> For his excretions also special arrangements had to be made, and this was torment to him every time. . . .

> But just through this most unpleasant matter, Ivan Ilyich
> obtained comfort. Gerasim, the butler's young assistant, always came
> in to carry things out. . . .
>
> After that Ivan Ilyich would sometimes call Gerasim, and get him
> to hold his legs on his shoulders, and he liked talking to him. . . .
>
> What tormented Ivan Ilyich the most was the deception, the lie,
> which for some reason they all accepted, that he was not dying but
> was simply ill.[18]

The passage provides a nondidactic humanistic purpose as a story about an illness. The story introduces characters who play varying roles in relation to the protagonist; it treats the intensity of Iliyich's inner feelings; and it elaborates the social setting—all features that contribute to an ethical calculus, but not to a particular ethical decision. One actually "gets inside" the unpleasantness involved in the care of the sick. The passage grows out of one of the story's most interesting components: Ivan's obsession with his health, which at first may lead us to believe that he is a "malade imaginaire," a hypochondriac. And it highlights the awkward and rigid family, professional, and social relationships that characterize life in illness and numerous aspects of his illness that could be the starting point for ongoing commentary and interpretation. Unlike the Rabbi Judah story, this Russian narrative has not had a history of didactic readings, but both stories can be portals to rich reflection. And one could add some of Tolstoy's "literary" strategies to a consideration of the Judah story, which lacks this kind of detail. Whereas the narrator describes Ivan's efforts at the toilet, the Judah narrative simply implies that discomfort through the metonymy that he constantly removed his tefillin. (The servant in each is the sensitive party in the environment.)

The Limits of the Binary—Halakhah vs. Aggadah

It should be clear that we are not limited to the conventional distinction between aggadah and halakhah, Bialik's famous dichotomy that reminded his readers of the admixture of one with the other. He affirmed the importance of aggadah's search for principles and values for fostering a desirable idealism (and we might add: sometimes helped justify a particular ethical conclusion). But aggadah, to Bialik's way of thinking, betrayed a softness that needed to be corrected by halakhah. (His metaphor: the molten ideals need the halakhic cooling into hard steel).[19] Bialik overstated his case, to my mind, for a Zionist purpose, and he should never be understood as a theoretical master of his own dichotomies. Among other reasons is the fact that there are many kinds of aggadah, and many literary components to aggadic presentations and to the entire domain of rabbinic narrative. Aggadah has sometimes been a more legitimate aid for developing *pesikah* (legal decision) than many believe, as Michael Chernick has demonstrated in a paper designed to probe instances of aggadic influence on halakhah.[20]

But the deep probing of the twentieth-century narrative theories that has characterized so much recent Jewish scholarship has been less evident in the realm of bioethics. And, despite the work of several bioethicists like Laurie Zoloth, Jonathan Cohen, and Noam Zohar, most of even our most imaginative scholars limit their thinking about "story" to aggadah as opposed to "halakhah."[21]

Narrative, then, need not be about drawing specific moral points from a story—although that happens frequently. In the story about the death of Rabbi Judah Ha-Nasi, countless commentators have found a kind of support for the halakhic prescription of the *Shulhan arukh* legal code that permits death to take its course, but does not permit hastening one's death. This is often expressed through the principle of the "Woodchoppers chopping" (a famous example from the medieval *Sefer Hasidim*), which is typically seen as a *mone'a'* (an impediment) to the natural dying process. One is permitted to turn away the impediment (*lehasir mone'a'*). The prayer in the Talmudic tale corresponds more or less to the woodchoppers whose noise famously was alleged to keep death at bay or—in contemporary terms—to the respirator that is keeping a patient alive against all neurological indicators that the patient has in fact expired.[22] The story of Rabbi Judah persisted as a popular Jewish favorite, demonstrating the power of narrative and our tendency to see stories as making a case for a particular ethical behavior.[23] This practice of reading an aggadah (or any story for that matter) as an exemplum, or as making an argument for a particular ethical resolution would be called, in Richard Lanham's terms, "looking through" a story to some meaning external to the story.[24] It is perhaps the most common reaction of readers, who look toward a moral point beyond a story. That tendency is consistent with all the generations of storytellers who have sought the "moral of the story." But a growing number of serious readers are looking "at" narratives for their technical formal features, for surprises within the story content that take one beyond the obvious expectations. In narratives one has the opportunity to find more broadly construed morality or virtue, and a fuller understanding of the general cultural context that the story brings to mind. And that is why Ivan Ilyich's narrative is so important for this conversation. Tolstoy's tale reminds us that the Talmudic story can be the base for probing the behavior of caretakers, for experiencing the duration of the illness and the patient's suffering within that duration, and for contemplating the significance of the heroic action (of the servant) against a norm. Like any good story, these two tales involve a breach of expectation; and they have a shape that affects their rhetorical power. As norms grow out of certain narratives, new narratives are used to expand the discourse around such normative conclusions.[25]

Of particular interest is the function of the narrative as revealing an imperfect world in which imperfect decisions are made. There are good arguments for keeping Rabbi Judah alive, even as there are the more obvious arguments for letting him pass away. The tale is not a story of *Kuli alma* . . . (a rabbinic phrase for universal agreement). As J. Hillis Miller has argued, stories narrate the epistemological limits that must be part of all ethical decisions.[26]

Some Background

Until the late Rabbi Immanuel Jacobowitz's early efforts, there was not much of a Jewish "bioethics" per se, and the galaxy of young scholars who began to devote serious time to the subject emerged only in the generation after Lord Jacobowitz's work. The American "boost" to this work was rendered by physician-rabbi Fred Rosner, who combined his experience as a doctor with his rich knowledge of Jewish law and practice.[27] Decades later, Israeli scholar Noam Zohar contributed his more contemporary notion of alternatives. Contemporary non-Orthodox thinkers, principally leaders within particular religious movements, have paved the way for the expanding discussion that has occurred since that early period. They began in the 1970s to move the bioethical discourse into modernity, with new ways to interpret halakhah by examining the principles behind the halakhic judgments, and by finding suitable analogies for medical practice filled with technologies that often seemed to render certain ethical principles obsolete.[28] "The narrative turn" in bioethics is an even later development, and it has enjoyed the scholarship of a significant group of scholars who have reflected brilliantly on the work of Martha Nussbaum and Robert Cover; on the respect for the "other" of Emanuel Levinas; and on some of the explications of Jerome Bruner, the legendary social philosopher and educator, who believed that "narrative thinkers" were a specific breed who thought inductively and who created meaning out of their inductions.[29] For Nussbaum, narrative forces us to explore virtue rather than to concentrate on specific answers to specific questions, and for Cover, one's "legal" decisions are both the product and progenitor of cultural meaning. Most recently, Jonathan Crane's doctoral dissertation concentrates on the rhetoric of Jewish thinking in regard to innovation in Jewish law. In his book, he provides a fuller treatment of various forms of narrative thinking and the other modern strategies that can be contrasted with narrative. Crane divides his separate categories (in chapter 2 of his book) into principlists, narrativists, and covenantalists.[30] I do not know where David Ellenson's argument about covenantal thinking would have developed had he concentrated on bioethics once he entered the discussion in 1985. He would certainly have been in some sort of vanguard, as I have noted, and his attention to covenantal thinking involved a significant degree of narrative sensibility. Following David Hartman and Eugene Borowitz, he promoted patient autonomy into a kind of theology that added a spiritual richness to the dichotomies of autonomy vs. beneficence-paternalism. I suggest his Jewish theology grows out of a particular narrative understanding of the Covenant, which is elevated to secular theory by Robert Cover's efforts to understand that all law occurs within particular narrative contexts. That perspective is not limited to Jews who followed in Cover's footsteps (Laurie Zoloth, Suzanne Last Stone and Rachel Adler, most prominently). It has been expressed simply by David Morris, author of *Illness and Culture in the Post Modern Age*, who embeds our ethical inquiry in the narratives with which we live and the narratives that organize our culture. With Morris, the endpoint of narratives (as in the didactic exemplum) is not what matters most, but the entire intellectual environment in which a good narrative takes place.[31]

A Reprise: What Can Narratives Do for Us?

Thus, to review the four ways in which narratives can function in the narrative universe: (1) there are stories with a didactic function, stories where there is a moral, or at least where a dilemma is put forth that requires an "up or down" vote. Such stories invite us to "look through" the story to an external purpose; (2) there is the narrative of patient or care provider, which influences their perspective and which explains how they use their autonomy; (3) there are formal features in a good narrative that prompt our awareness of the multiple factors that influence our ethical thinking; and (4) there is the broader social and historical "narrative" context of a "law" (or in this case an ethical conclusion) that must be included in our judgment about ethical behavior.

What all of this adds up to is a compromise of our certainty, a resistance to simplistic "flattening" and an acknowledgment of the aporias that accompany serious reflection. But that compromise accompanies a broad ethical vision.

Looking at narratives for their qualities rather than looking "through" narrative offers a kind of integrity but not a lot of efficiency; and there are times when, as Louis Newman has noted, decisions simply must be made.[32] When it comes to making a particular decision, there is an inevitable reversion to Bialik's argument about the need for the cooling into hardness of the molten material of aggadah.

Narrative approaches (which sometimes include covenantal thinking) provide a kind of roundness that principlists, logicians, and formal halakhists often resist in the interest of needing to make a decision, most commonly because their systems solicit specific answers. A good narrative privileges giving voice to counterargument, and it is surely an important tool for expanding the horizon of those involved in ethical discourse. Narrative, in many instances, asks different questions from those that more normative approaches are concerned with. But once the counterargument is posited, we are left with vital and much larger questions. Yes, we ought to be talking about end of life, and its beginnings, about priorities in the provision of who gets medical resources, and about the appropriateness of certain procedures for beginning pregnancy or ending pregnancy. But the "different" questions, the "soft" ethics I suggest above must not be ignored: a physician's awareness of the patient's deepest needs, the limits to private medicine in our country, the deeper listening that must occur between patient and healer, and similar intangible issues from the broader horizon.

Can a Religious Bioethic Tolerate Preference Rather than Solutions?

It seems possible to maintain a fixed point of view—a sense of what is ideally right in a certain circumstance—while accepting deviations from that anchor that are not compatible with preferred values. Is it possible that we are not using the word "ethics" in an adequate way? An action may be wrong, according to one or another religious tradition, without being "unethical." How, for example, may we honor social realities without devolving into a mushy relativism? Can we attach ourselves to—even sponsor—a tropism toward the notion that all life is of infinite value, maintaining that principle as an anchor in our thinking, while at the same time accepting the compromise that permits us to disregard that principle? Can we subscribe to the principle that we not prescribe a medicine that has not been researched adequately, and yet suggest that a physician might prescribe an illicit drug to relieve headaches or anxiety and the discomforts of cancer treatment? May we favor autonomy and yet require a recalcitrant nurse to take flu shots, or eject a child from school whose parents will not allow such an inoculation? Can we sponsor a patient who refuses to have a necessary amputation and who thus flaunts the spiritual notion that extending life is a supreme value? Can we insist that financial considerations not enter a family's deliberations about a loved one's end of life, while accepting the reality that such matters are part of the family's concerns? And when might we favor bootlegging medicine or any treatment for an ill loved one? And, is it even reasonable to discuss the ethics of abortion in a culture where sexual practices are fairly uninhibited but the same old physiology of conception continues? These are questions that will not be answered by fully conventional Jewish discourse—no matter how analogically we approach halakhic materials.

Our society continues to function with an anxiety that results from the uncertainty as to whether one's aging or ill parent or friend has no quality of life. Yet we do need to make decisions in the case of every dying patient, and many Jews inevitably default to extending life at almost any cost. But we need some correction to the disservice we perform by keeping people alive under the dubious notion that all life is of infinite value. And autonomy and redefinitions about the value of living will probably dominate tomorrow's ethical agenda. Marcia Angell's thinking will have to account for families who are exhausting their resources in the care of a morbidly ill parent without much quality of life, but the very narrative that will help us understand that problem may also push us toward a stubborn resistance to more lenient legislation, or to rejection of new moral sensibilities about the so called infinite value of all life.

Of course we live with the fear reflected in Woody Allen's fanciful proposal that we might need to "pull the plug" a little early because we are late for a dinner reservation; but we must face realistically families' fears of economic catastrophe as a factor in end-of-life decision making. Life as being of infinite value will eventually clash with the nearly inexhaustible costs of extending life. The various narratives of individual families, the American cultural narrative, and specific stories and aggadot that narrate the end of life will all be increasingly important as we address this gigantic issue. But it is still a specific issue. Those of us who work on narrative add some hope that studying "stories" may also help us have more empathy for our patients, understand their environments more fully, and see our work within the largest spiritual and social context possible.

A Caution

Let us not assume that halakhists ignore the importance of story or retreat from modern conundrums by hiding behind halakhah, or that halakhists produce nonequivocal answers to all questions of right or wrong. But I seek a system into which the ambivalence is built, and where ambivalence is an expectation in the discourse; when, to cite J. Hillis Miller again, narrative is the story of the renunciation of the less preferred resolution, and not a rejection of wrong as such.

An honest reading of more traditional *poskim*, either among the traditional halakhists (that is, the most relevant among the Orthodox) or among moderns like Washofsky, Dorff, Teutsch, Gordis, Mackler, Zohar, and Newman, will surely demonstrate openness to debate and discourse. One would be hard put to argue that these decisors simplify the truly complex dilemmas with which they attempt to deal. What some of our moderns *may* be simplifying is our relationship to texts, or they may be ignoring all that a text might do. So I invite more attention to looking "at" narrative for an understanding of a different kind of utility.

The goal of self-understanding, as enunciated by Martha Nussbaum, Rita Charon, or David Morris (as only three examples),[33] or the search for wisdom or a different set of goals when "doing" bioethics, is what drives the need for more sophisticated uses of narrative.

Conclusion: Too Much Faith in Story?

My essay argues for a renewed awareness of how different people have tried to find a reasonable way to do bioethics in our current environment. On the one hand, when it comes to Jewish practice, there may seem to be not much more to say about tradition's perspective on the end of life than has already been said in this extraordinary environment of creative scholars, thinkers, and intellectuals. On the other hand, we have not yet had the conversation that might bridge the interests and concerns of the various intellectual communities that tackle bioethical theory day by day. And we certainly have been afraid to take on—in Jewish terms, at least—a discussion of the right to die that includes much of the current thinking about narrative. We never adequately escape facile generalization or have enough empathy. Narrativists seek to honor story in a new way that gives weight to another part of the human experience: the softer ethics in which relations among the members of a community are considered as part of the ethical inquiry and in which we seek a different moral vocabulary for our time. We might call this aesthetics, as the most effective boundary breaker that respects the tradition it is always breaking.[34]

Stories cannot solve our current ethical dilemmas—neither the micro nor the macro—and it is not only through stories that we can open our minds to new ways of seeing old problems. Poets argue for their favorite genre, and philosophers for their professional discipline; art critics will find a narrative in the thousand paintings that depict death and dying; and narrativists still include those seeking to clinch a point through an illuminating story. But in facing our dynamic technological world, and in addressing the anthropology of those embedded in that world, narratives will be essential vessels for our imaginations and our intellects. We must constantly reflect along with narratives that promote empathy and respect for the "other" person and for alternative readings of her condition. And we must permit narratives to expand the definition of the problem we are addressing, and the people who are affected by our actions.

Notes

1. This last point is particularly germane to new narrative thinking promoted by Dr. Rita Charon of Columbia University, who argues for seeing all of the relationship between patient and physician through an ethical framework. See Rita Charon and Martha Montello, eds., *Stories Matter: The Role of Narrative in Medical Ethics* (London, 2002).

2. David Ellenson, "How to Draw Guidance from a Heritage," in *A Time to be Born and a Time to Die: The Ethics of Choice*, ed. Barry Kogan, 219–32 (Amsterdam, 1991). The essay was first delivered at Hebrew Union College as a conference address.

3. David Morris, "Narrative, Ethics, and Pain: Thinking with Stories," in Charon and Montello, *Stories Matter*, 196. Notable as another example of this kind of narrative thinking is an essay by the usually conservative Leon Kass: "Ordinary bioethics, as professionally practiced today, largely steers clear of these deep issues of living with, and against, mortality. . . . It takes its bearings not from life as ordinarily lived at home, work, and play, but from life as reconceived through encounters with the institutions of science, technology, and medicine" ("Cancer and Mortality" in *Malignant: Medical Ethicists Confront Cancer*, ed. R. Dresser [New York, 2012], 180).

4. This is a phrase used by Julie Myerson, in her review of *Far From the Tree*, by Andrew Solomon, *New York Times Book Review*, November 23, 2012, 1, 23. I cite this book because it captures the obvious fact that we live with varieties of experience that we think of as exceptional, but that are really more "mainstream" than we have often acknowledged. An expanded approach to narrative increases the likelihood of accommodating variety.

5. See Jonathan Crane, *Narrative and Bioethics* (New York, 2013). My essay draws significantly on Crane's work, while collapsing some of his distinctions, and I record here my gratitude to him for several enlightening discussions. In addition to his focus on narrative as one among several ethical methodologies, Crane's dissertation is concerned with the rhetorical level of the discourse—namely, the language that is used to convince readers of the rightness of an ethical conclusion. See Jonathan Crane, "Rhetoric of Modern Jewish Ethics" (PhD diss., University of Toronto, 2009). Another significant work on rhetoric and its relationship to innovation is Aaron Panken, *The Rhetoric of Innovation* (Lanham, Md., 2005).

6. I do not intend this note to include a complete inventory of the writing on one or another phase of narrative, though this essay draws significantly on some of the more theoretical works among them. But as examples, I would point out the number of narratives of personal illness, ranging from the autobiographical work of William Styron to the biographical narrative of Joan Didion and including the anecdotes and essays of illness contained in anthologies. I would point to the particularly intriguing work published by ethicists associated with an anthology from Washington University: Dresser, *Malignant*. In this field of narrative and medicine, one must always include one of the earliest works in this area: Arthur Frank, *The Wounded Storyteller* (Chicago, 1995), and I would like to thank especially the important theorist Shlomit Rimmon Kena'an, who altered her literary career to include a theory of illness narrative and who has inspired my work on numerous occasions. A remarkable number of contemporary Jewish commentators have published countless illness narratives in Jewish anthologies. See, for example, D. J. Kohn, ed., *Life, Faith, and Cancer* (New York, 2008). The existence of an entire journal devoted to studying narrative and medicine speaks for itself as to the increasing importance of the subject of narrative in the healing environment. See, for example, *Literature and Medicine*, general issue, 30, no. 1 (2012).

7. I am grateful for this phrase to Professor Rachel Adler, my trusted colleague, who often invokes the thinking of narrative scholar Robin West. And I am grateful to Lewis M. Barth who, as always, gave this paper a careful reading. Rabbi Gordon Tucker contributed significantly to my understanding of how he drew on narrative in important deliberations of the Conservative Movement regarding homosexuality.

8. I am thinking particularly about Dresser, *Malignant*, which includes the personal stories of several prominent ethicists, and their reports of the stories of others. The book addresses ethics in pursuit of virtue, rather than ethics seeking specific solutions in particular situations.

9. Numerous important books—too numerous to cite—have been published in recent years. The names of Richard Kirsch, Marcia Angell, and Ezekiel Emanuel are most prominent. Most recently, American businessman David Goldhill has entered the discussion from an "outsider's" point of view. See David Goldhill, *Catastrophic Care: How American Health Care Killed My Father* (New York, 2013).

10. Marcia Angell, "How to Die in Massachusetts," *New York Review of Books*, February 21, 2013, 27–29.

11. In this regard, Jonathan Cohen has written an interesting warning to those who wish to adopt narrative for its more "progressive" conclusions. See Jonathan Cohen, "Jewish Bioethics: Between Interpretation and Criticism," *Midrash and Medicine*, ed. W. Cutter, 263–73 (Woodstock, Vt., 2011). Cohen's rather difficult essay is a response to an enthusiastic endorsement of "story" by Leonard Sharzer, in the same volume: "Aggadah and Midrash: A New Direction for Bioethics?," 245–62.

12. See Joseph Heinemann, "The Nature of the Aggadah," in *Midrash and Literature*, ed. G. Hartman and S. Budick, trans. M. Bregman, 41–55 (New Haven, Conn., 1986). Along with this effort several scholars, although not directly central to this essay, have contributed to my understanding of the "way stories work" in classic Jewish literature, especially the work of Jeffrey Rubenstein, David Kraemer, Ruchama Weiss, David Stern, and Daniel Boyarin, in addition to specific works I shall cite below.

13. Geoffrey Hartman, "Narrative and Beyond," *Literature and Medicine* 23, no. 2 (2004): 340.

14. Bradley Lewis, *Narrative Psychiatry: How Stories Can Shape Clinical Practice* (Baltimore, 2012), discussed by Frank, *The Wounded Storyteller*. Similar descriptions from beyond the particular realm of Jewish bioethics have been contributed by James Childress, Adam Zachary Newton, Barry Wimpfheimer, and David Kraemer, not to mention specific "ethicists" who have specialized in the use of story, including Rachel Adler and Laurie Zoloth.

15. Practical contributions to the challenges toward more conventional halakhic thinking (accompanied by arguments for aggadah and other narratiive) have come from Jewish efforts by Peter Knobel, Leonard Sharzer, Byron Sherwin, Louis Newman, and Phillip Cohen.

16. Robert Cover, "Nomos and Narrative," in *Narrative Violence and the Law: The Essays of Robert Cover*, ed. M. Minow, M. Ryan, and A. Sarat, 95–172 (Ann Arbor, Mich., 1995). I should add here that a recent paper by Louis Newman for the Society for Jewish Ethics (2014), demonstrates that most non-Orthodox perspectives on Jewish behavior begin with a certain narrative. For Elliot Dorff it might be that "our bodies belong to God," and for Byron Sherman it might be that compassion overrides Jewish principle.

17. Israeli scholar Ofrah Meir has written an important essay on the formal issues involved in the several versions of the Rabbi Judah story: "Sipur Petirato shel Rabbi" [The Story of the Death of Rabbi Judah haNasi], *Jerusalem Studies in Hebrew Literature* 12 (1990): 147–77.

18. Leo Nikolayevitch Tolstoy, *The Death of Ivan Ilyitch*, trans. L. and A. Maude (1886; New York, 1981), 83–86.

19. H. N. Bialik, "Halakhah ve-Aggadah," *Kol Kitvei H"N Bialik* [in Hebrew] (Tel Aviv, 1938). Bialik's famous line from this essay is "Obligation is cruel" (my translation).

20. Michael Chernick, "Does Lore Subvert Law?: The Case of b. Ketubot 62b," delivered at the Society of Christian and Jewish Ethics, January 2010, Atlanta, Ga. Chernick is expanding his argument and elaborating the development of aggadic halakhot in his continuing work.

21. Many of the generation of scholars who are now in middle age have contributed vastly to our understanding of the internal "literary" or formalistic features of the rabbinic narrative: Daniel Boyarin, Jeffrey Rubenstein, David Stern, and David Kraemer among the best known. They have dealt variously with subjects like the subtext of rabbinic material, the structure of narrative, the nature of parables and metaphor, the richness of various manifestations of polysemy, and the not always apparent "ethical agenda" of various texts. I am grateful to my colleague Ruchama Weiss, of HUC-JIR, Jerusalem, with whom I have been able to study narrative each spring. Here I must record a special thanks to my colleagues in the Bioethics Interest Group of the Society for Jewish Ethics, who have worked industriously to break free of some of the canonical modes of rabbinic discourse: Leonard Sharzer, David Teutsch, Elliot Dorff, Peter Knobel, with special thanks to the interest group's chair, Dr. Sander Mendelsohn. Noam Zohar, who has served as editor of the group's published work, was one of the first contemporary scholars to approach bioethics as providing alternatives. See Zohar, *Alternatives in Jewish Bioethics* (Albany, N.Y., 1997)

22. See *Shulhan arukh*, "Yoreh Deah," para. 349

23. See Sharzer, "Aggadah and Midrash"; and my own studies of this story.

24. Richard Lanham, *A Handlist of Rhetorical Terms* (Berkeley, Calif., 1991).

25. Jonathan Crane, *Narrative and Bioethics*. And to quote James Childress of the University of Virginia: "Once generated, norms still require interpretations, and this interpretive process involves narratives" ("Narrative(s) vs. Norm(s): A Misplaced Debate in Bioethics," in *Stories and Their Limits, Narrative Approaches to Bioethics*, ed. Hilde Nelson, 252–72 [New York, 1997]).

26. J. Hillis Miller, *The Ethics of Reading* (New York, 1987).

27. Fred Rosner, *Biomedical Ethics and Jewish Law* (Hoboken, N.J., 2001).

28. Elliot Dorff, *The Unfolding Tradition* (New York, 2005); David Teutsch, *A Guide to Jewish Practice: Bioethics* (Philadelphia, 2005); and most recently, Mark Washofsky, "The Woodchopper Revisited, on Analogy, Halachah and Jewish Bioethics," in *Medical Frontiers and Jewish Law*, ed. W. Jacob, 1–62 (Pittsburgh, 2012). The woodchopper in the title references Louis Newman's essay "Woodchoppers and *Respirators*," *Modern Judaism* 10, no. 1 (1990): 17–42.

29. I must cite here one of the earliest efforts to draw on narrative techniques to consider the crosscurrents in bioethical discourse: Noam Zohar, *Alternatives in Jewish Bioethics* (Albany, N.Y, 1997). Zohar was good enough to publish an early attempt by the author of the current essay: William Cutter, "Do the Qualities of Story Influence the Quality of Life? Some Perspectives on the Limitations and Enhancements of Narrative Ethics," in *Quality of Life in Jewish Bioethics*, ed. N. Zohar, 55–66 (Lanham, Md., 2006).

30. Crane, "Rhetoric of Modern Jewish Ethics."

31. David B. Morris, "Narrative, Ethics, and Pain: Thinking with Stories," in Sharon and Montello, *Stories Matter*, 196–218. This little book includes some of the major scholars of narrative and bioethics, and considers a rich array of necessary topics ranging from learning to think empathically to the place of narrative in institutional settings. It is upon this book that the next generation of thinking about Jewish bioethics should be based.

32. Louis Newman, "The Narrative and the Normative: The Value of Stories for Jewish Ethics," in *Healing and the Jewish Imagination*, ed. W. Cutter, 183–92 (Woodstock, Vt., 2007). Newman argues here that the interpretive freedom invited by stories can be an impediment to decision making, and his cautionary case is the "other side" of the very argument I am making for using narrative more expansively.

33. Martha Nussbaum, *Love's Knowledge: Essays on Philosophy and Literature* (New York, 1990), 190.

34. I am particularly grateful to my colleague Mark Washofsky for pointing out the gap between the different ways in which each of us approaches narrative—he seeking norms, and I seeking a kind of ambient aesthetic approach. I want to thank here five good friends from the arts who devoted many hours to the Rabbi Judah talmudic narrative and who rendered responses to my own search to probe the story through their disciplines of theatrical or movie script, music, and the graphic arts: Bernard Kukoff, Stacie Chaiken, David Shire, Tom Freudenheim, and Richard Maltby Jr. Their contribution to my thinking will be the centerpiece of a forthcoming paper, "Aesthetics and The End of Life."

15

THOUGHTS ON FORGIVENESS IN PSYCHOANALYSIS AND JUDAISM

LEWIS M. BARTH

Life forces us to make difficult decisions.[1] To ask for forgiveness and to forgive are among the most problematic of these. "To err is Humane; to Forgive, Divine" is the phrase often quoted in reference to this subject.[2] Human beings by nature make mistakes. The capacity to forgive is a property of deity. God alone has this capacity, or perhaps God is required to manifest it as an expression of the divine nature.

The author of these packed seven words was the British poet Alexander Pope (1688–1744). He penned them in his "An Essay on Criticism," a brilliant, witty poem. Pope's goal was to attack literary critics who have little understanding or appreciation of the sublime nature of poetry and the poet. As with so many quotable quotes, Pope's words seem to contain so much wisdom. Similar to a biblical verse infused with rabbinic-midrashic meaning, they fly out of their original setting, cross centuries, continents, and cultures to land on our tongues and to say it all.

"*To err is Humane.*" We recall how we hurt or were hurt by another's words or actions. No one escapes shaming, betraying, or undermining. At some time, all of us have been perpetrator or victim, doer or done-to. Wounds can be very deep. Families break up; brother turns against brother; sister against sister; or friend against friend—they stop talking to one another. Perhaps years go by until one of the feuding relatives dies, and the family temporarily reconnects. No one remembers why the breakup occurred; or if they remember, the very "clear" narratives of the originating incident conflict with one another—with the result that the real reason for the rupture cannot be recovered. As the family temporarily gathers, one or another of its members might decry the fact that with just a little bit of acknowledgement, a genuine apology matched by an equally genuine expression of forgiveness, life would have been so different, so much better.

Why is it so hard to ask for or grant forgiveness? The answer, on the level of individuals—not nations or religious or ethnic groups—might be analogous to the difficulties people find in marriage. Two people come together with their separate histories, personalities, deep psychological structures, and ways of organizing experience. It is hard work to make a marriage last.

Or, from another perspective, human beings are, in so many ways, like the four children of the Passover Haggadah: "the wise, the wicked, the simple and the one who doesn't know how to ask." *The wise*: some have the capacity to really understand that his or her spouse, partner, relative, or friend is a complete human being with his or her own ways of constructing the world. *The wicked*: some don't care about other people, their feelings, their struggles—what are they to me? (Perhaps this attitude is similar to Martin Buber's concept of the I–It relationship as applied to persons when treated merely as objects). *The simple*: some cannot even imagine that others are fully human, that their differences in thought, temperament, judgment and feeling are simply differences, not good or evil. *And the one who doesn't know how to ask*: some cannot conceive of understanding the self or other because they have experienced such trauma or dysfunction that they have no emotional energy left or unconsciously lose their capacity to feel.

The questions of dealing with forgiveness are many and very hard. Here are several that are found scattered throughout the contemporary literature on forgiveness: Can or should people forgive? How are we to forgive? Can perpetrators genuinely understand what they have done and enter into such deep feelings of authentic guilt, shame, and contrition that victims can be moved from their desires for revenge to grant forgiveness? Is it possible to forgive if the perpetrator hasn't asked for forgiveness? These and other questions force us to ask ourselves how we respond when we recognize hurt caused or felt in which we are implicated.

Thinking about such questions in this volume honoring David Ellenson offers the opportunity to reflect on changes within and parallels between two "classical" traditions: psychoanalysis and Judaism.

Some Psychoanalytic Perspectives on Forgiveness

Scholars of the history of psychoanalysis have noted that in the century since

Sigmund Freud began to create the field and theories of psychoanalysis, psycho-analytic literature rarely dealt with the subject of forgiveness. There are many possible reasons for the century-long avoidance of this subject. The psychoanalyst Salman Akhtar introduces his list of possibilities with the comment:

> This omission is puzzling, since issues closely linked to forgiveness (e.g., trauma, mourning, guilt, the need for punishment) have been of utmost concern to psychoanalysis. Reasons for this neglect are unclear, though many possibilities exist.
>
> First, the tradition among psychoanalysts to treat Freud's work as a touchstone before positing their own views creates the risk that topics not addressed by the master will be ignored. Forgiveness is one such phenomenon. The word itself appears a mere five times in the entire corpus of Freud's work (Guttman, Jones, and Parrish 1980), and then in a colloquial rather than scientific manner. Second, forgiveness is a hybrid psychological concept with unmistakable interpersonal and social referents. Thus, it borders on areas where analytic theory traditionally has been at its weakest and prone to heuristic omissions. Third, originating in clinical concerns, psychoanalysis has devoted greater attention to morbid psychic phenomena (e.g., anxiety, hate) at the expense of positive and life-enhancing emotions (e.g., courage, altruism). This bias, admittedly rectified to a certain extent by writings on wisdom (Kohut 1971), tact (Poland 1975), hope (Casement 1991), and love (Kernberg 1995), is also reflected in the literature's inattention to forgiveness. Finally, the benevolence implicit in forgiveness gives religious overtones to the concept (à la "to err is humane, to forgive divine"). This link, strengthened in the mind if one regards sin as the fraternal twin of forgiveness, might also have given pause to analysts considering this topic.[3]

Deepening this last point, Melvin R. Lansky writes in a prologue subtitled "Forgiveness and Atonement" in a recent issue of *Psychoanalytic Inquiry*:

> Perhaps the psychoanalytic exploration of forgiveness and atonement were so late arriving on the psychoanalytic scene because the topic tends to suggest something that is antithetical to the psychoanalytic attitude, the advocacy in moral or religious terms of forbearance from retribution in responses to injustice or injury, for example,

the forgiveness of Joseph with his brothers or Jesus on the cross. It would be inimical to the psychoanalytic method to consider forgiveness or atonement to be basic psychoanalytic concepts, and even more problematic to regard them to be psychoanalytic values with the implication that one should forgive or should atone.[4]

The interest in the topic of forgiveness among psychoanalysts changed at the end of the 1990s. Since then, and especially in the last two decades, there has been a flood of psychoanalytic articles and books on this subject that parallels contemporary international interest and activity.[5] The broader historical context for the sudden intense focus on forgiveness may relate to cultural perspectives regarding several ethnic-religious horrors of recent years—Bosnia, Rwanda, Sudan, the terrorist attacks on Oklahoma City, the first World Trade Center attempt in 1993 and the second on 9/11—as well as significant reconciliation efforts in South Africa and elsewhere.[6] Whatever the reasons, the focus on forgiveness represents a considerable shift in psychoanalytic theorizing.

Steven Wangh, a playwright with a deep interest in psychoanalysis, wrote about processes—individual and communal—that permit a psychological move from a desire for revenge toward forgiveness and reconciliation and what it means to forgive a perpetrator who hasn't asked for forgiveness. In his article, "Revenge and Forgiveness in Laramie, Wyoming," Wangh describes the *Laramie Project*. A group of actors led by Moisés Kaufman interviewed people in Laramie, Wyoming, regarding the brutal and deadly beating of Matthew Shepard, the university student whose life was taken because he was gay. It was reported that at the sentencing hearing of Aaron McKinney—during which the prosecution would ask for the death penalty—Matthew Shepard's father, Dennis, concluded his moving eulogy about his son with these words: "I would like nothing better than to see you die, Mr. McKinney; however, this is the time to begin the healing process, to show mercy to someone who refused to show any mercy." Dennis Shepard ended by saying: "Mr. McKinney, I give you life in the memory of one who no longer lives. May you have a long life, and may you thank Matthew every day for it."[7]

Wangh comments on Kaufman's insight that "one has to let go before [one] can really be merciful," and says: "If forgiveness depends on letting go, perhaps that is because revenge is a magical activity by means of which the avenger holds on to the past. . . . The act of revenge serves to deny that the dead person or the past event is still operative."[8] What Wangh seems to mean here is that to forgive means to go through stages of mourning—denial and anger—to come finally to acceptance and moving on with life.

But we might raise the question here: Did Dennis Shepard's charge represent a full act of mercy and forgiveness, or did this also contain an aspect of vengeance and unforgiveness? Everett L. Worthington defines the terms *unforgiveness* and *forgiveness* as follows:

> Unforgiveness is a cold, emotional complex consisting of resentment, bitterness, hatred, hostility, residual anger and fear. Those emotions motivate people to avoid or reduce unforgiveness.

> Forgiveness is a juxtaposition or superposition of a strong positive emotion over the cold emotions of unforgiveness in such a way that the unforgiveness is contaminated and overwhelmed by the more positive emotions. . . . The positive emotions can be empathy for the perpetrator, compassion, agape love, or even romantic love. Other positive emotions, such as humility over one's own culpability and past transgressions and gratitude for one's own experiences of forgiveness, might intermix to contaminate the cold emotions of unforgiveness or replace the hot emotions of anger and fear.[9]

Worthington goes on to speak of emotions as embodied experiences, certainly "feelings," but "also . . . thoughts, memories, associations, neurochemicals within the brain, brain pathways within various brain structures, hormones in the bloodstream, 'gut feelings,' facial musculature and gross body musculature and acts of emotional expression."[10] In other words, emotions suffuse the whole person—a primary reason why it is so hard to move out of a position of unforgiveness toward forgiveness.

Some Jewish Perspectives on Forgiveness

It is with these ideas in mind that I want to shift over now to Judaism and look at a few biblical and rabbinic parallels to the ideas and examples presented above. We begin with passages regarding vengeance and the limits of forgiveness and then shift to the commandment, the mitzvah, that prohibits vengeance, and conclude with two contrasting rabbinic views on the foundational reasons for forgiving and dealing in a humane manner with other people. (Obviously, the few texts discussed here from the Hebrew Bible and rabbinic literature do not reflect all the rich and varied views found within Jewish tradition).

To the bane of those requiring theological consistency and to the delight of rabbinic sages, the God of the Hebrew Bible is depicted in contrasting and often paradoxical metaphors.[11] For our subject, this is a God of vengeance *and* a God filled with compassion *and* forgiveness. These characteristics—of vengeance, compassion, and forgiveness—are found in descriptions of the deity and in biblical commandments the Hebrew and Jewish people were instructed to follow.

For example, the command to exterminate a people known as the Amalekites is so important to the biblical writers that it occurs in both Exodus 17:14 as a description of God's intention—"Then the Lord said to Moses, 'Inscribe this in a document as a reminder, and read it aloud to Joshua: I will utterly blot out the memory of Amalek from under heaven'"[12]—and in Deuteronomy 25:17–19 as a more detailed discussion of what the Israelites are commanded to remember and do and why they were thus commanded:

> Remember what Amalek did to you on your journey, after you left Egypt; how, undeterred by fear of God, he surprised you on the march, when you were famished and weary, and cut down all the stragglers in your rear. Therefore, when the Lord your God grants you safety from all your enemies around you, in the land that the Lord your God is giving you as a hereditary portion, you shall blot out the memory of Amalek from under heaven. Do not forget!

On the command to blot out the memory of Amalek (Deut. 25:19), Rashi (1040–1105) specifies: "From man to woman, from infant to weaned child, from ox to lamb, so that the name of Amalek will not even be remembered concerning an ox or lamb; by saying this beast belonged to Amalek." Rashi's comment suggests that Amalek's name should vanish so completely from memory that anything that once belonged to Amalek, including a domestic animal, will be destroyed. The result is that no one could ever say, "Oh I remember that beast [ox or cow], it used to belong to Amalek." Ramban (1194–c. 1270) adds: "Do not forget, 'this refers to forgetting in the heart.'" In other words, according to Ramban, these commandments not only require vengeance, but also prohibit a positive change of heart toward an enemy that destroyed the weakest among the people. Never forget so you will never forgive!

Compare these verses and comments to Leviticus 19:18: "You shall not take vengeance or bear a grudge against your countrymen. Love your neighbor as yourself: I am the Lord."[13] A full midrashic expansion of Leviticus 19:18 is found in *Sifra*, Kedoshim 4:10–12 (f. 89b), presented here following Jacob Neusner's outline and translation, with minor additions and changes.[14]

4. A. "You shall not take vengeance [or bear any grudge]":
   B. To what extent is the force of vengeance? (Or: how far does vengeance go?)
   C. If one says to him, "Lend me your sickle," and the other did not do so.
   D. On the next day, the other says to him, "Lend me your spade."
   E. The one then replies, "I am not going to lend it to you, because you didn't lend me your sickle."
   F. In that context, it is said, "You shall not take vengeance."

5. A. ". . . or bear any grudge":
   B. To what extent is the force of a grudge? (Or: how far does bearing a grudge go?)
   C. If one says to him, "Lend me your spade," but he did not do so.
   D. The next day the other one says to him, "Lend me your sickle,"
   E. and the other replies, "I am not like you, for you didn't lend me your spade [but here, take the sickle]!"
   F. In that context, it is said, "or bear any grudge."

I shall deal with the conclusion of this passage (6:A–7C) below, but I simply want to emphasize that the above-mentioned prohibition against exacting vengeance (4:A–F) means that one is forbidden to treat the neighbor in the way he has treated you. This is an example of how not to apply the rabbinic concept "measure for measure" and certainly not even a metaphorical "eye for an eye." The prohibition against bearing a grudge (5:A–F) is concretized by a verbal thrust designed to demean the perpetrator, teach him a lesson, and make him ashamed of how he acted. In other words, it represents a full range of negative emotions projected onto the biblical phrase "or bear a grudge." "I'm not like you" implies "I'm better than you"—and the victim is prohibited from acting on such feelings!

Rabbi Elliot Dorff has written on the Jewish legal obligation to forgive, and he argues that the emphasis in Jewish law and tradition is not on inner emotional or psychological change. In contrast to this reading of the midrash cited and its implications, he offers reasons for deemphasizing the moral character of the action and why forgiveness in Jewish law is not based on moral reflection or psychological transformation but rather is a commandment to be fulfilled:

> Immanuel Kant, who emphasizes intention as the key element in determining the moral character of an act, would say . . . : Wait to act until you can do so out of a sense of moral principle. Judaism, however, stands at the opposite end of that spectrum: "A person should always do the right thing even for the wrong reason," the Rabbis say, "for in doing the right thing for an ulterior motive one will come to do it for the right motive (B. *Pesahim* 50b, et. al.)" Thus, even though a victim may have no desire to forgive, he or she must do everything possible to forgive the transgressor once the transgressor has gone through the process of return. In such cases, it is duty that is at work rather than charity; at some point, the victim may be able to forgive out of a sense of charity, too.
>
> This means, of course, that for Judaism forgiveness is not exclusively, or even primarily, an internal, psychological process. Typical of Judaism's emphasis on action, the concept of forgiveness that emerges out of the Jewish tradition stresses the actions that the perpetrator must take to return to God and the community and, in turn, the actions that the community must take in welcoming him or her back. It is, in other words, an *inter*personal process, not an *intra*personal one. Judaism certainly harbors the hope that the feelings of both the perpetrator and the community will ultimately follow along, thereby creating the foundation for reconciliation and even renewed friendship; but the essence of forgiveness, for the Jewish tradition, is not acquiring a new feeling about each other, but rather acting on the demands that the duty of forgiveness imposes on us so that we can live together as a community worthy of God's presence.[15]

Dorff's concluding emphasis on the relationship between forgiveness and living in a community, on the interpersonal level, reflects the deeply embedded consciousness of social context in addition to legal obligation in Jewish reflection on forgiveness.

It should be mentioned in passing that Dorff appears to hold a classical definition of psychoanalysis as dealing with *intrapersonal*—to use contemporary psychoanalytic terminology: *intrapsychic* processes. Contemporary psycho-analysis takes an entirely different view, emphasizing that all psychological processes and transformations are rooted in relationship, that is, in the *interpersonal*. On this point there is a vast literature based on theoretical positions found in self-psychology, relational psychoanalysis, and intersubjective psychoanalysis, to name but a few modern psychoanalytic schools and perspectives.[16]

A remarkable midrash reflects the power of *interpersonal* processes at work. The passage opens with a halakhic (legal) question:

> May our Master teach us [that is: provide an answer to the following question]: If there was strife between one person and another, how does one seek atonement for sin on Yom Kippur? Thus our Rabbis have taught: for transgressions between man and God, Yom Kippur provides atonement; for transgressions between one person and another, Yom Kippur does not provide atonement until one person seeks to appease the other (through an act of apology). If the person went to apologize and the other does not accept the apology, what should he do? . . . Rabbi Samuel b. Nachman said, let him bring ten people and stand them in one line and let him say before them, my brothers, there is strife between me and this man. I went to beg forgiveness and he refused to accept my apology. Immediately, God sees that the person humbled himself before Him, and God has compassion on him. (*Tanhuma*, Vayera 30)

I want to add one other dimension to the discussion of forgiveness in Judaism. For this we return to the concluding lines of the text and commentary in the *Sifra* on Leviticus 19:18:

6. A. "You shall not take vengeance or bear any grudge against the sons of your own people":
   B. [The anonymous creator of this passage then adds a hypothesis that is going to be rejected, for he infers from the words "or bear any grudge against the sons of your own people that] "You may take vengeance and bear a grudge against others." [In other words, you might think it is acceptable to take revenge or bear a grudge against non-Jews].

7. A. [But the concluding phrase of the biblical verse is now restated in rebuttal:] "but you shall love your neighbor as yourself [I am the Lord]":

    B. R. Akiva says, "This is a great [Neusner: 'the encompassing'] principle of the Torah."

    C. Ben Azzai says, "'This is the book of the generations of Adam' (Gen. 5:1) is a still greater [Neusner: 'more encompassing'] principle."

The disagreement between R. Akiva and Ben Azzai over which biblical verse is greater is universal in its reach. Both sages reject the notion of taking vengeance against non-Jews. More important, their disagreement is also essential to our understanding of the basis for ethical behavior in general. It implies the obligation to forgo taking vengeance against, or bearing a grudge toward anyone, no matter his or her origin. They justify the prohibitions on the grounds of two different perspectives regarding the nature of human beings. In emphasizing Leviticus 19:18, "you shall love your neighbor as yourself," Rabbi Akiva points to the essential characteristics of all people, an understanding that requires the victim to appreciate his shared humanity with the perpetrator. Perhaps a better way of translating *ve-ahavta lere'akha kamokha* might be: "You shall love your neighbor, he is just like you are."

Ben Azzai's citation of Genesis 5:1 is abridged, and we need to read the full verse he cites to understand why he thinks it contains a greater principle: "This is the book of the generations of Adam—When God created man God made him in the likeness of God [*bidmut elohim*]." Human beings are made "in the likeness of God." Many interpretations have been offered for that phrase. The late medieval commentator Sforno (c. 1475–1550) said that being created in the image or likeness of God means "having the power to make choices [*ba'al behirah*]."

Rabbi Richard N. Levy has suggested how far the biblical concept of human beings made in the "likeness" or "image" of God can push us. In a passage both challenging and disturbing he has written: "When Adolf Eichmann went on trial in Jerusalem for his crimes during the Holocaust, Martin Buber urged that the Israeli court not give him a death sentence, but commit him to live out the rest of his life working on a kibbutz, facing every day the very people he wanted to put to death. That brilliant "final solution" to radical evil expressed not only Buber's opposition to capital punishment, but even more his belief that there is something deserving of redemption in every child of the creation, because each person possesses a *tzelem Elohim* (an image of God)."[17] Buber's view is very much like the view of Dennis Shepard, and it could be argued that a vindictive substratum underlies the motivation of both of them, despite the justifications both Buber and Shepard provide.

Here is where, I think, psychoanalytic "tradition" in its contemporary theorizing and religious views of forgiveness, both biblical and rabbinic, converge. The process of forgiveness requires at least the five "Rs": Regret, Remorse, Repair, Restitution, and Reconciliation. Beginning with the inner emotions of regret and remorse, forgiveness demands the involvement of the whole person, whether perpetrator or victim; the capacity for self-examination; as well as the ability to see the other as a complete yet different human being, and paradoxically to see the other as just like oneself. Whether one believes in God or not, asking for or granting forgiveness presumes we have the Godlike capacity to make decisions (Sforno), but also, and more importantly, to act on them by engaging in repair and restitution. Human agency is fundamental for reconciliation.

Notes

This essay was presented in an expanded form to several audiences, beginning with the UCLA Institute on Aging (April 30, 2009) and ending with the Pacific Association of Reform Rabbis (April 30, 2012). It has benefited from the comments and questions of many individuals. Special thanks go to Joye Weisel-Barth and William Cutter for their suggestions.

1. I deal here with themes of forgiveness and vengeance and will not deal with broader questions and relationships between psychoanalysis and Judaism or issues about Freud's complicated perspectives on Judaism as a religion. See Louis Breger, *Freud: Darkness in the Midst of Vision* (New York, 2000), for numerous references to Freud, Judaism, and Jews. For thematic and theoretical perspectives, see Lewis Aron and Libby Henik, eds., *Answering a Question with a Question: Contemporary Psychoanalysis and Jewish Thought* (Boston, 2010).
2. Original quote. The 1709 edition of "An Essay on Criticism" uses the spelling "humane" for our more customary spelling "human." See the entry "human" in the *Oxford English Dictionary* for the historical development of the orthography of this word.
3. Salman Akhtar, "Forgiveness: Origins, Dynamics, Psychopathology, and Technical Relevance," *Psychoanalytic Quarterly* 71 (2002): 175–212. Sources cited in the quote from Akhtar are S. A. Guttman, R. L. Jones and S. M. Parrish, eds., *The Concordance to the Standard Edition of the Complete Psychological Works of Sigmund Freud* (Boston, 1980); H. Kohut, *The Analysis of the Self* (New York, 1971); W. Poland, "Tact as a Psychoanalytic Function," *International Journal of Psycho-Analysis,* 56 (1975): 155–61; P. Casement, *Learning from the Patient* (New York, 1991); and O. F. Kernberg, *Love Relations: Normality and Pathology* (New Haven, Conn., 1995).

4. Melvin R. Lansky, "Prologue," *Psychoanalytic Inquiry*, 29, no. 5 (2009): 358.

5. Lansky, *Forgiveness and Atonement*, 387, and references 360–361. Michael E. McCullough, Julie Juola Exline, and Roy F. Baumeister, "An Annotated Bibliography of Research on Forgiveness and Related Concepts," in *Dimensions of Forgiveness: Psychological Research and Theological Perspectives*, ed. E. L. Worthington Jr., (Philadelphia, 1998)., 193–317.

6. For our specific theme relating to the Holocaust, see the growing number of responses in the most recent edition of Simon Wiesenthal, *The Sunflower: On the Possibilities and Limits of Forgiveness* (New York, 1998), esp. 101–274.

7. Stephen Wangh, "Revenge and Forgiveness in Laramie, Wyoming," *Psychoanalytic Dialogues* 15 (2005): 4, quoting from Moisés Kaufman and the Members of Tectonic Theater Project, *The Laramie Project* (New York, 2001), 85.

8. Wangh, "Revenge and Forgiveness in Laramie, Wyoming," 6.

9. Everett L. Worthington, "Unforgiveness, Forgiveness, and Reconciliation and Their Implication for Societal Interventions," in *Forgiveness and Reconciliation: Religion, Public Policy and Conflict Transformation*, ed. Raymond G. Helmick, S. J., and Rodney L. Peterson (Philadelphia, 2001), 172–73.

10. Ibid., 175, and see his note there.

11. *Mechilta D'Rabbi Ismael cum variis lectionibus et adnotationibus*, ed. H. S. Horovitz and Israel A. Rabin [in Hebrew] (Frankfurt: 1928–1931.; repr., Reprint. Jerusalem, 1960), 219–20.

12. Translations of the Hebrew Bible are primarily taken from *Tanakh: A New Translation of the Holy Scriptures according to the traditional Hebrew Text* (Philadelphia, 1985).

13. See Leon Wurmser's discussion of aspects of this verse, its expansion in rabbinic literature and its meaning in a psychoanalytic context in his "The Superego as Herald of Resentment," *Psychoanalytic Inquiry* 29, no. 5 (2009): 389–90.

14. *Sifra d've rav: hu' sefer torat kohanimm*, ed. I. H. Weiss (Vienna: 1865; repr., New York, 1946), 89b; *SIFRA: An Analytical Translation I-III*, trans. J. Neusner (Scholars Press, 1988), 3:108–9.

15. Elliot N. Dorff, "The Elements of Forgiveness: A Jewish Approach," in *Dimensions of Forgiveness: Psychological Research and Theological Perspectives*, ed. E. L. Worthington Jr. (Philadelphia, 1998), 46, 55 n.8.

16. For a good introduction to contemporary psychoanalytic schools and theories, see Stephen A. Mitchell and Margaret J. Black, *Freud and Beyond: A History of Modern Psychoanalytic Thought* (New York, 1995).

17. Richard N. Levy, *A Vision of Holiness: The Future of Reform Judaism* (New York, 2005), 45.

16

ETHNICITY, RELIGION, AND SPIRITUALITY IN POSTWAR JEWISH AMERICA

LAWRENCE A. HOFFMAN

In 1975 Tony Judt arrived in America from England to find "nothing to suggest community—except the Church." Religion was "often the sole link to anything recognizably social, to a higher striving. If I lived in such a place," he concluded, "I too would join the elect."[1]

Judt was experiencing the surviving trace of what Peter Berger famously called a "sacred canopy"—the premodern era when everything in life seemed inescapably religious. Our teacher and friend David Ellenson has described this as the most influential metaphor he came across in his early study of religion. The modern Orthodox responsa in which he has specialized reflect an era in which the canopy was already coming down; the American town that Judt encountered had seen it shrink even more.

As tribute to David Ellenson's fascination with the condition of the cultural canopy, this essay explores a chapter in American history when both the American and the Jewish versions were in serious disarray: the post–World War II years saw America expanding in power and opportunity, while opening its doors to Jewish participation as never before.

Judt's observation to the contrary, the great century of Protestant domination was coming to an end, and the sacred canopy it had tried so hard to maintain was being replaced by a secular one. The changeover did not eliminate religion, however; it just shifted the authority structure in which religion is made manifest, allowing it to show up "outside the institutional church, in new religious movements, or in 'secular' cultural forms like literature, film, and art."[2] For Jews, it appeared as ethnicity: channeled into the study of world literature, on one hand; and the movement we call Conservative Judaism on the other. To understand the twists and turns of both, we need first to trace the uniqueness of America's religious landscape.

America has always been genuinely religious, although not, on that account, "unsecular." Rather, it has displayed its own unique mix of secularity and religion—with a twist: an ongoing tension between public church and private spirituality. It is not simply a case of secularization driving out religion, as classical secularization theorists predicted. Nor is it mere hybridization of the two, as postmodernists have alleged—a case, perhaps, of two enemies who become strange bedfellows. Rather, it is the more interesting tale of a ménage à trois: secularity, religion, and spirituality, coexisting in interesting ways. American history is unique for its spiritual awakenings, which challenge churches, which (in turn) adapt or fall—the most recent case being ourselves, when, again, mainstream religion is under attack for lacking spirituality.

William James chronicled the story as he saw it in his 1901–2 Gifford Lectures, which were published as *Varieties of Religious Experience* (1902). He saw established churches as "religion's wicked intellectual partner, the spirit of dogmatic dominion."[3] One hundred years after James, philosopher Charles Taylor pronounced James prescient, for in our time, too, privatization and spiritual search are the norm.[4]

How do we explain the ubiquitous success of institutional religion in America, coupled with the regularized critique of that very success? The most likely theory for the well-being of American religion relative to other industrial and postindustrial countries has cited disestablishmentarianism: the dismantling of official state support that made religion a market commodity competing for adherents. Churches that respond to market conditions survive; those that do not fail.[5]

This insight into American religion must be seen alongside the school of thought best represented by Steven Bruce, who insists that religion is in fact dying; its continued potency here and there in the world can be explained by the fact that religion succeeds when it provides a secondary gain by doing "something else."[6] Examples would be Poland during the Soviet era and French Canada prior to the rise of the Quebecois. Polish Catholicism remained strong as long as it served the nationalist goal of retaining Polish identity under Russian Communist hegemony; French Canadian Catholicism thrived as a means of protecting French identity when it was under siege by Canadian Anglo rule. When the Iron Curtain fell, Catholicism declined in Poland; with de facto local separatism in Quebec province, Catholicism declined there as well.

We can combine the "market" and the "secondary gain" hypotheses by saying that the American situation has permitted religion to respond to consumer needs, thereby allowing it to do the "something else" that was necessary for it to succeed. My two cases in point begin in the Eisenhower era, when a popular president who was fighting Godless Communism urged all Americans to attend the religion of their choice. "Our form of government," he said, "has no sense unless it is founded in a deeply felt religious faith, and I don't care what it is." By faith, he meant "honesty, decency, fairness, service, that sort of thing"[7]—nothing that might offend anyone.

With so broad a definition of faith, Jews had no trouble claiming a Jewish version of it, especially in the burgeoning Conservative Movement, which became the main recipient of Eisenhower's ideological largesse. Other Jews, however, had no use for religion at all. Raised in a traditionalist milieu where study was the highest aspiration, they redirected their efforts away from Jewish particularity into Jewish universalism—away from Talmud, that is, toward world literature. What bound the two groups together was their eastern European heritage coupled with prewar anti-Semitism, not just the virulent form that exploded so demonically in Europe, but the tamer American version that produced quotas in colleges and the *Gentleman's Agreement* explored by Laura Z. Hobson in 1947. Both groups thrived as uniquely American experiments in ethnic Jewish identity. Conservative Judaism became an "ethnic church," stressing internal issues of Jewish Peoplehood. The universalist counterexample (to which I now turn) transformed Talmudic study in the yeshivah into academic study at the university. As Jews had once studied Talmud, they now studied world culture, most particularly literature, which Norman Podhoretz described as playing "something like the role philosophy and theology have played at other periods."[8]

Podhoretz had in mind the New York Jewish intellectuals like himself who virtually took over the Columbia English department in the 1950s and '60s—"the Family" as he called it. The influx of Jews into academia generally was astounding in those years: from 1920 to 1940, for example, as quotas against Jews took hold, the Jewish population of Columbia Medical School alone dropped from 50 to 7 percent.[9] By contrast, from 1945 to 1960, when quotas were lifted, the Jews had become so dominant that literary critic Leslie Fiedler (a member of the Family) remembers finding himself "at the University of Bologna as one of four Americans [all of them Jewish] chosen to tell the Italians about American Puritanism."[10]

The Family, most of whose members were Jewish, revolved around Lionel Trilling, the first tenured Jewish appointee in the department. Fellow travelers, other than Podhoretz, included such people as Daniel Bell, Diana Trilling, Alfred Kazin, Hannah Arendt, and the two foremost art critics of the day, Clement Greenberg and Harold Rosenberg. Others dropped in on occasion, sometimes staying for a while, the most famous being Saul Bellow of Chicago and Leslie Fiedler, who taught until 1964 at the Montana State University in Missoula and then (until his death in 2003) at the State University of New York at Buffalo. Like most families, this one too was somewhat dysfunctional, as we gather from the ongoing debate between Greenberg and Rosenberg, whose "family rows" have been described as "no holds barred . . . the polemical style of the so-called New York intellectuals."[11]

They published regularly in *The Partisan Review* and later in *Commentary*. The *Review* featured an anti-Stalinist Marxist slant, which took up literary arms against the new critics of the South who saw literature as a phenomenon unto itself, entirely divorced from the political realities of life. Though not officially Jewish, it was Jewish (and Marxist) enough, in practice, for Edmund Wilson to call it *The Partisansky Review*.[12] *Commentary*, by contrast, was an official Jewish organ from its beginning—but for intellectuals focused on universal culture and politics, rather than Judaism per se. As Nathan Glazer, its editor in charge of culture, explained, "We could see no relation between Judaism and the Jewish life we knew and the culture, politics, and civilization to which we aspired."[13]

Commentary's founding editor, Elliott Cohen, had begun his publishing career at the *Menorah Journal*, which was "secular [and] humanist [but . . . outfitted with a] progressive Jewish consciousness."[14] It was there, for example, that Mordecai Kaplan chose to write his initial salvo demanding reconstruction of Judaism.[15] For Cohen, however, the *Journal* was merely a stepping-stone to what *Commentary* could become. Both Cohen and *Commentary* were committed to the secular and ethnic Jewish cause. "He [Cohen] had rejected Judaism as a form of worship, seeking to promote Jews and ethnic Jewishness without Judaism."[16]

The universalization of religious consciousness that marked the transfer of allegiance from the sea of Talmud to the ocean of world literature was hardly a Jewish invention, however. Impetus for this approach came originally from Matthew Arnold (1822–88). Seeing religion "admittedly in a state of collapse,"[17] Arnold had seized on literature as the new "Scripture" for the secular mind: "What made literature . . . a replacement for Scripture in an age of declining faith and the death of God was its excellence as literature, and its consequent critical immortality."[18] He was in tune with nineteenth-century romantics like Keats, Wordsworth, and Shelley, who flirted with atheism and identified with nature as their religion. They sought the reenchantment of nature in the wake of the Newtonian revolution, an effort traced at least as far back as Samuel Taylor Coleridge, who despaired at what Alistair McGrath calls "the failure of the religious imagination."[19] Relative to the poets, who were trying to imbue nature itself with transcendent mystery, Arnold was a romantic once removed, in that he saw God (or all that was left of God, anyway) in the poets. His secularized religious consciousness, channeled into world literature, led in a straight line to F. R. Leavis, whose journal of criticism, *Scrutiny*, attracted Podhoretz himself during a brief stint at Cambridge in the 1950s.

Trilling was Leavis's American alter ego, who had written his dissertation on Arnold and become Columbia's first Jewish tenured professor in 1939, a time when Jews were being weeded out of academic circles, not encouraged to join them. "We have room for only one Jew," the department chair had reported, "and we have chosen Mr. Trilling."[20]

The Family, then, was the specifically Jewish equivalent of Arnold's literary turn, "Culture as Secular Salvation for an educated elite,"[21] in the words of Leslie Fiedler, its sometime member, or, at least, visitor. The implicit identification of world literature as the functional equivalent of Talmudic study comes through clearly in its characterization by Podhoretz as "activity which is its own reward . . . a great respect for the thing in itself"[22]—an echo of the traditional Jewish championing of *torah lishmah* (the study of Torah for its own sake). Attending Columbia was what Daniel Bell called "a conversionary experience," where Podhoretz learned there were "more things in heaven and earth than were dreamt of in the philosophy of Brownsville."[23]

We can round out these general observations by looking in more detail at the careers of two members of the family in particular: Saul Bellow and Lionel Trilling.

Bellow personifies ethnic Judaism in the finest sense. He visited Israel to cover the Six-Day War as a literary correspondent, and he looked back with dismay at the fact that he had been "too busy becoming a novelist to take note of what was happening in the Forties. I was involved with 'literature' and given over to preoccupations with art, with language, with my struggle on the American scene, with claims for recognition of my talent or, like my pals of the *Partisan Review*, with modernism, Marxism, New Criticism, with Eliot, Yeats, Proust, etc.—with anything except the terrible events in Poland."[24] Bellow's ethnic consciousness surfaces also when, as Augie March, he recalls nostalgically what Jews brought with them from Europe: "For sadness the *Kaddish*, for amusement the *schnorrer* [beggar], for admiration the bearded scholar."[25] When faced with a negative review of *Humboldt's Gift* by John Updike, whom one of his friends, Samuel S. Goldberg, had labeled "that anti-Semitic pornographer," he responded angrily that "perhaps I should write my next book in Yiddish!"[26]

Actually, his letters are peppered with Yiddish anyway, the ethnic product of an environment where "you began life by knowing Genesis in Hebrew by heart at the age of four and grew up with . . . English, Hebrew, Yiddish and [for Bellow, whose family lived in Montreal] French."[27] His mother wanted him to become a talmudist, but like so many other Jews of the time, not just the famous variety, he had left his Orthodox upbringing far behind and had no spiritual moorings to take its place. He wrote the response concerning Updike on Yom Kippur.

Although he never actually did write in Yiddish—he was a universalist after all—his ethnic Jewish consciousness continued to value it as the language of eastern European Jewry and of the immigrant Jewish streets where he was raised. "The most ordinary Yiddish conversation," he judged, "is full of the grandest historical, mythological, and religious allusions." But Bellow's own literary efforts were universalist through and through. Believing that writing was a universal genus for which there could be no specifically Jewish species, he wrote Cynthia Ozick, calling "Jewish writers in America . . . a repulsive category!"[28]

To be sure, more than one analyst has nonetheless tried to find a Jewish component in Bellow's work.[29] Bellow himself refutes these claims, however, when he identifies the Jewish content of his works as simply "two fundamental qualities of the Jewish imagination . . . the tendency to overhumanize everything, to invest all things in the universe with intense human meaning . . . [and] the ability to respond to the human condition in a manner that teeters on the knife edge between laughter and trembling." This, he quickly adds, is true "of all mankind" even though it may characterize "Jews specially."[30]

Despite these and other attempts to link Bellow's humanism (and that is what it is) to Jewish models, it is just as easy to find the values he expresses in the American literary tradition. In 1977, for example, M. Gilbert Porter noted "the frequent appearance in Bellow's fiction of quotations from or allusions to the writings of the Transcendentalists."[31] Following Tony Tanner, he locates Bellow within the literary tradition of Emerson, Thoreau, and Whitman.[32] Bellow's intellectual expression is as much Transcendentalist American as it is religiously Jewish.

The claim for Bellow's Judaism boils down to ethical generality and ethnic generosity. Summing up the first is the overall contention that the Bellow protagonists are "like Abraham . . . stating the primal moral identification of ethical Judaism."[33] But what exactly is this ethical Judaism other than the universalist identification with humankind at large that also gave us ethical culture as an offshoot of, not a deep insight into, Judaism. Bellow's ethnic component, by contrast, is real enough. But it is a singular historical phenomenon, an experiment in Jewish identity for second-generation Jews who had embraced secularism, had abandoned religion, and were left with Jewish ethnicity as their only Jewish marker.

Lionel Trilling is my second case in point. Trilling too had traditionalist roots. His Bialystok father had even nursed aspirations to become a rabbi before settling into the business of manufacturing coats. But by the time Lionel was born, he had dropped Jewish religion to the point of eating shellfish without apology; the Trillings belonged to no synagogue and kept both Hanukkah and Christmas.[34] Lionel's literary career began with a series of essays and short stories published between 1925 and 1931 in the *Menorah Journal*. His contributions there, however, implied no deep commitment to identity as a Jew; what he was after, says his wife, Diana, was "a passport to publication. Understandably [she told him] you want to be in print and in order to be printed in the *Menorah Journal* one has to write as a Jew."[35]

By the thirties, Trilling had nothing to say about Judaism at all, and when he returned to the theme in 1944 he lamented, "As the Jewish community now exists, it can give no sustenance to the American artist or intellectual born a Jew. And so far as I am aware, it has not done so in the past."[36] Stephen Tanner quotes Mark Shechner as saying that Trilling's "Jewishness was eclipsed, old associations kept at bay, the instincts soft-peddled, the unconscious squelched, 'authenticity' taken to task, and *a curriculum of reading taken on as a prosthetic identity*."[37] My claim precisely is that world literature took the place of Jewish classics as the source for identity among these ethnic, but no longer religious, Jews. Zionism became a particularly symbolic issue for them, and Trilling rejected it.[38] Despite clear differences, his Judaism was more akin to that of England's Lucien Wolf, also an opponent of Jewish statehood. Without the state, however, it was not clear just what was left. "A friend," Wolf explained, "once said of me that my Judaism was not a religion at all but a cult of auld lang syne. I think he was right."[39]

A novelist's view of this ethnic nostalgia sans faith is provided by Julian Treslove, the non-Jewish protagonist in *The Finkler Question*. Treslove wishes with all his might that he were Jewish—even imagines sometimes that he is. He calls Jews "Finklers" after his Jewish friend of that name, but concludes about him, "Finkler was a Finkler, and Finkler had no faith."[40] However much Trilling differed from the fictitious Finkler, he would have agreed that his Judaism (like Finkler's British version) is Judaism without faith. Tanner concludes of Trilling, "It is difficult to think of Trilling as Jewish at all,"[41]

But such characterizations presume "Jewish" as a descriptor for religion. When I speak of universalizing Judaism through literature, I do not mean abandoning consciousness of being a Jew by ethnicity. Bellow (who was a Zionist) was nothing if not ethnically Jewish to his core, and even Trilling (who was not) kept a Passover seder—"the Seder service would always be important to Lionel," Diana Trilling recalls.[42] She properly sums up the matter by saying that she and her husband were "Jews without religion but Jews nonetheless"[43]—a characterization for my first case of Jewish ethnicity: not just for Trilling but Jewish academics in general following World War II, Podhoretz's "Family," the *Commentary* "crowd," the largely second-generation Jews who retained Jewish ethnic memories and identity but no religion to go with it.

The other ethnic Jewish option at the time was to forego Bell's conversionary experience at Columbia and take up residence in synagogues, primarily Conservative ones. The Conservative Movement reads itself back to Zacharias Frankel's European approach to tradition, but institutionally, it is fully an American phenomenon, established by Reform Jews who bought up a sleepy seminary on New York's Upper West Side and refurbished it as a place for eastern European immigrants to be socialized during the Great Migration of 1881 to 1924. By 1946 graduates of the seminary displaced the Reform board and declared independence as a movement, partly through its own journal (*Conservative Judaism*) and liturgy (the so-called Silverman Prayer Book).

Space restrictions prevent my fully stating the case for Conservative Judaism as a parallel ethnic trend among postwar Jews, but in order to make my upcoming claim regarding the current cultural move toward spirituality, I need at least to suggest the broad outlines of what the argument would be.

A signal study from the 1950s is Marshall Sklare's *Conservative Judaism,* a direct witness to the expansion of institutional religion in the Eisenhower era. Sklare spoke descriptively, blowing the whistle on the Jews he observed as only ostensibly religious. The extent of their ersatz religious commitment comes through best, however, in Herbert Gans's study of suburban Levittown, where the Conservative synagogue hired an Orthodox rabbi on condition that "he keep his personal religious practices to himself and promise not to demand observance from the children." The goal was "to maintain ethnic cohesion . . . to keep the children in the fold to prevent outmarriage, but to leave the adults uninvolved."[44] Sklare properly calls this the Jewish version of an ethnic church and predicts its demise in a world where only Judaism with some underlying transcendent commitment is going to make it.

Transcendent commitment was doubtlessly at the core of the Judaism that characterized the faculty of the Jewish Theological Seminary at the time. It revolved about the traditional concepts of Torah, mitzvot, and chosen peoplehood, with an accent on historical change. But that is not necessarily how even the seminary students saw it—Podhoretz thought the covert goal of seminary education to be Jewish survival, "the business of making Jews,"[45] without any clarity as to why. And, as both Sklare and Gans perceived, the Jews in the Conservative pews bought very little of it. They traded on issues of ethnicity, *yiddishkeit*, and pride in "authentic" continuity with the past. It was Conservative Jews whom Philip Roth's early work parodied in painfully memorable pastiches of an ethnic way of life that just will not last.

Jewish academia has not proved lasting, and Conservative Judaism is under attack, with numbers falling precipitously. In Philadelphia, for example, once a bastion of Conservative strength, a 2009 study revealed that Conservative Jews made up only 30 percent of the Jewish population. Worse still, the Conservative population aged sixty-two and older was 38 percent of the whole, while of those aged eighteen to thirty-nine, only 18 percent claimed adherence to Conservative Judaism. The Pew report of 2013 confirms the fall: only 18 percent of all American Jews now identify as Conservative.[46]

The Family was secular, universal, and, by now, long gone; Conservative Judaism is religious, particularistic, and still with us. Both, however, are cases of ethnic Judaism withering without a cause. But what cause? As it happens, both secularity and religion are under attack from our third partner in the ménage à trois to which I referred: spirituality.

The spiritual turn of our time has been amply chronicled in the spate of literature prompted by such by-now classic accounts as *Habits of the Heart* and *Generation of Seekers*.[47] It has found its way into equally influential literature on church (and synagogue) transformation—the work of Diana Butler Bass, for example—and been studied among Jews specifically.[48] It figures prominently in recent sociological accounts of religion to the point where its pervasive appeal cannot be doubted. Still, "the spiritual" is a category broad enough to cover a great number of things, including such secular pursuits as business and the arts;[49] and it is notoriously hard to study—"akin to shoveling fog," it has been said.[50] We should be clear about how we are using the term here.

Synoptic work by Courtney Bender and Omar McRoberts suggests three approaches.[51] The first is essentialist, an exclusively denoted identification of spirituality as a single something or other: yoga, perhaps, or (for Jews) the mindfulness approach favored by the Institute for Jewish Spirituality.[52] The problem with that approach is that it "risks occulting" the subject and rendering it too ethereal to be of use generally.[53] A second approach tracks the language of the spiritual as it turns up in such settings as law, politics and commerce. This more expansive approach, however, risks occluding from view the specific set of meanings that spirituality seems to have within the legitimate, albeit imprecise, conceptual field of American religion alone. The third approach eschews both the essentialist and the expansivist views by treating spirituality functionally as a catchall phrase for organized religion's loyal opposition during historical moments of religious ferment and regeneration called awakenings. I use "spirituality" here in this third sense, referring back to the last of the three terms with which I defined America's religious landscape at the outset: neither secular nor religious alone, but the spiritual critique that regularly turns up in surveys of American religious consciousness.

The problem is that studies of this "loyal opposition" have inappropriately emphasized only its most obvious aspect: personal conversion—the affective process of "seeing the light" and experiencing rebirth. From the conversionary sermons of George Whitefield to the camp meetings of Cane Ridge, popular attention has thus been focused on such phenomena as the "bodily effects" and "physical manifestations" that are the "distinguishing marks of the Spirit of God."[54] Even the philosophically inclined William James provided the testimonial of Stephen H. Bradley, who heard a revivalist preacher "on the second evening of November, 1829" and was seized by "the remarkable experience of the power of the Holy Spirit."[55] But James also cites the Transcendentalists, which is to say, the cognitive side of the spiritual challenge to ossified religious institutions. American spirituality has as much to do with Jonathan Edwards's reasoned reassertion of human depravity as it does the hordes of people swooning away at revivalist meetings. What both have in common is their appeal to American individualism at the expense of static liturgies on one hand and encrusted dogmas on the other.

Many factors go into the questionable viability of the two forms of ethnic Judaism that we have looked at here, the universalizing tendency of the academics and the particularizing alternative that became Conservative Judaism.

But insofar as we apply a spiritual critique, we may fasten either on their lack of affective experience or their failure to provide a compelling cognitive message. It is the latter that proves most interesting.

As long as ethnicity is the norm, no validating ideas are necessary. Basic Durkheimian sociology explains the phenomenon: simply count up (1) how many people interact with one another (2) for how long and (3) with what intensity and length of interaction; and you get a predictor of social cohesion. Take away ethnic neighborhoods, a threat from the out-group (anti-Semitism, for Jews), and the other forces that produce Durkheim's mechanical solidarity, and ethnicity fails. In its place we get the anxiety of individual identity: the need to determine who one is, if one is not, self-evidently, a Polish Jew, an Irish Catholic, or a Swedish Lutheran.

Charles Taylor emphasizes the power of ideas in affirming identity at its deepest level, what he calls "moral space."[56] There is no reason why failing ethnic groups cannot, in theory, confirm their members in their old ethnic identity not simply by effervescent experience (in Durkheim's terms) but by a "big idea," that compels attention. These will have to be arguable as part of public discourse—the same way religions are, given their American character as market phenomena.[57] They can hardly be recycled ideological claims associated with the failing church structures that are under attack already.

Jewish ethnicity has yet to receive the compelling rhetoric of sustaining ideas.[58] The Jewish camaraderie of "the Family" did have a potentially big idea embedded within it, as expressed by Norman Podhoretz when he called Jews themselves "a very big idea in the history of the world [such that] no one born into this idea can dismiss it or refuse to acknowledge the loyalties and responsibilities it imposes on him, without doing himself some violence." He went on to register his "conviction that one ought to feel a sense of 'historic reverence' to Jewish tradition even, or perhaps especially, if one is convinced that the curtain is about to drop on the last act of a very long play."[59] The words "reverence" and "piety" suggest, at least implicitly, some aspect of spirituality.

Conservative Judaism, our other test case, is also in need of a big idea with traction, but its rhetoric has so far focused on covenant, responsibility, and mitzvot—none of which seems any longer to prove compelling.[60] Whether it can locate a more effective spiritual claim remains to be seen.

In any case, the issue for both groups is the failure of ethnicity alone. The academics were secular, albeit proudly Jewish, while at the same time having displaced the Jewish love of religious truth onto the world stage of literature and letters. Conservative Judaism emerged in the postwar years as religious in rhetoric and practice even though, as Sklare's "ethnic church," its members rejected much of the religious core and replaced it with ethnic solidarity. The larger issue is the spiritualization of American identity and the lack of big ideas when ethnicity fails.

Notes

1. Tony Judt, "Voyage Home," *New York Review of Books*, May 27, 2010, 29.
2. Conrad Ostwalt, *Secular Steeples* (Harrisburg, Pa., 2003), 4, 5.
3. William James, *The Varieties of Religious Experience* (1902; repr., New York, 1994), 370.
4. Charles Taylor, *Varieties of Religion Today: William James Revisited* (Cambridge, Mass., 2002).
5. See, e.g., Steven H. Warner, "Work in Progress toward a New Paradigm for the Sociological Study of Religion in the United States," *American Journal of Sociology* 98, no. 5 (1993): 1044–93; Laurence Iannoccone, "The Consequences of Religious Market Structure: Adam Smith and the Economics of Religion," *Rationality and Society* 3 (1991): 156–77; Laurence Iannaccone and Rodney Stark, "A Supply Side Reinterpretation of the 'Secularization' of Europe," *Journal for the Scientific Study of Religion* 33, no. 3 (1994): 230–52.
6. Steven Bruce, *Religion in the Modern World* (Oxford, 1996).
7. Jon Meacham, *American Gospel: God the Founding Fathers, and the Making of a Nation* (New York, 2006), 176–77.
8. Norman Podhoretz, quoted in Philip French, *Three Honest Men: A Critical Mosaic* (Manchester, 1980), 80.
9. David A. Hollinger, *Science Jews and Secular Culture* (Princeton, NJ, 1998), 81.
10. Leslie Fiedler, *Fiedler on the Roof* (Boston, 2001), xi.
11. Irving Sandler, "Clement Greenberg and Harold Rosenberg: Convergence and Divergence," in *Abstract Expressionism*, ed. N. L. Kleeblatt (New Haven, Conn., 2008), 126.
12. Alfred Kazin, *New York Jew* (1978; repr., Syracuse, 1996), 44. Among "the many Jews" associated with *Partisan Review*, Kazin mentions "Trilling and Bellow, Philip Rahv, William Phillips, Delmore Schwartz, Meyer Schapiro, Harold Rosenberg, Paul Goodman, Irving Howe, Daniel Bell, Sidney Hook, Lionel Abel, Isaac Rosenfeld, Clement Greenberg, [and] Leslie Fiedler."
13. Nathan Abrams, *Commentary Magazine, 1945–59: "A Journal of Significant Thought and Opinion"* (London, 2007), 76.
14. Stephen L. Tanner, *Lionel Trilling* (Boston, 1988), 13.
15. Mordecai Kaplan, "A Program for the Reconstruction of Judaism," *Menorah Journal* 6, no. 4 (1920): 181–96.
16. Abrams, *Commentary Magazine*, 75.
17. Giles Gunn, *The Interpretation of Otherness: Literature, Religion and the American Imagination* (New York, 1979), 13, cited by Tracy Fessenden, *Culture and Redemption: Religion, the Secular and American Literature* (Princeton, N.J., 2007), 1.
18. Leslie Fiedler, *Essays on Bioethics, Theology and Myth* (Lincoln, Mass., 1996), 11.
19. Alister McGrath, *The Twilight of Atheism* (New York, 2006), 112.
20. Kazin, *New York Jew*, 42–43.
21. Fiedler, *Essays*, 7.
22. Norman Podhoretz, *Making It* (New York, 1967), 53.

23. Ibid., 16–17.
24. Saul Bellow, *Paris Review* Interview, *Writers at Work,* 3rd ser., ed. A. Kazin (New York, 1967), 182.
25. Saul Bellow, *The Adventures of Augie March* (New York, 1953), 78.
26. Benjamin Taylor, ed., *Saul Bellow, Letters* (New York: 2010), 331, letter dated September 15, 1975.
27. Eusebio L. Rodrigues, *Quest for the Human: An Exploration of Saul Bellow's Fiction* (Lewisburg, Pa., 1981), 77.
28. Taylor, *Saul Bellow, Letters,* 438, letter dated July 19, 1987.
29. See, e.g., Chester E. Eisinger, "Saul Bellow: Love and Identity," *Accent* 18 (Summer, 1958): 179–203; and Eisinger, *Fiction of the Forties* (Chicago, 1963); and L. H. Goldman, *Saul Bellow's Moral Condition* (New York, 1984).
30. Saul Bellow, introduction to *Great Jewish Short Stories* (New York, 1971), 78.
31. See M. Gilbert Porter, "Hitch Your Agony to a Star: Bellow's Transcendental Vision," *Saul Bellow and His Work,* ed. E. Schraepen (Brussels, 1978), 87; and Porter, *Whence the Power? The Artistry and Humanity of Saul Bellow* (Columbia, Mo., 1974), 192.
32. Porter, *Whence the Power,* 192–94, 197.
33. Earl Rovit, "Saul Bellow and the Concept of the Survivor," *Saul Bellow and His Work* (Brussels 1978), 192.
34. Diana Trilling, *The Beginning of the Journey: The Marriage of Diana and Lionel* (Orlando, Fla., 1993), 11, 38.
35. Ibid., 144.
36. Mark Krupnick, *Lionel Trilling and Cultural Witticism in America* (Evanston, Ill., 1986), 22, 23, 31.
37. Tanner, *Lionel Trilling,* 15 (italics mine).
38. He even disapproved, apparently, of the Zionist elements in *Daniel Deronda* and ignored "Leopold Bloom's dalliance with Zionist impulses in *Ulysses.*" See also his contribution to the *Commentary* symposium of 1949 in which he "sarcastically observed that T. S. Eliot's ideal of 'a homogeneous culture with a strong religious cast' . . . attracts many Jews, who, indeed, have put it into practice"—an apparent "allusion to the state of Israel" (Edward Alexander, *Lionel Trilling and Irving Howe: And Other Stories of Literary Friendship* [New Brunswick, N.J., 2009], 42).
39. Jonathan Schneer, *The Balfour Declaration: The Origins of the Arab–Israeli Conflict* (New York, 2011), 120.
40. Howard Jacobson, *The Finkler Question* (New York, 2010), 56.
41. Tanner, *Lionel Trilling,* 15.
42. Trilling, *The Beginning of the Journey,* 112.
43. Ibid., 44.
44. Herbert Gans, *The Levittowners* (New York, 1967), 76, 77.
45. Podhoretz, *Making It,* 46.
46. By comparison, in the Philadelphia study, 6 percent overall are Orthodox, 41 percent Reform, 3 percent Reconstructionist, 10 percent "just Jewish," 3 percent "secular," and 5 percent "other"; parallel figures for age eighteen to thirty-nine are Orthodox 9 percent, Reform 53 percent, Reconstructionist 3 percent, "just Jewish" 8 percent, "secular" 2 percent, and "other" 2 percent. See Jewish Federation of Greater Philadelphia, *Jewish Population Study of Greater Philadelphia 2009 Summary Report* (Philadelphia, 2009), 38. For Pew, see "A Portrait of Jewish Americans," Pew Research: Religion and Public Life Project, October 1, 2013, www.pewforum.

org/2013/10/01/jewish-american-beliefs-attitudes-culture-survey/. Parallel figures there are Reform, 35 percent; no denomination, 30 percent; Conservative, 18 percent; Orthodox, 10 percent; other, 6 percent.

47. Robert N. Bellah, et al., *Habits of the Heart* (Berkeley, Calif., 1985); Wade Clarke Roof, *Generation of Seekers* (San Francisco, 1993).

48. See Diana Butler Bass, *The Practicing Congregations* (Herndon, Va., 2004); Herndon, *Christianity after Religion* (New York, 2012). Steven M. Cohen and Lawrence A. Hoffman, "How Spiritual Are America's Jews?," Synagogue 3000, http://synagogue3000. org/howspiritual (accessed January 22, 2014).

49. See, e.g., N. J. Demerath III, "Varieties of Sacred Experience," *Journal for the Scientific Study of Religion* 39.1 (2000): 1–11.

50. Courtney Bender, *The New Metaphysicals: Spirituality and the American Religious Imagination* (Chicago, 2010), 182.

51. Courtney Bender and Omar McRoberts, *Mapping the Field: When and How to Study Spirituality*, SSRC (Social Science Research Council) Working Paper, October 2012.

52. Jonathan Slater, *Mindful Jewish Living* (New York, 2004).

53. Bender and McRoberts, *Mapping the Field*, 20.

54. From Jonathan Edwards, 1740 Commencement Address at Yale, cited in Sydney E. Ahlstrom, *A Religious History of the American People* (New Haven, Conn., 1972), 302, 303.

55. James, *The Varieties of Religious Experience*, 210.

56. Charles Taylor, *Sources of the Self* (Cambridge, MA, 1989), 28.

57. On religion's arguability as public discourse, see esp. work of Jürgen Habermas: e.g., his dialogue with Joseph Cardinal Ratzinger, *The Dialectics of Secularization* (San Francisco, 2006).

58. Laura Levitt cites Yiddishist debates from the 1950s as "arguments [that] remain relevant" but even if they are (debates on unionization, for example), their being ethnic Jewish issues at one time has no relevance to that continued relevance. See Levitt, "Other Moderns, Other Jews: Revisiting Jewish Secularism in America," ed. J. R. Jakobsen and A. Pellegrini, *Secularisms* (Durham, N.C, 2008), 112.

59. Norman Podhoretz, "Jewishness and the Younger Jewish Intellectuals," *Commentary*, April 1961, 310.

60. See, e.g., Steven M. Cohen and Arnold M. Eisen, *The Jew Within* (Bloomington, Ind., 2000), whose study turned up the general finding that "even the most observant and active of our interviewees expressed discomfort with the idea of commandment" (24).

17

COMPLICATING A JEWISH MODERNITY

The Jewish Theological Seminary, Columbia University, and the Rise of a Jewish Counterculture in 1968

RIV-ELLEN PRELL

David Ellenson was among the very first of the American Jewish baby boom generation to assume an international leadership position in a major Jewish organization. As he moved from his role as a distinguished scholar and teacher to become, in addition, the president of the Hebrew Union College–Jewish Institute of Religion, he brought with him the culture and ideas of, if not an entire generation, certainly of one of its significant subgroups. Ellenson was an important part of a national cohort of Jews, the Jewish counterculture, committed to integrating traditional Jewish practices with advocacy for political and cultural change in the United States.[1]

David Ellenson attended college during the 1960s, which was a period of cultural and political upheaval. His graduate education at Columbia University, his membership in the New York Havurah, and his ordination from HUC-JIR occurred in a similarly tumultuous period of the 1970s.[2] Manhattan's Upper West Side was a particularly compelling geographic space where young Jews not only participated in and led those political upheavals; they also created alternative organizations outside the umbrella of Jewish communal and religious life.

In this essay I will offer a case study of the critical days in the spring of 1968 at Columbia University and the Jewish Theological Seminary of the Conservative movement when a major student revolt occurred. David Ellenson

263

arrived in New York City three years after these events, but his life in New York was surely shaped by them. The Columbia events, reflected back through protests at JTS, led, in the case of some Jewish students, to an increasingly clear disaffection with institutions, leaders, and teachers, as well as with the nation's wars and politics. Jewish students began to press for changes that helped dramatically reshape American Jewish life.

These events of 1968 underline a shift in the discourse of American Jewish life from a concern with rationalizing Judaism with modernity and science to a concern for its authenticity. If the parents of baby boomers sought a way to make Judaism compatible with the preoccupations of modernity, their children rejected its rationalism and dichotomizing of tradition and modernity. If that parental generation sought large and substantial expressions of Jewish arrival in the middle class in their synagogue and philanthropic and defense organizations, many of their baby boom children sought face-to-face alternative communities that often rejected the trappings of suburban affluence. If their parents sought a new relationship to power, their children, in some cases, eschewed power and in others challenged it directly. These antimonies applied to issues about the State of Israel, liberal politics, and other issues identified by the historian Arthur Goren as central to the postwar Jewish consensus.[3] Many Jewish baby boomers judged the world of their childhoods harshly, whether it was about liberal politics, religious hollowness, or family expectations.[4]

The uprisings at Columbia and its aftermath at JTS were perceived by the student activists as much as a response to the failures of bastions of learning and science to uphold their ideals, as they were modes of asserting alternative ways of living in the twentieth century. For JTS students, among others, Judaism provided a crucial medium to critique the failures of American culture and its authorities, in addition to a set of practices with which to live in the world.

The Jewish baby boomers who participated in both the American counterculture and the Jewish American counterculture, as many scholars have argued, had an enormous impact on the society. However, they did not constitute the numerical majority of their cohort. Young Jews, nevertheless, were typical of the youth who identified with the American counterculture.[5] They hailed from the middle class. They were students in American universities during the mid-1960s to the early 1970s. They attended both public and private universities, as well as Ivy League schools in far greater proportions than the number of Jews in the United States in this period.

The New Left, the most political manifestation of the American counterculture, was populated with young men and women who hailed from families with deep sympathies with the Left and who counted themselves as liberals.[6] The Jewish students at Columbia University who participated in the events of 1968 to be described in this essay, did not participate as Jews, but simply as students with varying degrees of commitment to Leftist politics and anger over America's participation in the War in Vietnam and at Columbia's secret involvement with that effort, to be described below.

The JTS students who are the focus of this paper were rabbinical, undergraduate, and graduate students at the seminary, many pursuing joint degrees with Columbia University. The majority of them had been raised in middle-class Conservative Jewish homes, attended or worked at Camp Ramah, the movement's camp, had spent time in Israel, and were, by the standards of their movement, religious observant Jews.

I am, therefore, concerned with this group of students. However, their protests, writings, and organizing efforts were not limited to a small number of blocks on New York's Upper West Side. Jewish students at the University of California at Berkeley, the University of Chicago, the University of California at Los Angeles, Brooklyn College, and other colleges and universities participated both in campus protests and simultaneously created a "Jewish response" to these issues. Some were Zionist responses; some were secular; and some grew out of the Conservative movement. Comparable responses did not seem to flower from Orthodox and Reform roots, for reasons really never fully explored.

The Jewish baby boom cohort that was both most involved in campus protests and the development of a Jewish counterculture was, then, very much like its American counterpart in terms of class and education. Its Jewishness was, like the politics of the New Left, also linked to families and communities that nurtured a commitment to Judaism and Zionism.

The Jewish baby boomers who were deeply engaged in the cultural transformations of 1968 constituted a hinge generation, which was raised in a highly modern approach to Judaism that emphasized the integration of rationalism and science with the possibility of religious practice.[7] For the most part, American Jewish movements following World War II embraced the compatibility of Judaism with the perspectives of the natural and social sciences that were classically viewed as threats to religious life. For most of these movements, neither evolution, nor the application of scholarly approaches to the study of sacred texts (to greater and lesser extents) posed fundamental problems for Judaism. Sermons of the era, across the movements, drew from secular thinkers. Even the aesthetics of synagogues and worship, again to varying degrees, were presented as compatible with postwar American culture.

The period's great antimodernist religious movements were most often associated with Evangelical Christianity and the several strains of Hasidism found in various parts of New York that rejected science and a modern sensibility. These antimodern movements did not initially hold an attraction for this cohort of the baby boom, although that would change with time.[8]

Whether the first cohort of the baby boom came of age in a postmodern era is particularly difficult to claim since neither the time frame of postmodernism nor its definition may be clearly defined. I view them as a hinge generation since they moved in both directions. They were shaped by modern American life and developed ideas in opposition to it, but they were not fully postmodernists. Their opposition to the rationalism and compartmentalization of the Jewish practices that defined their youth, teens, and twenties was less "ironic" and "deconstructive," than the classic hallmarks of postmodernism. However, their combining and recombining halakhah and personal autonomy, a "return" to Jewish ideas, texts, and historical figures that were often dismissed or overlooked by their teachers, and an almost contradictory assertion of "tribalism" and "universalism" are often associated with the oppositions that characterize the postmodern era. The writers and activists involved with this nascent Jewish counterculture advocated for a generationally based vision of Jewish life that they viewed as a criticism of their families, synagogues, and religious educational institutions. They were, therefore, poised between two periods of time and two cultural formulations of American and American Jewish life.

Authority and Religious Transformation

This upheaval in Jewish life that undermined any simple dichotomy between "tradition" and "modernity," or even "religious" and "secular," fits a pattern identified by a number of scholars who are interested in the complexity of religious life in contemporary society, whether that was in the 1960s, 1990s, or the twenty-first century.[9] If, for example, Charles Taylor, Robert Wuthow, and others argue that the 1960s was a key transitional point in American culture's religious and cultural life, other scholars have argued that the 1960s was not a period of such radical transformation.[10] Whatever decade scholars will some day claim was the critical one for a variety of changes in religious life, or when cultural and social forms of authority sputtered out and new cultural patterns, forms of association and ideas sparked fires of change, the baby boom was clearly a critical generation in the process. For Jews, Manhattan's Upper West

Side, Chicago, Los Angeles, Boston, Washington D.C., Brooklyn, and other areas were all sites of these changes.

As important as social conditions are to explaining religious life—a fundamental tenant of the social sciences—religions continue to overflow the boundaries of these classic distinctions. Religions fail to disappear when it seems reasonable to assume that they might. Rather, they may take different turns, such as opposing power or supporting those who hold it. The very unpredictability of religious traditions has made religion a compelling site of study from the 1960s forward. Hence, the countercultural movements of the 1960s were both radically secular and religious, often most surprisingly embracing various religious traditions only to transform them. Just as baby boom activists attacked religious authorities—meaning both church or synagogue leaders and text and practices—for their complicity with political conservatism, many of them, including those in the Jewish counterculture, drew on their traditions to attack power and war.

I offer this brief case study of some of the generative events that gave rise to New York variations on that counterculture. I suggest that it brings into view, like a photograph emerging from a chemical bath in which it is developed, the frustrations with the modes of mobilization, and the promises of new forms of religious and cultural authority. It underlines the great complexity of terms like tradition, modernity, and authority in the context of American Jewish cultural and religious life during the counterculture.

Columbia University's Student Revolt

Mark Rudd, the most public face of Columbia's students protests, recounts in his memoir, *My Life with SDS and the Weathermen Underground*, how he and other students came to occupy university president Grayson Kirk's office at dawn on April 24, 1968.[11] This occupation was the culmination of several earlier events and lengthy debates and discussions that characterized the radically democratic processes that marked the protest.

On the previous day, following an on-campus demonstration, students marched to the construction site of a gymnasium being built in Morningside Park to protest Columbia's incursion into, and disregard for, the neighborhood.[12] The marchers included members of both Students for a Democratic Society and the Student Afro-American Society. They returned to campus after a confrontation at the gymnasium site, hoping to occupy a building in order to disrupt the normal flow of university life. About four hundred students occupied Hamilton

Hall that afternoon and presented the administration with a series of demands that included dropping probation for the six students who protested Columbia's relationship with the Pentagon's Institute for Defense Analyses and abandoning the gym project.[13] After an all-night debate over whether to blockade the building from other students, the African American students asked white SDS students to leave and to occupy their own building, as African American students declared their desire to "take our own stand in Hamilton."[14] This decision was to create the occupation of Columbia. Various student groups occupied different buildings and made different decisions about the nature of their protests, whether violent or nonviolent resistance. The racial politics of America in the 1960s were very much part of student politics as well.

Half of the remaining white students from the Hamilton Hall occupation walked over to Low Library. After some slight hesitation, a few of them took the plank from a nearby bench and broke one of the building's windows in order to enter the basement, climbed up Low's imposing staircase to the president's office suite, and finally proceeded to the "inner sanctum" after shattering more glass. Rudd and others were "awed" by the president's sumptuous office filled with art, leather sofas, and books on what appeared to Rudd to be "miles of built-in book shelves." Rudd walked over to the shelves to pull a book down and discovered that none of its edges had been cut. As he looked at one after another of the books, he discovered that they had obviously never been opened, handled or read. Rudd concluded that the president was, "as I expected, a phony."[15]

In recounting this story in his memoir, Rudd then reflected on what Columbia University meant to him as an "idealistic Jewish kid" who grew up in New Jersey knowing that the world consisted of "Jews and goyim." As he crossed the river to Manhattan to attend Columbia, he entered a world that was run by "them," those in control of America's great institutions. However, that moment in Grayson Kirk's office revealed to Rudd that at the top of this world were people who "violated their own principles," "lied," and put in practice "pro-war and racist policies."[16]

A week later Kirk brought a thousand police to campus to clear the occupied buildings, which resulted in the arrest of seven hundred students and injuries and hospitalization of more than one hundred. The next day a thousand of Columbia's students and a great many of its faculty declared a strike and refused to hold classes in the buildings.

On the first day of the strike, six blocks uptown from Columbia at the Jewish Theological Seminary of the Conservative Movement, two hundred faculty and students overflowed the seating of Unterberg Auditorium for a meeting that would address both what had happened at Columbia and students' ongoing frustrations with the seminary. JTS was linked to Columbia by far more than geographic proximity. It offered a joint undergraduate degree. Its graduate students enrolled at both institutions. Some members of its distinguished faculty also held dual appointments. And, not to be underestimated, it shared a subway stop with Columbia that brought students and faculty into daily contact with one campus on the way to the other. During April of 1968 that contact was for many students inspiring. One former rabbinical student recalled that "going from 116th to 122nd Street was going from the modern age to the middle ages."[17]

For many of the seminary's faculty, the blocks were far too close for their comfort, and what they saw at Columbia horrified them. Students of that era remembered members of their faculty telling them about those fears. For example, Fritz Rothschild, a professor of Jewish philosophy, had grown up in Germany and remembered Nazi youth massing in a plaza and screaming to expel Jewish students.[18] The 1968 protests at Columbia evoked that time for him and many other faculty members.

In contrast to the occupation of Low Library, this JTS gathering was sanctioned and relatively orderly. Some students formed the group Jews for Justice that initiated the meeting. They posted flyers around the seminary with an image of the golem, an anthropomorphic being made of inanimate material that appeared in Jewish folklore. On the student poster, the golem's forehead bore not the classic Prague version of the animating word *EMET* (truth), but "Revolution is the right of the people."[19]

Dean of Students Joe Brodie and dean of the Rabbinical School Neil Gillman presided. Tempers flared as students demanded that JTS take a stand to condemn the violence ordered by Columbia's administration the previous night. Some argued that Jewish tradition required it. Several students attending the meeting were bandaged from injuries received from encounters with police.[20] The seminary's chancellor, Louis Finkelstein, first appointed to his position in 1951 (serving as president beginning in 1940), rose to reply to them. He declared to those assembled that that the seminary would "need to look into the matter."

The students' responses were hardly respectful. They booed in outrage at this obvious denial, not only of what had happened a few blocks away but of its effect on the seminary's own students. A member of the education faculty, Joseph Lukinsky, rose to respond to Finkelstein in an effort to calm the students. "With all due respect," he began, "Dr. Finkelstein, you can see around you the results of what happened. The students have been in the middle of something quite disturbing that should not happen in any academic or social environment. People are hurt and that is not the way in which conflicts are resolved."

The chancellor shot back, "Rabbi Lukinsky, we don't know what happened and whether or not it was justified." He dismissed any notion of the students or Joseph Lukinsky's that this was a matter of injustice to be addressed by Jewish law. No one missed the obvious condescension in the chancellor's form of address. Though Lukinsky held a PhD from Harvard and was on the seminary's faculty, Louis Finkelstein addressed him "merely" as rabbi, suggesting that he was not worthy of being addressed as "Professor," that is, as a colleague or a scholar; he belonged in a pulpit rather than in academic life.[21]

If Mark Rudd found hollowness at the center of Columbia, JTS students recalled disillusionment with their institution. If Rudd looked on Columbia as a Jewish outsider, JTS students looked at an institution that they imagined would embody what they took to be Jewish engagement with a world of ethics and values. They too found something hollow in its leadership and curriculum.

Certainly no student at JTS doubted Chancellor Finkelstein's commitment to scholarship and Jewish observance. Nevertheless, there were students who viewed him as hypocritical. Michael Greenbaum, a scholar of the Finkelstein years at the seminary, explained that "the chancellor didn't engage in any particular social issues or events. He would always say 'that's not the job of the seminary; that's the job of the social action committee of United Synagogue.'"[22] Nevertheless, former students recalled Finkelstein's commitment to bringing public figures from the fields of religion and science together weekly to discuss the social issues of the day. Still, when called upon to take a real stand, Finkelstein refused. Arthur Green, a rabbinical student in the 1960s, labeled the seminary "morally disappointing."[23]

Like Rudd, many JTS students fled what they experienced as a conformist postwar Jewish suburban world in search of something more compelling and important. If their disillusionments were not identical, there is nonetheless something quite striking about the fact that students at Columbia and JTS saw the two institutions as failing their moral aspirations, thereby motivating them to seek alternatives.

A closer look at the events that stretched from April of 1968 to March of 1969 at JTS reveals an overlapping network of students from the seminary whose frustrations and disappointment, as well as vision and aspirations, led them to create important alternative cultural, religious, and political groups and projects. Almost all of these students aimed to integrate what they defined as Judaism, Jewish values, Jewish ethics, and Jewish culture with a New Left critique of American politics. Barely three years after these initial events, Jewish feminism became central to this set of concerns. These feminists were among the visionaries of a Jewish counterculture with its many branches that would ultimately challenge American Jewish life to its core. What many of the students at the Jewish Theological Seminary in 1968 sought was nothing less than the commitment as Jews to respond to the social crises of the time within a framework of religious obligation. They framed their actions in the discourse of Torah, mitzvah (commandment), and halakhah (Jewish law). Their understanding of war and peace, of rights and racial equality, inextricably linked their New Left convictions and their Judaism.

Arthur Green explained that integration: "We saw that it was possible to combine holiness with being progressive. We were in the throes of the civil rights movement. We learned there that religion can be a force for progressive social change. Prior to that the Jews who were progressives were mostly secular, even anti-religious. They were the old lefty Jews. Civil rights showed that religion was a positive force for social change."[24] Then Green referred to his teacher and mentor Rabbi Abraham Joshua Heschel, always referred to as Heschel: "That was what made Heschel's involvement with Civil Rights so magnificent. This was all very stirring because Heschel was also co-chair of Clergy and Laity Concerned with Vietnam."[25]

Many of the seminary students who filled Unterberg Auditorium were not only responding to the deeply troubling events of what they all called "the bust," when police were brought on Columbia's campus. Most had for years, in a variety of venues, come to understand that Judaism was in fact engaged fundamentally with the world that they wanted to transform. For many of them, Rabbi Heschel, a scholar, an observant Jew, and a refugee who had barely survived the Holocaust, was unique since he embodied that integration.[26]

A second event at JTS in March of 1969 both affirmed the emerging vision of what an engaged Jewish life might look like and revealed the limitations of the seminary to provide that life. Reuven Kimelman, then a rabbinical student at the seminary, described this event in the journal *Judaism*, under the title "A Jewish Peace Demonstration."[27] He recounted the story of Burton Weiss, a student who had studied at JTS one summer. In December 1968 Weiss refused to submit for induction into the Armed Forces on the grounds that he would not take a life and would on the designated day be instead at the synagogue of JTS. He explained that he would be with people who "wish to give me aid and comfort, argue with me and pray, study and sing."[28] Indeed, it was at the seminary that Weiss surrendered to federal marshals.

Kimelman's article focused on the process that the JTS students engaged in to support Weiss. They debated whether it was simply sufficient to offer "to support a fellow Jew in his time of need," and concluded that what was required was to directly support the refusal to take a life because the "Torah refuses Temple sanctuary to a murder."[29] One hundred students signed a petition of support, not sure if there would be consequences for them as rabbinical students. They discussed the place of nonviolence in Judaism by studying relevant texts. They referred to the day as a "learn-in," echoing such civil rights terms as "sit in," or "pray in." However, according to Kimelman, this event was not an attack on the seminary, nor did they expect the administration to offer "sanctuary" to Weiss as a draft resister as some churches had throughout the United States.[30]

The day Weiss surrendered was devoted to services at the seminary's synagogue, as well as study of a variety of traditional texts and singing songs of peace. Kimelman commented, "We were not studying text but Torah. This was not a normal experience of learning the past wisdom of our Sages. We found them speaking to us in our situation. . . . Issues of war, peace, non-violence and the ethics of protest flowed naturally from our study." He concluded that "we had realized a Jewish ideal, the total integration of our religious, moral and personal concerns within the context of our Torah."[31] Other students at the seminary may have disputed Kimelman's view that this gathering constituted JTS's "ideal."

The third set of events that transpired during this brief period was the students' demand that the curriculum for rabbinical education had to change. While there was a stirring in the institution among some of the deans and faculty about the need to change the curriculum, the student protests may well have created a greater urgency for this change. Following the gathering in Unterberg Auditorium, a few rabbinical students, including Steve Shaw and Robert Sacks, met with Chancellor Finkelstein and other administrators. Robert Sacks recalled, "We had an opportunity to make our case." Steve Shaw proclaimed to those gathered that the Seminary was a "pediatric institution that infantilized its students."[32] The era when students were expected to feel that "it's an honor to be admitted here, and you sat in class and learned what you were told to learn" was over, according to Michael Greenbaum.[33] A new generation of students was never again going to spend five years in this world in order to become rabbis.[34]

Sacks, like other students, recalled a curriculum that was rigid and that only a handful of faculty had any interest in relating their studies to the issues that deeply moved so many of the students. He remembered at last studying the Prophet Jeremiah, the powerful voice for justice, in one of his courses. But he was only asked about what, from his perspective, was "to master and memorize the Hebrew text. We never grappled with it, asked what it meant, or what it had to say about contemporary life." He added, "I still recall an examination question, Where were (trees) mentioned in Jeremiah?"[35]

Both Columbia and JTS were fundamentally transformed by the events of 1968, even if it was, in both cases, too little for many, and certainly too late. Shortly after the Weiss Learn-in, Reuven Kimelman met with a group of people, including rabbinical and graduate students at JTS and Columbia, to create a new kind of Jewish community, an alternative to a synagogue that would become the New York Havurah.[36] New signs appeared on the walls of the seminary that invited people to be part of a group where you could "pray and protest together." Kimelman recalled being criticized by various faculty members at the seminary for creating such a group who thereby isolated themselves from existing synagogues.[37]

In the fall of 1969 Hillel Levine and Steve Shaw, both students at the seminary during the period of the Learn-in and Jews for Justice, were key organizers of a successful protest at the annual meeting of the General Assembly of the Council of Jewish Federations that resulted in Levine speaking. He called for new priorities. Funding for younger Jews followed and led to, among many other initiatives, the birth of a dynamic Jewish press where arts, politics, history, and Zionism were all debated.[38]

In 1971 a group of women, many of whom were members of the New York Havurah, formed Ezrat Nashim, a type of consciousness-raising group, which studied the role of women in Jewish law to prepare to challenge limitations placed on them. They launched the campaign for the equality of Jewish women in religious life and ordination of women rabbis in the Conservative movement when they presented a "Call to Action" at a 1972 meeting of the Rabbinical Assembly.[39]

These examples in no way exhaust the engagements closely involving students from JTS and Columbia in the late 1960s. Nor were Columbia and JTS the only centers of Jewish student activism. In particular, leftist and radical Zionists played an important and complex role in the Jewish Student Left as Zionism was marginalized from the Left beginning in 1968 at the Conference for New Politics.[40] Radical Zionists were among the most political "branch" of the Jewish counterculture. They understood themselves to be involved within the student left more so than many other Jewish activists of the time, particularly those who wanted to create alternative Jewish organizations. When they were rebuffed at the Conference for New Politics by the student left who identified with Third World alliances, the sense of the Left as a home for Jews who identified with the social movements of the sixties became problematic and unsettling.

This explosion of politics, art, culture, and even the dramatic growth of the field of Jewish studies were all the outcome of shaking what appeared to be the solid foundation of American Jewish life. If scholars and commentators claim that the Six-Day War of 1967 was primarily responsible for transforming American Jewry into becoming more interested in Judaism and Jewish identity, more concerned with the Holocaust, and other matters, they miss the centrality of the events of 1968. That cultural and historical moment also launched a remarkable transformation through what came to be called the Jewish counterculture and its many components, including the Jewish New Left and Jewish feminism. Its publications, protest marches, and organizations avidly pursued interests in Jewish memory that differed from the settings in which they were socialized. Jewish leftist traditions in the United States, Europe, and Palestine were of keen interest, as were alternative approaches to prayer. Like many of those involved in American student movements of the 1960s, these Jews in their twenties and early thirties both sought out a different narrative of Jewish culture and set about creating new "alternative" Jewish institutions.

America's social movements of the 1960s and early 1970s were a complex mix of cultural and political protests, a struggle for rights matched by a struggle for liberation, a sweeping analysis of the evils of liberalism, imperialism, and capitalism, as well as engaged grassroots activism and mass protests. Many of them focused on radically transforming the self and the world. Leftist movements have a long tradition in Russia, Europe, Israel, North America, and elsewhere, particularly among youth groups, of placing the principle of wholeness at the center. Fragmentation is the enemy of utopian movements. Authenticity, integration of the self, and the close bond between self and others have all had many articulations across time and space, whether it was the beloved community of the civil rights movement or the promises of the Old Left. They were the forerunners of the "personal is the political" of feminism and the anti-bureaucratization of the New Left. It was not, therefore, impossible to imagine that a struggle for a relevant curriculum, the demands for an institution to be responsible to its neighborhood, and the opposition to America's fight against North Vietnam could coexist in a single student movement. Nor was it unlikely that women who had participated in the left and civil rights movements could understand their lives in those terms notwithstanding the ridicule of the hypermasculine New Left.

In the context of JTS, Jewish students refused to choose between their politics and their Jewish practice—whether it was in a Jewish way to mark draft resistance or a Jewish feminism. While JTS may have been committed to the scientific study of Judaism, its 1960s generation, often in the mode of Abraham Joshua Heschel, refused to engage in such a compartmentalization of Jewish practice and the world in which it was embedded.

In this sense, the JTS students addressed a great weakness of the New Left: its failure to see beyond a myopic universalism and cosmopolitanism that considered difference dangerous. JTS students insisted that the specificity and deep religious and cultural grounding of their politics was not a political disadvantage, but instead a far richer obligation, even a requirement of Jewish law. They rejected the totalizing quality of the Marxist critique that focused on class, and hence inspired but often ultimately failed movements for social transformation based on gender and race. Mark Rudd's Jewish marginality and a number of JTS students' passion for Jewishness and wholeness paradoxically met in April of 1968 on six blocks of Manhattan's Upper West Side when, in different ways, they were convinced they could change the world.

Jewish Tradition and Change

The Jewish baby boomers who launched a Jewish counterculture came into their own political, cultural, and religious maturity in a way that challenged many traditional notions of religion, secularity, and modernity. The JTS rabbinical and graduate students shared a common concern. They insisted that Judaism as a practice could not be separated from the world in which they lived and acted.

They challenged the world of Conservative Judaism, in particular, in which prayer and observance were systematically differentiated from scholarly approaches to Talmud and Bible pioneered by earlier generations of scholars in the Wissenschaft des Judentums movement. This bifurcation was one of the chief targets at which their protests took aim.

Their ideas, rituals, study, and politics should be understood, in part, as a shift in American Jewish religious life. Talal Asad has called on scholars of religion to analyze how religious authority is used as a dynamic process, how it is made real and convincing through symbolic discourses in political life. Asad has challenged the cultural notion of religion as a set of ideas and symbols cut off from power and conflict. He has advocated, instead, for a more dynamic and contested view of religious life in society.[41] The year of protest and confrontation at JTS revealed a dynamic Judaism that, for example, made the Conservative movement's seminary a contested arena for redefining the nature of American Jewish life, the training of rabbis, and most importantly the way to negotiate Jewish life in the context of American political conflict. The JTS students, one important group among many of that hinge generation raised on the ideals of a modern, rational Judaism joined their radical cultural and political protest to Judaism. They did not leave or abandon Judaism or Jewish practice, but set about undertaking its transformation. They radically altered notions of Jewish authority when women and their male allies demanded a fundamental change in how women (and later gays) could participate in the tradition. At the same time they sought "authenticity" by reclaiming submerged traditions such as Hasidism, engaging with the language of spirituality, and studying Jewish texts as part of their political life.

The most common complaint made against the generation that pioneered *havurot* and Jewish feminism was that they were "pick and choose Jews." Many commentators of the time claimed that they questioned traditional sources of authority in some settings but not others. Their Judaism was therefore "suspect" from the perspective of various rabbis and lay people in their own movement. They abandoned the community's institutions and insisted that their approach was superior.[42]

These Jewish baby boomers challenged an American postwar engagement with Jewish modernity under the banner of authenticity, wholeness, and the conviction that Judaism offered a counterculture to embrace. More than fifty-five years have passed since 1968, a year that transformed the United States, European nations, Mexico, and many other countries in both small and large ways. Nothing remained static about the vision that grew out of the JTS protests. However, the central engagement of the Jewish baby boom with issues of power and change marks those events as an important launching of a transformation in American Jewish life.

Notes

This chapter is based on a paper originally presented in May 2012 at the conference Jews and the Left at the Center for Jewish History. My thanks to David Myers for his thoughtful comments on an earlier version.

1. Works on the Jewish counterculture include Riv-Ellen Prell, *Prayer and Community: The Havurah in American Judaism* (Detroit, 1989); Michael Staub, *Torn at the Roots: The Crisis of Jewish Liberalism in Postwar America* (New York, 2002).
2. I consider the context of David Ellenson's development as a rabbi and scholar with deep appreciation for his work as a public intellectual and rabbi, for his commitment to the equality of women in Judaism, for his scholarship, and above all for his friendship and colleagueship.
3. Arthur Goren, "A Golden Decade for American Jewish: 1945–1955," in *The American Jewish Experience*, ed. J. Sarna, 2nd ed. (New York, 1976), 294–313.
4. Examples of these frustrations may be found in James A. Sleeper and Alan L. Mintz, eds., *The New Jews* (New York, 1971).
5. For two excellent works on the American environment that gave rise to the counterculture, see Thomas Engelhardt, *The End of Victory Culture: Cold War America and the Disillusioning of a Generation* (Boston, 2007); James Gilbert, *A Cycle of Outrage: America's Reaction to the Juvenile Delinquent in 1950* (New York, 1986).
6. Kenneth Keniston, *Young Radicals: Notes on Committed Youth* (New York, 1968).
7. Some of these developments began in the 1930s. See Jonathan Sarna, *American Judaism: A History* (New Haven, Conn., 2004), 274–83.
8. See Lynn Davidman, *Tradition in a Rootless World: Women Return to Orthodox Judaism* (Berkeley, Calif., 1991) for an example of the attraction of traditional orthodoxy.
9. There is an extensive literature on the issues of religion and modern society. What was once called "secularization theory," which was most often associated with the sociologists Peter Berger and Thomas Luckmann, was questioned in the 1980s. Berger himself backed away from those earlier ideas in Peter L. Berger, *The Desecularization of the World: Resurgent Religion and World Politics* (Grand Rapids, Mich., 1999). The sociological foundations for these views of religion and society emerged out of the late nineteenth and early twentieth centuries, and came under a different type of scrutiny in the intellectual upheavals of the 1970s. I have discussed the relevance of these concerns within Jewish studies in "Boundaries, Margins, and, Norms: The Intellectual Stakes in the Study of American Jewish Culture(s)," *Contemporary Jewry* 32, no. 12 (2012): 189–204.
10. Charles Taylor, *A Secular Age* (Cambridge, Mass., 2007); Robert Wuthnow, *The Restructuring of American Religion* (Princeton, N.J., 1988); Mark Oppenheimer, *Knocking on Heaven's Door: Religion in the Age of Counterculture* (New Haven, Conn., 2003).
11. Mark Rudd, *Underground: My Life with SDS and the Weathermen* (New York, 2009), 69.
12. *The Columbia Spectator*, the student newspaper of Columbia University, provided a day-by-day description of the events related to the protests and strike. These articles are digitally available.
13. Rudd, *Underground*, 66.
14. Ibid., 68.
15. Ibid., 70.
16. Ibid., 71.
17. Robert Sacks, interview by telephone, April 2012, Washington, D.C.
18. Reuven Kimelman, interview by telephone, March 2012, Boston.
19. Hillel Levine, interview by telephone, April 2012, Boston.
20. The only written version of these events I have been able to locate appears in Baila R. Shargel, "Textures of Seminary Life During the Finkelstein Era," in *Tradition Renewed: A History of the Jewish Theological Seminary of America*, ed. J. Wertheimer

(New York, 1997), 552–53. The following people (including their relationship to the seminary in 1968) provided memories of these events by phone interview or e-mail: the late Sylvia Ettenberg (Dean of Teacher's Institute), Hillel Levine (rabbinical student), Danny Margolis (graduate student), Patty Margolis (undergraduate, joint program), Robert Sacks (rabbinical student), Ed Greenstein (rabbinical student), Steve Shaw (rabbinical student), Susan Shevitz (undergraduate, joint program), Arthur Green (recently ordained rabbi). Michael Greenbaum (rabbinical student) recalled hearing about it.

21. Danny Margolis, interview by telephone, Boston; Patty Margolis, interview by telephone, Boston. Baila Shargel reports another exchange between Chancellor Finkelstein and Professor Lukinsky in which Lukinsky commented on curriculum change at the Teachers College of Columbia. She notes, as former students recalled, that Finkelstein lectured those assembled on the structure of Columbia's various schools, including Teachers College. Shargel learned from oral interviews that the chancellor apologized to Lukinsky several days later and thanked him for "saving my life," meaning that he deflected some of the students' concerns toward curricular change. See Shargel, "Textures of Seminary Life," 564n.134.

22. Michael Greenbaum, interview by telephone, April 2012, New York City.

23. Arthur Green, interview by telephone, March 2012, Boston.

24. Ibid.

25. Ibid. Edward R. Kaplan, *Spiritual Radical: Abraham Joshua Heschel in America 1940–1972* (New Haven, Conn., 2007), discusses Heschel's involvement in this cause and others. Kaplan did not have information about Heschel's involvement in student activism at JTS (e-mail communication, March 20, 2012).

26. Abraham Heschel's life in Poland and Germany is described in Edward Kaplan and Samuel Dresner, *Abraham Joshua Heschel: Prophetic Witness* (New Haven, Conn., 1997).

27. Reuven Kimelman, "A Jewish Peace Demonstration," *Judaism* 18, no. 3 (1969): 354–57. Baila Shargel provides a different version of these events and refers to them as "a stunt," although she cites Kimelman's article. She focuses on the organizers' attempt to "embarrass the Seminary." She claims that organizers "convinced" students to attend the morning minyan (prayer quorum) falsely. It is unclear what her sources for this version of the events were and why she is dismissive of their importance to the students to which Kimelman attests in his article and interview (Shargel, "Textures of Seminary Life," 553–54). I also interviewed Neil Gillman, then dean of the Rabbinical School, about these events, March 2012, New York City, by telephone.

28. Kimelman, "A Jewish Peace Demonstration, 355.

29. Ibid.

30. Ibid., 356. Indeed, the presence of Rabbi Abraham Joshua Heschel was important to those protesting that day. Kimelman reported that Rabbi Heschel pulled up to the seminary in a taxi and joined them. His presence was viewed as fortuitous. However, Neil Gillman, then dean of the Rabbinical School, believes that he was asked to go to the gathering to keep a close watch on what was happening (Gillman, interview).

31. Kimelman, "A Jewish Peace Demonstration, 356.

32. Steve Shaw, e-mail correspondence, January 2010.

33. Michael Greenbaum, interview by telephone, March 2012, New York City.

34. Baila Shargel discusses this challenge to the curriculum in "Textures of Seminary Life," 547. David Ellenson and Lee Bycel, "'A Seminary of Sacred Learning': The JTS

Rabbinical Curriculum in Historical Perspective," in *Tradition Renewed: A History of the Jewish Theological Seminary of America*, ed. J. Wertheimer (New York, 1997), 564, argues that the most significant changes in the JTS curriculum in the 1960s in fact upheld the "ongoing commitment of the Seminary to Jewish learning and modern scholarship."

35. Robert Sacks, interview by telephone, April 2012, Washington, D.C.

36. Arthur Green moved to Boston in 1968 to study for his PhD at Brandeis University. He was the founder of the first havurah, Havurat Shalom, in Sommerville, Massachusetts. It provided an inspiration for the New York Havurah. However, the members of both groups also viewed the communities differently. The New York Havurah was explicitly interested in integrating politics with Jewish life. Havurat Shalom was viewed as committed to "spirituality." Havurat Shalom was initially envisioned as a seminary for the training of rabbis, and thus provided those men affiliated with it with the "4 D," a deferment from military service. The New York Havurah considered that option but ultimately did not claim that status. In 1968 and 1969 the issue of the draft for men of college age and beyond was a particularly important issue. See Prell, *Prayer and Community*, 92–95.

37. Reuven Kimelman, interview by telephone, March 2012, Boston. Kimelman recalled the original meetings for the New York Havurah taking place at the apartment of the now deceased Eugene Wiener, who was then a student adviser at JTS and subsequently made aliyah. He recalled those attending the first meeting included Alan Mintz, Peter Geffen, John Ruskay, Ron Kronish, Michael Swirsky, Sam Heilman, and Steve Cohen (although he does not recall attending). Many of them did not become part of the havurah. He could recall no women attending those meetings, although women were among the group's founders.

38. For a discussion of this event see, Staub, *Torn at the Roots*, 194–95.

39. See Beth S. Wenger, "The Politics of Women's Ordination: Jewish Law, Institutional Power, and the Debate Over Women in the Rabbinate," in *Tradition Renewed: A History of the Jewish Theological Seminary of America*, ed. J. Wertheimer (New York, 1997), 488–89. "Paula Hyman," in the Jewish Women's Archive, http://jwa.org/feminism/_html/JWA039.htm (accessed February 3, 2014).

40. The important Conference on New Politics in 1967 in Chicago was a watershed in separating socialist Zionism from the student left as well as being a key catalyst in the feminist movement.

41. Talal Asad, "Toward a Genealogy of the Concept of Ritual," *Genealogies of Religion: Discipline and Reasons of Power in Christianity and Islam*, 55–83 (Baltimore, 1993).

42. The classic example of this critique was Marshall Sklare's review of the *Jewish Catalog*: Marshall Sklare "The Greening of Judaism," *Commentary* 58 (1971): 51–57.

18

REFORM RABBIS, BETTY FRIEDAN, AND THE USES OF "TRADITION"

CAROLE B. BALIN

David Ellenson had a total of three female colleagues in 1977 when he was ordained a rabbi. A year later, that number more than doubled when four additional women received ordination and entered the Reform rabbinate.[1] In the fall of 1978 these pioneering women found themselves at the center of a political maelstrom that had erupted earlier that summer in Toronto at the annual meeting of the Central Conference of American (Reform) Rabbis (CCAR). On the floor in Toronto, the membership of the CCAR had debated rescinding a contract with the Hyatt Regency Hotel in Phoenix, Arizona, the site of its meeting the following March, because of the state legislature's refusal to ratify the Equal Rights Amendment. The battle tested the fiber of a longstanding tradition of Reform Judaism: its commitment to equality between the sexes in religious life. The telling of this story roughly coincides with the fortieth anniversary of women in the rabbinate, whose ranks now include more than six hundred women, among whom is Jacqueline Koch Ellenson, the beloved wife of our distinguished honoree.

When feminism burst onto the American scene in the final decades of the last century, Jewish women were able to ride that second wave all the way to the *bimah* (the pulpit). However, not long after Sally Priesand's historic rabbinical ordination in 1972, the leadership of North American Reform Jewry began to fret about the "significant number of women" who would be flowing into the rabbinate. Ordaining women was one thing, integrating them into the movement was quite another.

Apprehensive about the "theatrical and circus-like atmosphere" that might result in congregations if and when female clergy walked through the temple doors, the leaders of the three official bodies of Reform Jewry (i.e., the Union of American Hebrew Congregations, the Central Conference of American Rabbis, and the Hebrew Union College–Jewish Institute of Religion [HUC-JIR]) sent representatives to a strategy meeting in September 1976 to devise ways to stave off such scenes.[2] As a result of the meeting, two task forces were established to acquaint Reform laity and clergy with female rabbinical students lest the latter be regarded as "something strange and unique."[3] Meanwhile, well aware of the extraordinary nature of their professional futures, female rabbinical students at the New York campus of HUC-JIR had already linked up with their counterparts at the Reconstructionist Rabbinical College in Philadelphia to address shared concerns. The fifteen women in attendance at a meeting on February 8, 1976, organized themselves into the "Women's Rabbinical Alliance" and invited their peers in Cincinnati and Los Angeles to join them.[4] Cincinnati students declined the offer, having already established the "Rabbinical Students' Organization for Women," which welcomed male students into its ranks. Neither group would want for members—by 1978, 62 of the 209 students enrolled at HUC-JIR's Rabbinical School were female.[5]

While it would obviously take the CCAR, with its membership of over 1,200 rabbis, many decades to catch up to the HUC-JIR's three-to-one gender ratio, its support of women seemed unequivocal at the time. At its eighty-sixth annual convention in 1975, for instance, it passed a resolution in favor of the proposed twenty-seventh amendment to the United States Constitution, stating in no uncertain times:

WHEREAS we are heirs of a prophetic *tradition* which ever sought to repair the damaged world, and

WHEREAS in our efforts to restore the world to sanity we affirm the following position which we take knowing full well the complexity of such an issue but knowing also that we cannot be silent,

BE IT THEREFORE RESOLVED that we urge the speedy ratification of the Equal Rights Amendment and pledge our efforts in the various states to work for its ratification, recognizing that it is an important step toward insuring equal rights for women and men.[6]

Like millions of women and men across the country, Reform rabbis had been anticipating ratification of the Equal Rights Amendment (ERA) since 1972, when the Senate passed the amendment (a year after the House). By law, three-quarters of the states—or thirty-eight states—would need to ratify the amendment within seven years for it to become an amendment to the Constitution. While thirty states ratified it within the first year, the process slowed as anti-ERA forces mobilized with the intent of instilling fear that its passage would deprive women of privileges, such as exemption from the military draft and the ability to be supported by their husbands. Others dismissed such claims, including the Reform rabbinate, which in 1976 reiterated its support of the amendment, adding: "We deplore the slowness with which our country has moved in approving the ERA and we again urge its speedy ratification by the States."[7]

As the 1979 deadline for ratification drew near, supporters of the amendment beefed up their efforts in nonratifying states. Among CCAR members, there was talk of relocating their 1979 convention scheduled for Arizona, a nonratifying state, to one that favored the ERA. In June of 1978 the CCAR Executive Board met for its usual preconvention meeting. Regarding the issue of Arizona, the executive board voted 10 to 6 in favor of "issu[ing] a carefully worded statement expressing the sentiments of the Executive Vice President [Joseph Glaser] concerning our unwillingness to rescind our former commitment to hold our 1979 convention in Phoenix, AZ, regarding such areas as business ethics and Constitutional problems." The board further instructed that the statement contain a reaffirmation of "our support" of the ERA and that the "CCAR go on record not to make further contractual arrangements in any state that had not adopted the ERA so long as the ERA remains a viable issue." Later in the same meeting, a motion was adopted to reconsider the issue, but it lost in a vote of 8 to 12.[8]

When the 1978 convention formally opened with 441 registered members, including four newly ordained female rabbis, the site of the next convention weighed on the participants' conscience. At a plenary business session, the membership voted 117 to 44 to overturn the executive board's decision to confirm Phoenix as the site of the 1979 convention. It was further moved to direct the officers "to make the best available arrangement for a site for the 1979 convention in a state on record as approving the ERA."[9] The motion carried by a vote of 132 to 85.

But the matter was not over. During the summer, the executive board found that the discussion and motions relating to rescinding the commitment in Phoenix "were not in accord with standard parliamentary procedure, by which the Conference is bound by its Constitution." Therefore, on advice of legal counsel [i.e., Weil, Gotshal, and Manges], the Board deemed the "entire discussion . . . null and void."[10]

Rabbi Deborah Prinz did not mince words in her response to this decision. She sent a letter to CCAR president Ely Pilchik, asserting that "the moral imperative of constitutional protection for equal rights for women must be pursued forcefully by boycotting non-ratified states."[11] A mere three months after being ordained as the fourth female Reform rabbi and attending her first CCAR Conference and only weeks after assuming the post of assistant rabbi at Central Synagogue in New York, Prinz put forward her argument for relocating the March 1979 meeting.[12] First of all, she reminded the president, the conference had already indicated its support for the proposed twenty-seventh amendment in no uncertain terms in a resolution adopted in 1975. She additionally pointed out that the CCAR's fellow Reform organizations, the National Association of Temple Educators (NATE) and the UAHC, had elected to hold their conventions only in ratifying states and, in one case, had "even altered plans in the midst of contractual negotiations with [a] hotel."[13] Moreover, Prinz maintained, the CCAR's 1973 boycott of table grapes and head lettuce in support of the United Farm Workers Union had created a precedent for exerting "financial pressure" as a protest strategy. She then examined and dismissed the possibility of legal action against the Conference ("It is unlikely that a religious organization would be sued [for breach of contract] on what is clearly an ethical/moral issue") and of financial loss ("some members . . . offered monetary support . . . and . . . lay members of the Reform Jewish community would also be supportive"), and closed with the ringing exhortation: "In order to maintain its *tradition* of advocacy for equality for women, I urge the CCAR Executive Board to make alternate [*sic*] convention arrangements and not go to Phoenix."

In historical terms, Prinz's invocation of the word "tradition" to describe Reform Judaism's aspiration to secure religious equality between the sexes is apt. The march toward gender equality among reform-minded Jews began in continental Europe at a private school in Berlin in 1814 when the first confirmation of Jewish girls took place.[14] In no time, the ceremony, including boys as well, spread in Prussia and beyond, to Denmark and France. Confirmation's egalitarian ethos and doctrinal essence appealed to those seeking to adapt

Judaism for the modern age. Three decades later, a cluster of liberal-leaning rabbis who met in Breslau in 1846 raised the general question of women's status in Judaism. In their words "the female sex" was the "religious equal of the male" with regard to "obligations and rights."[15] To that end, they proposed expunging the prejudicial benediction "*she-lo 'asani ishah*" (who has not made me a woman) from the liturgy, obligating women like men to religious instruction and public worship, and raising the age demarcating girls' religious maturation from the talmudically established twelve to thirteen, so as to match that deemed appropriate for boys.[16] In the same year, reformer Max Lilienthal imported the egalitarian spirit to America when he inaugurated confirmation at New York's Congregation Anshe Chesed. Others immediately followed suit, including Isaac M. Wise at his temple in Cincinnati.[17]

Like his German predecessors, Wise assigned women a strategic position in the project of Jewish reform. Coeducational confirmation was one of several activities—along with "allowing girls to read the Thorah on that occasion," "admit[ing] females to the choir," and "introduc[ing] family pews into the temple"—that Wise believed would hasten the progress of reform. As he argued in 1876, "With the admission of mothers and daughters to a recognizable place in public worship, came order and decorum. . . . But we cannot stop here." In addition, women needed a "voice and a vote." Enfranchisement would allow their uniquely female "heart[s] and piety" to hold sway over congregational meetings and their maternal "influences" to benefit the Sabbath-schools. Wise insisted that "the principle of justice, and the law of God inherent in every human being, demand[s] that woman be admitted to membership in the congregation, and be given equal rights with man" so that "her religious feelings be allowed scope for the sacred case of Israel."[18]

Wise was under no illusion that men and women were created equal. His worldview was bifurcated along gender lines: he regarded women as "priestesses of the home," whose virtues were considered essential for the moral upbuilding of the family as well as the synagogue. Women's contributions to congregational life would lead to a purer, more moral, more "reformed" Judaism for all.

Wise's campaign to give women the congregational vote developed against the backdrop of the suffragette movement, which retrospectively became known in American history as first-wave feminism, to distinguish it from the next wave in the following century. Elizabeth Cady Stanton and Lucretia Mott convened the first conference on women's rights in Seneca Falls, New York, in 1848—approximately two hundred miles from Wise's home at the time in Albany. As circumstances would have it, Wise and Mott met face to face in Boston in 1867 at the founding meeting of the Free Religious Association, an interfaith organization of liberal religious leaders attempting to shake free of the orthodoxies of their respective denominations.[19] While the degree to which the suffragettes directly influenced Wise can only be conjectured, the pages of his two newspapers, *The American Israelite* and its German supplement *Die Deborah*, written for a female audience, demonstrate unabashed support of women's rights.[20]

Although Wise did not live to see women gain the vote, his colleagues raised the issue at several conventions. At its 1912 convention, the CCAR membership debated the matter of women's suffrage and concluded that it was "inadvisable for the Conference, as a body, to take action thereon." The shillyshallying persisted for half a decade, until 1917, when the CCAR went on record in support of granting women the vote: "We feel it is our solemn duty as ethical leaders and as preachers of a religion which has stood throughout the centuries for justice and righteousness to assert our belief in the justice and righteousness of the enfranchisement of the women of our country."[21] For some, the passage of the Nineteenth Amendment in 1920 aroused an expectation that all barriers to women's equality in American society would subsequently fall. For the CCAR, it meant opening a discussion on women's ordination.[22]

Such a discussion transpired at the 1922 CCAR Convention, but only after HUC professor Jacob Lauterbach, a member of the organization's Responsa Committee, presented what he called "the attitude of traditional Judaism on this point."[23] The weight of his evidence pointed toward "debarring women from the rabbinate," a view he regarded as "strictly adhered to by all Jewry all over the world throughout all generations even unto this day."[24] As to the question of whether Reform Judaism ought to follow tradition in this regard, Lauterbach stated:

> We [Reform rabbis] are still carrying on the activity of the rabbis of old who traced their authority through a chain of tradition [*shalshelet hakabalah*] to Moses and the elders . . . even though in many points we interpret our Judaism in a manner quite different from theirs. We are justified in considering ourselves the latest link in that long chain of authoritative teachers who carried on their activity of teaching, preserving and developing Judaism, and for our time we have the same standing as they had.[25] . . . We should, therefore, not jeopardize

the hitherto indisputable authoritative character of our ordination. We should not make our ordination entirely different in character from the traditional ordination, and thereby give the larger group of Jewry, following traditional Judaism, good reason to question our authority and to doubt whether we are rabbis in the sense in which this honored title was always understood.[26]

In other words, Lauterbach feared that the authority of all Reform rabbis would be questioned, and perhaps diminished, were they to allow women to enter their profession.

The lively discussion that ensued focused on the fact that, while Lauterbach had opined on the so-called traditional Jewish view on the subject, he had failed to express the Reform perspective. As Louis Witt (Temple Shaare Emeth, St. Louis, Mo.) contended, "It is not a matter of *tradition* at all. I must confess that I was not the least interested in Rabbi Lauterbach's presentation. . . . I honor [him] for the learning contained therein but the point he presents is not the point at issue. . . . I cannot believe that a religion . . . so splendidly . . . forward-looking as our[s] will stand in the way of [the women's] movement."[27] Similarly, Joseph Rauch (Congregation Adath Israel, Louisville, Ky.) reminded his colleagues that "in every line of endeavor in our temples, we have proceeded on the theory that woman is the equal of man."[28] Others maintained that Lauterbach's fear of creating a schism in Israel had never informed CCAR decisions. Had that been the case, according to Henry Englander (registrar and professor of biblical exegesis and biblical history at HUC), "[W]e would not have taken stands on many subjects." He continued, "Years ago this Conference put itself on record favoring absolute religious equality of women with men. Are we going back on our action?"[29] Paradoxically, it would seem, the discussion participants had transformed their nontraditional approach to Jewish tradition into a hallowed Reform tradition. Like bygone generations of Reformers who had handed it down to them, they, too, hoped to transmit it to future generations.

Meanwhile the discussion persevered, and the CCAR membership voted and approved a motion that "the courtesy of the floor be extended to the wives of rabbis" in order to gain a female perspective on the subject.[30] Of the three women who participated, all favored women's ordination. Mrs. Ephraim Frisch explained how she initially opposed the notion on account of the practical concern of "how a woman could attend to the duties which devolve upon a rabbi and at the same time be a true home-maker." But she changed her view after listening to the arguments, adding, "I love the work of the rabbinate so much that could I have prevailed upon myself to forget the joys that come with wife-making, I should have become a rabbi."[31] To most at the meeting, the idea that a woman could fulfill her roles as wife and mother while leading a congregation seemed unlikely. Though Joseph Leiser (Congregation Beth El, Helena, Ark.) disagreed, saying, the "thesis that the rabbinical profession . . . involves the totality of life to the preclusion of . . . motherhood is not valid and is no more applicable to the Jewish woman as rabbi than . . . [as] lawyer, doctor, dentist, newspaper writer, musician, business woman or teacher."[32] In the end, with a nod to its own tradition, the CCAR's resolution affirming the ordination of women carried the day in a vote of 56 to 11.

A half century would lapse before the promise was fulfilled. And even with the advent of female rabbis, or arguably because of this reality, the CCAR was forced to confront its tradition of egalitarianism once again. As Rabbi Laura Geller observed, "When women's voices are heard, a tradition changes."[33]

Indeed, Rabbi Deborah Prinz's voice resounded in 1978. In response to her objections to the CCAR conference being scheduled for Phoenix, she received a three-page, single-spaced letter, in which the executive vice president painstakingly refuted each of her points. To her argument that the boycott of produce on behalf of the UFW had set a precedent in this instance, he retorted:

> You cannot in truth say that the CCAR has established a precedent for this when it urged the boycott of table grapes and head lettuce. . . . You are calling here for something else—a secondary boycott: illegal based on its immorality. Your statement that "this is not a boycott against Hyatt Hotels, but rather support for the states which have ratified ERA" bears examination. First of all, pulling out of Hyatt really hurts only Hyatt. The State of Arizona will absorb the loss. The ranchers and miners against ERA don't give a hang. Then, too, it doesn't ring true about support for the other states. This whole operation is to punish Arizona, and everybody in it, in what I am afraid is a spiteful approach, an intervention of non-violent violence, which will lead to horrendous repercussions, into the constitutional, deliberative process of American democracy. Every pressure group in existence— anti-abortion, anti-homosexual, anti-anything and everything, will take its lead and turn our country upside-down.[34]

After weighing the issue, "thoroughly and deliberately" on four different occasions, he explained, the CCAR Executive Board "has come down on the side of

business ethics . . . of not punishing the guiltless and the powerless."[35] In closing, he urged Prinz to "go into the lion's den" and attend the convention in
Arizona "instead of sulking off somewhere else, unnoticed." At the same time,
he expressed his fear that staging "an alternate simultaneous convention"
would militate against the integration of women rabbis. This "would create a
havdalah [ritual of separation between the Sabbath and the rest of the days of
the week] in the minds of many—indeed, maybe even a *mechitzah* [separation
between women and men during worship]—and neither of us want [*sic*] that."
Tone notwithstanding, Glaser apparently conveyed Prinz's sentiments, along
with those of other protesters, to the executive board, which reopened the
matter at its fall meeting.[36]

In a last-ditch effort to settle the affair once and for all, the board sent a
letter to its membership on October 19, indicating that, as a result of direct
negotiations with the management of the Hyatt Regency Hotel in Phoenix,
there had been an offer to release the CCAR from its contract upon payment
of $20,000.[37] The board was requesting an immediate response regarding this
proposition from every one of its 1,262 members, as each would be "levied
a general assessment to cover the $20,000 penalty" (i.e., $15.85 per member)
should the CCAR withdraw from its Phoenix contract. The letter contained
arguments on both sides of the issue, along with a brief note that the U.S.
Congress had recently extended the deadline for passage of the ERA to 1982.[38]
In the end, the membership did not put its money where its mouth was, so to
speak, and the contract remained intact. Consequently, planning continued
apace for the conference in Phoenix, including the scheduling of additional
activities designed to educate about and express support for women's rights.[39]

In the wake of the decision, the six female members of the CCAR were torn
between the desire to boycott the convention as a pro-ERA gesture, on the one
hand, and the need to be involved in the CCAR by participating in its convention, on the other.[40] They turned to an improbable but judicious source for guidance. As luck would have it, the brother of Laura Geller (the third woman to be
ordained a Reform rabbi) maintained a friendship with a childhood friend by
the name of Jonathan Friedan. Geller called his mother, Betty, for advice on the
issue.[41] Betty Friedan suggested that the women attend the convention and also
hold a rump convention where she would speak. And so they did.

Hundreds of rabbis crammed into a small room at the Hyatt Regency
Hotel in Phoenix, to hear Friedan speak. The room was the only space made
available by the conference and hotel, and even that was rented with monies
donated by a male colleague rather than CCAR funds.[42] Although this was not

the first time Friedan had addressed a Jewish group in support of the ERA, it was the first time on record that she explicitly mentioned her Jewish roots as being dispositive in her own actions on behalf of women.[43] She opened with an explanation of how she came to write *The Feminine Mystique* (1963), which is often credited with launching second-wave feminism in America:

> What made me do it? Probably the simplest answer is that my whole life made me do it, or that I grew up as a Jewish girl in Peoria, Illinois. I grew up isolated and feeling the injustice, the burning injustice of the subtle and not so subtle anti-Semitism that was the experience of my generation. . . . Then, too, I grew up in an era when Jews, if they could, would try to pass. . . . When I went to Smith some wealthy girls from Cincinnati would talk in whispery voices and hold their hands behind their backs so they wouldn't talk with their hands. And when there was a resolution to open the College to any of the victims of Nazism and to ask President Roosevelt to undo the quotas that kept the Jewish refugees from coming here, the Jewish girls from Cincinnati didn't vote for that resolution. I, who was a freshman from Peoria, Illinois, with hayseed in my hair, was horrified. I had this burning feeling, all that I am I will not deny. It's the core of me. I had this feeling as a Jew first. First as a Jew before I had it as a woman. All that I am I will not deny.[44]

Friedan went on to describe how Jewish self-awareness led her to question injustice against others in American society, especially women. And in an effort to make democratic principles like human freedom, dignity, and equal opportunity gender-blind, she started the women's movement. The mother of second-wave feminism publicly thanked her "spiritual daughters (some of whom are in the room)" for teaching her that it is "profoundly Jewish" to "take actions, not words, to break through barriers that keep us from participating."[45]

Friedan's actions on that afternoon in Phoenix did not go unnoticed. Two weeks after the convention, she received a letter of thanks addressed to "Ms. Friedan" from the Office of the Executive Vice President of the CCAR. Rabbi Glaser expressed regret for not having had "an opportunity to provide the appropriate setting" for her presentation and explained that he was enclosing a check from the "Treasury of the CCAR" for $600, which he understood from Laura Geller and Deborah Prinz would cover her expenses, "inasmuch as [her] appearance did become part of the official program of the Conference."[46] Glaser's wish to transform Friedan's impromptu appearance at the Phoenix conference into an officially sanctioned event is not consistent with the chain of events that brought her there. It is as though the executive vice president's sleight of hand swept months—indeed decades—of rancorous debate over the Reform tradition of supporting religious egalitarianism under a revisionist rug. The reality was that CCAR board members, though theoretically supportive of the idea of gender equality in religious life, were, at the least, ambivalent about the advent of female colleagues. The Phoenix conference forced a confrontation with their tradition and, in the end, challenged the very meaning of the word. As David Ellenson has maintained, "Tradition, it is clear, is constantly involved in the process of *reform*ulation."[47]

Notes

1. They include Sally Priesand (1972), Michal S. Bernstein (1975; who subsequently left the rabbinate), Laura Geller (1976), Karen Fox (1978), Rosalind Gold (1978), Deborah Prinz (1978), and Myra Soifer (1978). Ben Gallob, "Special to the JTA Record Total of 75 Women to Study for Reform, Reconstructionist Rabbinate in 1978," *Jewish Telegraphic Agency*, August 24, 1978.
2. Eugene Mihaly, minutes for "Meeting of representatives of the CCAR, UAHC and HUC-JIR on the significant number of women rabbis who will be ordained beginning with June of 1978," September 22, 1976, 1, MS-677, American Jewish Archives, Cincinnati (hereafter referred to as AJA).
3. Ibid., 1–2. In due time, the two merged into a single "Task Force on Women in the Rabbinate," which Sally Priesand initially chaired.
4. In 1980 both groups gave way to form the Women's Rabbinic Network (WRN), which functions today as an auxiliary of the CCAR. See Carole Balin, "From Periphery to Center: A History of the Women's Rabbinic Network," *CCAR Journal*, Summer 1997. Jacqueline Koch Ellenson serves as the executive director of the WRN.
5. Gallob, "Special to the JTA." In 1975 women constituted 2 percent of all ministers in the United States, while female enrollment in some seminaries jumped to more than 30 percent. See *American Jewish Year Book* (1977): 68.
6. "Resolution Adopted by the CCAR," 1975, CCAR: Central Conference of Reform Rabbis, www.ccarnet.org/rabbis-speak/resolutions/1975/equal-rights-amendment-1975/ (accessed October 11, 2012) (my italics).
7. Resolution on the Equal Rights Amendment adopted by the CCAR at its 87th Annual Convention, 1976.
8. "Minutes of the Executive Board," Central Conference of American Rabbis *Yearbook* (1978): 12. (Inexplicably, the tally for the second vote is greater than that for the first.) Central Conference of American Rabbis *Yearbook* (hereafter referred to as CCARY).
9. Ibid., 193.
10. Ibid., 193.
11. Rabbi Deborah Prinz of Central Synagogue, New York to Rabbi Ely Pilchik of B'nai Jeshurun, Short Hills, N.J., September 18, 1978, 2, SC-1692, AJA. Note that on

February 21, 1979, Judge Hunter of the District Court for the Western District of Missouri, Central Division, held that action against nonratified states is a form of free speech and is not subject to restraint under the antitrust laws. In an ironic twist, Prinz until recently served as the director of program and member services and director of the Joint Commission on Rabbinic Mentoring at the CCAR.

12. The proposed ERA would have amended the Constitution to read: "Equality of rights under the law shall not be denied or abridged by the United States or by any state on account of sex."

13. The UAHC annulled its contract with a Chicago-based hotel for a biennial assembly meeting and held it in another state, largely due to pressure exerted by the National Federation of Temple Sisterhoods, according to Glaser. See Joseph B. Glaser to Deborah R. Prinz, September 20, 1978, SC-1692, AJA (my italics).

14. Michael A. Meyer, "Women in the Thought and Practice of the European Jewish Reform Movement," in *Gender and Jewish History*, ed. M. A. Kaplan and D. Dash Moore (Bloomington, Ind., 2010), 141.

15. W. Gunther Plaut, *The Rise of Reform Judaism* (New York, 1963), 253–55.

16. Riv-Ellen Prell has convincingly argued that Jewish reformers transformed the *legal* status of women, but failed to challenge the gendered *cultural* practices in which men still dominated. See Riv-Ellen Prell, "The Dilemma of Women's Equality in Reform Judaism," *Judaism* 30 (Fall 1981): 418–26, and, in a similar vein, Karla Goldman, "Women in Reform Judaism: Rhetoric and Reality," in *Women Remaking American Judaism*, ed. Riv-Ellen Prell, 109–33 (Detroit, 2007).

17. Bruce L Ruben, *Max Lilienthal: The Makings of the American Rabbinate* (Detroit, 2011), 69, 85–86.

18. Isaac M. Wise, "Women as Members of Congregations (1876)," in *Selected Writings of Isaac M. Wise with a Biography*, ed. D. Philipson and L. Grossman (Cincinnati, 1900), 398–99.

19. Wise and Mott were among the thirty-seven founding members of the Free Religious Association, which included Ralph Waldo Emerson as well. See Richard A. Kellaway, "The Free Religious Association," Collegium conference paper (2010), 5.

20. Benjamin Maria Baader, *Gender, Judaism, and Bourgeois Culture in Germany, 1800–1870* (Bloomington, Ind., 2006).

21. The Conference actually affirmed the nondecision three years later. See *CCARY* 25 (1915): 133, and for the decision *CCARY* 27 (1917): 175.

22. The ratification of the Nineteenth Amendment only indirectly sparked discussion on women's ordination. The direct issue at hand was the request of Martha Neumark, a seventeen-year-old student at HUC in Cincinnati, to be assigned, like her male rabbinical school classmates, to a High Holy Day student pulpit. Her request raised the possibility that Neumark, daughter of an HUC faculty member, might ultimately present herself as a candidate for ordination. Consequently, the HUC Board of Governors asked the Responsa Committee of the CCAR to answer the question: Shall women be ordained as rabbis? See *CCARY*, 32 (1922): 156–77; and Pamela Nadell, *Women Who Would Be Rabbis: A History of Women's Ordination 1889–1985* (Boston, 1998), 62–66.

23. Jacob Z. Lauterbach, "Responsum on Question, 'Shall Women Be Ordained Rabbis?'" *CCARY* 32 (1922): 156.

24. Ibid., 156, 160.

25. Lauterbach validates the Reform rabbi's authority on the basis of the dictum that every group of three that has acted as a *bet din* [court] over Israel is on a level with the *bet din* of Moses (bRosh 25a).

26. *CCARY* 32 (1922): 160–61.

27. "Discussion [of Lauterbach Responsum] *CCARY* 32 (1922): 163 (my italics). Witt had argued in favor of women's rights before the Arkansas legislature in 1917 when he served Congregation B'nai Israel in Little Rock.

28. Ibid., 166.

29. Ibid.. Englander referenced the CCAR's anti-Zionist stance as one illustration.

30. Ibid., 171.

31. Ibid.

32. Ibid., 172.

33. As quoted in Dana Evan Kaplan, *American Reform Judaism: An Introduction* (New Brunswick, NJ, 2003), 197n25.

34. Joseph Glaser to Deborah Prinz, September 20, 1978, 1, SC-1692, AJA.

35. Ibid., 3.

36. In his response to Prinz, Glaser referred to other letters that had been sent to the board in protest. See Elliot Stevens (CCAR Administrative Secretary) to Balfour Brickner, September 19, 1978, 1–3, SC-1692, AJA.

37. Ely Pilchik to CCAR Membership, October 19, 1978, 1–2, SC-1692, AJA.

38. Only thirty-five states ratified the ERA by the 1979 deadline. Even by 1982, no additional states ratified the amendment. Arguments in favor of paying for release of the contract and seeking an alternative site: (1) the CCAR plenum voted in Toronto not to hold the convention in Phoenix; (2) the most effective support for ERA is to refuse to hold the convention in a non-ERA state; (3) for the sake of movement unity, the CCAR should follow the lead of the UAHC, which refused to hold its next biennial in a nonratifying state. Arguments in favor of retaining the contract and holding the convention in Phoenix: (1) the most effective advocacy of the ERA is to bear witness in Phoenix in the convention itself, through plenum sessions, classes, etc. as well as in visits to the Arizona legislature, public statement and demonstration; (2) rejection of the notion of secondary boycotts in attempts to secure state ratification; (3) the sole beneficiaries of the payment would be the (local) Hyatt; (4) the UAHC was able to negotiate a release from its Chicago contract because it had eighteen months' lead time.

39. Activities would include, among other events, an optional visit to the state legislature, where an ecumenical worship service would be led outside the state capitol, and an invitation to hear Lea Goodman, the Arizona Coordinator of the National Organization for Women (NOW). See Conference Program, *CCARY* (1979).

40. Letter of Karen Fox, Laura Geller, Rosalind Gold, Sally Priesand, Deborah Prinz and Myra Soifer to CCAR Colleagues, March 26, 1979, 1–2, SC-1692, AJA.

41. Laura Geller, telephone conversation, October 12, 2012.

42. Male colleagues helped the women arrange for Friedan's speech, including securing the room and putting up the funds for its rental. One rabbi told me privately that he became persona non grata at the CCAR as a result of his assistance. According to Judea Miller, a group of men who were longtime members of the CCAR decided to boycott the 1979 convention in support of the ERA. See Miller's letter in *New York Times Magazine*, December 2, 1984.

43. Friedan appeared before 350 delegates of the National Jewish Community Relations. See "Friedan Says ERA Is a Jewish Concern," *Jewish Telegraphic Agency*, July 2, 1976.

44. For Friedan's full address, see *CCARY* 89 (1979): 180–87. This excerpt appears on p. 180.

45. Ibid., 182.
46. Ibid. (my italics).
47. David Ellenson, "German Jewish Orthodoxy: Tradition in the Context of Culture," in *After Emancipation: Jewish Religious Responses to Modernity* (Cincinnati, 2004), 245 (my italics).

19

ON *MEMENTO*

Remaking Memory from the Outside In

WENDY ZIERLER

Modern Jewish Learning in Reverse: Reel Theology

In his draft address "Upon the Opening of the Jüdisches Lehrhaus," Franz Rosen-zweig sees the modern Jewish turn to "the realms of alien knowledge of the 'outside book'" as occasioning the birth of a new kind of Jewish learning: "It is learning in reverse order. A learning that no longer starts from the Torah and leads into life, but the other way around: from life, from a world that knows nothing of the Law or pretends to know nothing, back to the Torah. That is the sign of the time."[1] Rosenzweig refers to post-Emancipation Jewish alienation from the Torah and traditional Jewish learning—that is, from Jewish textual memory—as a form of illness that begets its own cure, allowing one to draw on the resources of one's outside learning to return to and strengthen one's Jew-ish core. Arguably, there is no more central Jewish experience than memory; Rosenzweig fittingly closes his remarks on the opening of the Lehrhaus with a blessing that imagines the Jewish intellectual return from periphery to cen-ter as an experience of "inner remembering": "May the hours you spend here become hours of remembrance, but not in the stale sense of dead piety that is so frequently the attitude toward Jewish matters. I mean another kind of remem-brance, an inner remembering, a turning from externals to that which is within, a turning that, believe me, will and must become for you a returning home. Turn into yourself, return home to your innermost self and your innermost life."[2]

The present essay, a work of Rosenzweigian "learning in reverse order," looks at a work of secular culture that deals with the implications of memory loss as a means of reimagining Jewish memory. It is an outgrowth of a course that my colleague Dr. Eugene Borowitz and I have been teaching at HUC-JIR for more than a decade, entitled "Reel Theology," in which we use close readings of film, television, and other popular media as a springboard for Jewish religious conversation. We refer to this kind of learning as "inverted midrash." Rabbinic midrash often elucidates or underscores the meaning of a classical text by introducing a parable. The rabbis explain a verse and then introduce a story or real-life application with the words *mashal le-mah ha-davar domeh*—a parable, to what can the saying be likened? Today, many Jews in synagogues are inadequately acquainted with classical sources; exposure to such texts is as likely to puzzle as to inspire. We teach our potential rabbis, cantors, and educators, then, to be practitioners of inverse midrash. That is, we begin our learning with the profound matters that are raised in contemporary secular culture in its thoughtful and artistically rendered books, movies, or television shows and seek to show how they lead back to the Torah, to Jewish practice, thought, memory, and knowledge.

On the most basic level, the learning practice at work in "Reel Theology" aims to complicate the simple dichotomy between tradition and modernity, a theme that characterizes David Ellenson's scholarship overall and serves as the organizing principle of this volume. Ellenson's study of German Orthodox rabbi Esriel Hildesheimer, for example, highlights Hildesheimer's attempts "to mediate between the pull of tradition and the demands of modernity," which made him a "paradigmatic practitioner of the dialectical interplay between tradition and change."[3] "Reel Theology" similarly avoids a crude dichotomy between traditional and modern conceptions of Jewish learning. It recognizes and reckons with, as Rosenzweig did, the major rupture that beset Jewish culture in the wake of modernity with its pull toward secular materials, not by segregating or opposing these materials, but by attempting to construct a meaningful dialogue and comparison between them.

Over the years, the syllabus for "Reel Theology" has shifted with the emergence of new films, books, and cultural phenomena. One of the few films to remain consistently on the syllabus, however, is Christopher Nolan's *Memento* (2000). Viewing this film quite literally involves a process of learning/viewing in reverse—much of the film proceeds backward rather than forward in time—and highlights a number of contemporary issues concerning the malleability and construction of memory, on both a personal as well as collective level. *Memento* is a film that, on one level, throws into serious doubt the very notion that it is possible, via memory, to locate or return to the past or to identify an "innermost self," as Rosenzweig refers to it. The self, necessarily rooted in memory, is as unstable as is memory, and therefore vulnerable to manipulations and changes. A wide gap yawns, it would seem, between Rosenzweig's call for memory and the postmodern condition of memory loss and destabilized interpretation, which the film *Memento* so aptly represents. And yet, borrowing again from Rosenzweig, I'd like to suggest that the illness here—the absence, instability and/or malleability of memory, as presented in *Memento*—also has its salutary aspects. While our culture, secular and Jewish alike, has lost its sense of certainty surrounding collective and personal memory, it has come to embrace the idea of memory as story that we actively reconstruct, reimagine, and retell, thereby endowing our lives with some coherence and meaning. Yosef Hayyim Yerushalmi's 1982 classic work on Jewish history and Jewish memory, *Zakhor,* directly opposes the modern practice of historiography with the tradition of Jewish collective memory, suggesting that in the pursuit of hard historical data about the past, the modern Jew often loses collective memory, and by extension, tradition. In more recent years, however, under the influence of postmodernism, scholars have attempted to undermine this history/memory binary, noting commonalities among historiography, storytelling, and memory, and acknowledging the subjectivity and unsettled nature of all interpretation. This essay engages the film *Memento* as a way of contributing to the conversation about the ongoing relevance and contemporary practice of Jewish memory.

Reading *Memento*

An acknowledged technical and narrative masterpiece, avidly studied not just in film schools, but by scholars of literature, narrative theory, and philosophy, *Memento* is the story of a former insurance investigator named Leonard Shelby who, as a result of a blow to the head, suffers from profound anterograde amnesia. Since his injury, which occurred simultaneously with his wife's rape and (supposed) murder, Leonard has lived outside the regular flow of memory and time. While he can summon forth memories from before the assault, he cannot store and integrate any new memories. Painfully aware of the absence of his former life but unable to recall how much time has passed or what has transpired since the trauma, Leonard lives for the sole, detached purpose of finding and killing "John G," the man who allegedly raped and murdered his wife and took away his memory.

Leonard's prior training as an insurance investigator had equipped him with skills of detection and deduction, which he hopes to employ in his search.

Yet these skills are rendered almost useless by the inability to remember anything or construct a narrative in time. Leonard attempts to impose order
on the chaos of his anterograde mind by employing a system of mnemonic
devices. He writes notes, takes Polaroid photos of places and people, which
he labels for future reference, and inscribes tattoos on his body with what
he believes to be key "facts" of the case. But because he cannot remember
anything for longer than ten minutes, he cannot integrate, internalize, and
utilize these memory aids in any reliable way. Leonard's condition also makes
him vulnerable to the nefarious manipulations of others, including a rogue
cop named Teddy, who lures Leonard into killing a drug dealer named Jimmy
Grantz (on the false pretense that the latter is Leonard's John G, so that Teddy
can steal Jimmy's drug money), and Jimmy's girlfriend Natalie, who ultimately
helps Leonard kill Teddy.

All this seems fairly comprehensible and straightforward, though it is
not so at all when one actually watches the film. Instead of taking the viewer
from point A to point B in Leonard's story, the film radically breaks up the
time, order, and even the color of Leonard's story, so that the viewer shares no
small measure of Leonard's disorientation and confusion. The film begins in
color with Leonard's taking a Polaroid photo of the dead Teddy, but in reverse.
Rather than watching the image of the dead Teddy develop on the Polaroid,
the audience watches it disappear back into the camera, which becomes symbolic both of Leonard's memory loss and the viewer's immediate and increasing loss of certainty with regard to the trajectory and meaning of the story.

The film proceeds with two alternating storylines that coincide only
toward the movie's end. The first is shown in color; it moves in reverse chron-
ological order, from Teddy's murder to the immediate aftermath of Jimmy
Grantz's murder. The other appears in black and white and moves forward in
time. In order to stitch together the pieces of the colored strand, each of the
color sections ends with a repetition of an image from the color section that
preceded it, suggesting a kind of stutteringly fragmented process of reconstruction, what Stephen Owen refers to in his book *Remembrances,* as "a 'pointing,' an index of absence."[4]

In the black and white sequence, which takes place sometime before the
aforementioned murders, Leonard sits in a nondescript motel room, trying to
figure out exactly where he is. "So where are you? . . . It's kind of hard to say;
it's just an anonymous room."[5] Leonard's description of his surroundings and
condition is provided in a "voiceover," which represents not only his inner
thoughts but also our own confusion over where we are in the sequence of the

narrative. Leonard then talks on the phone—we are not sure to whom—about a man named Sammy Jankis. This black and white sequence covers a relatively short period of time, but since it is broken up and stretched out over much of the movie, it seems far longer, accentuating the distortions of time and memory that characterize Leonard's anterograde life.

The choice in a contemporary film to use black-and-white instead of color often evokes a nostalgic past or conveys a sense of documentary truth. The first element seems to obtain for *Memento* as the black-and-white sections of the film clearly antedate the serial experiences of violence and corruption that characterize the colored portions. Instead of providing a linear documentary account, however, the black-and-white sections take on an almost mythic quality, with Leonard repeatedly invoking Sammy Jankis, whose name is inscribed in a handwritten tattoo on his hand. Leonard refers at the very beginning of the black-and-white sequence to the Gideon Bible that he finds in the motel room night table and that he claims (somewhat flippantly) to "read religiously." It is not the Bible, however, that Leonard reads religiously but his "Remember Sammy Jankis" tattoo, the story of which he tells as a kind of pseudo-biblical credo or prayer, a guiding text for his life.

According to Leonard, he repeatedly tells Sammy Jankis's story because it helps him understand his own situation. It turns out that Sammy was at the center of Leonard's first big case as an insurance investigator. Like Leonard's current circumstance, Sammy, too, had suffered an injury, making the storage of new memories impossible. Leonard was sent by his employer to determine whether Sammy's memory problems were really the result of physical injury or a symptom of psychosis (which would not be covered by his insurance policy). According to Leonard's understanding of the neuroscience of memory, even with damage to his hippocampus, Sammy should have been able to demonstrate habit memory, or to achieve some learning through conditioning.[6] But when tested, Sammy proved unable to make new habit memories, leading Leonard to the conclusion that Sammy's problem was psychological, not physical, and that he lacked the discipline or resolve to overcome it.

Saddled with medical bills and anxious to determine the true nature of Sammy's condition, his wife gives him her own test, repeatedly telling him that she needs her insulin shot, even though Sammy has already given it to her. She hopes that if Sammy's condition is psychological, the seriousness of her medical condition will jog him out of his memory loss before he repeatedly (and fatally) injects her with insulin. It does not, however, and she dies of an insulin overdose. Sammy's story, as Leonard tells it, is an object lesson on the mortal dangers of memory loss in the absence of a self and system to overcome it. Though Sammy had kept notes, they ultimately confused him. Leonard, in contrast, uses habit, repetition, and routine to bring order to his life. And he has a reason to make his life work—revenge.

Sammy's story is painful to Leonard because of the part he played in rejecting Sammy's insurance claim and in the sad demise of his wife, and because it ironically foreshadows Leonard's own condition. Nevertheless, Leonard seems to recount Sammy's story not so much to punish himself as to remind and admonish himself not to repeat Sammy's mistakes. Consequently, throughout most of the film, Leonard proffers the imperative: "Remember Sammy Jankis." But as Yosef Hayim Yerushalmi writes in *Zakhor*, "memory is always problematic, usually deceptive, sometimes treacherous."[7] Leonard's personal injunctions to remember prove unreliable in their own, complicated way.

Indeed, everything asserted or demonstrated in *Memento* is subsequently questioned, challenged, or undercut. As William G. Little notes, the film's "disruptiveness is not limited to making problematic the viewer's desire to put events in 'proper' order. Equally unsettling is the fact that no character's point of view can be considered reliable."[8] For example, Natalie is initially presented as a somewhat sympathetic character, until she is shown mocking and taunting Leonard with the knowledge that he will not remember anything ten minutes later. From the very beginning of the film, Teddy is presented as a smarmy, untrustworthy figure. But at the film's end, a possibility emerges that Teddy is the only truth-teller in the lot. According to Teddy, who claims to be the police officer assigned to Leonard and his wife's case, Sammy Jankis didn't even have a wife. Rather, it was Leonard's wife who was the diabetic. Moreover, he claims that Leonard's wife survived the attack that robbed Leonard of his memory; and it was the anterograde Leonard, not Sammy, who unwittingly killed his wife by insulin overdose. Teddy avers that Leonard's repeated invocation of "Remember Sammy Jankis" is merely the latter's attempt to repress the truth of his own deeds and to condition himself to retain a false memory, saving him from culpability for his own wife's murder. Deborah Knight and George McKnight thus argue that in killing Teddy, Leonard "kills the only person who could afford him any self-understanding because he kills the only person who challenges his own narratives about the past."[9]

There are plenty of reasons, scientific and otherwise, not to take Teddy at his word. While researchers of memory loss have indeed found evidence of anterograde patients' ability to form new habit memories,[10] Teddy alleges that the brain-damaged Leonard produced an entirely new episodic or declarative memory about Sammy Jankis in order to transfer his own guilt onto Sammy, which, though not inconceivable, would seem highly unlikely for a total amnesiac.[11] And, as I will discuss below, Teddy's revelation occurs against a backdrop of other, overarching lies, which make him an unlikely arbiter of truth.

Still, there are several visual clues spliced into the film that support Teddy's contention: there is a brief tableau of Leonard sitting in a chair in a mental hospital, in the same pose as Sammy Jankis, suggesting that Sammy's story is somehow really Leonard's. Leonard rejects Teddy's account on the grounds that his wife was not a diabetic. And yet, the film includes split-second images that belie Leonard's view: (1) Leonard's preparation of an injection, (2) his injecting insulin into his wife's thigh, and (3) his wife lying in bed, first blinking and then with eyes rigidly open, as if she is suddenly comatose (from an overdose). There is a whole subfield within psychology, dating back to Hippolyte Bernheim in 1889, that deals with the way in which therapists, law enforcement personnel, and others can manipulate the memories of others and/or plant memories in other people's minds.[12] Do these images constitute "facts" then, or are they simply ideas that appear in Leonard's mind as a result of Teddy's bullying suggestions? The film teases us by constantly juxtaposing competing interpretations. All of this, as Michael McKenna observes, places us in an interpretive quandary, emblematic of the postmodern condition: "Given the available evidence, there simply is no settled, proper interpretation of reality. As between competing and inconsistent interpretations, we are completely ill-equipped to settle on which, if any, is veridical."[13]

Memento and (Post)modern Jewish Memory: The Meaningfulness of Partial Truths

On the most basic level, *Memento* suggests that in the absence of memory and functioning sense of narrative time, one cannot have a coherent sense of self, a working interpretive framework, or an ethical system. Jewish tradition presages this attention to the urgent ethical importance of memory, both personally and collectively. In the Decalogue, the commandment to "Remember the Sabbath to hallow it"[14] immediately precedes the ethical commandments to honor your parents, not to murder, commit adultery, steal, or bear false witness, suggesting that ethics are entirely contingent upon our remembering God's role in creating the world in six days and resting on the seventh. As Yerushalmi notes in *Zakhor*, the Bible's "injunctions to remember are unconditional, and even when not commanded, remembrance is always pivotal. Altogether the verb *zakhar* appears in its various declensions in the Bible no less than 169 times, usually with either Israel or God as the subject, for memory is incumbent upon both."[15] If one has no memory, like Leonard, the entire structure runs the risk of collapse.

Most of us are not thoroughgoing amnesiacs. Or are we? On one level, Leonard's condition might be seen as an extreme version of the kinds of routine memory lapses and distortions that we all experience. "Like the amnesiac lead character in the 2000 film *Memento*," writes Jonathan Gottschalk in his recent book, *The Storytelling Animal* (2012), "we all go through life tattooed with indelible memories that didn't happen the way we remember them. . . . Our memories are not precise records of what happened, and many of the details— small and large—are unreliable."[16]

And on a collective level, as David Ellenson writes in "History, Memory and Relationship," "ours is a world seemingly afflicted with amnesia. Many Jews and Christians either forget or ignore their history. . . . The pluralism offered by the modern world makes tradition and the weight of tradition and memory an unattractive option for many people."[17]

That said, Jewish forgetfulness is not necessarily new or unique to the (post)modern condition. Regarding the issue of memory lapses or competing values, Jewish tradition frankly acknowledges that we all have a tendency to forget our core principles, hence the need for a system of mnemonic devices or reminders. Deuteronomy 6, for example, commands us to love the Lord our God, insisting that this credo be "upon your heart"[18] and taught diligently to one's children through repetition (*veshinantem*), so as to ensure that it be instilled in their memories.

As if assuming that this learning-by-heart will not stick on its own, the passage further enjoins us to employ various visual memory prompts as reinforcements: "And you shall bind them for a sign upon your hand, and they shall be as circlets between your eyes; And you shall write them on the doorposts of your house and in your gates" (Deut. 6:8–9).[19] Visual reminders appear in Numbers 15:39, as well in the commandment to place a fringe on one's garments "that you shall see it and be mindful [remember] of all the Lord's commandments and you shall do them. And that you go stray after your heart and after your eyes, after which you used to go whoring."[20]

In the Bible, memory is seen as a necessary and stabilizing element and a means of preserving one's self and one's central tenets. At the same time, even in the Bible, memory is presented as ephemeral, elusive, and unpredictable. As Adriane Leveen notes in her study of memory in the book of Numbers, memory introduces havoc into the camp; a collective, public remembering of the Egyptian delicacies triggers a series of disastrous events that end up over-turning memory as a stabilizing influence.[21]

In biblical terms, at least, memory is as critical and necessary as it is desta-bilizing and unreliable. As Leonard Shelby avers in *Memento*: "No, really. Mem-ory's not perfect. It's not even that good. Ask the police, eyewitness testimony is unreliable. The cops don't catch a killer by sitting around remembering stuff. They collect facts, make notes, draw conclusions. Facts, not memories: that's how you investigate. I know, it's what I used to do. Memory can change the shape of a room or the color of a car. It's an interpretation, not a record. Memories can be changed or distorted and they're irrelevant if you have the facts."[22] In our "learning in reverse" context, Leonard, out on his own trying to find the truth, might be regarded as a kind of empiricist, set out to discover hard data through careful, ground-up investigation. One simply has to know the right method for arriving at these truths.

Of course, it suits Leonard to make an argument here against the efficacy and reliability of memory, since his no longer works. But at what cost does one uphold "facts" and eschew memory entirely? Certainly Leonard's faith in "the facts"—especially given that throughout the film, they are shown to be manipulated and falsely adduced—is naïve in its own right.

All this calls to mind, once again, Yosef Hayim Yerushalmi's *Zakhor*. As memory and facts are to Leonard, so collective memory and history are to the great scholar. As mentioned earlier, Yerushalmi presents his vocation as a Jewish historian, in search of hard data (like Leonard!) as representing a deci-sive break with the habit of Jewish remembering:

> Memory and modern historiography stand, by their very nature, in radically different relations to the past. The latter represents, not an attempt at the restoration of memory, but a truly new kind of rec-ollection. In its quest for understanding it brings to the fore texts, events, processes, that never really became part of Jewish group memory even when it was most vigorous. With unprecedented energy it continually recreates an ever more detailed past whose shapes and textures memory does not recognize. But that is not all. The historian does not simply come to replenish the gaps of memory. He constantly challenges those memories that have survived intact.[23]

The opposition presented here between (collective) memory and history was anticipated many years earlier, albeit in a different form, by French sociologist and anthropologist Maurice Halbwachs in his writings on the social context of collective memory. In recent years, however, scholars have challenged or attempted to modify both Halbwachs's and Yerushalmi's positions.[24] As Yael Zerubavel has argued, "Halbwachs's desire to highlight the unique qualities of collective memory appears to have led him to overstate its contrast to history. He therefore portrays them as two polar representations of the past."[25] Nowadays historians commonly acknowledge the constructedness not just of memory but also of history: "In fact, historians not only share the basic premises of collective memory but also help to shape them through their work, as the history of national movements has shown."[26]

So, as Leonard Shelby might say, where are we? I have thus far presented the relevance of *Memento* to a discussion of the necessity as well as the slippery nature of memory, and to the supposed opposition between modernist (empiricist) and postmodern (subjective, less stable) approaches to Jewish history and collective memory. We have shown that while memory is selective and constructed, the supposed realm of facts—historiography—shares, at least in some measure, these same features. With regard to the film itself, if we, the viewers, are detectives in our own right, attempting to discern the truth of this story, our conclusion may well be nihilistic, that is, that there are no "true facts" to be found. And yet, as Eugene Borowitz noted toward the end of one of our class discussions of *Memento*, a logical contradiction arises from that premise: if there is no truth, then this supposed "truth" about the lack thereof itself needs to be toppled (that is, a version of the "liar's paradox"). For decades Borowitz has been making a plea for a middle ground between the Enlightenment faith in human reason with its abrogation of the past and the nihilism of postmodernism: "Against the teaching of so much present-day philosophy and science," Borowitz wrote in 1974, "we find that we do not consider the universe empty of values and man thus free to adopt any form of behavior whatsoever."[27] In a similar vein, Borowitz announced to the students in our "Reel Theology" class: "You cannot leave it at that," referring to the nihilistic postmodern message of the film. Turning to me before departing to catch his imminent train home, his charge to me was, pointedly, "I trust you will not leave it at that."

In response, I would like to argue that the film itself does not "leave it at that"—at least, not in any simple or straightforward way, which is why it serves as such an effective catalyst for discussion about the current understanding of (Jewish) memory.

To this end, let's return to the film to consider its climax. In the denouement, Leonard murders Jimmy Grantz and realizes, traumatically, that the latter was not his John G, after all. When Leonard confronts Teddy with the realization that he has just killed the wrong man, Teddy attempts to evade the truth and convince Leonard that Jimmy really is his John G. Against this backdrop of lies, Teddy rolls out his supposedly "true" version of Leonard's past, including the revelation that over a year ago, Teddy helped Leonard track down the real John G, but Leonard had not remembered this event. Over the course of this conversation, Teddy dissolves the few remaining memories and principles that Leonard has lived by. In addition, Teddy betrays his willingness to use his knowledge of Leonard's disability to his own crass advantage. Given this "reality," Leonard consciously decides to "forget" Teddy's would-be "truths" and to "remember" only his venal lies. Leonard thus burns the Polaroid photo of the dead Jimmy, labels the Polaroid shot of Teddy with the words "DO NOT BELIEVE HIS LIES," and tattoos Teddy's license plate number to his thigh—clues that with Natalie's help, will lead him eventually to kill Teddy, as if he were John G.

One student asked: Why doesn't Leonard simply kill Teddy right there and then when he realizes what Teddy has done to him? Why does he delay by inserting Teddy into the story of his ongoing quest for his wife's rapist and murderer? Doesn't Leonard's manipulation of the "facts" here represent the worst kind of betrayal both of memory and "truth"?

Michael McKenna would have responded to my student that, at this point in the film, Leonard's "desire for revenge has outstripped what is true. . . . In this moment, Leonard forsakes his allegiance to the truth as he cynically says to himself, 'Do I lie to myself to be happy? In your case, Teddy, yes I will.'"[28]

Perhaps. And yet, one might also argue that this moment of cognitive fabrication on Leonard's part represents the only assertion of meaningfulness and agency in a life otherwise stripped of it. Leonard, desperately seeking justice and truth but suddenly aware of the extent to which his injury has mired him in the opposite, chooses to forget some things and "remember" others out of his tenacious desire to believe that his actions still have meaning. In the context of this film, where many views are presented but all are challenged, Leonard makes a pluralistic claim for the partial truth of his grievance against Teddy and for the larger abiding truth of his quest for justice in the face of his wife's and his own suffering.[29] Leonard's decision to fold Teddy's misdeeds into the memory of what John G did to him and his wife represents a reassertion of the ongoing meaningfulness of his own personal story.

Let me be clear, I am neither advocating for lying and murder as a defensible way of life nor attempting to justify the wholesale, self-conscious invention of one's past. Leonard is an extreme case: a flawed and pathetic hero, whose pursuit of justice, truth, and meaning is sorely compromised and whose agency is woefully limited; he is, at best, an awfully weak illustration of Rosenzweig's call to the inner self.

That said, given a choice between competing truth claims, between a version of the past touted by one exposed as a greedy murderous manipulator, and another version that, though potentially faulty or partial, allows one to seek the punishment of that wrongdoer while at the same time maintaining one's dignity—is the latter not preferable? Teddy dismissively says to Leonard "So you lie to yourself to be happy. Nothing wrong with that—we all do."[30]

But this, our tendency to fictionalize, or to construct a better version of our past is itself an important truth. "We are all tellers of tales," writes psychologist Dan P. McAdams in his book *Stories We Live By*: "We each seek to provide our scattered and often confusing experiences with a sense of coherence by arranging the episodes of our lives in to stories. This is not the stuff of delusion or self-deception. We are not telling ourselves lies. Rather, through our personal myths, each of us discovers what is true and is meaningful in life. In order to live well, with unity and purpose, we compose a heroic narrative of the self that illustrates essential truths about ourselves."[31] What this means is that each of us emphasizes selective details from our past so as to construct a narrative that propels our lives forward, generatively. Given Leonard's compromised state, resolving to construct a narrative that will lead him to kill his current aggressor, Teddy, is probably the best that he can muster. And the moral consequences are quite disturbing, to say the least.

Torah she-be'al peh: Memory and the Imagination

Throughout the film, when Leonard attempts to conjure up details from his distant past or to fix an image in his mind, he is shown either looking up and away from the camera or closing his eyes. In one scene, Natalie asks him to tell her about his wife: "Close your eyes and remember her," she says. Leonard closes his eyes and consequently is able to call forth and describe a past memory of his wife that that is textured, emotional, and commanding[32]: "You can only feel details. Bits and pieces, which you didn't bother to put into words. And extreme moments you feel even if you don't want to. Put it together and you get the feel of the person, enough to know how much you miss them, and how much you hate the person who took them away."[33] Here the amnesiac Leonard "remembers" not by using the externalized memory aids of his written notes, photos, and tattoos, but by looking inside himself and insisting on what he sees in his own mind's eye—a preference shared by the ancient Greeks. As critic Tony Jackson claims:

> As Plato prophesied long ago, the importance of memory in human affairs changes drastically with writing. Over time, writing usurped the place of what we may call public or communal memory, the oral means of handing on the past that is the only kind of history accessible to non-literate community. Plato charged that writing is unnatural, in that if you ask questions of it, it cannot respond; said another way, with writing, our words are no longer a function of the body. Because writing removes our words from our voices and our histrionics and some specific flesh and blood communicative context, we cannot be as sure of the success of our linguistic intentions as we typically can be in speech.[34]

Leonard is exceptional. Yet, we all share something of his problematic dependence on externalized written (or digitized, as the case may be in our day and age) memory. Our reading practices, which consign learning to written form, abet this. As Robert Darnton describes, a reading revolution took place in the West around 1800. Before then people read "intensively": "They had only a few books—the Bible, an almanac, a devotional work or two—and they read them over and over again, usually aloud and in groups, so that a narrow range of traditional literature became deeply impressed on their consciousness. By 1800 [people] were reading 'extensively.' They read all kinds of material, especially periodicals and newspapers, and read it only, then raced on to the next item."[35]

Rosenzweig seems to register an awareness of the Jewish version of this phenomenon. In the beginning of his essay on the opening of the Lehrhaus, he argues: "It is to a book, the Book, that we owe our survival—that Book which we use, not by accident, in the very form is has existed for millennia . . . Everything was really within the learning of the Book . . . Then came the Emancipation."[36] Rosenzweig's educational project, described at the beginning of this essay, aims to reverse the process and thereby return Jews to an intensive reading of the Book, though not merely in an atavistic or an externalized sense. His hope is that this new form of learning, albeit influenced by our extensive outside reading, will result in "inner remembering." But what might inner remembering look like?

What comes to my mind in this context is Judaism's insistence on the importance not only of *Torah she-bi-khtav* (the written Torah) but also of *Torah she-be'al peh*, what Martin Jaffee refers to as "Torah in the Mouth." According to Jaffee's research on writing and oral tradition in Palestinian Judaism, "the written texts of the Torah in the mouth, that is to say, are not *Torah* at all as long as they remain merely written on inscribed material surfaces; the real inscription of Torah in the mouth must be in memory, as memory is shaped by the sounds of the teacher's own rendition."[37] Jaffee describes an ancient learning community, where one studied, memorized, and shared aloud the teachings of one's master for the purpose of being imaginatively transformed by them. "The privileged path to such transformation lay in emulating the living embodiment of that knowledge in the writings and deeds of one's teachers, and their teacher's teachers. In the person of the philosophical Sage, the instructional text came alive.[38]

We are unlikely to return to those premodern days of remembering; our sense of what constitutes learning has forever changed. We are similarly unlikely to revive the ancient tradition of memorization, though if contemporary Jewish literature is any indication of our current disposition, our community is evincing a renewed interest in engaging Jewish memory in new and creative forms. In a 1997 *Tikkun* magazine symposium on the New Wave in American Jewish literature, nearly all the critics and writers included noted the centrality of Jewish memory in the work of the current wave of Jewish American writers.[39] One writer of this New Wave, Jonathan Safran Foer, whose debut novel *Everything Is Illuminated* tells the story of a young American writer who journeys to the Ukraine to recover the story of his family's pre-Holocaust past, goes so far as to say that "Jews have six senses: Touch, taste, sight, smell, hearing . . . memory."[40] It is significant to note, however, that a good deal of this book's investigation and evocation of the past involves the creation of a fictional(ized) shtetl populated by imaginary "Slouchers" and "Uprights."

Even in the time of the Rabbis, Jewish remembering required a commitment not only to memorization but also to acts of the imagination. And forgetting this commitment posed special kinds of risk, as Rabbi Dostai ben Yannai says in the name of Rabbi Meir: "He who forgets a single word of his studies, Scriptures considers it as if he were liable for his life; for it is written (Deut. 4:9) 'But take care and watch yourselves closely, so as not to forget the things that your eyes have seen.'"[41]

This Mishnah functions as a kind of Jewish memento mori—not in the sense of being a reminder of one's mortality, but of the potential danger to one's integrity should one lose one's memory. Note that in the Mishnah the very proof-text adduced for the notion that one's life depends on remembering what one has learned hangs on an act of the imagination. When Moses speaks to the people in Deuteronomy 4 and admonishes them not to forget what "your eyes have seen," he is speaking to that post-wilderness generation of Israelites who didn't actually see the Exodus with their own eyes. As the Tiferet Yisrael explains, it couldn't possibly be that the text is referring here to actual sight, as the Torah was written for all of Israel, and the latter generations, of which we are a part, did not witness any of the miracles.[42] Rather, the biblical text seems to be referring to "the eye of one's intellect,"[43] adjuring that one ought not forget the formative ideas and stories that one sees—dare I say, invents?—in one's own mind.

David Ellenson writes that "the paradox of the modern world is that its conditions also engender community and allow for the renewal and re-creation of tradition and memory. Modernity releases the bonds and frameworks that tied persons to the practices and perceptions of the past. It simultaneously permits an experimentation with and return to tradition and memory that many have never known, but which offers the promise of security and warmth, community and memory."[44]

At the ordination ceremony for the 2012 graduating class of rabbis and cantors at HUC-JIR, New York, Rabbi Cantor Angela Buchdahl delivered a stunning address in words and song that took this teaching a step further: "They say 'You can't change history.' But here's the radical thing—you can change memory. In every generation, as we remember anew—we actually *re-form* Jewish memory itself. We come out of a new Egypt, we change the faces of those who stood at Sinai, we add new leaders who received authority from the very hands of Moses. . . . You who have been studying these letters, interpreting the words and decorating the text with your own understanding. . . . You will become memory makers."[45] Buchdahl offered her notion of memory-making against the backdrop of the commemoration of two historic events that occurred the year she was born (1972): the ordination of Sally Priesand as first woman rabbi in the American Reform movement and the release of Debbie Friedman's *Sing unto God,* a landmark occasion in terms of the history of Jewish feminist liturgy and song. Within a single generation (according to the forty-year reckoning in the book of Exodus), these watershed events have brought about a radical reimagination or rerembering of synagogue leadership and practice, forever changing, as if retrospectively as well as for generations to come, the very picture of the rabbi and the very sound of a prayer.

Might Franz Rosenzweig have had something like this in mind when he envisioned the new enterprise of "learning in reverse"? A reading of a secular film about memory that itself resists easy explication, as a means of reencountering and reimagining the tradition of Jewish memory as storytelling or imaginative recollection? A reading of the current state of Reform Jewish leadership and prayer as a way of creatively reenvisioning the very notion of Jewish tradition? An embrace of "inner remembering," not in some naïve, romantic, anti-intellectual way; not without awareness of amnesia, alienation, rupture, and change, but with a brave willingness to reshape the familiar in light of the alien, and the past in light of the present? "In being Jews we must not give up anything," wrote Rosenzweig, "not renounce anything, but lead everything back to Judaism. From the periphery back to the center; from the outside, in."[46]

Notes

1. Franz Rosenzweig, "Upon the Opening of the Jüdisches Lehrhaus," in *On Jewish Learning*, ed. N. N. Glatzer (New York, 1955), 96.
2. Ibid, 102.
3. David Ellenson, *Rabbi Esriel Hildesheimer and the Creation of a Modern Jewish Orthodoxy* (Tuscaloosa, Ala., 1990), x.
4. Stephen Owen, *Remembrances* (Cambridge, Mass., 1986), 66.
5. See Christopher Nolan, *Memento*, scene 2, www.imsdb.com/scripts/Memento.html (accessed March 14, 2014).
6. For more on the difference between declarative or episodic memory and habit memory see Brenda Milner, Larry R. Squire, and Eric R. Kandel, "Cognitive Neuroscience and the Study of Memory," *Neuron* 20 (March 1998): 445–68. See also Daniel Schachter, *Searching for Memory: The Brain, the Mind and the Past* (New York: Basic Books, 1996), 134–60.
7. Yosef Hayim Yerushalmi, *Zakhor: Jewish History and Jewish Memory* (New York, 1989), 5.
8. William G. Little, "Surviving *Memento*" *Narrative* 13, no. 1 (2005): 67.
9. Deborah Knight and George McKnight, "Reconfiguring the Past: *Memento* and Neo-Noir," in *Memento: Philosophers on Film*, ed. Andrew Kania (New York, 2009), 163.
10. Brenda Milner's famous studies of H.M., who suffered from anterograde amnesia, showed that despite his brain damage, H.M. was able to develop a new skill by practice and conditioning (drawing a star by looking into a mirror). This proves that amnesiacs have been able to retain and build on habit memory. See Milner, Squire and Kandel, "Cognitive Neuroscience and the Study of Memory," 448, 456.
11. According to Israeli neuropsychologist Daniel Levy, "a pure amnesiac would indeed not be able to remember a post-amnesia-onset incident at all, nor assign it to a new context or frame. However, I have had contact with patients who had very bad but not total amnesia. Such a person might conceivably form a gist memory of a very salient, emotionally charged, event, and then associate it with preserved knowledge acquired pre-morbidly. So Leonard Shelby could have linked the very powerful impression of a woman dying of an insulin overdose administered by her husband with the case of Sammy Jankis, with which he was familiar from the period before the injury that caused his amnesia. That would not be a case of

repression, but of confabulation, trying to make sense of a fragment of memory lacking a context by associating it with a preserved pre-morbid memory" (e-mail correspondence, November 1, 2012).

12. See Hippolyte Bernheim, *Suggestive Therapeutics: A Treatise on the Nature and Uses of Hypnotism* (New York, 1889). On the subject of police investigators or psychotherapists suggesting false memories into existence see Elizabeth Loftus, "Our Changeable Memories: Legal and Practical Implications," *Nature Reviews* 4 (March 2003): 23–233. See also Schachter, "Reflections in a Curved Mirror," *Searching for Memory*, 98–133.

13. Michael Mckenna, "Moral Monster or Responsible Person? *Memento*'s Leonard as a Case Study in Defective Agency" in Kania, *Memento*, 25.

14. Exod. 20:8. Translation from Robert Alter, *The Five Books of Moses* (New York, 2004), 431. All subsequent biblical translations are from this source.

15. Yerushalmi, *Zakhor*, 5.

16. Jonathan Gottschalk, *The Storytelling Animal* (Boston, 2012), 168.

17. David Ellenson, "History, Memory and Relationship," *Memory and History in Christianity and Judaism* (Notre Dame, Ind., 2001), 171–72.

18. Alter, *The Five Books of Moses*, 913.

19. Ibid., 913

20. Ibid., 760.

21. Adriane Leveen, *Memory and Tradition in the Book of Numbers* (Cambridge, 2008), chap. 11, p. 21.

22. Nolan, *Memento*, scene 44.

23. Yerushalmi, *Zakhor*, 94.

24. See Amos Funkenstein, "Collective Memory and Historical Consciousness," *History and Memory* 1 (Spring/Summer 1989): 5–26.

25. Yael Zerubavel, *Recovered Roots: Collective Memory and the Making of Israeli National Tradition* (Chicago, 1995), 4–5. For responses to Yerushalmi's *Zakhor*, see "Forum: Recalling Zakhor: A Quarter-Century's Perspective," *JQR* 97, no. 4 (2007): 487–544. For more on the notion of history as construction or the transformation of chronicle into story, see Hayden White, *Metahistory: The Historical Imagination in Nineteenth-Century Europe* (Baltimore, 1973).

26. Zerubavel, *Recovered Roots*, 5.

27. Eugene Borowitz, "God and Man in Judaism Today: A Reform Perspective," *Judaism* 23, no. 3 (1974): 303.

28. McKenna, "Moral Monster or Responsible Person," 35.

29. On the subject of the pluralism of partial truths see Irving (Yitz) Greenberg, "The Principles of Pluralism," *Sh'ma*, April 1999, 4.

30. Nolan, *Memento*, scene 174.

31. Dan P. McAdams, *The Stories We Live By: Personal Myths and the Making of the Self* (New York, 1993), 11. See also Michael White and David Epston, *Narrative Means to Therapeutic Ends* (New York, 1990), 10; and Donnel Stern, *Partners in Thought* (New York, 2010).

32. In using the adjective "commanding," I am referring to a distinction recently made by Yehuda Kurtzer between history and memory: "*Where history informs, memory commands*. History enables standing apart, outside, above the past . . . Memory, meanwhile, whether by design or accident, wields a commanding over those who

remember" (Yehuda Kurtzer, *Shuva: The Future of the Jewish Past* [Waltham, Mass., 2012], 26).

33. Nolan, *Memento*, scene 25.

34. Tony E. Jackson, "Graphism and Story-time in *Memento*," *Mosaic* 40, no. 3 (2007): 53, 54. The reference here to Plato is from *Phaedrus*, particularly in Socrates' speech at the end of the dialogue. See Plato, *Phaedrus*, available at the Internet Classics Archive, http://classics.mit.edu/Plato/phaedrus.html (accessed January 26, 2014).

35. Here Darnton is summarizing the theory of Rolf Engelsing. See Robert Darnton, "First Steps toward a History of Reading," *The Kiss of the Lamourette: Reflections in Cultural History* (New York, 1990), 165.

36. Rosenzweig, "Upon the Opening of the Jüdisches Lehrhaus," 95–96.

37. Martin S. Jaffee, *Torah in the Mouth: Writing and Oral Tradition in Palestinian Judaism 200 BCE–400 CE* (New York, 2001), 155.

38. Ibid, 147.

39. See the Symposium on "The Jewish Literary Revival," *Tikkun* 12, no. 6 (1997).

40. Jonathan Safran Foer, *Everything Is Illuminated* (New York, 2003), 198.

41. Translation adapted from "Ethics of the Fathers: Mishnah Pirkei Avot," available at Sharei Shechem website, www.shechem.org/torah/avot.html#chap3 (accessed January 26, 2014).

42. Commentary on Pirkei Avot by Israel Lifschitz, German rabbi (1782–1860).

43. Cited in Pinkhas Kehati, *Mishnayot mevo'arot: Seder Nezikin 2*, commentary on Avot 3:8, "*Rak hishamer lekha*" (Jerusalem, 1977), 352.

44. Ellenson, *Rabbi Esriel Hildesheimer*, 174.

45. Angela Buchdahl, "Ordination Address," Temple Emmanu-El, New York, 2012. Quoted with permission from the author. For a full copy of the address, see http://accantors.org/acc/system/files/Ordination+Address+Angela+Buchdahl+2012.pdf.

46. Rosenzweig, "Upon the Opening of the Jüdisches Lehrhaus," 98.

20

AT THE CENTENARY OF AGNON'S "VE-HAYAH HE'AKOV LE-MISHOR"

A New Reading

ARNOLD J. BAND

The angel of historiography, unlike Walter Benjamin's dour angel of history, challenges us to wrest meaning out of an examination of historical events. While Benjamin's angel was inspired by a painting of Paul Klee, the angel of historiography I allude to derives from a more familiar locus: Genesis 32:23–33 and its many commentaries. The angel of historiography may struggle fiercely, but might finally yield insight. In our study of historical events, we might choose to study a movement, a period, or, if we are so attracted, a person whose deeds or writings intrigue us. David Ellenson, in his pervasive fascination with the transition from tradition to modernity in the religious life of Jews, was intrigued by the figure of Rabbi Esriel Hildesheimer, a paragon of modern Jewish orthodoxy who both served as a community rabbi and founded the Orthodox Rabbinical Seminary in Berlin in 1873. Hildesheimer's activities as an active community rabbi and a leading educator-scholar provided Ellenson with a perfect subject for his interests in the sociology of religion, as well as in the dialectical relationship between tradition and modernity.

Intrigued by similar historical phenomena, but temperamentally attracted to literature more than the history of religion, I found my avatar in the Hebrew author Shmuel Yosef Agnon, who fused modern prose fiction with the Hasidic tale and dominated Hebrew prose fiction for the first half of the twentieth century, and even beyond his death in 1970. A comparison of Hildesheimer with Agnon regarding the historical transition from tradition to modernity is illuminating since for Hildesheimer this historical transition generated a dialectical, existential situation in which he had practical problems to solve, legal decisions to make, institutions to create, while for Agnon this dialexis became instrumental. It provided him with a framework in which to create his fictions. He employed his prodigious knowledge of Hebrew texts of all periods to create a style that, though linguistically traditional, could convey the complex concerns of a modern writer that were often expressed in ambiguities and ironies.

His penchant for ambiguities, embodied in the characteristic Agnonic style first adopted in his novella "Ve-hayah he'akov le-mishor" ("And the Crooked Will Become Straight," 1912) was both his vehicle for dealing with the tensions between tradition and modernity that obsessed him, and for creating fictions that embodied these concerns.[1] In the current year, the centenary of this masterly story is being celebrated in Israel, and I will take this opportunity to offer some reconsiderations of this pivotal story in the light of the tradition/modernity dialectic. I call this story pivotal since, as I have documented in my book on Agnon, in his first stories published between 1903 and 1911, he was clearly searching for a contemporary narrative style of Hebrew to tell his stories.[2] In late 1911 he adopted a style that fused traditional texts of all previous periods of Hebrew writing to tell his stories. "Ve-hayah he'akov le-mishor" is the first story written in that style, which critics have subsequently called Agnonic. Written in Jaffa, where Agnon had been living as of 1908, it was published by Yosef Hayyim Brenner first in the journal *Ha-po'el ha-tsa'ir* and then as a separate volume in 1912. And while Agnon either scrapped or relentlessly rewrote stories he had published before 1912, his editing of "Ve-hayah he'akov le-mishor" for later editions of his works, though significant, is relatively minimal. Obviously, this early story (he was twenty-four when he wrote it) still met the approval of this notoriously self-critical writer decades after its first publication. Ironically, while it is a seminal work in modern Hebrew literature, it has not yet been translated in full into English, though it was published in German as early as 1918 by Max Strauss.

My own preoccupation with this novella goes back more than fifty years. More recently, I have been intrigued by the implications of a collection of major essays on this novella edited by Yehudah Friedlander in 1993.[3] Much significant, productive work has been done, mostly on studying the rich sources of the novella and trying to determine their implication for the understanding of the story. The interpretations of the story have become more complex; among the twelve essays in this collection, one finds at least six or seven distinct interpretations. Why, I wonder, are there so many different interpretations of this text? This hermeneutic profusion is generated, I would argue, by the unique narrative style and stance Agnon adopted in writing this novella, which differs radically from anything he had written before late 1911. My own reading of this story has also become more complex in that I am now more convinced than ever that a proper reading of this story and much of Agnon's subsequent writing must begin with a concentration on the author and his manipulation of his readers' responses by using the dialectic between tradition and modernity as an expressive instrument.

To focus on the choice of style he made in writing this novella, I bring a statement made by Agnon and quoted by the Hebrew author Yehoshua Radler-Feldman, known as Rabbi Binyomin: "I tell you, Rabbi Binyomin, that Mendele's style is not the last word in Hebrew fiction."[4] In this retrospective article written in 1933, the addressee of this statement, Rabbi Binyomin, recalls his meetings with Agnon in Jaffa in 1908–11, when both were young, aspiring writers. In one memorable scene, the two were walking along the Mediterranean shore when Agnon protested that Mendele, for all his monumental stature, was not "the last word in Hebrew fiction." Agnon was obviously referring to the publication of the collected Hebrew fiction of Mendele that began to appear in 1909 and was the obvious challenge to an ambitious young writer who wanted to make his mark in Hebrew fiction. The author Rabbi Binyomin, recording this event after Agnon had published the four volumes of the first edition of his collected works in 1931, implies that Agnon had indeed succeeded in forging a new prose idiom in Hebrew, something that transcended Mendele.

There are at least two features of Agnon's narrative technique in "Ve-hayah he'akov le-mishor" that differ from that of Mendele. First, while Mendele does employ Hebrew of all periods, in contradistinction to the biblically oriented Hebrew of Avraham Mapu, for instance, he is trying to create a narrator who is a modern person. Agnon, in "Ve-hayah he'akov le-mishor," creates a narrator who talks to us in a Hebrew style evocative of the Hasidic raconteur. The Hebrew style has all the distinctive charm of the naïve, pious raconteur. Second, while Mendele's narrator is not too interested in psychological motivation, the narrator of "Ve-hayah he'akov le-mishor" is profoundly obsessed by his hero's emotions and thoughts. Agnon learned this obsession both from the neo-romantic German and Scandinavian writers of the period and from the Hebrew fictions of Micha Yosef Berdichewski and Yosef Hayyim Brenner, the dominant author in Jaffa of that period and a close friend. Here it is crucial for us to distinguish between the author S. Y. Agnon and the narrator he created to tell his tale. For, while the narrator is a quasi-naïve Hasidic raconteur, the author is a skillful manipulator of plot, tone, and the creation of character. This novella is thus both traditional and modern, and the reader is constantly challenged to interpret which mode of discourse—if any—is dominant. In fact, Agnon's ambiguities and ironies are the predominant aspects of the game he plays with his readers, who are expected to participate in this interpretive contest.

The name of the novella is, itself, a challenge. The title comes, obviously, from Isaiah 40:4:

> Let every valley be raised,
> Every hill and mound made low,
> Let the rugged ground become level
> And the ridges become a plain.

The third stich here, in Hebrew "Ve-hayah he'akov le-mishor" is translated in the JPS translation as "Let the rugged ground become level," but is rendered in the King James as "And the crooked shall be made straight." Agnon's implied and actual Hebrew reader knew this verse well since it is chanted in the synagogue on the Sabbath after Tishah Be-Av, the Sabbath named after this portion of the prophets, "Shabbat Nahamu." This stirring prophetic verse from Isaiah heralds the return to Zion in 538 BCE after the Babylonian Exile and evokes cosmic yearning for national redemption. It is used here, however, as the title of a tale about the financial ruin and social decline of a shopkeeper, Menasahe Hayim; his extreme personal suffering; and his somewhat questionable redemption at the end of the novella. From the very title of the novella, one begins to wonder what Agnon actually means.

This is evident from the very first lines that mock the naïve content heading of certain Hasidic tales that summarize and comment on the story we are about to read, often offering the moral lesson the reader is supposed to derive. The brief summary is expanded in the narrative text. The protagonist, Menashe Hayim, a pious Hasidic shopkeeper, a *kohen*, lives happily with his wife, Kreyndel Tcharne, in Buczacz, Galicia (Agnon's hometown). As in a typical folktale, their happiness is marred by one failing: they have no children, and thus, Menashe Hayim has no prospects for posterity, a serious lacuna in the life of a pious man. Their love, however, is deep, portrayed in detail, and Menashe Hayim would not consider divorcing his wife even though, by Jewish law, he could do so since she had not born him children after ten years of marriage. In addition, when another shopkeeper opens a shop across the street from Menashe Hayim's store, he is financially ruined by his competitor. One would expect that Menashe Hayim, a pious man, would be redeemed somehow from this difficulty through his deep piety, but this is Agnon's story, not one of the uplifting tales of the Besht (the spiritual founder of Hasidism). In the spirit of the nineteenth-century realistic novel, the author devotes much attention to his hero's financial, and hence social, decline. Menashe Hayim has no money to restock his shop, no credit from his suppliers, and decides to try to solicit alms from individuals in other towns. This fateful decision was motivated by the couple's refusal to have Menashe Hayim earn his living as a *melamed* (a teacher of young boys), which he could have done since he was a learned man; that lowly profession would imply a significant loss of status in the community. Armed with a letter of recommendation from his rabbi, he leaves home to seek donations from individuals in other towns. His wife is forced to set up a stall in the Buczacz town market to earn enough to support herself. Due to Menashe Hayim's financial decline, the hero loses everything: his shop, his home, his status in town, his family life.

As a man of self-respect, Menashe Hayim has to adapt himself to the life of a beggar, which Agnon describes in painful detail. After a while, he stops writing to his wife and stays on the road well after the anticipated period he had set for himself. Bit by bit, he collects enough money and, overcome by yearning for his wife, he decides to return home. At that point, he meets a beggar who offers him a huge sum of money for the letter of recommendation from his rabbi. Figuring that he no longer needs the letter, Menashe Hayim succumbs and thus sells away his identity, clearly the cardinal sin he commits in this novella. Before returning home, he decides to visit the fair at Lashkovits to buy goods to restock his shop in Buczacz. The author constructs the fair as a grotesque Walpurgis Night. Menashe Hayim, inflamed by all he saw there, takes a room in an inn, eats a sumptuous meal, including much liquor. When he awakes from his stupor in the morning, he finds himself thrown out into the street, bereft of both his wallet and his phylacteries. Totally disconsolate, he has no alternative but to return to the road to resume his life of beggardom, but this time without the rabbi's letter of recommendation.

While Menashe Hayim is back out on the road, Agnon adds drama to the story by having the beggar who bought the letter die in a fit of drunkenness. When bystanders happen onto the letter he bought from Menashe Hayim, they assume that its original owner is dead and relay the news back to Buczacz. Agnon thus generates a crucial situation of mistaken identities, for if Menashe

Hayim is dead, and his death can be certified, then his wife Kreyndel Tcharne is a widow. She remarries and, shortly afterward, bears a child—exactly what she was unable to do during her marriage with Menashe Hayim, when she was considered barren. She has no idea that her first husband, whom she still loves, is in fact alive, nor that she is actually illegally married and her child is a bastard. Agnon, for his part, assumes that his readers know that this situation violates traditional Jewish law, and they are thus drawn into a suspenseful situation. Menashe Hayim has no clue of what has transpired and continues on his way, begging for alms. Finding no success on the road, for he has no letter of recommendation, he decides to return home to the woman he loves. When he reaches Buczacz, people do not recognize him, since he has been begging on the roads for years. Meeting a group of children, he learns from them that they are going to the celebration of the impending circumcision of the child of Kreyndel Tcharne. Hearing this, Menashe Hayim is thoroughly shocked; he runs out of town, and falls to the ground crying.

Agnon's reader knows that Menashe Hayim is faced with an impossible dilemma: if he were to go home, he would ruin his wife's life and disgrace her child. He could, furthermore, not remarry her since he was a kohen and could not marry a woman in such marital circumstances. But if he did not go home, he would be allowing her to live in sin. Agnon thus creates a peculiar narrative situation by crafting a complicated version of the predicament of the *agunah*, the "anchored" or "chained" wife whose husband has disappeared, left her without a *get* (a bill of divorce) and thus rendered incapable of remarriage. The hero hides in forests and cemeteries lest he be discovered and wanders from place to place hoping to die. This, for him, is the only solution, though as a pious Jew, he is prohibited from committing suicide. As his strength begins to fail him, he comes upon a cemetery where the guard befriends and feeds him. One day he notices the guard, who also served as a stone carver, engraving a handsome stone with the name "Menashe Hayim" on it. Hearing from the guard that it was ordered by a lady for the headstone of a certain beggar, her husband, Menashe Hayim, our Menashe Hayim realizes that it was Kreyndel Tcharne who ordered the stone for him, since she thought he was dead. Menashe Hayim finally confesses his story to the guard. Shortly afterward, he dies happy in the thought that his wife still loved him and that he had resisted the temptation to reveal the truth and ruin her life. When he dies, the guard places over his grave the stone ordered by his wife for the other grave that she thought was his. Though childless, his name was not forgotten among his people, since his wife would come to weep over his grave.

Agnon ends his story with the five letter Hebrew acronym one finds on a traditional gravestone: Tav. Nun. Tsadi. Bet. Heh. "May his soul be bound with the bond of the living." This acronym, more prominent in the 1912 edition than in later editions, is an apt closing for a pious text written in the style of a Hasidic tale. Eliezer Meir Lifshitz, one of the first literary critics to publish an article about this story, as early as 1912, complained about the dissonance of this ending: Menashe Hayim is given a happy ending, a proper burial even though his reticence allowed his wife to live in a sinful marital status. Lifshitz, significantly, had been Agnon's literary editor and mentor in Buczacz "before Agnon became Agnon" and when he still published under his original name, Czaczkes. Lifshitz clearly understood the responsibility of the author of this story.

The novella begins with a title that raises questions (can it apply to Menasheh Hayim's story?) and ends with an epitaph that is more than ambiguous (can Menasheh Hayim be considered virtuous, or blessed at the end of the story?) The reader must recognize that any simple reading will not suffice. The hero's name is Menasheh Hayim (he makes forgotten/erases life) while his wife's name is Kreyndel Tcharne (black crown). Even the brief summary of the story I have presented above should alert the reader to the author's artful emplotment of the novella with its surprising turns, mistaken identities, and legal complications. While the well-wrought ambience is that of traditional pious Jews in the middle of the nineteenth century, the skillfully charted financial decline of the hero, his accompanying social degradation, his deep, detailed love for his wife, his psychological anxieties, are all evidence of a modern sensibility. Similarly, a close study of the text, beyond the scope of this paper, but well documented in several of the essays in the Friedlander volume, offers abundant evidence of pervasive authorial manipulation. The attentive, competent reader is intrigued by the pervasive play with traditional texts to express very modern sentiments, a narrative technique so persistent as to call attention to the presence of the author in every line. The reader is thus consistently engaged with Agnon's fusion of the traditional with the modern and challenged to interpret the rich complexities emerging from the story's many ambiguities.

While such critics as Yosef Hayim Brenner and Fishel Lachover praised the novella effusively upon its publication, such luminaries as Michah Yosef Berdichevsky and Hayim Nahman Bialik found it too mannered. Agnon himself had the good sense to know when to modify this style. In the novel *Hakhnasat kalah* (The Bridal Canopy, 1931), which takes place in Galicia of the early nineteenth century, he returns to this quasi-Hasidic style, but in the novel *Sipur pashut* (A Simple Story, 1935) set in the early twentieth century, he forged a style that exploits many of the rabbinic or Hasidic locutions, but does not sound like an intertext of a Hasidic tale. His awareness that the style of his first great novella, "Ve-hayah he'akov le-mishor," could not be used for all situations is added evidence that he knew that the stylistic fusion of the traditional and the modern offered the writer a rich variety of creative possibilities.

Notes

1. S. Y. Agnon, *Ve-hayah he'akov le-mishor* (Jaffa, 1912).
2. Arnold J. Band, *Nostalgia and Nightmare* (Berkeley, Calif., 1968).
3. Yehudah Friedlander, *"Al Ve-hayah he'akov le-mishor": Masot 'al novela shel Shay Agnon* (Ramat Gan, 1993).
4. Yehoshua Radler-Feldman, *Mishpehot soferim: Partzufim* (Tel Aviv, 1961), 280.

CODA

From Tradition to Radicalism

Jewish Women in Pre-Holocaust Poland

PAULA E. HYMAN

The focus of my lecture today is on Jewish women in Poland and how their radicalism, even more than their secularism, transformed Polish Jewry. The three million Jews who lived in interwar Poland constituted the single largest European Jewish population at the time.

The Jewish women of Poland are forever fixed in our mind as we imagine them to have been in the late nineteenth century. They are "bobbes," pious ancestral grandmothers, wearing their scarves, or tikhls, forever unchanging. That image has been reinforced by the pictures we see of contemporary Hasidic women, living in Boro Park or Monsey. Yet modern Jewish women, who rebelled against their place in traditional Judaism or in the traditional Jewish family, had emerged in full force in Poland in the last quarter of the nineteenth century. In fact, their presence heightened the issue of how Jews were to be modern in tsarist Russia and interwar Poland. The question of women, as well as the activity of women, was central to political and cultural debates in the Jewish community.

It was hard to be a Jew, male or female, in Poland, or as Polish Jews would have it, "Shver tsu zayn a yid." Jews living in the twentieth century in Poland had hoped that the demise of tsarist Russia, which had absorbed Poland into its territory, would put the lie to that assessment. In the newly independent Poland, they presumed, they would be treated as equals, as fellow citizens.

That did not happen. The 1920s and '30s were difficult times for Jews in Poland, as they found that in the new Polish State they were alien, other, not only because of their religion but also because of their nationality—what we Americans would call their ethnicity. The history of Polish Jewry before the Nazi invasion that signaled the outbreak of World War II is a story of economic impoverishment and disillusionment. Jews were subject to increasing anti-Semitism, supported by the government, and ultimately to economic boycotts and the imposition of quotas, and Jewish benches, in higher educa-tion. That story of Polish Jews includes the many strategies that they created to fight against the "Jewish problem" of "otherness"—of being considered as outside the cultural space that defined what it meant to be Polish. There were a variety of Jewish strategic responses. These included struggling for their rights in the state and municipalities with a number of political parties ranging from Orthodox to socialist to Zionist, working to sustain their insti-tutions, their community, and their culture, and preparing youth for aliyah, immigration, to Palestine. All these strategies were ultimately unsuccessful, but they reflect a vibrant and diverse population, who could not know that their futures would be brutally cut short.

Women comprised 52 percent of the more than three million Jews of Poland, yet they remain virtually invisible in the pre-Holocaust histories of twentieth-century Polish Jewry. This is not because of the misogyny of his-torians, or at least not only because of that tendency. The destruction of Pol-ish Jewry severed the connection between the generations of historians, and particularly destroyed the tradition of social history that was developing in eastern Europe. Much gender-sensitive scholarship has derived precisely from developments within social history. Also, the issues that seemed so critical to the fate of Polish Jews were political. The struggle between nationalities (Jews vs. Poles) and the struggle between classes (workers vs. the bourgeoi-sie) engaged contemporaries far more than the struggle between the sexes. Women were easy to ignore because they were not major leaders in Jewish political parties. The Orthodox Agude, which was the single largest Jewish party in interwar Poland, opposed female suffrage and stated that political activity was unseemly for women. But even in the Zionist and Bundist parties women leaders were few, and women's issues were considered secondary to the larger questions of national and socialist liberation. Historians shared the general conviction that public events were truly what mattered. Only in the past few years have some scholars of East European Jewry acknowledged that the experience of women offers a new vantage point to explore the culture, and even the politics, of East European Jews.

If Jews were considered the Other in Poland, Jewish women confronted a double otherness. They shared the otherness of all Jews and the discrimination that this engendered in the world of work and higher education. As women, they faced the prejudices that confronted all women in Poland who sought expanded opportunities for employment and education. Some historians of

Jewish women—for example, Marion Kaplan, writing about Germany in the late nineteenth and early twentieth centuries—have found that Jewish women experienced more discrimination because of their gender rather than because of their religio-ethnic identity. That was not the case in interwar Poland, where anti-Semitism was strong and pervasive and increasingly supported by the government. Yet, to their consternation, in addition to the discrimination they encountered in Polish society as Jews and as women, Jewish women also confronted marginalization within their own communities.

In some ways, Jewish society offered greater opportunities to its daughters than did Polish society. As Polish census data indicate, a greater percentage of Jewish women studied in university than did non-Jewish women, even as restrictions against all Jews in universities grew. Middle-class Jewish families expressed strong support for the education of their children, and extended that support to the secular education of their daughters. In fact, both the social historian Shaul Stampfer and the literary specialist Iris Parush have written that as early as the second half of the nineteenth century, Jews from traditional families often sent their daughters to public schools or provided teachers in foreign languages and literatures because it was appropriate to educate girls, just not in traditional Talmud study. Parush describes this gendered distinction in education as an example of the "advantages of marginality." Traditional Jewish culture also produced images of strong women who were respected as long as they did not defy social convention.

Why, then, did some Jewish women in Poland feel socially marginalized? How did they succeed in transforming their anger at constraining gender norms into recognition of a broad social problem that had to be addressed? What paths of social activism did they choose to achieve recognition as full members of the Jewish community?

These questions, of course, do not apply to all Jewish women in Poland. Even in the interwar years at least a third—and perhaps up to a half—of Polish Jewish women were religiously traditional in their perspectives and looked to their rabbis for guidance. The single largest number of women's societies among Polish Jews were dedicated to maintaining mikvehs (ritual baths) under the auspices of the Agude. Jewish women were diverse, divided by their level of urbanization, their region of residence, their educational attainments, and their social class. The vast majority were concerned with sustaining their families in difficult economic conditions, and not with activism of any stripe.

There were women of the middle classes, however, who articulated a strong case for women's equality, for the end of the Otherness of women within the Jewish community. They based their argument, in part, on the assertion that it was both good for, and necessary for, the Jewish community. There were also women who participated in revolutionary political movements whose case for the equality of women was a corollary of their socialist politics. No one woman is typical of the substantial numbers of female activists, but sometimes an unusual individual, if not typical of her generation, can represent issues that disturbed broad circles within the Jewish community.

I have one such person in mind, a woman named Puah Rakovsky. An English version of her Yiddish memoirs, which I edited and annotated, was published in 2002 under the title *My Life as a Radical Jewish Woman: Memoirs of a Zionist Feminist in Poland.*

Puah Rakovsky, hardly a household name, but a woman whose struggles against "female otherness" in the Jewish community of Poland, reveals much not only about Jewish women but also about how Polish Jews who departed from Orthodoxy constructed their self-definition and vision of the future in the twentieth century. Moreover, Puah's story reveals that even before the second wave American feminism of the 1970s, the personal *was* political.

Rakovsky's perception of women's differentness within the Jewish community began in her childhood. Descended from a long line of rabbis (though her father, who had *smikha*, was a businessman), she was born in 1865 in Bialystok. She begins her Yiddish memoirs (which were published in 1954) with the memorable sentence: "I was born in 1865 to a fifteen-year-old mother and a seventeen-year-old father." Her personal experience of the disparity in Jewish educational ideals for boys and girls forced her to confront the subordination of women. Raised in a fairly prosperous (and large) traditional Jewish family, Puah received a good Jewish education, first at a heder and then through private tutors. But her intellectual achievements were considered a waste; her father commented ruefully, "It is a shame that you were born a girl and not a boy." Moreover, her education was halted completely when her parents determined, when she was sixteen, that she should be married. Following custom, they chose her bridegroom with every consideration for his brilliance as a yeshivah bokher (Talmud student) but with no consideration for her wishes. (No groom would have pleased her; she simply did not want to get married at that point).

Puah's education was unusual for a middle-class Jewish girl in the attention given to Hebrew and Jewish texts. But many daughters in financially comfortable Jewish families were educated well beyond our stereotype of the ignorant female. They received a secular education, mastering foreign languages and reading general literature. Their Jewish education, however, as I've mentioned, tended to be minimal. Rakovsky determined, when she directed her own girls' school in Warsaw, to address the abysmal ignorance of Jewish girls in Jewish culture.

In establishing her school and writing about the education of Jewish girls, Rakovsky contributed to a Jewish communal debate. By the end of the nineteenth century and well into the twentieth, some Jewish leaders lamented the fact that so many Jewish women were taking the lead in assimilation, the most radical form of secularization. On the eve of the First World War, one journalist wrote in *Der Fraynd*, a Yiddish newspaper published in St. Petersburg, that Jewish women were now better educated and more elegant than their husbands. While the Jewish man had a common language with his son, he had to speak to his daughter in a foreign language, Polish or Russian. "Jewish women," asserted the writer, "were taking revenge on Jewish men for their former sins." This polemical article, written with irony, is much exaggerated. Still, there is some statistical and much more anecdotal evidence that Jewish girls were being educated in secular culture to a higher degree than their brothers were. Even in Hasidic families, where boys studied traditional texts exclusively, their sisters would be enrolled in public schools or in private Jewish schools that provided little instruction in Jewish subjects. The Jewish education of girls did not matter to traditionalists and was of minimal importance to secularists, who favored European-style education. Journalists and rabbis alike were becoming aware of the consequences of this gender disparity.

Women like Puah Rakovsky entered this communal discussion and left an imprint on East European Jewish culture. They argued that as future mothers, girls were too important to the Jewish community to be left ignorant of Jewish learning. In the Orthodox community Sarah Schenirer, a seamstress from a Hasidic family, established a study group for Jewish women in Cracow. In 1918 she established the first Beys Yaakov school. She succeeded in her endeavor because she sought and received the support of the Belzer rebbe and ultimately of the Agude, which absorbed the school as its educational agency for women. It is likely that her action, as well as the general communal debate, prompted the Agude to act and inspired the Chofetz Chaim, the leading rabbinic authority in Poland, to issue a *psak* (halakhic decision) that authorized formal Jewish education for females: "It is surely a great mitzvah to teach girls the Pentateuch and also the other books of Scripture and the ethics of the rabbis . . . so that our holy faith will be verified for them. Because if not, the girls are likely to stray completely from the path of the Lord and transgress the foundations of our religion, God forbid."

Puah Rakovsky did not operate within the constraints of the Orthodox Jewish community, and therefore her activism was more sustained and her leadership more direct than Schenirer's. She secured a job teaching in a Jewish school for girls in Lomza in 1889, and within two years she had moved to Warsaw to teach in a newly organized Zionist girls' school. Two years later she decided to open her own school, becoming the principal of what several sources call the first modern Hebrew school for girls in Warsaw; Hebrew and Jewish texts were a significant component of the curriculum. Until its demise in 1915 as a consequence of the German invasion of Poland the school flourished. In addition to its middle-class clientele, who paid tuition, it provided free classes in the evening to poor girls.

Rakovsky saw education as the sine qua non for equality for women, a goal that she embraced in her youth. In a 1937 article in *Dvar ha-poelet*, a labor Zionist paper for women, she wrote that she knew by the age of thirteen that she wanted to be a teacher. As early as 1894 she began to publish articles in the Yiddish press, and later pamphlets as well, to promote her ideas. She was drawn to education as a tool for achieving women's equality in part because of her personal experience of educational discrimination, in part because of her familiarity with political developments both within Russia and to the West. (Incidentally, in addition to Yiddish, Hebrew, Russian, and Polish, she knew German and French, and after her school was forced to close she supplemented her income as a translator of books, primarily from German and French, to Yiddish).

Rakovsky was a secular Zionist, but her analysis of the deleterious consequences of the failure to provide a solid Jewish education to girls was similar to that of the traditionalists. As she commented in her memoirs, "Our people paid dearly [for the traditional view that it was wrong to teach Torah to females]. If our grandfathers and fathers . . . had reversed themselves . . . so that Jewish daughters, exactly like sons, should be educated in our Torah, in our culture and moral doctrines, who knows how many thousands of Jewish mothers would have been saved from assimilation . . . and thereby also Jewish sons, whom we have lost because of their education, which they received from their assimilated mothers?"

This is a conservative argument that sees women's education as crucial because of their maternal role, but Rakovsky went beyond this. She may have initially framed her calls for Jewish education for women and for recognition of women's value in terms of their role as maternal teachers, but her concern for women was as persons in their own right, and not just as instruments of cultural transmission and national survival. She modeled for her students, and for the Jews of Warsaw, where she was well known, the way that education permitted women independence and assertiveness. And, as she later wrote, she was concerned with providing women with the means to acquire "personal and social liberation."

Female Jewish activists also assumed the right to act politically to erase their "otherness" in the Jewish community by achieving political and social equality. Although most women in Russian Poland and in the independent Polish state (including Jewish women) were not politically active, most anti-tsarist radical political groups that sprung up at the end of the nineteenth century in theory offered women equality. On the Jewish street—which was how Russian Jews referred to their own communities—the socialist Bund did so as well. Indeed, one historian of the Bund asserts that "women's status within the movement was indistinguishable from men's." Still, less than 20 percent of Bundist activists were female (because political activism was extremely difficult for women with families). The Zionist movement was more ambivalent about the role of women. In 1902 Rakovsky wrote in a Yiddish paper that Herzlian Zionism was more open to women than were "the first bearers of the idea of *Hibbat Zion* [Love of Zion], the rabbis and pious Jews [who] did not admit women into their circles." Yet, although political Zionists gave women the right to vote at Zionist Congresses, the *haluts* was a male figure, and local leaders saw no need for women to do more than collect funds for the cause.

Women like Puah Rakovsky responded to this situation in two ways: by bringing the specific needs of women to the attention of male political leadership, and by organizing women. Women in the Bund, who saw the party and its apparatus as supreme, participated in a women's auxiliary, the YAF (Yidishe Arbeter-Froy), founded in the early 1920s to bring working women into the party. In independent Poland women comprised a substantial segment of the Jewish working force. In 1931, according to census figures that did not include "helpers" in family businesses, they were 27.5 percent of primary breadwinners and 44.5 percent of Jewish wage earners (55.9 percent in 1921). Despite the fact that the primary goals of the male Bundist leadership were recruitment to the party and labor unions, the YAF did pragmatically provide day care and education to women. Women unionists, however, complained of mistreatment by their male peers and demanded the organization of separate unions for women. The separatist demands of female activists in the YAF as well, as their calls for recognizing the specific needs of women as women, flew in the face of the Bund's ideology that men and women were equal and hence the same. The YAF remained small in membership and subordinate to the party as a whole, never more than a "bit player" in the Polish Bund.

Yet, Daniel Blatman, a younger Israeli historian of the Bund, has argued that the women activists in the YAF transformed the role of women in the Bund from revolutionaries who ignored specific women's issues to activists who were concerned with meeting women's needs as they defined them. The question of women's place in the Bund, he concludes, offers an opportunity to examine a general issue, the dialectic tension between political ideology and the changing realities of Jewish life in the interwar period.

Before the Bund established the YAF, Puah Rakovsky recognized the need for a separate women's Zionist group. Toward the end of the First World War Rakovsky devoted her efforts to organizing Bnos Tsiyon, a women's Zionist group under the leadership of women (despite its affiliation with a Zionist party). She had long harbored a passion for Zionism. From the time of her arrival in Warsaw in 1891, she had been involved in the Hibbat Zion (Love of Zion) movement, and she recognized that early Zionist leaders' antipathy toward women kept many middle-class women from participation in the movement. Although one Zionist meeting in Minsk in 1902 inspired her to write that there was some evidence of progress in the movement's treatment of women and she persisted in her own Zionist activism throughout her life, in her memoirs she considered Zionist attitudes toward women as a significant factor in Jewish women's greater attraction to secular rather than nationalist organizations. In a 1937 presentation to a seminar of women workers in Palestine, she noted with sadness, "When I wanted to raise the question of women's indifference to Zionism, they [male leaders] didn't understand me. I tried several times to write about this subject, but they didn't publish my impressions."

In 1918, under the auspices of Bnos Tsiyon, Puah published a pamphlet in Yiddish, *Di yidishe froy*, which called on Jewish women to become more active in Zionist work, especially since women were so important in all movements for social reforms. Both the Jewish question and the woman question, she asserted, could be solved only through self-determination, a popular slogan at the end of the war. Jewish women could do their part by founding a national Jewish women's organization (in Poland) and by pressing for the adoption of female suffrage in Jewish communal elections. (This was blocked by the Orthodox). Rakovsky combined her feminist message with an appeal to ethnic Jewish pride: "It is not possible that we Jews, who were the first bearers of democratic principles, should in this regard lag behind all civilized peoples and close the way for women to achievement of equal rights and to the first step in that direction—to participation in the community."

Rakovsky was committed to the concept of separate women's organizations that would place women's concerns at the center of their activities. Otherwise, she felt, issues important to women would be defined as secondary and would be deferred until "more significant" problems were solved. She and her colleagues were not averse to using their clout as organized women when necessary. In the aftermath of World War I, the leaders of Bnos Tsiyon established a women's council, on which Rakovsky served, to direct their recruiting efforts. At first (and I'm drawing here on the narrative of the Polish Zionist leader Yitzhak Grinbaum) the members of the Zionist Central refused to recognized the women's council and did not want to provide financial support for its activity, despite their earlier promise to do so. The members of the women's council thereupon resigned in protest. Working independently, they were enormously successful, expanding their branches in the provinces to seventy-two—at which point they won recognition from the Central. Rakovsky's strategy of autonomous organizing was effective in this case.

Following her published call for a separate Jewish women's organization in Poland that would appeal to broad sectors of women, Puah Rakovsky joined with colleagues, in particular Leah Proshansky and Rokhl Stein, in establishing a nation-wide organization in the early 1920s. Its orientation was explicitly feminist and pro-Zionist (though it was not affiliated directly with the organized Zionist movement). It was called YFA (Yidishe Froyen Organisatsie) and was considered the women's organization of the middle classes, as opposed to the Bundist YAF, which was socialist and working class. Most importantly, unlike the Bundist organization, the YFA was controlled by women and explicitly addressed women's needs.

The YFA promoted women's equality on a number of fronts, including support of women's suffrage in Poland and in Palestine. It published a short-lived monthly journal and pamphlets on the modern women's movement, calling on women to assume an active role in political and social activity in this period of change. As the editors of the journal *Froyen-shtim*, Rakovsky, Stein, and Proshansky undertook a propaganda campaign that they described in an editorial as "enlightenment work among Jewish women, because the doors of the Yiddish press are for us women closed with seven locks." They hoped "to awaken . . . the Jewish woman to take her fate in her own hands, herself to demand and defend her rights." "For those of us who can speak," they noted, "our journal offers the opportunity for their voice to be heard." The editorial reflected Rakovsky's message of female self-empowerment and her recognition of the need for middle-class women—"those of us who can speak"—to assume responsibility for effecting social change, as equals with men.

In addition to proclaiming the need for woman "everywhere to take the same part as man" in creating new social and political patterns, the YFA addressed the manifold social problems of women and children, the most vulnerable of Jews, in Poland. As Rakovsky noted, it directed its attention to the poorest women and their families, providing vocational education and classes in literacy, administering a home for children, establishing cooperatives, and running day care centers and summer camps for children and youth. It labored to find solutions for *agunot*, chained wives, who could not marry without a divorce. And it provided courses and public lectures (in Yiddish) on Jewish and Polish literature, politics, and public events so that Jewish women of all social classes would be able to function as educated citizens. As a pro-Zionist organization, it also sponsored Palestine-centered work. In a 1928 circular letter of the organization, Rakovsky pointed out that working with YFA led to women's self-education and development, a goal toward which the organization strove. Rakovsky also spoke for the YFA when she published a second Yiddish pamphlet, *Di moderne froyen-bavegung* (The Modern Women's Movement) in 1928. It placed the Jewish women's movement within an international context. In Poland, as elsewhere, she argued, women had to organize on their own behalf to secure civic and political equality, equal rights to work and equal pay, and equal opportunities for education. Other Jewish feminists in Poland concurred. Summing up the condition of Jewish women in a Yiddish pamphlet, *Froyen-problem*, Rokhl Kaplan-Merminski wrote, "The Jewish woman was wounded on three fronts: as a woman, as a Jew, and as a human being." Celebrating women's potential for effective social action, as had been demonstrated by the YFA, she concluded her pamphlet with a powerful combination of radical rhetoric and Jewish imagery: "Let woman rise up! She is going to pluck the apple from the Tree of Life."

Rakovsky's strategy of separate organizations for women, I would argue, was the right one for her time and place, and she pursued it even when she met opposition from her male colleagues. The fact that the YFA did not become a major political or social service force among Polish Jewry is easy to understand, given the economic circumstances of the time, the implacable hostility of the Polish authorities, and the failure of all Jewish political groups in interwar Poland. What is harder to understand is the absence of any reference to YFA in the historical literature until now—despite its publications and the occasional document it left behind.

The YFA suggests how female activists could define women's needs and attempt to place them on the agenda of the Jewish community. It continued the traditional role of women's philanthropy, but with a difference. It proclaimed that in their social welfare work women were acting as social and political equals within a community reluctant to grant them that status.

Puah Rakovsky also provides evidence of the ways in which some women assumed agency in response to their subordination in the Jewish community and particularly to the ways that Jewish law discriminated against them. The personal, in other words, became political. Most of these cases involved marriage, or more specifically, getting out of marriages, especially arranged marriages. Rakovsky, as you may recall, was married at the age of sixteen to a yeshivah student some ten years her senior. Because her husband was a full-time student of Talmud, she was able to use the traditional gender ideal of women supporting their scholarly husbands to acquire higher education for herself. In her very early twenties, when her husband had already lost her dowry and she was the mother of two small children, she convinced her husband and parents (who would take care of her children) to permit her to live with her grandparents and study as an extern for a teachers' diploma. When she received her teaching license, she returned home and promptly asked for a divorce (which she did not receive for six years). Only when she threatened to convert to Christianity, and to convert her children as well, did her rabbi grandfather, who wielded great authority within the family, persuade her husband and her parents to accept the need for divorce. There is some evidence from memoirs and Russian court records that Rakovsky was not alone in this attempt to evade the provisions of Jewish law. I recommend to you a new book that confirms my assertion, Chae-Ran Freeze's *Jewish Marriage and Divorce in Imperial Russia*.

I am convinced from reading her memoirs and the comments that contemporaries made about her that she considered the choices she made in her personal life as a component of the revolutionary she felt herself to be. Remember that she called her reflections *Memoirs of a Revolutionary Jewish Woman*. As early as the 1890s she was the subject of a roman à clef, published in Hebrew and called "Rabbi Shifra." (Shifra and Puah were the names of the two midwives in the Exodus story, and readers of a Hebrew novella would know that). "Rabbi Shifra" recounted the story of a divorced Jewish woman who was well educated in Jewish matters and whose love for her cousin had been thwarted by her family (as Rakovsky's was). Rabbi Shifra was clearly a curiosity, but she was also presented as an admirable figure. She illustrated new possibilities available to women and the type of woman who would take advantage of them.

In addition to her career as teacher and director of a school, and her success in freeing herself from a miserable marriage, Puah Rakovsky was also recognized as a radical because of her third marriage. After the marriage imposed on her when she was a teenager, she married twice more, both times for love. (She nursed her second husband, stricken by tuberculosis, for six years before he died). When she married a man ten years her junior, she was the talk of intellectual circles in Warsaw. An older woman marrying a younger man was a radical act that defied the gender conventions of the time.

Women like Puah Rakovsky who acquired secular education but remained immersed in Jewish culture, without necessarily continuing religious observance, raised the issue of female equality as a challenge to the Jewish community. They applied the Jewish demand for equality in the larger society to the Jewish community itself, by arguing that women shared with Jewish men the need for recognition of their equality regarding education, economic opportunities, and political leadership. They also laid bare the constraints placed on women by widely accepted gender norms. That women were not equal in Orthodox circles was clear. That women were marginalized as well within secular movements like Zionism or radical parties like the Bund required female activists to provide powerful arguments in word and deed to support their assertions. What their activism and their writing demonstrated was the social costs that the Jewish community paid for its failure to treat women as equals and to draw on their talents.

The status of women in any society points to the distribution of power within that society and reveals its core values. In Jewish society in interwar Poland, the status of women was shifting, during a period when all Jews faced significant economic and educational barriers. Like men, Jewish women varied in social class, in level of education, in religious practice, and in their mode of self-definition as Jews. Yet all experienced a double otherness, as Jews in Polish society and women in Jewish society. Female activists, ranging from Sarah Schenirer, the founder of Beys Yaakov; to the Bundist Dina Blond; to the educator, Zionist, and feminist Puah Rakovsky, pushed their sectors of a diverse Polish Jewish society to accommodate to the demands of women for something more than they were offered. To achieve their goals they had to become radical or at least to have radical ideas that challenged things as they were.

Jewish women's gains in interwar Poland are hard to evaluate. The history of the Jews in Poland came to an abrupt and horrifying end before female activism could fully develop and its impact penetrate throughout the Jewish community. The years between the two world wars are so distant from us because of the abyss of the Holocaust. Still, the recovery of the history of Jewish women in this place and time, however fragmentary it may be, is important. It reminds us that we cannot understand the intimate world of family life or the public life of the community, the religious sensibilities of Jews or their very identity, if women and their concerns remain invisible.

BIBLIOGRAPHY OF WORKS
BY DAVID ELLENSON

"Ellis Rivkin and the Problems of Pharisaic History." *Journal of the American Academy of Religion* 43, no. 4 (1975): 787–802.

"Emil Fackenheim and the Revealed Morality of Judaism." *Judaism* 25, no. 4 (1976): 402–13.

"A Jewish Legal Decision by Rabbi Bernard Illowy of New Orleans and Its Discussion in 19th-Century Europe." *American Jewish History* (December 1979): 174–95.

"Modern Orthodoxy and the Problem of Religious Pluralism: The Case of Rabbi Esriel Hildesheimer." *Tradition* 17, no. 4 (1979): 74–89.

"The New Ethnicity, Religious Survival, and Jewish Identity: The 'Judaisms' of Our Newest Members." *Journal of Reform Judaism* (1979): 47–60.

"Accommodation, Resistance, and the Halakhic Process: A Study of Two Responsa by Rabbi Marcus Horovitz of Frankfurt." In *Jewish Civilization: Essays and Studies Honoring the One Hundredth Birthday of Rabbi Mordecai Kaplan*, volume 2, *Jewish Law*, edited by Ronald Brauner, 83–100. Philadelphia: Reconstructionist Rabbinical College Press, 1981.

"Rabbi Esriel Hildesheimer and the Quest for Religious Authority: The Earliest Years." *Modern Judaism* 1, no. 3 (1981): 279–97.

"Rabbi Zvi Hirsch Kalischer and a Halachic Approach to Conversion." *Journal of Reform Judaism* (Summer 1981): 50–57. Co-authored with Robert Levine.

"American Courts and the Enforceability of the Ketubah as a Private Contract: An Investigation of Some Recent U.S. Court Decisions." *Conservative Judaism* (Spring 1982): 35–42. Co-authored with James S. Ellenson.

"The Role of Reform in Selected German-Jewish Orthodox Responsa: A Sociological Analysis." *Hebrew Union College Annual* 53 (1982): 357–80.

"Church-Sect Theory, Religious Authority, and Modern Jewish Orthodoxy: A Case Study." In *Approaches to the Study of Modern Judaism*, edited by Marc Raphael, 63–83. Atlanta: Scholars Press, 1983.

"The Evolution of Orthodox Attitudes Towards Conversion in the Modern Period." *Conservative Judaism* (Summer 1983): 57–73.

"Jewish Religious Leadership in Germany: Its Spiritual and Cultural Legacy." In *Genocide: Critical Issues of the Holocaust: A Companion Volume to the Film Genocide*, edited by Alex Grobman and Daniel Landes, 72–81. Los Angeles: Simon Wiesenthal Center, 1983.

"Jewish Tradition, Contemporary Sensibilities, and Halakha: A Responsum by Rabbi David Zvi Hoffmann." *Journal of Reform Judaism* (Winter 1983): 49–56. Co-authored with Robert Levine.

"The Dilemma of Jewish Education: To Learn and to Do." *Judaism* 33, no. 2 (1984): 212–20. Co-authored with Isa Aron.

"The Holocaust, Covenant, and Revelation." *Encounter* (Winter 1984): 53–59.

"Liberal Judaism in Israel: Problems and Prospects." *Journal of Reform Judaism* (Winter 1984): 60–70.

"Jewish Covenant and Christian Trinitarianism: An Analysis of a Responsum on Jewish-Christian Relations in the Modern World." In *Jewish Civilization: Essays and Studies*, edited by Ronald Brauner, volume 3, 88–103. Philadelphia: Reconstructionist Rabbinical College, 1985.

"Jewish Legal Interpretation: Literary, Social, and Ethical Contexts." *Semeia* 34 (1985): 93–114.

"Representative Orthodox Responsa on Conversion, and Intermarriage in the Contemporary Era." *Jewish Social Studies* 47, nos. 3/4 (1985): 209–20.

"Abraham Geiger," "Esriel Hildesheimer," "Samson Raphael Hirsch," "David Hoffmann," "Samuel Holdheim," and "Isaac Eichanan Spektor." In the *Encyclopedia of Religion*. New York: Macmillan, 1986.

"Eternity and Time." In *Contemporary Jewish Religious Thought*, edited by Arthur A. Cohen and Paul Mendes-Flohr, 189–94. New York: Charles Scribner & Sons, 1986.

"The Integrity of Reform Within Kelal Yisrael." *Yearbook of the Central Conference of American Rabbis* 96 (1986): 19–32.

"Mordecai Kaplan." In *Biographical Dictionary of Social Welfare in America*, edited by Walter Trattner, 432–34. New York: Greenwood Press, 1986.

"'Our Brothers and our Flesh': Rabbi Esriel Hildesheimer and the Jews of Ethiopia." *Judaism* 35, no. 1 (1986): 63–65.

"The Orthodox Rabbinate and Apostasy in Nineteenth Century Germany and Hungary." In *Jewish Apostasy in the Modern World: Converts and Missionaries in Historical Perspective*, edited by Todd Endelman, 165–88. New York: Holmes and Meier, 1987.

"Modernization and the Jews of Nineteenth Century Frankfurt and Berlin: A Portrait of Communities in Transition." Dworsky Center for Jewish Studies, University of Minnesota, Paper Number 2 (1988): 1–23.

"Scholarship and Faith: David Zvi Hoffmann and His Relationship to Wissenschaft des Judentums." *Modern Judaism* 8, no. 1 (1988): 27–40. Co-authored with Richard Jacobs.

"Traditional Halakhic Sources and the Construction of Liberal Jewish Thought: Limitations and Possibilities." *The Reconstructionist* (March 1988): 28–30, 32.

"The Validity of Liturgical Pluralism." *The Reconstructionist* (June 1988): 16–18.

"A Jewish Response to Jack Verheyden: On the Christian Doctrine of God." In *Three Faiths—One God*, edited by John Hick and Edmund S. Meltzer, 58–62. London: MacMillan, 1989.

"Modern Challenges to Halakhah." *Judaism* 38 (1989): 358–65.

Tradition in Transition: Orthodoxy, Halakhah and the Boundaries of Modern Jewish Identity. Lanham, Md.: University Press of America, 1989.

Rabbi Esriel Hildesheimer and the Creation of a Modern Jewish Orthodoxy. Tuscaloosa: University of Alabama Press, 1990.

"Sacrifice and Atonement in the Literature of German Orthodoxy: Defense of a Discarded Institution." In *Versohnung in der Liturgie*, edited by Jakob Petuchowski, 27–40. Freiburg: Verlag Herder, 1990.

"'Who Is a Jew?' Issues of Jewish Status and Identity and Their Relationship to the Nature of Judaism in the Modern World." In *Berit Mila in the Reform Context*, edited by Lewis M. Barth, 69–81. Secaucus, N.J.: Carol Publishing, 1990.

"The Continued Renewal of Jewish Theology in North America: Some Recent Works." *Journal of Reform Judaism* (Winter 1991): 1–16.

"German Orthodoxy, Jewish Law, and the Uses of Kant." In *The Jewish Legacy and the German Conscience: Essays in Memory of Rabbi Joseph Asher*, edited by Raphael Asher and Moses Rischin, 73–84. Berkeley: Judah L. Magnes Museum, 1991.

"How to Draw Guidance from a Heritage: Jewish Approaches to Mortal Choices." In *A Time to Be Born and a Time to Die: The Ethics of Choice*, edited by Barry Kogan, 219–32. Hawthorne, N.Y.: Aldine de Groyter, 1991.

"Jewish Identity in the Changing World of American Religion: A Response to Jonathan Sarna." in *Jewish Identity in America*, edited by David Gordis and Yoav Ben-Horin, 105–10. Los Angeles: Susan and David Wilstein Institute of Jewish Policy Studies, 1991.

"The Other Side of S'vara." *S'vara: A Journal of Jewish Law and Philosophy* 2 (1991): 8–10.

"Reform Judaism in Present-Day America: The Evidence of The Gates of Prayer." In *Threescore and Ten: Essays in Honor of Rabbi Seymour J. Cohen*, edited by Abraham Karp, 377–85. Jersey City, N.J.: Ktav, 1991.

"A Theology of Fear: Liberal Jewish Thought and the Nuclear Arms Race." In *Confronting Omnicide: Reflections on Weapons of Mass Destruction*, edited by Daniel Landes, 142–63. Northvale, N.J.: Jason Aronson, 1991.

Translation from the Hebrew of Jacob Katz's "Contributions Towards a Biography of the Hatam Sofer." In *From East and West: Jews in a Changing Europe 1750-1870*, edited by Frances Malino and David Sorkin, 233–66. Oxford: Basil-Blackwell, 1991.

"Religious Pluralism in Israel: American Jewish Perspectives and Policy Options." *American Jewish Committee* (1992): 1–27.

"American Values and Jewish Tradition: Synthesis or Conflict." *Judaism* 93, no. 42 (1993): 242.

Bits of Honey: Essays for Samson H. Levey. Atlanta: Scholar's Press, 1993. Co-edited with Stanley Chyet.

"Conservative Halakha in Israel: A Review Essay." *Modern Judaism* 13, no. 2 (1993): 191–204.

"Eugene Borowitz." In *Interpreters of Judaism in the Late Twentieth Century*, edited by Steven Katz, 17–39. Washington, D.C.: B'nai B'rith Books, 1993. Co-authored with Lori Krafte-Jacobs.

"German Jewish Orthodoxy: Tradition in the Context of Culture." In *The Uses of Tradition: Jewish Continuity in the Modern Era*, edited by Jack Wertheimer, 5–22. New York: Jewish Theological Seminary and Harvard, 1993.

"A Note on Peter Berger's 'Charisma and the Social Location of Israelite Prophecy.'" In *Bits of Honey: Essays for Samson H. Levey*, edited by Stanley Chyet and David Ellenson, 229–32. Atlanta: Scholar's Press, 1993.

"Sociology and Halakha: A Response." *Tradition* (1993): 5–22.

Between Tradition and Culture: The Dialectics of Jewish Religion and Identity in the Modern World. Atlanta: Scholars Press, 1994.

"Eugene Borowitz: A Tribute on the Occasion of His 70th Birthday." *Jewish Book Annual* 51 (1994): 125–36.

"Retroactive Annulment of Conversion: A Survey of Halakhic Sources." In *Conversion to Judaism in Jewish Law*, edited by Walter Jacob and Moshe Zemer, 49–66. Tel Aviv: Rodef Shalom Press, 1994.

"Zion in the Mind of the American Rabbinate: A Survey of Sermons and Pamphlets of the 1940s." In *The Americanization of the Jews*, edited by Naomi Cohen, Norman Cohen, and Robert Seltzer, 193–212. New York: New York University Press, 1994.

"Wissenschaft des Judenthums," "Samson Raphael Hirsch." In *HarperCollins Dictionary of Religion.* New York: HarperCollins, 1995.

"Artificial Fertilization and Procreative Autonomy: Thoughts Occasioned by Two Israeli Responsa." In *The Fetus and Fertility in Jewish Law*, edited by Walter Jacob and Moshe Zemer, 19–38. Tel Aviv: Rodef Shalom Press, 1995.

"A Disputed Precedent: The Prague Organ in 19th Century Central European Legal Literature and Polemics." *Leo Baeck Institute Yearbook* 40, no. 1 (1995): 251–64.

"Reform Zionism Today: A Consideration of First Principles." *Journal of Reform Zionism* 2 (March 1995): 13–18.

"A Sociologist's View of Contemporary Jewish Orthodoxy: The Work of Samuel Heilman." *Religious Studies Review* 21, no.1 (1995): 14–18.

"Emancipation and the Directions of Modern Judaism: The Lessons of *Melitz Yosher*." In *Studia Rosenthaliana*, edited by Emile Schrijver, 118–36. Assen: Van Gorcum, 1996.

"Envisioning Israel in the Liturgies of North American Liberal Judaism." *Envisioning Israel: The Changing Ideals and Images of North American Jews*, edited by Allon Gal, 117–48. Jerusalem: Magnes Press, 1996.

"Interreligious Learning and the Formation of Jewish Religious Identity." *Religious Education* 91, no. 4 (1996): 80–88.

"Moshe Zemer's *Halakhah Shefuyah*: An Israeli Vision of Reform and Halakhah." *CCAR Journal* (Spring/Summer 1996): 31–41. Co-authored with Michael White.

"Orthodox Reactions to Modern Jewish Reform: The Paradigm of Germany." In *The Routledge History of Jewish Philosophy*, edited by Daniel H. Frank and Oliver Leaman, 732–58. London: Routledge, 1996.

"A Responsum on Fundraising." *Judaism* 45, no. 4 (1996): 490–96.

"A Separate Life." In *Jewish Spiritual Journeys: 20 Essays Written to Honor the Occasion of the 70th Birthday of Eugene B. Borowitz*, edited by Lawrence Hoffman and Arnold Jacob Wolf, 93–101. West Orange, N.J.: Behrman, 1996.

"Symposium on Jewish Belief." *Commentary* (August 1996): 12–13.

"Transformation of the Rabbinate: Future Directions and Prospects." In *Women Rabbis: Exploration & Celebration Papers Delivered at an Academic Conference Honoring Twenty Years of Women in the Rabbinate 1972–1992*, edited by Gary Zola, 93–108. Cincinnati: Hebrew Union College–Jewish Institute of Religion Rabbinic Alumni Press, 1996.

"Max Weber on Judaism and the Jews: A Reflection on the Position of Jews in the Modern World." In *What Is Modern about Modern Jewish History?*, edited by Marc Raphael, 78–88. Williamsburg, Va.: College of William and Mary, 1997.

"Modern Liturgies" Commentaries. In *Minhag Ami/My People's Prayer Book*, edited by Lawrence A. Hoffmann. Woodstock, Vt.: Jewish Lights Publishing. 1: The Sh'ma and its Blessings (1997); 2: The Amidah (1998); 3: P'sukei D'zimrah (Morning Psalms) (1999); 4: Seder K'riat HaTorah (The Torah Service) (2000); 5: Birkhot Hashachar (Morning Blessings) (2001); 6: Tachanun and Concluding Prayers (2002); 7: Shabbat at Home (2003); 8: Kabbalat Shabbat (Welcoming Shabbat in the Synagogue) (2004); 9: Experiencing Nightfall: *Minhah* and *Ma'ariv* for Shabbat and Weekdays (2005); and 10: Shabbat Morning: *Shacharit* and *Musaf* (Morning and Additional Services) (2007).

Preface to Rachel Adler, *Engendering Judaism*, viii–xi. Philadelphia: Jewish Publication Society, 1997.

"'A Seminary of Sacred Learning:' The JTS Rabbinical Curriculum in Historical Perspective." In *Tradition Renewed: A History of the Jewish Theological Seminary of America*, edited by Jack Wertheimer, 527–91. New York: Jewish Theological Seminary, 1997. Co-authored with Lee Bycel.

"Zionism." In *Jewish Women in America: An Historical Encyclopedia*, volume 2, edited by Paula Hyman and Deborah Dash Moore, 1544–48. New York: Routledge, 1997.

"Jakob Petuchowski: The Man and His Thought." In *Studies in Modern Theology and Prayer*, edited by Jakob Petuchowski, xi–xvii. Philadelphia: Jewish Publication Society, 1998.

"The Rabbiner-Seminar Codicil: An Instrument of Boundary Maintenance." In *Through Those Near to Me: Essays in Honor of Jerome R. Malino*, edited Glen Lebetkin and Jerome R. Malino, 200–207. Danbury, Conn.: United Jewish Center, 1998.

"Autonomy and Norms in Reform Judaism." *CCAR Journal* (Fall 1999): 21–28.

"A Conservative Rite from Israel: Reflections on Siddur Va'ani Tefillati of the Israeli Masorti Movement." *Studies in Contemporary Jewry* 15 (1999): 151–68.

"The Direction of Modern Jewish Thought: A Comment." In *Contemporary Jewish Religious Thought*, edited by Elliot N. Dorff and Louis E. Newman, 498–501. Oxford: Oxford University Press, 1999.

"The *Israelitischer Gebetbücher* of Abraham Geiger and Manuel Joel: A Study in Nineteenth-Century German-Jewish Communal Liturgy." *Leo Baeck Institute Yearbook* 44, no. 1 (1999): 143–64.

"Mordecai Kaplan." In *The Routledge Encyclopedia of Philosophy*, 433. London: Routledge, 1999.

"Samuel Holdheim on the Legal Character of Jewish Marriage: A Contemporary Comment on His Position." In *Marriage and Impediments to Marriage in Jewish Tradition*, edited by Walter Jacob and Moshe Zemer, 1–26. Tel Aviv: Freehof Institute, 1999.

"Samuel Solomon Cohon." In *American National Biography*, edited by John A. Garraty. Oxford: Oxford University Press, 1999.

"Visions of Gemeindeorthodoxie in Weimar Germany: The Positions of N. A. Nobel and I. Unna." In *In Search of Jewish Community: Jewish Identities in Germany and Austria. 1918–1933*, edited by Michael Brenner and Derek Penslar, 36–55. Bloomington: Indiana University Press, 1999.

"Commentary on Einhorn and Hirsch." In *The Jewish Political Tradition*, edited by Michael Walzer, Menachem Lorberbaum, and Noam Zohar, 373–78. New Haven: Yale University Press, 2000.

"History, Memory, and Relationship." In *Memory and History in Christianity and Judaism*, edited by Michael Signer, 170–81. Notre Dame: University of Notre Dame Press, 2000.

"A Jewish Legal Authority Addresses Jewish-Christian Dialogue: Two Responsa of Rabbi Moshe Feinstein." *American Jewish Archives* (2000): 113–28.

"A Jewish View of the Christian God." In *Christianity in Jewish Terms*, edited by Tikva Frymer-Kensky et al., 69–76. Boulder, Colo.: Westview, 2000.

"Marcia Falk's *The Book of Blessings*: The Issue Is Theological." *CCAR Journal* (Spring 2000): 18–23.

"David Hartman on the Modern Jewish Condition." *Modern Judaism* 21 (2001): 256–81.

"Gender, Halakhah, and Women's Suffrage: Responsa of the First Three Chief Rabbis on the Public Role of Women in the Jewish State." In *Gender Issues* in Jewish Law, edited by Walter Jacob and Moshe Zemer, 58–81. New York: Berghahn Books, 2001.

"Interpretive Fluidity and P'sak in a Case of Pidyon Sh'vuyim. An Analysis of a Modern Israeli Responsum as Illuminated by the Thought of David Hartman." In Judaism and Modernity: The Religious Philosophy of David Hartman, edited by Jonathan Malino, 341–67. Burlington, Vt.: Ashgate, 2001.

"Jewish Legal Interpretation and Moral Values: Two Responsa by Rabbi Hayyim David Halevi on the Obligations of the Israeli Government towards its Minority Populations." CCAR Journal (Summer 2001): 5–20.

"Judaism Resurgent? American Jews and the Evolving Expression of Jewish Values and Jewish Identity in Modern American Life." Studies in Contemporary Jewry 17 (2001): 156–71.

"A Vindication of Judaism: The Polemics of the Hertz Pentateuch: A Review Essay." Modern Judaism 21 (February 2001): 67–77.

"Women and the Study of Torah: A Responsum by Rabbi Zalman Sorotzkin of Jerusalem." Nashim: A Journal of Women's Studies and Gender Issues 4 (2001): 119–39.

"Jacob Katz on the Origins and Dimensions of Jewish Modernity: The Centrality of the German Experience." In The Pride of Jacob: Essays on Jacob Katz and His Work, edited by Jay Harris, 97–123. Cambridge, Mass.: Harvard University Press, 2002.

"Parallel Worlds: Wissenschaft and Pesaq in the Seridei Eish." In History and Literature: New Readings of Jewish Texts in Honor of Arnold J. Band, edited by William Cutter and David Jacobson, 55–74. Providence: Brown Judaic Studies, 2002.

"Rabbi Samson Raphael Hirsch to Liepman Philip Prince of Amsterdam: An 1873 Responsum on Education." The Edah Journal 3, no. 2 (2003): 2–5.

After Emancipation: Jewish Religious Responses to Modernity. Cincinnati: Hebrew Union College Press, 2004.

"A Portrait of the Poseq as Modern Religious Leader: An Analysis of Selected Writings of Rabbi Hayyim David Halevi." In Jewish Religious Leadership: Image and Reality, Volume 2, edited by Jack Wertheimer, 673–93. New York: Jewish Theological Seminary Press, 2004.

"Wissenschaft des Judentums, Historical Consciousness, and Jewish Faith: The Diverse Paths of Frankel, Auerbach, and Halevy." The Leo Baeck Memorial Lecture 48 (2004): 1–15.

"On Conversion and Intermarriage: The Evidence of Nineteenth-Century Hungarian Orthodox Rabbinic Writings." In Text and Context: Essays in Modern Jewish History and Historiography in Honor of Ismar Schorsch, edited by Eli Lederhendler and Jack Wertheimer, 321–46. New York: Jewish Theological Seminar Press, 2005.

"American Rabbinic Training." Encyclopaedia Judaica, 17:23–31. 2nd ed. New York: MacMillan 2006.

"Rabbi Leo Baeck: A Personal Appraisal and Appreciation." European Judaism 39, no. 2 (2006): 58–64.

"American Jewish Denominationalism: Yesterday, Today, and Tomorrow." *The Reconstructionist* (Spring 2007): 5–15.

"'Creative Misreadings' in Representative Post-Emancipation Halakhic Writings on Conversion and Intermarriage." In *Napoleon's Influence on Jewish Law: The Sanhedrin of 1807 and Its Modern Consequences*, edited by Walter Jacob and Moshe Zemer, 79–93. Pittsburgh: Solomon B. Freehof Institute of Progressive Halakha, 2007.

"The Talmudic Principle, 'If One Comes Forth to Slay You, Forestall by Slaying Him,' in Israeli Public Policy: A Responsum by Rabbi Hayyim David Halevi." In *Studies in Mediaeval Halakhah in Honor of Stephen M. Passamaneck*, edited by Alyssa Gray and Bernard Jackson, 73–79. Jewish Law Association Studies 17. Seattle: Jewish Law Association, 2007.

"An Ideology for the Liberal Jewish Day School: A Philosophical-Sociological Investigation." *Journal of Jewish Education* 74 (2008): 245–63.

"Michael A. Meyer and His Vision of Reform Judaism and the Reform Rabbinate: A Lifetime of Devotion and Concern." In *Mediating Modernity: Challenges and Trends in the Jewish Encounter with the Modern World, Essays in Honor of Michael A. Meyer*, edited by Lauren B. Strauss and Michael Brenner, 17–24. Detroit: Wayne State University Press, 2008.

"Laws and Judgments as a Bridge to a Better World, *Parashat Mishpatim*." In *Torah Queeries: Weekly Commentaries on the Hebrew Bible*, edited by Greg Drinkwater, David Shneer, and Joshua Lesser, 98–101. New York: New York University Press, 2009.

"Heschel and the Roots of Kavanah." In *New Essays in American Jewish History: Commemorating the Sixtieth Anniversary of the Founding of the American Jewish Archives*, edited by Pamela S. Nadell, Jonathan D. Sarna, and Lance J. Sussman, 345–66. Cincinnati: The American Jewish Archives of Hebrew Union College–Jewish Institute of Religion, 2010. Co-authored with Michael Marmur.

"Rabbi Hayim David Halevi on Christians and Christianity: An Analysis of Selected Legal Writings of an Israeli Authority." In *Transforming Relations: Essays on Jews and Christians Throughout History in Honor of Michael A, Signer*, edited by Franklin Harkins, 340–61. Notre Dame: Notre Dame Press, 2010.

"Colleagues and Friends: Letters between Rabbi Samuel Belkin and Rabbi William G. Braude." In *Continuity and Change: A Festschrift in Honor of Irving Greenberg's 75th Birthday*, edited by Steven Bayme and Steven Katz, 63–79. Lanham, Md.: University Press of America, 2011.

"German Orthodox Rabbinical Writings on the Jewish Textual Education of Women: The Views of Rabbi Samson Raphael Hirsch and Rabbi Esriel Hildesheimer." In *Gender and Jewish History*, edited by Marion A. Kaplan and Deborah Dash Moore, 158–69. Bloomington: Indiana University Press, 2011.

Pledges of Jewish Allegiance: Conversion, Law, and Policymaking in Nineteenth- and Twentieth-Century Orthodox Responsa. Stanford: Stanford University Press, 2012. Co-authored with Daniel Gordis.

"The Rock from Which They Were Cleft: An Review-Essay of Haim Amsalem's *Zera Yisrael* and *Mekor Yisrael*." *Jewish Review of Books* (Winter 2012): 41–43.

"A Zionist Reading of Abraham Geiger and His Biblical Scholarship." In *Making a Difference: Essays on the Bible and Judaism in Honor of Tamara Cohn Eskenazi*, edited by David J. A. Clines, Kent Harold Richards, and Jacob L. Wright, 121–31. Sheffield: Sheffield Phoenix Press, 2012.

"Mothers and Sons, Sisters and Brothers: The Women of Reform Judaism and Hebrew Union College–Jewish Institute of Religion." In *Sisterhood: A Centennial History of the Women of Reform Judaism*, edited by Carole Balin, 72–85. New York: Ktav, 2013. Co-authored with Jane Karlin.

"Rabbi Eliezer Berkovits in Conversion: An Inclusive Orthodox Approach." *Shofar: An Interdisciplinary Journal of Jewish Studies* (Summer 2013): 37–53.

Jewish Meaning in a World of Choice. Lincoln: Jewish Publication Society and the University of Nebraska Press, 2014.

CONTRIBUTORS

RACHEL ADLER is the David Ellenson Professor of Modern Jewish Thought at Hebrew Union College of Los Angeles. She is the author of *Engendering Judaism* (1999), which won the National Jewish Book Award for Jewish Thought, and many articles.

ISA ARON, Professor of Jewish Education at the Rhea Hirsch School of Education, Hebrew Union College–Jewish Institute of Religion, was the founding director of HUC's Experiment in Congregational Education, and is currently codirector of the B'nai Mitzvah Revolution. She was recently the author of *Sacred Strategies: Becoming a Visionary Congregation* (2010), winner of the 2010 National Jewish Book Award.

CAROLE B. BALIN is a professor of history at Hebrew Union College–Jewish Institute of Religion in New York. She is a coeditor, with Wendy I. Zierler, of the forthcoming *"To Tread on New Ground": From the Hebrew Writings of Hava Shapiro (1878–1943)* (forthcoming 2014).

ARNOLD J. BAND is Professor Emeritus of Hebrew and Comparative Literature at UCLA. He has published books and articles on a variety of topics in Hebrew literature, both modern and biblical, has been a visiting professor at various universities in the United States and Israel, and has directed thirty doctoral dissertations in Hebrew and comparative literature.

LEWIS M. BARTH, Rabbi, is Professor Emeritus of Midrash and Related Literature, and former Dean of Hebrew Union College–Jewish Institute of Religion, Los Angeles. His academic and teaching interests have been in the areas of midrash, tales of the Rabbis, manuscript editing, and psychoanalysis.

WILLIAM CUTTER is Emeritus Professor of Hebrew Literature at Hebrew Union College–Jewish Institute of Religion, Los Angeles, where he is also Emeritus Steinberg Professor of Human Relations. He concluded a teaching career of forty-eight years in June of 2013. He publishes in the area of educational theory, pastoral education, and the history of Hebrew literature.

ELLIOT N. DORFF, Rabbi, is Rector and Distinguished Service Professor of Philosophy at American Jewish University and Visiting Professor at UCLA School of Law. He has edited or coedited fourteen books on Jewish thought, law, and ethics, and he has written more than two hundred articles and twelve books on those topics.

ARNOLD EISEN, who currently serves as the Chancellor of the Jewish Theological Seminary, previously taught Jewish Studies and Religious Studies at Stanford, Tel Aviv, and Columbia Universities. He is the author, among other works, of *Rethinking Modern Judaism: Ritual, Commandment, Community* (1998) and *Galut: Modern Jewish Reflection on Homelessness and Homecoming* (1986).

ADAM S. FERZIGER is senior lecturer and vice chairman of the Graduate Program in Contemporary Jewry at Bar-Ilan University, Ramat-Gan, Israel. He has served as visiting professor at University of Shandong in Jinan, China, and University of Sydney in Australia, and he is presently a visiting fellow at Wolfson College and the Oxford Centre for Hebrew and Jewish Studies, University of Oxford.

LAWRENCE A. HOFFMAN is an ordained rabbi and the Barbara and Stephen Friedman Professor of Liturgy, Worship, and Ritual at the Hebrew Union College in New York. He has written or edited forty books and is cofounder of Synagogue 3000, an organization devoted to helping synagogues become spiritual and moral centers for the twenty-first century.

PAULA E HYMAN was the Lucy Moses Professor of Modern Jewish History at Yale University. She was the author of numerous seminal works, including *From Dreyfus to Vichy: The Remaking of French Jewry, 1906–1939*; *Gender and Assimilation in Modern Jewish History*; and *The Jews of Modern France*. She also edited several significant works, including (with Deborah Dash Moore) *Jewish Women in America: An Historical Encyclopedia*.

DEBORAH E. LIPSTADT is Dorot Professor of Modern Jewish History and Holocaust Studies at Emory University. Her two most recent books are *The Eich-*

mann *Trial* (2011) and *History on Trial: My Day in Court with a Holocaust Denier* (2006). The latter is her personal reflection on her experience as a defendant in a British court when she was sued for libel by Holocaust denier David Irving.

STEVEN M. LOWENSTEIN has written many books and articles about German Jewish social, demographic, and cultural history. Since retiring from his position as professor of modern Jewish history at the American Jewish University in Los Angeles, he has been a psychiatric social worker for the Los Angeles County Department of Mental Health.

MICHAEL MARMUR is the Jack, Joseph and Morton Mandel Provost and Assistant Professsor of Jewish Theology at the Hebrew Union College–Jewish Institute of Religion in Jerusalem. His doctoral dissertation, a number of articles, and a recently completed book all deal with the work of Abraham Joshua Heschel.

RABBI DALIA MARX is Associate Professor of Liturgy at the Jerusalem campus of Hebrew Union College–Jewish Institute of Religion and teaches in various academic institutions in Israel and Europe. She is the author of *When I Sleep and When I Wake: On Prayers between Dusk and Dawn* (2010, in Hebrew) and *A Feminist Commentary of the Babylonian Talmud* (2013, in English).

MICHAEL A. MEYER is Adolph S. Ochs Professor of Jewish History Emeritus at Hebrew Union College–Jewish Institute of Religion in Cincinnati. He is the author, inter alia, of *Origins of the Modern Jew: Jewish Identity and European Culture in Germany, 1749–1824* (1967) and *Response to Modernity: A History of the Reform Movement in Judaism* (1988).

DAVID N. MYERS is Professor of Jewish History and Chair of the UCLA History Department. He is the author of numerous books in the field of modern Jewish intellectual and cultural history.

RIV-ELLEN PRELL, an anthropologist, is professor of American studies and director of the Center for Jewish Studies at the University of Minnesota. Among her publications are *Fighting to Become Americans: Jews, Gender, and the Anxiety of Assimilation*.

JONATHAN D. SARNA is the Joseph H. and Belle R. Braun Professor of American Jewish History at Brandeis University, and chairs its Hornstein Jewish Professional Leadership Program. Author or editor of more than thirty books on

American Jewish history and life, his *American Judaism: A History* (2005) won six awards including the 2004 Everett Jewish Book of the Year Award from the Jewish Book Council.

JACK WERTHEIMER is professor of American Jewish History at the Jewish Theological Seminary. He writes on trends in the religious, philanthropic, and educational spheres of American Jewish life since 1945. His current research focuses on aspects of Jewish day school education in the United States.

WENDY ZIERLER is professor of Modern Jewish Literature and Feminist Studies at Hebrew Union College–Jewish Institute of Religion. She is the author of *And Rachel Stole the Idols: The Emergence of Modern Hebrew Women's Writing* (2004), and coeditor with Carole Balin of *The Selected Writings of Hava Shapiro* (2008, in Hebrew) and the forthcoming *To Tread on New Ground*, an expanded English volume of Shapiro's writings.

ZVI ZOHAR is Chauncey Stillman Professor of Sephardic Law and Ethics at Bar Ilan University, where he teaches in the Faculty of Law and in the Faculty of Jewish Studies. His research relates to the history, development, and current application of halakhah, with special focus on the creativity of Sephardic/Oriental rabbis in modern times.

INDEX

Abrabanel, Isaac, 198

academia, 251, 256, 283. *See also* education

Active Learning Network, 103

Adam 1 "Majestic Man," in *Lonely Man of Faith,* 211

Adam 2 "Lonely Man of Faith," 211–12

"Adam and Eve" (Soloveitchik, edited by Shatz and Wolowelsky), 215–16

Adler, Nathan Marcus, 88–89

aggadah, 224–28

Agnon, Shmuel Yosef (Czaczkes), 312–14, 318–19. *See also* "Ve-hayah he'akov le-mishor"

Aish HaTorah, 68–69, 72–73

AJC (American Jewish Committee), 177

Akiba: Scholar, Saint and Martyr (Finkelstein), 201–2

Akiva, 125, 194, 197, 200–204, 246

Akiva's Orchard (Brandes), 204

Allgemeine Zeitung des Judenthums (newspaper), 90

Alon, Eli, 132–33

America: baby boom generation in transition of religious and cultural life, 266–67; "can do" spirit, 222–23; Civil War, 88–89; ethnic identity, 114; Jewish newspapers in, 81; narratives about health care system, 223; New Left in counterculture of, 264–65; Orthodox outreach workers in, 69–70, 77; Reform Judaism in, 53–54, 62–63; religion in, 28, 250; social movements of 1960s and early 1970s, 274; spirituality

in, 258; supplementary schools in, 101; as treifene medinah (unkosher state), 81; UAHC, 112–15, 281, 283, 291n13. *See also* Central Conference of American Rabbis (CCAR)

American Conference of Cantors, 111, 115

American Jewish Committee (AJC), 177

American Jewry: attacks by Zionist thinkers, 176; baby boom generation and transformation in life of, 276; Conservative, 257; expressions of Jewish identity, 114; growing estrangement from Israel, 62–63; intermarriage, 98; movements following World War II, 265; Orthodoxy's contextual view of Reform Jews, 56–57; Reform movement concerns about integrating women into rabbinate, 280–81; shift in discourse of, 264

American law, Jewish law compared to, 45–46

amnesia: anterograde, 296–300, 309n10; pure, 309–10n11

Angell, Marcia, 223, 231

angels of history and historiography, 312

Anglican Church, 112

aniconism, 82, 87, 91

anti-Semitism: focus on, by Zionist vs. Diaspora Jewish thinkers, 178–79; in interwar Poland, 322; political, in the Netherlands, 161; prewar, and Jewish universalism, 251

anti-tsarist radical political groups, women's status within, 326